"Once you start reading, you will not be able to stop. A compelling look at one of the most influential and controversial figures in baseball history. A new generation needs to know the story of Jim Bouton: a man who never wearied of gleefully and hilariously skewering the establishment but who also had the old-school drive to will his dreams into reality. Above all, a lifetime love of baseball shines through in every chapter—a true reflection of Bouton himself."

—BRIAN KENNY, host for MLB Network and author of
Ahead of the Curve: Inside the Baseball Revolution

"When Mitchell Nathanson . . . approached Bouton about writing his biography, the pitcher gave his blessing, on one condition: that Nathanson write about him with the honesty he'd tried to bring to the game of baseball. . . . Nathanson moves crisply through the deep backstory, though he knows a good detail when he sees one."

—JOHN SWANSBURG, *New York Times Book Review*

"An astute writer on the game, [Nathanson] is at his best on the Bouton-Shecter collaboration—late nights at the Lion's Head Bar in Greenwich Village; Shecter making sense of Bouton's scrawls on stationery, envelopes and toilet paper; the pair noodling over the manuscript stripped down to their underwear in Shecter's airless Chelsea apartment. . . . Nathanson is good, too, with Bouton wisecracks."

—MAXWELL CARTER, *Wall Street Journal*

"Half a century after Jim Bouton's *Ball Four* hilariously let the air out of Major League Baseball's inflated self-image, one of the game's most fascinating characters finally gets the biography he deserves. Unfettered and unfiltered, like Bouton himself, *Bouton* will make you laugh, make you cry, and make you wanna pound that Budweiser. To paraphrase the late, great Joe Schultz, 'Attaway to go, Mitchell Nathanson!'"

—DAN EPSTEIN, author of *Big Hair and Plastic Grass:*
A Funky Ride through Baseball and America in the Swinging '70s

"For years people have told me that they fell in love with baseball after reading *Ball Four*. Jim Bouton was a unique character on the baseball stage, a figure of historical importance. It's time we all knew him better, and Mitchell Nathanson's book gets that done."

—MARTY APPEL, New York Yankees historian and author of
Pinstripe Empire and *Casey Stengel*

"Nathanson goes beyond tracing Bouton's life, focusing instead on explicating the roots of *Ball Four*. In so doing, [*Bouton*] becomes an inside-publishing exposé, showing how the publication and selling of *Ball Four* changed our expectations of what a sports book could be.... In addition, the book provides fascinating details about Bouton's post—*Ball Four* life, including his fling at acting and his turn as an entrepreneur, developing the successful bubble-gum product Big League Chew. A welcome look at one of baseball's signature mavericks."

—MARK LEVINE, *Booklist*

"One of the best baseball biographies in recent memory. Nathanson is a fantastic storyteller, capable of juxtaposing Bouton's recollections with those of his contemporaries and situating these stories within their historical context."

—CLAYTON TRUTOR, *Reason*

"A well-researched and fascinating read that tells how the free-thinking Bouton always marched to the beat of his own drummer."

—JOHN WERNER, *Waco Tribune-Herald*

"*Bouton* is a book that deserves space next to *Ball Four* on the bookshelf. Nathanson has done a thorough job of presenting the life of a complex man who changed the game of baseball, not by what he did on the field, but what he observed on the field, in the clubhouse and on the road."

—BOB D'ANGELO, *Sports Bookie*

"Nathanson's source list is deep and insightful and his writing is crisp. And his access to Bouton's *Ball Four* notes provides answers to some lingering questions."

—DENNIS ANDERSON, *Peoria Journal Star*

"Readers who choose to visit *Bouton* will feel pleased to have made the acquaintance of a truly unique player in the panorama of American sports."

—J. KEMPER CAMPBELL, *Lincoln Journal Star*

Bouton

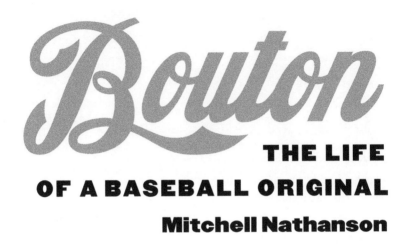

THE LIFE
OF A BASEBALL ORIGINAL

Mitchell Nathanson

University of Nebraska Press | Lincoln

Library of Congress Cataloging-in-Publication Data
Names: Nathanson, Mitchell, 1966– author.
Title: Bouton: the life of a baseball original / Mitchell
Nathanson.
Description: Lincoln: University of Nebraska Press,
2020. | Includes bibliographical references and index.
Identifiers: LCCN 2019044481
ISBN 9781496217707 (hardback: alk. paper)
ISBN 9781496229854 (paperback)
ISBN 9781496221308 (epub)
ISBN 9781496221315 (mobi)
ISBN 9781496221322 (pdf)
Subjects: LCSH: Bouton, Jim. | Baseball players—United
States—Biography. | Baseball—United States.
Classification: LCC GV865.B69 N37 2020 |
DDC 796.357092 [B]—dc23
LC record available at https://lccn.loc.gov/2019044481

Set in Sabon Next LT Pro by Mikala R. Kolander.

For John Gleeson
teacher, coach, friend

With rebellion,
awareness is born.

—ALBERT CAMUS

Contents

Acknowledgments

In the late summer of 2016 I dragged my family out to the Berkshires so that I could sit down with who I hoped would be the subject of my next book—Jim Bouton. "Dragged" is most definitely overstating it. We were leaving hot, humid Philadelphia for the cool breezes of western Massachusetts—who would refuse such an offer? It would be a baseball-themed trip, as I also had a talk scheduled at the Baseball Hall of Fame in conjunction with another book, so I sold the excursion to my wife and kids as one where we'd spend a few days in the town that celebrated the baseball establishment and then head on over to meet the man who upended all of that in one fell swoop.

I had no idea how my meeting with Bouton and his wife, Paula Kurman, would go; he hadn't been receptive to the idea of my taking on his life's story at first. Or upon reflection, for that matter. Why, he wanted to know as we exchanged emails, would he agree to have me write his story when he'd spent his life doing that himself? I persisted, for what reason I don't really know, other than the fact that I'd had my eye on his story for nearly two decades by that point; he just fascinated me in so many ways. In my opinion the three most influential ballplayers of the 1960s were Curt Flood, Dick Allen, and Jim Bouton. There were a few great biographies on Flood, and I had just written a biography of Allen; at this point Bouton was my white whale.

Eventually, I heard from Paula, who suggested the get-together to see if something could be worked out so as to enable me to write my book while not completely upending their lives. Hence the trip to the Berkshires. I had no idea what to expect as I waited by the cvs near my motel in Great Barrington for Jim to pick me up in his beat-up

Subaru wagon. (Don't even try to figure out how to find their house using GPS, Paula warned. They were so far out in the middle of nowhere that the satellites had long since given up trying to locate them.) I was nervous as to how I'd be received; Dick Allen wanted nothing to do with me when I was working on his biography, and I feared another cold shoulder. I should add that I understood Allen's reticence; it's just that I didn't enjoy it and wasn't looking to experience that once again. More important, though, I knew going in that I was not going to do the book if I couldn't get Bouton's cooperation; unlike Allen's, I was convinced that Bouton's story couldn't be told without access to the man himself. So this meeting was an all-or-nothing experience for me. I'd either walk out of their house with my next project or be back at square one.

About thirty minutes into our meeting I began to feel comfortable. Jim was open and ebullient, Paula had pulled up a chair and was freely relaying stories I thought I'd have to wait months to hear and then only if I was lucky, the birds were whistling (and Bouton was whistling back at them), the frogs were croaking, life was good. I finally ginned up the courage to ask if they would mind if I turned my tape recorder on. Why not? Paula replied. You'd better make sure you get everything down if you're going to do this. From that moment on, whenever I asked to speak to them they were similarly open and forthcoming. I cannot even begin to thank them enough for the many hours of their lives I have taken up with my questions regarding nearly anything and everything I could think of that touched Jim Bouton's extraordinary life. Working with them has been the sort of gift I can only hope other writers get to experience when they seek similar access to their subjects.

I am also extraordinarily grateful for the time Bobbie Bouton-Goldberg spent with me, similarly answering whatever I asked, no matter how personal and intrusive. I could not have written this book without her patience and cooperation.

For reasons I won't get into here, this book's path to publication was unusually odd and hazardous, with numerous dead ends along the way. There is no way on earth I could have reached my destination without the skill, guidance, and encouragement of my agent, Farley Chase. Thank you, Farley, for never losing faith in either me or the project.

Eventually, the book found a loving home at the University of Nebraska Press, and for that I have Rob Taylor to thank, along with everybody there who worked on the manuscript along the way. Nobody does baseball the way Nebraska does baseball, and for that I am most appreciative.

There were also dozens who helped me one way or another, either through agreeing to be interviewed or by directing me to one resource or another I'd never have been able to locate without their help. Barbara Bair at the Library of Congress deserves special mention; she oversaw the acquisition of the Bouton Papers by the LOC and has been their enthusiastic champion since they arrived. Thank you, Barbara, for spending the time and energy going through the *Ball Four* collection with me. And to the following, thank you all as well: Marty Appel, Jill Baer, Gary Bell, Ira Berkow, Bob Bouton, Pete Bouton, Rick Cerrone, Marge Champion, Lou Charlip, Jim Charlton, Stephen Cohen, Jerry Colangelo, Larry Colton, Howard Cronson, Bruce Cunningham, Tommy Davis, Larry Dierker, Peter Dreier, Pierre Dulaine, Chip Elitzer, Sam Elitzer, John Feinstein, Richard Feuer, John Florio, Tom Flynn, Sonny Fulks, Cliff Gelb, Peter Golenbock, Al Gornie, Bill Hall, Donald Honig, Lou Hoynes, Ellen Isaacs, Fred and Barbara Jacobeit, Steve Jacobson, Jim Kaat, Irv Kalb, Marvin Kitman, Keith Korman (the son of Theron Raines), Robert Lipsyte, Yvonne Marceau, Sal Marchiano, Dr. Mike Marshall, Greg Martin, Dermot McEvoy, Larry Merchant, Norm Miller, Rob Nelson, Jeff Neuman, Neil Offen, Keith Olbermann, Gary "Pops" O'Maxfield, Peter Osnos, Frank Peters, Fritz Peterson, Robert Peterson, Steve Pokotilow, Jeremy Schaap, Lynne Schalman, Joe Schillan, Bill Schonely, Alan Schwarz, David Scribner, Ouisie Shapiro, Brad Shaw, Al and Rosa Silverman, Dennis Snelling, Brad Snyder, Marco St. John, Steve Steinberg, Art Stewart, Jim Swanson, John Thorn, George Vecsey, Maclain Way, Senator Loretta Weinberg, and Rick Wolff.

Finally, nothing would be possible without the love and support of my wife, Joanne, and children, Alex and Jaclyn. Thank you for listening to all of my Jim Bouton stories over the past few years and for laughing in all of the appropriate places. For the most part, anyway.

Ultimately, the question inevitably arises as to how well anybody can ever know anybody else. For the biographer this question is a particularly pointed one. While I can't say that I have the answer, I can attest to the fact that spending a few years immersed in the life of Jim Bouton is about as much fun as any biographer can ever hope to have. Which might be the most we can expect out of anything in life.

Prologue

Publication Day

The banging on the door was not going to stop. That was clear enough from both its frequency and its force. Norm Miller sat naked on the bed as the cacophony engulfed him—on one side of the room the persistent ringing of the telephone, on the other the banging on the door. His roommate was taking care of the telephone, for the moment at least, engaging the reporter on the other end of the line. Miller had lost count by now of the number of calls his roommate had received already; as soon as he nestled the receiver into its cradle, off it would go again within seconds. Never before had the arrival of the perennial sad-sack Houston Astros to New York generated this much attention. But never before had anybody on the club or in the game of baseball drawn attention to themselves or the game in the way Jim Bouton just had.

Bouton tried his best to talk over the pounding on the door, but the louder he spoke the more persistent it became. Finally, he pleadingly eyed Miller, and Miller realized that he had no choice but to answer the door. He rose from the bed and, in his full glory, opened it to behold a scowling Howard Cosell, swathed in his rumpled trench coat and fedora. No matter what the weather, no matter what the circumstance, Cosell always looked as if he were in an early stage of melt; the morning's glorious late-spring sunshine had no bearing on his visage in the least. Cosell looked right through Miller and lasered in on his target. Not waiting for an invitation from the naked utility outfielder, Cosell brushed by him and headed straight for the phone, grabbing it out of Bouton's hand. He sneered his nasal twang into the mouthpiece, cutting off in his staccato cadence the voice on the other end of the line in midsentence—"This ... interview ... is ... terminated!"—and slammed the receiver down. Now, for the moment at least, there was silence. No ringing of the phone. No knocking on the door. Miller returned to his bed and considered pulling up the covers. Instead, he slowly stretched out to listen. No matter. He could have lit himself on fire, and Cosell would not have looked away from Bouton. Because Cosell was where every sportswriter, sportscaster, and baseball fan wanted to be—standing face-to-face with the man who had just blown up the national pastime.

The June 2, 1970, edition of *Look* magazine had hit the stands just hours earlier, and in it was a ten-page excerpt of *Ball Four*. In those ten pages, a century of baseball mythology was set aflame and vaporized. Therein, readers were assaulted with tales of greenies, carousing, "beaver shooting," and players making out—with stewardesses, groupies, and, after a few drinks, each other. But most scandalous of all was a portrayal of baseball's golden boy, Mickey Mantle, drunkenly staggering into the batter's box and somehow hitting a home run. What's more, another bomb was promised in the next issue, two weeks hence. The book hadn't even reached bookstores yet, and already everybody wanted to speak with the journeyman pitcher who had written it.

Much of America was, by 1970, coming apart at the seams. Only baseball seemed stitched tightly enough to resist the forces of change, wound as it was deep into its mythic past. Or so it had appeared. When the June 2 edition of *Look* hit the stands, myth became exposed as such, and baseball for the first time looked very much like the real world in which it was played. Cosell might have been oblivious to a lot of what was happening in Miller and Bouton's Roosevelt Hotel room that Friday morning, but he was keenly aware of one thing: that he was bearing witness to the dawn of a new era. Baseball had spent more than a century building itself up as something otherworldly. With the release of *Ball Four* Jim Bouton brought it down to earth. Cosell, who liked to brag that only he could "tell it like it is," was at last staring down a man who really did. If it appeared odd that it was a Major League Baseball player, of all people, who had unmasked the cloistered world of the professional athlete, it made perfect sense that Jim Bouton would be the MLB player to do it. Already, at age thirty-one, it was a role he seemed destined to play his entire life.

Bouton

PART ONE   The Bulldog

1 Warm-up Bouton

On the day Jim Bouton was born, Generalissimo Francisco Franco declared a total blockade of all Republican-controlled ports in Spain, threatening to torpedo any and all ships that entered what he now declared his waters. A day earlier Mahatma Gandhi ended a four-day fast over the issue of constitutional reform in Rajkot, and a day before that, back in the States, the United Automobile Workers amended its constitution to officially bar communists from its ranks. Jim Bouton might have been born into the weight of history when he arrived on March 8, 1939, but to his good fortune he had likewise been born into a family that was hardly imprisoned by it. It could very well have been— the Boutons can trace their roots back to sixteenth-century France, where Nicholas Bouton was better known as Count Chamilly, Baron Montague de Naton, and his son not only claimed a title himself but a spot on the portrait wall in the gallery of French nobles at Versailles. More recently, Daniel Bouton was bayoneted by a British infantryman at the Battle of Bunker Hill in 1775, becoming the first, but certainly not the last, Bouton the establishment desired to see filleted.

But it wasn't their history that defined the Boutons. Instead, it was their desire to upend and redirect it. On both sides, Jim Bouton's lineage was dotted with tinkerers, with fiddlers, with people who saw things as they might be rather than merely as they were. Both grandfathers were inventors of a sort—his maternal grandfather patented several variations on the pressure cooker (his company was later bought out by the pressure-frying behemoth Hobart), and his paternal grandfather obtained patents while at Westinghouse on an elevator system for efficiently ferrying fighter planes from the underdeck of aircraft carriers to the flight deck. If his family had one defining characteristic, his brother Bob recalled, it was in "making it up," things and otherwise.

Both families resided in prim, proper Park Ridge, Illinois (the Rodhams lived nearby; Hillary would not arrive until 1947), where Jim's parents met and eventually became a couple. They weren't yet married when Jim's mother, Trudy, became unexpectedly pregnant with him in 1938. Once word got around, the moral arbiters of the neighborhood made it clear that that would not do in Park Ridge; they were encouraged to seek residence elsewhere for the duration of the pregnancy. Left with little choice, Jim's parents withdrew from high school and went to live with a grandparent in the more socially tolerant New York City area. For Jim's father, George—a swimming, diving, and track star at Park Ridge's Maine Township High School—this meant the abandonment of his formal education. He turned down athletic scholarship offers from Duke and Brown as he headed east to look for work to support the new family he suddenly had responsibility for.

After a time the Boutons settled in Rochelle Park, New Jersey, where, during the war, George had spent time in the navy. Without a college degree, his options were limited; eventually, his father-in-law got him a job with his company selling pressure cookers. Soon he began taking night classes in an effort to regain some of what he had lost earlier. "When I was real young," Jim recalled years later, "Dad sold pressure cookers in a department store all day; went to Columbia University at night, and still had time to do things like build an addition on the house."[1] Jim's brother Pete recalled a man who rarely came home unrumpled. "He had his feet in both worlds, blue-collar and white," he remembered. He was smart and industrious, but lacking the credentials that would firmly place him in a position of safety from market forces. "Whatever job he had, it was the one that they got rid of whenever times got tough," said Pete.

Regardless, for much of Jim's youth the Boutons were a traditional one-income family. Trudy was a stay-at-home mother, tending to the expanding Rochelle Park house along with Jim and his brother Bob, who came along nearly two years later. She joined the neighborhood bridge club, organized get-togethers with neighbors, and lived a life on the proverbial midcentury suburban front porch. For a time she was a Gray Lady volunteer at a local hospital. The Bouton boys—Jim, Bob, and a few years later baby brother Pete—were, like many boys of the era, on their own for most of the day. "Moms, at the time," Pete recalled, "weren't too involved with boys. They'd get kicked out of the house in the morning and wouldn't come home until the streetlights came on. We'd be out playing all day long, and Mom would call us in for lunch or dinner, but that was about it. We'd do our own thing—go down to the playground or into town or wherever. She had no idea where the hell we were." Wherever they were, they were rarely bored.

Traversing the environs of Rochelle Park wasn't difficult; there wasn't much of Rochelle Park to traverse. Located in southwest Bergen County, it was, Jim remembered, more of a cartographic afterthought than anything. "On local maps it appears as a dot west of Hackensack. On larger maps, it doesn't even have its own dot." All three Bouton boys shared a bedroom in their home on Central Avenue—one they couldn't wait to escape as soon as the sun rose. Because they were closer in age, Jim and Bob would often pal around together, stopping at Slupow's candy store for Sugar Daddies before heading over to the viaduct under Route 17, where they'd gird themselves for the rocks hurled at them by the hobos sleeping there if they arrived too early and startled them. Little Pete occasionally played the role of prop— Jim and Bob would send him up unsuspecting doorsteps and ring the bell, claiming he was a starving orphan. Although the ruse rarely worked—in a town of seven thousand nearly everybody knew everybody else—Pete would often walk away with a handful of cookies anyway, which he'd share with his brothers, who were hiding in the bushes. One time their target called their bluff and invited Pete inside for a meal, leaving Jim and Bob to stew in the bushes. Eventually, they had to ring the doorbell to retrieve him. That was all they left with; Pete walked out full but empty-handed.[2]

It wasn't long before preadolescent Jim was in business for himself. The feeling of independence that came from walking into Slupow's with purchasing power intoxicated him by the time he was eight: "I liked the fact that I had my own ability to feed myself. Any time there was something in the newspaper—sell chocolates door-to-door, whatever—okay, good. I'd send away for a kit. . . . I liked having money in my pocket and I liked having control over my life."[3] He and Bob started a "sports club" and collected dues from the neighborhood kids, found old newspapers to sell to scrap dealers (they would store them in the garage until there was no room for George's car, at which point Bob would call the scrap dealer for the pickup), and gathered empty ice cream cups at George's fast-pitch softball games. "If you collected twenty cups you got a free ice cream from 'Joe Slush,'" who sold them out of the back of his truck at the games.[4] Jim was always entrepreneurial, Pete recalled. "He could see an opportunity and get right on it. He was great at figuring out what other people's needs were and filling them." By the fourth grade he had business cards made up: "You name it, we'll do it," they read. Whenever someone named it, he and Bob did it—mowing lawns, shoveling snow, whatever. Recognizing an opportunity shortly after the war, Jim started his own scrap-metal business. "I'd be walking home from school and I'd see a bolt or a fender and I'd grab it, take it home with me, and store it in the woods part of my backyard. After a while I had a tremendous pile." At that point he'd flag down the man driving through the neighborhood looking for scrap metal himself. The man paid by the pound. "I think I got over fifty dollars, which is an enormous amount of money for a guy who's in third grade."

When it came to sports the Bouton boys had to "make it up" here as well. Rochelle Park was too small for organized youth leagues, so the summers and school-year afternoons were dominated by pickup games of one sort or another. "Every day you went down to the park and you chose up sides," Jim remembered. Occasionally, they'd play stickball under the viaduct, stopping whenever a car passed through. He also played catch with George and Bob and learned very early how to throw a ball far and hard. Soon he figured out how to make it curve. When he was ten he turned to the back of a Wheaties box and saw a photo of old-time pitcher Dutch Leonard along with a description of how to throw a knuckleball—a pitch that has baffled pitchers, catchers, and batters alike since it was introduced in the late nineteenth century. "Batsmen who are accustomed to working against speedy pitchers find the floater very bothersome," wrote a perplexed Cleveland sportswriter in 1908. "The ball looms up to the plate as big as a Halloween pumpkin, and just as it arrives seems to assume the proportions of a pea and fall to nothing at all."[5] Leonard "used two fingers, but my hands were too small so I had to use three," Jim remembered. "I started to throw them to my brother [Bob], and finally I got one to break. He had his hands up here [by his chest], and it dropped and hit him on the kneecap. I spent the rest of that summer trying to break my brother's kneecaps." It was a difficult pitch to master, but he kept at it until he did. "His knuckleball was so good," Bob remembered, "that you could not follow it. It would dip, go up, down, sideways. Even he didn't know where it was going. It was dangerous." That Wheaties box would alter the course of his life. Not just that he saw it but that he saw it when he did. "The knuckleball is like the violin in that it is better learned by children," he once said. "A split-finger you can pick up in an hour and a half."[6] Gripping the ball behind the seams seven decades later, he still had the ability to make it dance: "If learned with a child's grip, you'll remember it the rest of your life."

The pickup games may have been informal, but to Jim, at least, they meant as much as any World Series game. "I was a terrible kid," he said years later. "I always had to win. I was a poor sport.... None of the kids liked me. I was a bad loser. I'd sulk, kick, cry and stomp. I was awful."[7] Bob had a front-row seat for all of this throughout their years in Rochelle Park. "He could not handle a situation where somebody made an error. If there was a pop fly and the second baseman dropped it, Jim would run towards him, berate him, and maybe even give him a little nudge or a kick.... It was very important to him not to lose." Eventually, he had a difficult time finding teammates; few eight-year-olds wanted to be reminded of their athletic shortcomings whenever a ball came their way. If they were looking to be on the winning side, however, there was nobody better. From the first pitch he was intense and competitive. "I'm here and you're gonna have a tough time" was his worldview, said Pete. "You may beat me, but it ain't gonna be easy. Let's go."

"I was a pretty good little ballplayer back then," Jim remembered. "Very little."[8] When he was eleven he played formal ball for the first time, having made his Midland Elementary School's fifth grade team. One problem—there were no uniforms small enough to fit him; Trudy had to stitch his herself. On the mound, in his homemade Midland Lions uniform, Jim realized that this is where he wanted to be: with the ball, in control, staring down a hitter.[9] The dynamic was the purest distillation of his competitive fire and, as such, the biggest thrill of his life. Nothing would, nothing could, ever supplant it.

George, himself a pitcher—for Jack's Tavern—would oftentimes bring Jim to his softball games. As the oldest and most athletically inclined, Jim seemed to be George's favorite, or at least that's how his brothers interpreted things. Before games little Jim Bouton would be out there with the men, shagging flies during batting practice. He was usually the only kid out there. "George," Jim remembered one of his father's teammates admonishing him when he first sent his son out with the guys, "your boy there, he's in a lot of trouble. They're hitting line drives. He's gonna get hurt." "No," George replied, "he's not gonna have any problem at all." A few minutes later there was a screaming line drive into short center field, and Jim ran, dove, and caught it. The teammate was impressed: "I guess you're right, George. I guess he's okay." From the start George not only had confidence in Jim, but was also eager to demonstrate that confidence publicly. This filtered down. "I always felt like I could do anything."

His competitiveness and confidence, combined with his short stature, put Jim on the side of the underdog early on. Aside from the reality that the smallest kid on the field had no choice but to prove himself each and every time, it was just more fun to be on that side than with the guys who expected to prevail. "Whenever we chose up sides for something like basketball, if there were an odd number of guys, I always wanted to be on the side where it looked like it was an impossible situation. I loved the underdog role. I'd rather lose in that sort of situation than make it easy." It was the challenge of it all he loved the most, the fun of overcoming the odds—or not, but at least trying to. In this way he was the epitome of blue-collar Rochelle Park. "Nobody rooted for the Yankees in Rochelle Park," Jim would say. "It didn't seem sporting—like shooting fish in a barrel." Yankee fans were the kids who wanted to be on the side with five guys rather than four, who only liked the bedtime stories with happy endings. "Yankee fans, we believed, were the sons of bankers who lived in towns with bigger houses and nicer lawns." Roger Angell once described the Yankees as "the rich family up on the hill."[10] Rochelle Park was at the bottom of that hill. So Rochelle Park kids rooted for either the Giants or the Dodgers.

When they could swing it the brothers trekked over to the Polo Grounds to root on their team of choice, the New York Giants. They'd bring their lunches—tuna fish or peanut butter sandwiches that would befoul the air by the third inning on a warm day—and cheer on Willie Mays, Whitey Lockman, and the rest.[11] Whenever possible they'd arrive well before game time to try to catch the players as they were entering the stadium to ask for their autographs. This, by itself, was not unusual; there were dozens of kids there every time. But little Jim Bouton was no doubt the only one to make sure to reserve a space between the signatures of Mays and Amalfitano for his own autograph, which he would add after the game. "I wanted to see how I would sign when I was a big-league player," he said later.[12] Not "if," "when."

By the time Jim was thirteen, George was doing a little better financially, so the Boutons packed up and headed for Ridgewood, New Jersey, home of the bankers with the bigger houses and nicer lawns. Monochrome, white-collar, comfortable Ridgewood. Where the Yankee fans resided. Whatever rough edges Rochelle Park presented, Ridgewood smoothed away. Here would be where young Jim Bouton would finally have the space to get serious about school and plan for his future, or at least that was the thought. Quickly, however, it became obvious to everyone that Jim was singularly focused—he wanted to be a base-ball player. So it was Bob whose academic star rose as he became the designated engineer in the family, urged by his parents and relatives to carry on the Bouton tinkerer tradition (he would eventually grad-uate with an engineering degree from Cornell). "Bob was more of a student, got very good grades," Pete recalled. "Jim was a decent stu-dent, but his focus was baseball. He was good, but he didn't have the focus on grades that Bob did." Thus did Bob become the engineer-in-waiting and Jim become the ballplayer.

Summer mornings would arrive with Jim urging Bob to get out of bed already because there was a ball game somewhere and they needed to be a part of it. Why are you just reading books? Jim would ask Bob. Why are you studying? he wanted to know. Why sit at home when there are games to be played? "I was the student," Bob recalled, "and he was the athlete." More than simply participate, Jim had an overwhelming desire to run the entire enterprise, no matter what it might be. "He liked to be the show maker," said Bob. "He wanted to call the shots." He had in his head a vision of what needed to be done to make whatever it was, to him at least, better and more fun, "even though that might not have been something other people wanted to do," Bob remembered. No matter. Jim would push them forward, bending them toward his will, undaunted.

This portrait of Bouton's childhood perhaps clashes with the future image of him among his professional teammates and many of the scribes as something of a thinker—a cleated philosopher—but only upon first glance. In truth, he was very much a thinker, albeit an untraditional one who was always open to acquiring knowledge from unconventional sources—people, circumstances, the streets—rather than simply textbooks. He was every bit the tinkerer as anyone else in the Bouton household, although his smarts didn't evidence them-selves on his quarterly report cards. He was simply interested in things that weren't tested in school. To the surprise of many (today, but not then), he was never much of a reader; about all he read with any regularity were the sanitized "Chip Hilton" books written by former bas-ketball coach Clair Bee.[13]

Starting with the football-themed *Touchdown Pass* in 1948, these sports-themed novels for boys presented wholesome life lessons through baseball, football, and basketball that were little different from the ones sportswriters were penning for their fathers in the dai-lies. Typically, Chip and his teammates faced obstacles that threatened their sense of teamwork and fair play. By the end sportsmanship won out, good triumphed over evil, and virtue had been restored. The over-whelming theme of the Chip Hilton books was that to do good, one had to *be* good and that the good teammate was the one who subli-mated his own interest for the good of the team. If he were fictional-ized, Mickey Mantle could have been Chip Hilton, given how he was typically portrayed.

Jim thrived in Ridgewood. He professionalized his business cards, printing dozens of them in the school's print shop, and generating enough business doing whatever for whomever to ensure that he always had money in his pocket. Although he may have been so-so in the classroom, once the bell rang and after-school sports began, there was nobody better. In monochrome Ridgewood, where white families were comfortable and black ones mostly a rumor, a kid like Jim—who wanted it more than anyone else, who needed to win—couldn't help but succeed. He was an all-sports star in high school, excelling no matter what the sport, no matter what the season. He may not have been the biggest or the fastest, but nobody in Ridge-wood High competed harder than Jim Bouton. Provided he never left its protective bubble, that would be enough.

In 1954 after his freshman year at Ridgewood, the bubble burst. By that time George had long since moved on from selling pressure cookers to become an operations manager at American Manganese. Offered an opportunity to run their plant in Indiana, George jumped and relocated the family just across the state line in Homewood, Illi-nois. That quickly, Ridgewood High was in Jim's rearview mirror.

Homewood, itself, was not all that different from Ridgewood, but it, along with many of the neighboring towns, lacked its own high school. Instead, it served as one tributary of many to sprawling Bloom Township High School, which took students from all of them. Located in Chicago Heights, one of the most industrial communities in the country after World War II, Bloom was everything Ridgewood High was not. It was large, it was diverse, and it could be brutal. Each town, monochromatic as it might have been, sent its young to Bloom, where everyone was stirred together. Chicago Heights would have been a culture shock on its own, replete as it was with factories, steel mills, and foundries—the prototypical lunch-bucket community. Add in the multitude of races, classes, and ethnicities from the neighboring towns, and it became a salad bowl of American society. "This was not Ridgewood," Bob remembered. Instead, "This is where the real world is." It was an eye-opener in more ways than one.

Bloom had nearly four thousand students in all; when Jim arrived he became little more than simply one of approximately a thousand sophomores, more of a statistic than a star. "I had acne and braces and I was miserable," he recalled years later. Worse, "no one knew I was a hero."[14] He was hardly that—Bloom was a factory for athletes, merely making a squad was an accomplishment, forget about being the star. Just as he had in Ridgewood, he tried out for the varsity football and basketball teams. He was cut by both. In the spring he tried out for the baseball team and barely managed to survive the final cut for the freshman and sophomore squad. Little matter, as he barely played anyway. He was "Warm-up Bouton," as he liked to describe himself years later—always in the bullpen, never in the game. Looking back, most notably in *Ball Four*, he always described this period with great humor, but at the time the competitor in him seethed. His confidence was such that he knew he was every bit as good as the kids out there; he just wasn't being given the chance. As he saw it there was an entrenched star system at Bloom, with the coaches' handpicked favorites being given the starting positions before the seasons even began. Nothing offended his competitive nature more deeply. Although there

was little he could do to change the coaches' minds, he was determined to at least show the stars themselves that he was very much
their equal. He recruited Bob, along with a ragtag collection of kids
from the neighborhood, and challenged the first teamers to a game
of street football, to be played not on the manicured football field in
Bloom's state-of-the-art stadium but in the backyards of Homewood,
among the rocks, trees, hills, and ridges. With Jim at quarterback and
Bob as his receiver, they won. They challenged them again and beat
them once more. And then again. Perhaps the stars didn't take the
game seriously; it was simply an after-school backyard get-together to
them. But to Jim the games meant everything. He was not going to
lose. And so he didn't.

Now more than ever he identified with the underdog. No longer
simply a fun construct self-created to test himself, this time the status
was imposed on him by the structure and culture at Bloom. Nearly
every day he bore witness to some form of manifestation of the strong
preying upon the weak. Pete, however, bore the brunt most directly.
Ripped from his comfortable existence in Ridgewood at nine years
old, he was thrust into a world he was hardly prepared for. "What
a terrible time for me," he recalled. "It was fighting on your way to
school, fighting on your way from school. I was bullied all the time."
Although Jim and Bob continued to tease Pete mercilessly themselves
(one time devising a rigged Ping-Pong tournament in the basement
with a milkshake for the "victor," then throwing the games to Pete,
compelling him to down the concoction spiked with salt and vinegar
as his "prize"), Jim began stepping in to recalibrate the scales whenever he noticed an imbalance of power. Jim appointed himself Bob's
protector, and Jim and Bob both took charge of protecting Pete. "One
day I was followed home by a group of boys who wanted to beat the
crap out of me," Pete recalled. "There was a foray on a neighbor's lawn
where I was getting jabbed in all directions by three different guys—
you didn't know who to defend yourself from first. Suddenly Jim and
Bob showed up. I was crying; there were at least six kids jeering at
me, poking and grabbing at me. [Jim] said to them, 'You're not going

to all fight him at once. You want to fight him, you fight him one at a time? So they picked out one of the kids, and I beat the shit out of the kid while [Jim and Bob] held the other kids back. Then they said, 'You want to do this again? Then come on over, one at a time.' I never saw those kids again." In the school yard as well, whenever he'd see a kid crying he'd step in to see what was wrong. "He was always looking out for the kids who couldn't defend themselves," said Bob. He'd then administer his own form of justice by punching their tormentors in the nose. Sometimes he'd apologize later for bloodying them. Still, the message had been sent.

As an underdog himself, he soon recognized the steps he'd have to take to rebalance the scales in his own life. Reluctantly, he decided to rechannel his energies away from football and basketball and focus solely on baseball. It was the only way he could ever even have a hope of making the varsity before graduation. Years later he believed that the pressures of Bloom turned him into a Major League pitcher. "If I had stayed at Ridgewood and had it easy I probably wouldn't have made it. I'd have played all sports, been a jack of all trades and master of none."[15] The benefits were not immediately forthcoming. The coaches might have had their handpicked favorites, but there were some legitimate stars on every squad. On the varsity baseball team future National Basketball Association (NBA) executive Jerry Colangelo was a southpaw curveball specialist who was the ace of the staff and drawing the interest of professional scouts. Other players were being recruited by major colleges, such as powerhouse Arizona State. Once Jim lasered in on baseball, he succeeded in making the varsity as a junior but rarely made it into the games. He was still "Warm-up Bouton," as coach Fred Jacobeit often turned to infielders or outfielders when he needed a relief pitcher rather than the skinny 145-pound kid loosening up in the bullpen.

"I was the number-one pitcher, and Jimmy was behind me," Colangelo recalled. "To say he was having trouble adjusting [to the level of competition at Bloom] was an understatement. He was very, very competitive. I saw that firsthand. . . . There were times when, out of frustration, Jim frustrated some of the guys. I remember one day by our lockers I had to break up a potentially bad scene between Jim and another athlete. . . . He could be a little edgy from time to time." Ultimately, he had someone on his side—one of those coaches he dismissed upon his arrival at Bloom for playing the star system. Coach Fred Jacobeit may have at first passed Bouton over for his infielders and outfielders when the games were on the line, but at heart he was a scrapper, a competitor just like Jim was. "He was all banged up all the time" was how Colangelo remembered Jacobeit. Hobbling onto the field with two bad knees wrapped in braces, he never begged off, no matter what. Jim didn't realize it yet, but Jacobeit was just the sort of coach who would see the value in what he had to offer. "Jim was a fireballing right hander," Jacobeit remembered. A kid who seemingly threw everything he had into every pitch, so much so that his hat flew off nearly every time. Throughout his career, coaches—professional as well as those who simply considered themselves experts—would shake their heads in disapproval whenever they watched him pitch, admonishing him to adjust his delivery. Not Jacobeit. "They'd tell him, 'You've got to see that ball go into the glove. Your head has gotta come through before the rest of your body.' And you looked at him—he was darned near looking at first base when he ended up, he followed through so far." But he was throwing harder than the kids who were practicing what the ordained experts preached. So be it, Jacobeit figured. If it worked for Jim, that was good enough. Regardless, there simply wasn't a spot for him in the rotation during his junior year. The talent was seemingly bottomless at Bloom; short, skinny Jim Bouton just could not get on the field. "Jim was so deep in the varsity pitching staff," John Meyers, a local sportswriter who covered the squad recalled years later, "it was hard to find him."[16]

After a lost season in the Bloom bullpen he tried out for a Chicago Heights American Legion team managed by Earl Detella. Here, he figured, he might have a shot at taking the mound in an actual game; many of his teammates at Bloom took the summers off and didn't play Legion ball. Regardless, he was taking no chances. "I was the first kid at the ball park along the Dixie Highway," Jim remembered. "Earl was already there, and he said, 'What are you?' I told him I was a pitcher and he told me to throw a few to him. The same thing happened the next night and then Earl said, 'You'll start our first game.'" He not only pitched but also helped manicure the field before games and get it into shape after it rained.[17] "Bouton, you're my pitcher," he remembered Detella telling him, words he hadn't heard in a long time.[18] Given the opportunity, he thrived, quickly becoming the ace of Detella's staff. Meyer covered these games also. He was impressed. So impressed that he penned an open letter in the *Chicago Heights Star*, suggesting to Jacobeit that he would do very well to take a long look at Jim Bouton the following spring when baseball season started again.[19]

Jacobeit was reaching the same conclusion on his own. He incorporated ballroom dance in his physical education classes and was impressed by how easily Bouton took to it, by how well and athletically he moved. Soon they developed a rapport such that Jim would wait on the corner every morning for Jacobeit to drive by and pick him up on his way to school. This time there was little chance that Bouton would be just another anonymous arm when baseball resumed in the spring. And Meyer, Detella, and Jacobeit weren't the only ones who by this point had taken notice of him. William K. (W. K.) Fred, a Chicagoland bird-dog scout who once had a loose affiliation with the St. Louis Browns, caught a few of Bouton's Legion games and tipped off a friend of his, Art Stewart, who managed another area Legion club, this one with a higher level of talent than Detella's. Stewart had a loose affiliation of his own—he was a part-time scout with the New York Yankees, who had him run a club in the Chicago area called, appropriately enough, the Chicago Yankees, in the hope that maybe he'd unearth a gem or two in the process. Fred made his living by taking the streetcar from one Chicago park to another, looking for players he could recommend to the full-time scouts. Even though he made his living on the run, he was at all times dressed in a suit and tie, topped always by a fedora. Many of his fellow straphangers naturally assumed the nattily attired man standing next to them was most likely a banker on his way to a real estate closing; he hardly fitted the mold of the grizzled hustler beating the bushes for raw, unpolished baseball talent.

"I was always nice to [Fred]," Stewart recalled. "That was why he'd tip me off on things, even though I worked for the Yankees. So he told me, 'You know, there's a young junior over at Bloom. He'd be worth taking a look at and having on your club. He could help you.'" Fred was a friend, but there was more to it than that. Fred wanted to see how Bouton would fare against better competition than he was facing with Detella's squad. If he performed well, maybe Fred could recommend the young pitcher to one of the full-time scouts he knew and perhaps collect a commission for doing so. Stewart marked Bouton's name down in his notebook and then promptly forgot about it.

2   Take a Hike, Son

Art Stewart and W. K. Fred lived in a world that Bouton barely knew existed. His extended little farther than Homewood and the Bloom High campus. Where, as far as he was concerned, life had moved on. Fall had arrived, school was back in session, baseball was on the distant horizon, and he had by now given up his pursuits of football and basketball. Facing the void, he rediscovered a childhood passion: watercolors. He had always had an interest in art; his great-aunt had graduated from art school, and as a child he enjoyed watching her work.[1] And in art it didn't matter if you were too small to grip a knuckleball the way Dutch Leonard showed you on the back of a Wheaties box.

As he grew and learned how to throw hard, baseball began to dominate his life. Still, he never completely abandoned this other interest. Now, at Bloom, it flourished. Sometimes when asked he'd say that Hoyt Wilhelm was his hero, but sometimes he'd say no, Wilhelm was great, but his true hero was John Marin, the early- to midcentury abstract art pioneer who specialized in watercolors. At Bloom he took some art classes, which rekindled his passion. Once he had enough for a portfolio of watercolors, charcoals, and oils, he entered a contest held by the Homewood-Flosswood Women's Club.[2] He placed third, good enough for an all-expenses-paid two-week course at the Art Institute of Chicago.[3] This led to an invitation to show his work at the avant-garde Gold Coast Art Show on Rush Street. Jim and Bob piled his paintings and etchings into the back of the family car and set off, setting up alongside artists of various stripes. While most artists considered the show primarily a platform by which to display their work, Jim and Bob saw it differently. Whereas the other artists priced their work at $400 or $500 apiece,[4] Jim and Bob held, in essence, an "everything-must-go" closeout sale, undercutting the competition by offering Jim's paintings for $4 each: "$3.98, two for $7."[5] Despite being perhaps the most inexperienced artist there, his quickly became the most popular booth at the show. Crowds swelled around the high school art student from Homewood. Within two hours his inventory was gone.[6] Jim and Bob returned home fifteen paintings lighter and with about $60 in their pockets.

He then expanded into jewelry making. When he could find it, he'd melt silver or gold. When he couldn't, other metals would do. Whatever he could scrounge up. He learned how to make wax impressions and then cast them in plaster to create a mold in which to pour his metals. He'd look for interesting driveway stones to polish as centerpieces for the rings, bracelets, and necklaces he'd create and then sell; few of his customers realized that the ring they were admiring was largely composed of discarded materials strewn about their neighborhood just days earlier. The cold slap of athletic reality at Bloom caused Bouton to wonder whether his future lay as a commercial artist rather than as a pitcher. Art, he realized, could be a satisfying means toward a financial end. He loved art itself, but he also loved the attention it brought him along with the idea that people would pay him for his work. On its own, art was a hobby. But blended with his knack for making a buck and ability to draw a crowd, he saw how this could be a lifestyle.

He burnished other interests while waiting for baseball season to start up again. He took a deep dive into the Chicago music scene, although here he was more in the audience than up on the stage. He fell in love with blues, jazz, and soul music after his dial found an obscure radio show broadcast out of the South Side late one night. "This is Sam Evans," the show would begin, "and I'm in the basement with the blue light on drinking Orange Tommy: the screwdriver in a bottle, and you're listening to *Jammin' with Sam*." Jim and Bob would listen, enraptured, through the night and early morning, keeping the volume down so as not to wake the rest of the house. Sam would tell stories and spin records. Real records. Black records, "before they were co-opted by whites," Jim would say. And real stories. Not ones that had been scrubbed, rinsed, and sanitized. Told not by a polished, professionalized DJ but by a guy sitting in his basement on the South Side of Chicago drinking supercharged screwdrivers. They had never heard anything like it. Later Jim took a job with the Chicago Heights Park District, where he organized pickup games for inner-city kids. The games, themselves, were fun, but what he really enjoyed was listening to the stories these kids told him every time he went there, the language they used, the banter between them. All of it—unedited, unpolished—fascinated him. Often he'd come home full of tales and anecdotes, looking for someone to unload them on. Most of the time he found Bob and shared with him everything he had heard.

As he matured, so did his tastes. As soon as it was released, he became enamored of the movie *On the Waterfront*, along with its star Marlon Brando. Brando's cool "yoked together defiance and vulnerability," a critic would later write, "the side-glances of thwarted hope with kinetic explosions of righteous anger."[7] All of this spoke to him. In the dockworker and shamed boxer Terry Malloy, Jim witnessed the melding of defiance and vulnerability as well as what another critic at the time described as "a single human soul caught in the contradictions and absurdity of modern life."[8] This was no Chip Hilton story. The film offered up an antihero for a protagonist—a conflicted individual who remained "unsatisfied and alone as the credits roll[ed]."[9] So when Jim leaned over the Wrigley Field dugout at about this time to get Giants shortstop Alvin Dark's autograph (as he recounted in *Ball Four*), he could not have been shocked at Dark's response: "Take a hike, son. Take a hike."[10] After all he'd experienced since leaving the cocoon of Ridgewood, he knew by now that life was far more complex and messy than the sanitized tales he'd ingested as a child. If anything, Dark's "Take a hike" could only have suggested to him that baseball was in fact no different from anything else. The sportswriters were wrong; in his own backhanded way, Dark had imparted upon him a fundamental truth.

At long last spring rolled around. Even before the ice melted it was clear that, finally, he was going to get his shot. His successes in Legion ball, along with the open letter in the *Star* and his burgeoning relationship with Jacobeit, made it impossible for him to fade into the background any longer. More immediately, Colangelo had all but thrown out his arm by this point and, worse, suffered a broken hand in the off-season, leaving what was left of his arm shrunken and withered. Jacobeit now had a need in the rotation; somebody would have to step up. Jacobeit gave Bouton the ball and watched him become a star. As a senior he flourished and led Bloom to the state finals, where he pitched fourteen innings in a 2–1 defeat. "Warm-up Bouton" was now the ace. Testament to how far he had come at Bloom since his arrival came eight years later when the school inaugurated the "Jim Bouton 110% Award," given to the athlete who put forth the most effort in any school sport during the previous year. It paid for the fifty-seven-inch trophy with the money Bouton refused to accept upon returning to Bloom a few years later for a sports banquet.[11]

Despite Bouton's successes on the Bloom High mound, Art Stewart was none the wiser. The note he jotted down at W. K. Fred's insistence the previous summer was by this point swimming in the sea of names, places, and other details he had accumulated in the months since, seemingly lost amid the marginalia. Thankfully, for Stewart as much as Bouton, fate would intervene. One afternoon Stewart got word that Colangelo was going to take the mound again. So he, along with a busload of other scouts who had likewise had their eyes on Colangelo for a while now, trekked over to Bloom to see if he still had it. Colangelo warmed up but right before game time felt a twinge in his arm and was scratched. At that point the busload of scouts began chatting among themselves about a third baseman from Kankakee, Indiana, who was worth taking a look at. It was only a short drive across the state line to see him, so they all piled back into their cars and headed off. Stewart stayed. "I was a young scout at the time," he recalled. "And I was ready to go, too. And then I remembered something that one of the greatest scouts who ever lived told me." The scout was Paul Krichell, the famed Yankee scout who signed Lou Gehrig, Tony Lazzeri, Whitey Ford, and Phil Rizzuto, along with dozens of other household names. "One of the things he always told me was this: when you get to the ballpark, never leave early, no matter what. So with that I stayed."

Stewart settled in, more out of professional obligation than anything else. Suddenly, he was drawn to the sound, rather than the sight, of Colangelo's replacement, who was loosening up on a nearby practice mound. "I'm hearing this smack, smack, smack down the line of this kid warming up. He's only about five-ten and 150, 160 pounds, and I said, jeez, this kid's got a pretty good arm. I went to the coach and said 'What's his name?' He says 'Jim Bouton,' and then it all came back to me." Stewart searched through his notebook and found the tip from Fred. The young pitcher then took the mound and dominated, striking out sixteen batters. Fred had been right. Jim Bouton could help him. In more ways than he could possibly know at the time.

3 Joliet

Once he had discovered Bouton, Art Stewart made sure that nobody else did. "I pitched him out of Chicago as much as I could," he recalled. His favorite diamond for his diamond in the rough was the one inside the barricaded walls of the infamous Joliet Correctional Center. Here was where some of the most hardened rapists and murderers served their time and, occasionally, played ball on a beautifully manicured field designed by the Cubs' longtime head groundskeeper, Bobby Dorr, and maintained by a lucky few of them. Professional scouts routinely followed Stewart's club around, but they found reasons to be elsewhere when he scheduled games against one or another of the region's penitentiaries. It was in these games that Stewart would unleash his brightest prospects, the prison walls affording him the privacy to judge their abilities away from the prying eyes of his scouting competitors.

The visuals were surreal as Stewart's Legion Yankees took the Joliet prison-yard field in old New York Yankee uniforms, supplied by the big club itself. Stewart wore Rizzuto's old, frayed number 10 on his back. "I remember the first game Jim pitched there," Stewart said. "About fifteen to twenty minutes before the game, they marched the prisoners out—there were over a thousand of them—and Jim's warming up and throwing pretty hard." Sizing up the competition, the prisoners began to make their wagers. "They bet cigarettes. Most of them would bet against the home team because they hate them because they get the opportunity to work on the field and play ball while the rest of them sit in their cells." After watching Bouton warm up, the heavy money, or tobacco, was on him. He delivered. After throwing a two-hitter and striking out several of the inmates, he left the field to a thunderous roar.

Stewart could hide him for only so long. Competing within the Chicago Parks League, he had no choice but to pitch him in the play-off games, in front of everybody. In this era before the implementation of baseball's amateur draft, scouts were continually at war with each other, each attempting to hoard their finds for their respective clubs. As a Legion coach as well as a part-time scout, Stewart faced an unsolvable conflict of interest. As a coach his job was to win games and play his best players, but as a part-time scout his loyalty ran to the New York Yankees, who, Stewart hoped, might promote him to full-time if he was able to present them with top-notch talent. In Bouton Stewart knew he had a bona fide prospect on his hands, and after Bouton pitched his club to the Legion World Series in Battle Creek, Michigan, every other scout did as well. "He pitched against one of the big powerhouses," Stewart remembered, "and beat 'em. There were about forty scouts in the stands, and I said, 'Uh-oh. That's it. They all know about Jim Bouton now.'"

Although he could have entertained offers from numerous scouts at that point, Jim, guided by George, decided that another year of amateur seasoning was preferable. After driving past the Western Michigan University (WMU) campus one day and admiring its baseball diamond, George doubled back, picked up some brochures from the admissions office, and took them home to his son.[1] Western Michigan had a strong baseball program that intrigued the Boutons for a couple of reasons: it had sent a large handful of players to the Majors over the course of the previous two decades but was small enough to be a place where Jim might once more be able to stand out. Unbeknownst to Jim, at around this time a top catching prospect from Detroit was also considering Western Michigan. His name was Bill Freehan, and in 1958 he did in fact enroll. He transferred shortly thereafter to Michigan, however. Freehan would himself write a controversial baseball memoir, *Behind the Mask*, which was a diary of his 1969 season with the Detroit Tigers and released a few months before *Ball Four* in 1970.[2]

But for a couple of last-minute decisions by both Bouton and Freehan, WMU might very well have fielded, at least in retrospect, baseball's first "tell-all" battery.

The scouts might have been courting Jim, but the coaching staff at WMU had never heard of him. George fixed that; he sent the head coach an anonymous letter praising the phenom from Bloom High School. He stuffed the envelope with Jim's press clippings as an exclamation point. The coach was intrigued. He called Jim, took him to lunch, and eventually agreed to put him on the freshman squad to see what he had. If he did well, he might gain a scholarship and join the varsity as a sophomore, he offered.[3] George and Jim found the arrangement acceptable, so in the fall of 1957 Jim headed off for Western Michigan University, where, rather than being a professional pitcher in one of the organizations willing to sign him that summer, he would begin the season as the fourth starter on the freshman team.

Once settled in at WMU, he joined the baseball frat, Delta Sigma Phi, and very quickly made a name for himself among his brethren. One day, frat brother Jim Charlton remembered, "he led his pledge class on an elaborate raid of the fraternity house. It was an old Victorian mansion, and the raid involved bringing in farm animals, a smoke machine, and bricking up the front door so you couldn't get out. It was a very elaborate and time-consuming plan." He then decided to run for a leadership position within the fraternity. It didn't go well. While his brothers appreciated his sense of humor, some chafed at the range, as well as the amount, of Bouton's opinions. He received only four votes. It was an early indicator to him that life offered up choices, and here was one of them. With his looks, ability, and charisma, he would have little trouble being backslapped into the cloistered world of the insider if he constrained himself to conform to the insider's code. Or he could speak his mind and not worry about the code but reside on the outside looking in. Events like this one, minor in the grand scheme of things, reminded him that there was no escaping the choice. At Delta Sigma Phi, as he would everywhere else over the next half century, he chose the latter.

Baseball went better. By the end of the year he was the number-one pitcher on the freshman squad and primed to be promoted to the varsity the following season. Although his practical side pulled him toward finance as a major, his artistic side drove him toward WMU's art department. After sizing up its offerings, he decided to enroll in an advanced watercolors course. Upon being informed that he first needed to take several preparatory courses before he would be eligible for the class, he balked. Eventually, he argued his way into the class, making an arrangement with the professor that if he couldn't keep up with the more advanced students, he would drop the course. He wound up with an A.[4] At around the same time he was enrolled in a communications class when another student tried to argue her way into *that* course. She was Barbara Heister, a fellow freshman from Allegan, Michigan, who was trying to switch classes after the second semester had already begun. The professor left the decision to admit her up to the students. Led by Jim, several of the boys clapped their approval, and she was in.

A few weeks later it was "Twirp Week" at WMU, their version of Sadie Hawkins Day, where "the woman is required to pay." Barbara (or Bobbie, as she was called) asked out the good-looking guy who stood up for her earlier in the semester. They went to the student union, where Bobbie did most of the talking and on the subject she was most passionate about: baseball.[5] She was not only a rabid Detroit Tigers fan but also the official statistician for her high school newspaper and kept score for the baseball team. At WMU she continued to keep score, although this time unofficially from the stands. She had only made it to the varsity games; she had no idea that her date was pitching on the freshman team. Finally, he fessed up. They talked some more baseball but about other things as well. Bobbie started showing up at the freshman games, and soon they became a couple. It didn't take her long to realize that her new boyfriend was not a typical jock. He was knowledgeable about politics and causes and liked talking about both. He introduced her to costume jewelry making, and she soon developed an interest in that as well (after they were married they bought buffers and grinders and each made their own lines of jewelry).[6] "He was not one-dimensional," Bobbie recalled. His interests were wide-ranging, but undergirding all of it was the heart of a bulldog. "He certainly was competitive, and that would come out in just playing cards or putting together a jigsaw puzzle, but that's probably what made him succeed."

Bobbie helped him measure his success; she soon began charting his starts, keeping track of his innings pitched, strikeouts, walks, earned runs, and overall performance. In the far-right-hand column of her personalized Jim Bouton stat sheet came her overall assessment of each start—Excellent, Good, Fair, or Bad.[7] She never had the opportunity to chart one of his games for the varsity, though. Although in retrospect Bouton is often recalled as being one of the "greats" in WMU baseball history, he never advanced beyond the freshman squad; he was gone before he could. His best game at WMU was most likely not even an official one, coming in the annual alumni game the fall of his sophomore year, shortly before he signed with the Yankees.[8]

Jim and Bobbie would continue to date over the course of the next few years. Eventually, she graduated (Jim never did, although he returned several times to take various classes and then took more classes at Farleigh Dickinson after he joined the Yankees) with a degree in social psychology. She moved to suburban Philadelphia and became a social worker, dealing with delinquent adolescents. This amused Jim to no end; he liked to tell people that he was her first client.[9] On December 23, 1962, they were married in Bobbie's hometown of Allegan. Jim was in the U.S. Army Reserve stationed in Fort Dix at the time, so Bobbie had to make all the arrangements. On the day of the ceremony Bob officially assumed the role he had played throughout his brother's childhood. He was Jim's best man.

4   You Should Write a Book

After his successful season on the freshman squad at WMU, Bouton returned to Art Stewart and the Chicago Yankees for a second season of Legion ball with that club. He dominated again, and again the scouts appeared to be curious. After some back-and-forth that revealed their limited interest in him as a prospect, George decided to become proactive and force the issue. He drew up a letter announcing that his son would sign for $30,000 and sent it to every scout that at one time or another had at least shown cursory interest. Maybe, he hoped, he could ignite a bidding war. Letters went to scouts from the White Sox, Braves, Indians, Phillies, Dodgers, Yankees, Cardinals, and Tigers.[1] It was a decidedly unsophisticated campaign—the letter to the Philadelphia scout identified his employer as the "Phillys."[2] W. K. Fred also sent some letters. The goal was to smoke out those who had genuine interest and to cause those who were more reluctant to rethink their positions. George was confident that Jim would sign somewhere eventually, as he told him in a letter congratulating him on his successful start in the fall game against the alumni: "Was glad to ... hear how well you did against some 'pros.' They're human too so can be fooled, but it takes real control, stuff and resourcefulness to fool the big leaguers consistently. That's the main thing you'll develop in your first pro years." George explained to Jim that his letters to the scouts "should bring the whole thing to a head real soon." If anyone was sufficiently interested, they'd sign. "Otherwise we'll stop the whole matter 'till after school next spring."[3] In the meantime, George assured Jim that he was maintaining contact with Art Stewart; through it all the Yankees seemed to be Jim's most likely destination.

The initial returns were not promising. The White Sox and Dodgers returned unresponsive responses, and the Braves recommended that Bouton return to school for at least another year, if not two. At that point, perhaps, the Braves' Chicago-area scout suggested, "I think he will be a valuable prospect." He reiterated that his prior offer to sign Jim (made in Battle Creek, Michigan, at the Legion tournament) still stood but that $30,000 was too rich for his blood.[4] That amount in 1958 dollars certainly sounded, on the surface, like a lot, but as George and Jim were to learn, sometimes $30,000 wasn't exactly $30,000.

Upon Stewart's urging, however, the Yankees responded more favorably. The great Yankee second baseman Jerry Coleman had just retired and was named personnel director as preparation for a new career in the front office. One of his first official duties was to work with Stewart to sign Bouton. "He was learning all the facets of the front office," Stewart recalled, "so they gave him the figures to give to me. He called me from Washington during the Winter Meetings." One day Coleman himself showed up to help woo Jim, which set the whole Bouton house abuzz. Still, Stewart remained the driving force in Jim's signing. "Knowing Jim and playing for me, we were close. The folks invited me for Thanksgiving dinner, and we signed him—over Thanksgiving dinner, 1958."

On Coleman's authorization, Stewart was able to meet George's demand for a $30,000 contract ($30,250 to be exact), but when he broke it down for them, it was clear that this contract was hardly too rich for anybody's blood. In actuality Jim's bonus upon signing a contract with the most successful organization in American sports was a big, fat zero. Instead, his "bonus" was to be paid in $5,000 increments over each of the next three years. On top of this he would receive a typical Minor League salary of $500 per month for the three six-month playing seasons during that time. The final $6,250 was waiting for him if he ever happened to make it to the big leagues.[5] Annually speaking, $9,000, when it was all added up, was certainly not bad when considering that the minimum Major League salary at the time was $6,000 but hardly terms that projected confidence on behalf of a club that they were signing a top-drawer prospect. Nevertheless, the signing would alter the lives of the two people most directly involved in it—Bouton's, obviously, but also Art Stewart's. Bouton's signing was Stewart's first, and in a few years Bouton would also be the first of his signings to make it to the big leagues. Once Jim won twenty games with the Yankees, Stewart's career was made. "Now, among your fellow scouts and competitors, you're recognized—'Hey, that guy signed Jim Bouton.'" Stewart would go on to sign seventy future Major League players, such as Carlos Beltran and Johnny Damon, but Jim Bouton would be the springboard to all of that.

One person whose life was not altered by the signing was W. K. Fred's. Neither Stewart nor the Yankees threw anything his way for his initial tip to Stewart two years earlier, so Fred began hounding George and Jim for a cut of the signing bonus and subsequent salaries once he reached the Yankees. A couple months after Bouton signed with the Yankees, Fred found out about it thirdhand and wrote Bouton to remind him of his role in his development. Fred made it a point to let Jim know that although a couple of scouts from the Orioles were likewise impressed with his performance as a member of Earl Detella's Legion squad, "It was W. K. Fred, the part-time man, who made contact with you. Jim, I outlined a plan to you that your parents approved, which would afford you opportunity to pitch for a good ball-club, gaining experience and incidentally placing your pitching wares on display before important people. I am certain that the Bouton family will not be slow to acknowledge that my plan successfully produced in every respect." Fred went on: "I . . . consider that Mr. Stewart was very remiss in failing to contact me, bringing me up to date. It must be that Stewart long since has informed his N.Y. Yankee Brass [sic], where and how he was able to come up with pitcher Jim Bouton. That fine lad and Pitcher proceeded to be the Ace [sic] of Stewart's pitching staff for two seasons. All of this resulted in material gain to all parties concerned to date—with one exception."[6] After going on to inform Jim that his mother had passed away six years earlier and "I continue to miss her terribly," he signed off as Jim Bouton's "Friend and Discoverer." The letters would continue over the course of the next several years. Some would gently prod the Boutons for a share of Jim's salary; others would not so gently prod. After Bouton won twenty games in 1963 Fred suggested that he was "entitled to $1,000–$2,000" of his $10,500 salary.[7] Eventually, Bouton sent him some money, but still the letters persisted.

Bouton reported to the Yankees' Class D affiliate in Kearney, Nebraska, in the spring of 1959 to begin his professional career. It was a short-season league, and he struggled from start to finish, ending with a 5.40 earned run average (ERA). Regardless, he wasn't afraid to be a man apart. When the Topps Bubble Gum people sent him a contract for a whopping five bucks in exchange for the right to put his picture on a baseball card, he refused to sign, believing the terms to be unfair. He was the only Minor Leaguer to refuse to sign the contract.[8]

From Kearney he moved on to Auburn, another Class D club in the New York–Penn League, to finish the year and once again struggled, compiling a 5.73 ERA before breaking his pitching hand on a line drive hit back to the box. He was used inconsistently on both squads, sometimes starting, sometimes relieving, never being able to settle into any sort of rhythm. He also struggled with some of the cultural realities of professional baseball. Before a game against the Holdredge White Sox, manager Jim Gleeson encouraged his pitchers to throw at a Holdredge hitter whom Gleeson suspected of filing his spikes. On the clubhouse wall was an outline of the player in his batting stance, "with sections marked like the cow illustration in the butcher shop," Bouton recalled years later. "It was a contest for the pitchers, with certain areas worth more points." Bouton entered the game in relief and, as instructed, threw his first pitch behind the batter's head, in a high point zone. The batter froze, and the ball just missed his helmet, hitting his bat instead. It dribbled to Bouton, who threw him out. The experience shook him up; he never intentionally threw at a batter again, although he managed to plunk more than his share throughout his career, if inadvertently.[9] On another night in Kearney he was exposed to a cultural reality of a different sort when he and three teammates were jumped by eight local toughs who wanted to teach what they considered these privileged interlopers a lesson. Although not much came of it physically, Bouton bore witness to what he would later describe as the disconnect between the "people looking to get back at the world and the ballplayers walking around like they own it."[10]

He returned home after the 1959 season frustrated but also full of stories. Around the dinner table he would recount them to George and Trudy. Funny stories, sad stories, stories of the real life of the professional baseball player. He would express his frustrations over how he was used, how his teammates got along, or not, and how they viewed the outside world as well as how the outside world viewed them. They were not the sorts of stories that could be found in the sports section, so to George and Trudy they were fascinating—surprising, revealing, humorous, poignant. You should write a book, Trudy suggested one evening. Yeah, right, was essentially Jim's response.

He had more immediate concerns. He needed to do something before the 1960 season if he wanted to keep his Major League dream alive. Convinced that he needed to bulk up if he hoped to succeed, he put himself on a high-fat diet in preparation for the season. He downed three or four milkshakes fortified with raw eggs daily, dipped everything in gravy, and ate no matter what his stomach told him.[11] In two months he had put on thirty pounds and given himself a stomach condition that would plague him for the rest of his life. He also took steps to extricate himself from the Yankee organization. He enlisted Fred to air his grievances over how his coaches used him during the '59 season and to nose around other organizations to see if they might be interested in trading for him. It was a breach of baseball etiquette that was not well received. White Sox scout Jack Sheehan replied to Fred's entreaty with a stern admonition:

Apparently Bouton has much faith in you and I think you might do him a favor by pointing out to him that Pro Baseball is probably the most competitive business in the world and each year he will have to compete with others to prove he is better and that every

Major League System is primarily interested in each and every one of their players becoming big leaguers just as fast as possible and they never do anything to prevent that. He had an ordinary record with a 5.40 E.R.A. He was injured and the club took good care of him and he should be appreciative rather than critical.[12]

Despite his struggles in Class D ball, Bouton was promoted in 1960 to the Yankees' Class B affiliate, Greensboro, in the Carolina League. He arrived in town hard on the heels of the civil rights movement: the Greensboro Woolworth lunch-counter sit-in had begun just two months earlier. The town was in chaos, but his concerns were more personal. Just as he had in 1959, he struggled on the mound. At one point George, Trudy, Bob, and Pete decided to take a trip to see him pitch. "We all got in the car. It took about a day and a half to get down there," Bob recalled. "We were saying, 'We may never see this again.' He was about five levels down in the bottom of the barrel of the Minor Leagues." If they were ever going to see him pitch professionally, they figured that they had better do it now. "We could at least say, 'Gee, we saw Jim pitch as a professional baseball player. Wasn't that a nice thing to see.'"

After a few games the family left, but shortly thereafter Bob returned, this time with Bobbie, and they began to follow Jim around the Carolina League. Their presence seemed to settle him, and he began to have some success. Bob had about six weeks of free time during the summer to kill, but because Bobbie was working her way through WMU, she had to have a job if she was going to spend a significant amount of time in Greensboro. Jim very badly wanted her there with him, so he finagled a job for her in a restaurant along with a place to stay. With that she quit her job in Michigan and headed south. When she arrived she found her new employer accommodating; she was allowed to arrange her schedule such that she was usually free come game time. While the games provided a sense of familiarity for Bobbie, nearly everything outside of the ballpark was as if it were in a foreign language. Almost nothing in Allegan was as it was in a civil rights–era southern town. Everything was different—the food, the mores, everything. Race was sucking up most of the oxygen; it hovered over the totality of everyone's life. At work the conversation among the waitresses often turned to the Woolworth's sit-in and what they might do if a black customer attempted to be served in their restaurant. Most were adamant: they would ignore him. Bobbie said otherwise, but this was within the cocoon of their conversation, without the glare of the nation on her as the customer sat in her presence with a menu in his hand. There was seemingly no end to the otherwise meaningless interactions that were now fraught with complications. One day Bobbie was walking on the sidewalk in town and noticed a black man walking in the other direction toward her. Right before their paths crossed, he stepped off the sidewalk and continued on, in the street. Bobbie stopped, turned to him, and pleaded, "Oh, no. Please don't do that." He just smiled and kept on walking.

As the season progressed, Bouton thrived. He ended the season going 14-8 with a sparkling 2.73 ERA. He was the staff workhorse, starting twenty-four games and completing half of them. He led the staff in innings pitched and, even though he wasn't throwing at anybody, batters hit by pitch. He was one of the hardest throwers on the club but also the wiliest—he had a number of different pitches in his arsenal that he might throw at any given moment. Sometimes he had no idea where they were going. The only thing he was sure of was that he was going to outthink, outwork, and, in the end, beat the competition. And he was not shy about saying so. The offensive star of the club was future Yankee utility infielder Phil Linz, who was often on the receiving end of Jim's coffee-shop theories on what made a winner and what separated the winners from the losers. Bouton would tell Linz that there were two types of people in the world—those who thought like winners and those who thought like losers—and if one was able to train his brain properly, he could overcome nearly anything. To Linz, he appeared to be walking proof of that.[13]

When he arrived in St. Petersburg for spring training in 1961 he was full of confidence but, to the Yankee brass, little more than a Minor League roster filler. Pitching coach Johnny Sain took an interest in him, though, and one day pulled him aside. You've got four good pitches, he told Jim, but none of them were outstanding. If he wanted to make it to New York, he'd need to drop his lesser pitches and concentrate on his big three—fastball, curve, and changeup. Drop the knuckleball, at least for now, Sain advised. Even more, focus on your number one—either the curve or the fastball—and work on that until you've mastered it. Once you've got a pitch you know you can throw in a tight spot, you can start to see yourself in Yankee pinstripes, he counseled.[14] Bouton did Sain one better, dropping the change as well and working almost exclusively with his fastball and curve.

The Yanks assigned him to AA Amarillo that year, and once again he dominated. He finished second on the club in wins (with thirteen) and led it in strikeouts. His games weren't always pretty, as sometimes his fastballs and curves missed their mark by a wide margin, but as the season wore on he gained more control, as well as more confidence, in them. He spent the season once again with Linz, and this year they were joined by Joe Pepitone. Together they formed an irreverent trio, emerging as the stars and, perhaps, the future of the Yankees, at least in their eyes. Occasionally, Jim would check out the big club to see how the pitchers were faring. Chip Hilton would have been pleased with what was being reported in the papers—the Yankees were running away with the American League (AL) once again. But Jim now knew firsthand that Chip Hilton existed only in storybooks. Sure, the Yankees were "his" organization, but it wasn't all for one and one for all in Amarillo. Nor had it been in Greensboro, Auburn, or Kearney. As all the Minor Leaguers understood, success in New York meant fewer available roster spots on the big club the following spring. And that was bad news for all of them. Closer to home, the definition of individual success from an organizational perspective was largely relative. How well did you do compared to your fellow pitchers? Were you better than the guy lockering next to you who pitched the day after you did? In professional baseball, rooting interests were intensely local, often extending no farther than the tip of your finger. Clair Bee never wrote anything about that.

5 A Long Way from Amarillo

Six months later, and to the surprise of absolutely everybody, Jim Bouton was a New York Yankee. He never forgot the experience of entering the Yankee clubhouse for the first time. It was April 9, 1962, and what struck him first was how funereal it was. Sunken in the bowels of Yankee Stadium, it was "like a large subterranean living room," he recalled, apparently designed to keep the world outside at bay.[1] Wall-to-wall grayish green carpet swallowed idle chatter; the windows facing the three walls of walk-in lockers were frosted to allow only diffuse shafts of light from the street above in and even less from the clubhouse out. The overhead lighting was subdued, as was everything else—painted a muted gray-green to match the carpet, even the exposed ductwork in the darkened ceiling above. The space was intensely private, cloistered. Babe Ruth had dressed here, as had Gehrig and DiMaggio. Everything about it seemed to be telling you to keep it down, show some respect. You were in the presence of something beyond the mere mortal here.

It was a long way from Amarillo. Even a few weeks earlier it would have been unthinkable that Bouton would be standing in that hushed, reverent space. The Bombers never let up in '61, winning 109 games and then steamrolling the Cincinnati Reds in the World Series for their nineteenth championship trophy. Heading into spring training the following year, the Yankees were stacked like few teams in baseball history had ever been. Mickey Mantle was the game's premier power hitter, having smacked fifty-four home runs in '61, exceeded only by his teammate Roger Maris, who had broken Ruth's single-season record with sixty-one. Their catcher, Elston Howard, hit .348

with twenty-one home runs, and his backup, Johnny Blanchard, hit .305 with twenty-one home runs of his own. On the mound Whitey Ford, with twenty-five wins, and Ralph Terry, with sixteen, were at times outshone by Bill Stafford, who had an ERA a half-run less than either of them. Coming into the 1962 season the Yanks did not appear to want for much of anything, let alone a pitcher who was barely even on their radar when the trucks were loaded up two months earlier and driven south to Florida with the tools for what appeared to be yet another championship run.

Yet he had made it nevertheless. Given a chance to shine in the club's pre-spring-training camp after his strong showing in Amarillo, he made the most of the opportunity. The advance camp had by 1961 become a Yankee tradition. It was started by former manager Casey Stengel a dozen years earlier, who referred to it as his "instructural school." Each year the club invited a large handful of Minor League pitchers to the camp to show their wares and, perhaps, open some eyes. Nobody opened more eyes than Bouton. After a couple of weeks, manager Ralph Houk pronounced him the camp's best pitcher. "Bouton's a young pitcher with a big league future," Houk said. Not only that, Houk added that "he's going to get every chance to make the club here. We're going to pitch him. Make no mistake about that." Sain was also impressed, even though Bouton trotted out his knuckler once again. This time he was able to throw it consistently for strikes. "Normally," Sain said, "you would discourage a young pitcher from fooling around with a knuckleball. That's a tough pitch to master. What I mean is you don't learn to control it overnight. But in Bouton's case, he didn't come by his knuckler overnight. This boy has been throwing the knuckler since he was about 11 years of age. He's 22 now, so you can easily see he's lived with this knuckler for a while."[2]

His "instructural school" success led to an invitation to formal spring training with the big club. This year it was held for the first time in Fort Lauderdale, where everything felt new and exciting. There were young people on the beach, on the streets, in the bars. After the '61 season the Yanks departed dowdy St. Petersburg, dubbed "God's waiting room" by many of the scribes, for their new spring-training digs, and the vibe everywhere was of youth, of change. The feeling infected even the Yankees, despite the polished mahogany out of which the organization was fashioned. Pepitone and Linz were there, and now so was Bouton. Possibility perfumed the air. A strong few weeks might very well land the three of them on the big club's roster.

Jim Bouton had those strong few weeks. Whenever the coaching staff turned around he seemed to be getting hitters out one way or another. Houk was impressed anew, as now he was doing it against Major League talent. More than that was his tenacity. He just refused to be beaten. New York Post sportswriter Maury Allen nicknamed him "the Bulldog," and it stuck.[3] As the Grapefruit League schedule was winding down, Art Stewart broached the topic of Jim Bouton with the front-office folks he was chatting up one afternoon. How's my boy doing? he wanted to know. If he keeps it up, he'll very likely skip Triple-A and head north with the varsity, was the reply. He did and he did.

Which was how he came to be standing in the Yankee clubhouse for the first time the morning before opening day. The season was to begin with a game against Baltimore the following afternoon, so Bouton, along with his new teammates, wasn't expected at the stadium until later in the day for a final preseason workout. He was so excited to have made the club, though, that he couldn't sleep. After tossing and turning for what felt like an eternity, he arose, dressed, and left his parents' house in Ridgewood, New Jersey (they had recently moved back to the East Coast), at seven that morning to head to the ballpark. He was greeted by clubhouse man Pete Sheehy, who decades earlier was charged with bringing Ruth his daily "bicarb and coffee" upon the Bambino's arrival and keeping his mouth shut while doing so. "Your locker is right here by the door," Sheehy told him. Bouton followed him to his assigned space, grinning as he passed Whitey Ford's locker.[4]

After settling the young pitcher, Sheehy returned to his work preparing for the season. Bouton waited and then, when he was sure Sheehy was out of sight, reached out and, with some hesitation, reverently touched the uniform, number 56, that hung in his locker. A few moments later, after convincing himself that he was alone, Bouton tried on his jersey, then his pants, and then, finally, his cap. He studied himself in the mirror. All of it fitted perfectly.[5] He was now, undeniably, a Yankee. He had made it.

Now the battle would be to remain. He was a forgotten man during the season's first month, appearing only once, in middle relief during a late-April game against the Indians. It was the first game of a doubleheader, and Houk had little choice but to throw him out there; the Yanks were being blown out 7–1 after five innings, and there was another game that followed this lost cause. Better to use up the back end of his pitching staff now and save his quality arms for the nightcap. Bouton pitched three scoreless innings, though, and the Yanks climbed back into the game. They still lost, but he was impressive after a shaky start (he walked the first batter he faced on four pitches and then started the next with two balls before recovering). Still, another dozen games would go by without Bouton appearing in any of them.

Finally, on May 6, Houk decided to start him in the second game of a doubleheader against the Senators. Among the 23,940 fans in the stadium that afternoon were George, Trudy, and about three dozen other family members and friends. Again he started off shaky, walking the first batter. After clearing the bases by inducing a double-play grounder, he walked the next hitter and then gave up a single. He got out of the inning with a fly ball to left and no permanent damage. The Yanks got three in the bottom of the first, and neither they nor Bouton looked back after that. As the offense added to the lead throughout the game, he worked himself into and out of trouble nearly every inning. In all he gave up seven hits—all singles—and another seven walks. Not only did he not give up any runs, but no Senator even reached third base until the game was out of reach in the ninth. Partially heeding Sain's spring training advice from a year earlier, he threw primarily fastballs and curves but mixed his knuckler in here and there as well as an occasional palm ball.[6] Two hours and thirty-four minutes later, Danny O'Connell's fly ball landed in Mickey Mantle's glove, and Bouton had his first big-league victory, complete game, and shutout all at once in the Yanks' 8–0 win.

After the game he was corralled by Yankee announcer Red Barber, who interviewed him on his postgame show. Meanwhile, Mantle collected all of the clubhouse towels and laid them end to end from the clubhouse door to Bouton's locker. Mantle deputized Johnny Blanchard to stand guard at the door to prevent Jim from entering before everything was ready. For the final touch Whitey Ford ran over to relief pitcher Luis Arroyo's locker and swiped his 1961 Fireman of the Year award, placing it in Bouton's locker instead. When he was finally permitted entry to the clubhouse, it hardly resembled the hushed enclave he stood in nearly a month earlier. His teammates gave him a rousing ovation as he made his way—floated, really—across the towels toward the trophy in his locker.[7] From Barber to Mantle to Ford, it was anointment by royalty.

He came down to earth in his next start, going only 3.1 innings before being removed after giving up three runs on six hits and three walks. Thereafter he settled into a role of swingman, occasionally getting a start but usually coming in during the anonymity of the game's middle innings. He finally found the spotlight after he entered a game against Detroit in the sixteenth inning and pitched seven innings of shutout ball. "He just pitched the bats right out of their hands," catcher Yogi Berra said after the game. "He had plenty on his fast ball and he threw one of the best curve balls I've seen all year." Houk, however, refused to commit to Bouton as a full-time starter. "We would like to spot him around," he said. "There is no need to rush him."[8] Still, Houk found more opportunities to give him the ball in important situations, and by the middle of July he was, for the most part, a starter. While he retained his multipitch arsenal, he began relying more heavily on his overhand curve, drawing praise whenever he threw it. More than one player called it the best curve they'd seen outside of Camilo Pascual.[9]

Whenever he was scheduled to pitch, Bobbie took the train from her apartment in Media, Pennsylvania, to root him on and chart his starts. Bob, as well, would come, catching nearly every home game that summer. Often, he acted as the chauffeur to the club's New Jersey residents. Bobby Richardson, Elston Howard, Bill Skowron, and others would wait outside their homes in Englewood, Teaneck, and elsewhere for twenty-year-old Bob to drive by and pick them up for the trip over the George Washington Bridge to Yankee Stadium. If this car flips over, Bob would tell himself while driving, I will have single-handedly cost the city of New York a pennant.

In so many ways Bouton introduced an everyman spirit to the regal Yankees. With his hat flying off on nearly every pitch, nonroster uniform number (he refused Sheehy's offer to trade his number 56 for one more associated with big-league pitchers once he had established himself), along with the effort he seemed to exert every moment he was on the field, he looked very much like a fan who had somehow managed to con his way onto baseball's most glamorous team. "I always felt I was a souped-up Volkswagen in the Indianapolis 500," he later said. "If the glove compartment flew open, I was in the infield."[10] Before he even enjoyed much success on the mound, he connected with the masses in the seats. If they were ever to play big-league ball, they imagined, they'd look like him out there. The feeling was mutual. When he was taking notes for the book that was to become *Ball Four* a few years later, Bouton contemplated an incident where police beat the hell out of a few fans who had run onto the field during a game. Why'd they beat them up? he wanted to know. So they don't do it again—they don't belong on the field—was the answer. "I sympathized with the guys who ran on the field," he jotted down on a scrap of paper.[11] Mantle might have been the star, but for thousands who watched the Yankees play, Bouton was their avatar.

He was also Johnny Sain's avatar in many ways. Sain was a marginal prospect a generation earlier and had to fight just to be noticed.[12] He was once released from a Class D club but managed to fight back and eventually become a workhorse for the Boston Braves of the late 1940s. During one stretch he pitched nine complete games in twenty-nine days and refused to be relieved. Other than one game where he agreed to be pulled from a meaningless start in order to rest for the World

Series, he finished every game he won between 1946 and 1948. He was unorthodox in mind and in spirit and open to nearly everything—he learned how to perfect his signature changeup from a twenty-year-old kid he met at an Arkansas feed store who himself had learned to throw it by studying a photo of the grip. As a pitching coach he didn't believe pitchers should run between starts, didn't believe there was any value in going out to the mound to talk to a struggling pitcher during the middle of an inning, and didn't believe he should dress with the other coaches in the locker room. Better, he believed, for him to dress with his pitchers so they could more easily approach him with questions. He, like Bouton, was convinced that more ball games were won with the mind than the arm. "Pitchers who control themselves control the game," he said. Ultimately, he saw pitching as a con game; in order to succeed, a pitcher had to keep hitters off-balance, guessing, never sure what was up his sleeve. Once a hitter figured out a pitcher's tricks, the game was over. Conversely, a pitcher who could master his thoughts and outthink his opponent could master hitters for years.

He was furiously protective of his pitchers. And make no mistake about it, to Sain they were very much "his" and not the manager's or anybody else's. Everybody in baseball thinks they know all there is to know about pitching, says Jim Kaat—another Sain prodigy—and has no qualms second-guessing every decision on the mound. Sain pushed back every chance he got. "If a manager would make a suggestion," Kaat said, "Johnny would say, 'This pitcher is twenty-one years old, and he has more experience than that manager ever had.'" Ted Williams liked to say that pitchers were dumb, that they were on the mound because they couldn't do anything else. Sain elevated the position by listening to his pitchers, trusting them, and protecting them from the rest of the clubhouse. In so doing he gained their trust, so much so that they'd read the positive-thinking literature he'd leave in their lockers, books like Napoleon Hill's *Think and Grow Rich* and others that championed the idea of mind over matter.

Wherever Sain went, twenty-game winners followed: Whitey Ford, Ralph Terry, Mudcat Grant, Jim Kaat, Earl Wilson, Denny McLain, Wilbur Wood. And one day Jim Bouton. Sain gravitated toward Bouton and Bouton toward Sain; when they scanned baseball's expanse they saw the same things. They saw the factions, suspicions, and overarching fear of anything that ran counter to tradition. Sain took his new ideas and threw his lot in with his pitchers, angering his managers and fellow coaches, who considered the position of pitching coach as little more than ceremonial—a spot for another drinking buddy and, when push came to shove and it was time to choose up sides, an ally who should be one of them instead. Which was why, despite his successes, he kept getting shown the door. Within a few years Bouton would refer to Sain as one of his heroes, one of the great men in the game. But baseball had no place for heroes like Johnny Sain, Bouton realized. "Baseball takes its best people and hides them and snuffs them out because they don't want to hear from them," he said.[13] When Bouton saw Sain he saw so much of himself, only a generation too soon. Sain saw the same in Bouton, only a generation later. It was no surprise they threw in with each other. And that eventually they'd become factions unto themselves.

But that wouldn't be until later. As long as the Yankees were winning, nobody made too much of the fissures that would become glaring in a few years. As they glided toward yet another pennant, the infusion of youth that was Bouton, Linz, Pepitone, and Tom Tresh seemed to spark the club and imbue it with the sort of energy that experience drains away. Toward the end of the season a toy pop-out-of-the-box mongoose made its debut in the clubhouse, causing shrieks of surprise and laughter that rattled the staid space. The kids were insistent upon having fun along with winning ball games, and the veterans put up with it, even though they considered the mongoose as well as the shrieking to be inconsistent with the Yankee way. Still, the '62 Yanks remained *their* club, and when they formally clinched yet another pennant, they celebrated their way—by retreating to a back room where they watched the Sonny Liston–Floyd Patterson fight on TV. After Liston knocked out Patterson the veterans showered, dressed, and headed off to the Stadium Club, where they enjoyed steaks and champagne along with a three-piece orchestra. In all the celebration reminded a writer from the *New York Times* of one "in the manner of a man who has just been informed he'd become a father for the 10th time." The kids were a different story. They sprayed the locker room with champagne, doused each other and Houk with it, and clowned for the cameras, making things at least marginally bearable for announcer Mel Allen, who was doing all he could to convey to his viewers a sense of excitement that was largely absent.[14]

Bouton watched the 1962 World Series from the bullpen. He never made an appearance in the seven-game series, won once more by the Yankees, this time over the Giants. It was their twentieth World Series championship, and in that sense it was business as usual. But time was starting to take its toll. The Yankees hit all of .199 in the Series, and Mantle was particularly weak, scratching out only two singles and a double in twenty-five at bats. The kids—Tresh, Tony Kubek, Clete Boyer—led the way, generating whatever offense the sputtering Yankee machine could muster. Change, it seemed, was in the air. After a particularly rough game during the Series, Mantle stared into the mirror affixed to one of the posts of his locker and repeated the catcall directed at both him and Willie Mays, who also struggled, from the bleachers earlier that afternoon. "Hey, Mick," the guy yelled. Mantle turned around. "We came to see which one a youse was better. And now we're trying to figure out which a youse is worse."

Taking in the media horde from his stool in the Yankee clubhouse, Bouton couldn't help but reflect on just how removed all of this was from the Joliet prison yard he strolled into only a few years earlier. Joliet to Kearney to Auburn to Greensboro to Amarillo to the New York Yankees World Series locker room in half a decade's time. From pitching to the cheers of society's outsiders, locked away and wagering tobacco sticks, to dressing among the ultimate insiders—Major League Baseball's royal family. Despite not pitching in the Series, the experience for him was sparkling and effervescent. He had so much he wanted to say, so many stories of his journey from nowhere to the center of the baseball universe. But the writers were too busy filling their notebooks with the mutterings of Mantle, no matter what he said. Whenever he deigned to turn his gaze their way, no matter how cold it was, they took down every syllable. Even every half syllable. Same with Whitey Ford, and with Berra, competing as they did to transform his banalities into cornpone witticisms they would attribute to him in the next day's editions. This was as it should be, he knew. They were the stars. They were the ones readers were expecting to hear from when they opened up their papers. But he was there, too. And he had so much he wanted to say.

6 Fucking Shecter

Although, geometrically speaking, baseball is a game that starts at the southern tip of home plate and expands outward into infinity, for decades it had been the narrow-mindedness of the people involved in it that dominated the game on and off the field. Mistrust and fear abounded, to the point where seemingly everybody was wary of everybody else. The suspicious nature of baseball showed itself most obviously when it came to the relationship between the players who played the game and the writers who covered it. These were the men—they were all men—charged with conveying the story of baseball to their readers, adding new chapters after every game. Because they controlled the narrative, they held tremendous sway over the players, even though none of them could hit or field or throw. A negative story could damage the image of a player, costing him his reputation as a good guy or charitable man. This could affect his career more than a few strikeouts. Most players dealt with this outsider threat by ignoring the outsiders whenever possible. Because they felt that the press could only make trouble for them, they ran from the media, said *Newsday*'s Steve Jacobson, offering only the rote responses that had gone down like dry toast for aeons or, better yet, literally running away by hiding in the trainer's room. Yankee coach Frank Crosetti once explained the nonanswer answers he liked to provide by remarking that talking to the media was like looking for smallpox. There was no sense in venturing out on that expedition.

That didn't mean that Crosetti, along with his fellow coaches and Houk, had no use for the press. They were an effective embodiment of the "other," those outside forces threatening their well-being that justified the battlefield mentality that pervaded most clubhouses. There may have been factions and divisions among the ball club itself, but at least everyone could join in common cause against the sportswriters. Houk liked to demonstrate his disdain for the writers by spitting tobacco juice on their shoes during interviews. He was also not above physically roughing up a writer if doing so might cause his club to coalesce around him. Once, after Maury Allen had written a critical piece during spring training, Houk picked him up by his lapels and banged his head against the cinder-block wall of his office. It was a very public display, done with his door open and the other writers and entire club looking on. The next day he pulled Allen aside and apologized. The apology, however, was made in private.[1]

But it was the players who most vehemently saw the press as the enemy, and not for show. *San Francisco Examiner* sportswriter Wells Twombly saw this as inevitable, given the incestuous relationship between the writers and management. Why wouldn't the players perceive the writers as their nemesis? he wondered. "They see the club's policy being repeated word for word, without question, in the daily sports pages. They see reporters in the company of general managers and publicity men on the road. What else are they to think?"[2] After the Yanks clinched the pennant in '61, Johnny Blanchard took after one of them, picking him up and dunking him in a garbage can filled with ice and beer. He then held him there, finally relenting and letting him out.

In his unpublished memoir *Newsday*'s Stan Isaacs wrote that many writers identified too closely with the teams they were covering.[3] In New York they all clamored to cover the Yankees because the Yankees were winners. Therefore, they were winners also. Almost nobody wanted to cover the expansion Mets because the Mets were bound to be awful. As such the writers who were on that beat feared being branded as second-rate losers themselves. For many writers it was the relationship with the organization they covered that mattered most. So they made sure not to damage it. Tarnishing the ball club would be the same as smearing themselves, something they would never do.

By the middle of the century this symbiosis had become the accepted norm within the sports pages. Remember, Houk would admonish the press in his office, we're all in this together. The writers promoted the agendas of the clubs they were covering and helped them sell tickets by glorifying their stars and ignoring nearly everyone else. Grantland Rice may have been a legend in his field, but he served up a "hero sandwich," according to a later account of his career.[4] In the *New York Times*, Arthur Daley won a Pulitzer but was "not so much a columnist as a sports master of ceremonies, introducing and promoting sports figures he liked and ignoring those he didn't." Given this environment, it was no wonder that men like Crosetti would divvy up the media not between those who were honest and dishonest but between those who were loyal to the organization and those who were not.[5] "When I first showed up," Robert Lipsyte recalled, "[Houk] wanted to know if I was a 'booster' or a 'ripper.'" To Houk these were the only options. And not many were selecting option B. The sports media was full of "star fuckers," Isaacs said of the state of the profession when he joined it in the mid-1950s.[6] Publicists and cheerleaders masquerading as journalists.

Leonard Shecter changed all of that. That sportswriter whom Blanchard dunked in the icy garbage can? It was Shecter—Yankee beat man for the *New York Post*. If ever a writer fitted Crosetti's definition of disloyal, it was he. Along with Isaacs he made a career of pissing off the Yankees one way or another. Recalling his time with Shecter on the Yankees beat, Isaacs wrote: "We had an irreverent attitude about the team. We didn't think it was a rare privilege to be allowed to associate with the Yankee ball players, however talented and lordly they were. We treated the Yankees and baseball for what it was—grown men playing a little boy's game. We asked questions that weren't always appreciated."[7] Shecter was provocative and acerbic, never afraid to ask a difficult question. Politically, he was far left of center, which made him a unicorn in a clubhouse dominated by conservative management types and culturally suspicious farm boys. He was a tough son of a bitch, more than one of his fellow writers observed. Fearless. Houk liked to think he was tough, Lipsyte of the *Times* said, but Shecter was tougher. He would always have a scotch at his desk, Jacobson remembered, but it never dulled his edge. "He could cut you with a knife, and you'd never even feel it," said Jacobson. He was that subtly sharp. Many of the players avoided him because they knew he would dig deeper than the old-school writers and get to the truth, no matter where it led and no matter how it shaded a reputation, said Larry Merchant, Shecter's replacement at the *Post*. But not all of them ran when he approached. Mantle and Whitey Ford might cringe when Shecter honed in on them, but they'd speak with him nevertheless. Shecter was the only writer who could write critically of Mantle without fearing that Mantle would turn his back on him the next day. The most Mantle would say was "Ripped me, Lenny." And then he'd submit to more questioning from his executioner of the previous day.

Other, lesser, players likewise welcomed Shecter when he came by their lockers. These were the players the old-school writers mostly ignored, who didn't get much ink because they weren't stars. They had things to say and were dying to say them. Things having to do with how they were treated by management during contract negotiations, how the club was being run, how the game looked from their perspective away from the limelight in the seventh spot in the lineup or in the darkened recesses of the dugout. Talking to a writer like Shecter, who was hardly promanagement and who had an eye for the offbeat, would bring them some much-wanted attention. So they spoke to him. Soon they would have more than just Shecter and Isaacs to talk to.

Coming up behind Shecter and Isaacs was a generation of young sportswriters who emulated their style rather than that of the cheerleading Arthur Daley. Writers such as Jacobson, Merchant, Lipsyte, George Vecsey, Phil Pepe, and others. To them, Shecter and Isaacs were their heroes, the new standard-bearers of locker-room reporting. "[Shecter] was the guy the young people tried to emulate," Jacobson said. "If we worked the same events, I would read his piece to see what I could or should have done. Sometimes I'd say 'Gee, I did a better piece than Lenny did,' but lots of times there were insights that only he had." Insight was something that, at last, was needed in the dailies. By the late '50s games were starting to be televised; many fans already knew the score by the time they opened their newspaper the next morning. Something more was needed, something that could add to what they already knew. This was particularly true of the afternoon papers—if some fans knew the score by the time they opened their morning paper, all of them knew it by the time the afternoon papers hit the stands. The *Post* was an afternoon paper, so Shecter's editor encouraged him to seek out different, deeper, angles on the teams he was covering.

By the early '60s Shecter was of his era. "It was a time of change," said Merchant. "Not just in journalism but in society." More and more, the angle was "anti this, anti that. The women's movement was coming; the civil rights movement was coming. There were now black players in the big leagues. Reporting on those changes and the conflicts that might have come with them" was now fair game. Soon, the Vietnam War would dominate the front pages of the papers, along with the antiwar protests. "Some of these issues resonated with some of the players," Merchant recalled. The younger reporters gravitated toward the younger Yankees, players like Linz, Tresh, and Pepitone. And, most of all, Jim Bouton. "I remember in spring training, when they told me I was going to make the team," Bouton said. "They said, 'When you get to New York, watch out for this guy Shecter. Fucking Shecter. I was hearing all of these stories about this guy, Fucking Shecter. I thought, well, he must be a real tough guy. Then I met him. He came right over to my locker, with his big bug-eyed glasses and a big smile, and introduced himself. I said to myself, 'He doesn't look like a tough guy at all." They hit it off immediately. Even though Bouton had a nondescript rookie season, Shecter routinely came by his locker and chatted him up. Not because he had done anything to win the game but because he offered a fresh perspective on things. Soon Shecter had company—hordes of young writers were gathering around Bouton's locker, even though he played no part in the outcome of the game. The older writers were dismissive. "Look at them," Jimmy Cannon said one day as Pepe, with his prominent tooth profusion, was laughing it up with Bouton and the other young writers around his locker. "A bunch of chipmunks."[8]

The comment was derisive, but the young writers wore it as a badge of honor. Soon they referred to themselves by that name, using it to distinguish themselves from the old-school cheerleaders they wanted no part of. Headed by Shecter, Isaacs, and Merchant, the Chipmunks "were the guys who looked for things that were funny, who looked for insight into people. We weren't godding-up the Yankees," said Jacobson. "We were looking for personality, looking to write about people," rather than mythical figures. They found all of that in the new generation of Yankees. They were young; they were irreverent; they were funny. They were everything their older teammates weren't. There was a growing culture clash within the Yankee locker room, and the Chipmunks were the first to see it. Houk, Crosetti, Mantle, Ford, and Hank Bauer were relics of the old Yankees—the strong, silent type. On opening day it was not unusual for the club's elders to school the newcomers as to how to behave as a New York Yankee, George Vecsey remembered. Bauer would approach a young Kubek and say, "Don't fuck with my World Series check." In other words, shut up and play ball. Into this clubhouse came Jim Bouton, who would talk and talk and talk. Linz and Pepitone would see this and feel less encumbered as well. All of it drove the traditionalists nuts. This was not how a Yankee behaved. But the more they talked, the larger the crowd around their lockers became.

The Chipmunks considered the old-guard Yankees boring and limited. Bobby Richardson was revered by the traditionalists, who saw him as something of an intellectual. But when Isaacs interviewed him, he saw a man interested only in himself.[9] Mantle was unquestionably a superstar on the field, but in the locker room he would turn his back on the writers, offer one-word responses to their questions, or simply stare right through them.[10] Despite all of his talent, there was only so much they could write about him, given how little he was providing them. So they turned to Bouton. "He was a refreshing guy," Vecsey said. "We'd go into the locker room before the game and after the game, and there was Bouton. And he was talking to people. He was a little bit off-center, given the post-'50s conservatism of baseball, particularly in the Yankee clubhouse." Breaking from tradition, "Bouton was capable of responding seriously to interview questions," Lipsyte recalled, while being at the same time "breezy and happy to be in the bigs." He could, and freely did, speak about things beyond the ball field. To the Chipmunks, who were in search of exactly that, he was the tonic for everything that ailed them in that stuffy space.

For the better writers, like Shecter, Isaacs, Jacobson, Lipsyte, Pepe, and Vecsey, Bouton would provide color to their stories. For the lesser writers, he would take over their stories altogether. More than a few bylined pieces consisted of little more than a string of Bouton quotes. Rather than analyze a play or a decision themselves, these writers would simply transcribe Bouton's take on them.[11] This was particularly the case when he was pitching but also occurred on the days when he wasn't. "Everybody would go to him, win or lose or even when he didn't play," Vecsey recalled. He was always available and always willing to provide his take on nearly anything. "He was a go-to guy if you needed a comment on something," Merchant remembered. "He enjoyed being in the baseball scene and generally had a smile on his face."

All of this broke with long-standing Yankee custom. "Whitey Ford had established his credentials" was how Jacobson described the accepted clubhouse guidelines for speaking to the media. "He could be a charming fellow, and nobody would be negative about that because he had earned his pinstripes." The newcomers were a different story: Who the hell were these Linz, Pepitone, and Bouton characters? They hadn't done anything to talk about. As Bauer had suggested to Tony Kubek a few years earlier, just shut up and play ball. The chattiness of the younger players particularly irked Blanchard and Clete Boyer, who considered Bouton an insufferable chatterbox.[12] Lipsyte recalled the looks and eye rolls Bouton's teammates directed his way whenever he prattled on to the press. Bouton didn't care. "The older guys would walk by me making noises and gestures," he said at the time, "indicating that I was a loudmouth. . . . I don't care what anybody says. I don't get on those guys who don't talk to reporters and I don't want anybody on me because I do talk to them. I have as much right as anyone to set the pace."[13] In a game largely devoid of it, Bouton was the personification of cool. He was authentic, independent, and fiercely resistant of the societal norms of the clubhouse. He was like nothing, at least in baseball, that had come before.[14] The music world was just starting to reckon with Bob Dylan. Shecter and his Chipmunk acolytes were determined to give voice to his pinstriped counterpart, whose mere presence was a walking indictment of baseball culture. The Yankee freight train rolled on in 1962, but things were hardly as they had been. Or would ever be again.

7 All 'Bout Bouton

Going into 1963 the freight train appeared to be picking up speed, if anything. The Yankees were not only the defending World Series champs but also young, with the average age of their extended forty-two-man roster being just twenty-six and a half. The older generation might have been slowing just a bit, but that did not seem to be much cause for alarm. Yankee tradition dictated that the young shall replace the aged, and the process of regeneration appeared to be under way once more. So much so that there wasn't a spot in the rotation for Bouton. True, he hardly dazzled in '62, but he was solid and would have been penciled into most clubs' starting rotation, based on the promise he showed. Ralph Houk, however, could find no room for him there. "My, how Bouton can throw that ball," he exclaimed to a reporter during spring training.[1] He would throw it, however, in relief.

From the get-go, he felt particularly strong. He would be abandoning the knuckler this year, he promised, and was going to rely instead on purely the hard stuff. Fastball and his overhand curve. "I've got a strong arm and I'm not going to waste it by trying to come up with a lot of gimmick pitches," he said. He took up the knuckler as a kid, he explained, only because he was so small that he had trouble getting it up to the plate at all. "And when I did, they'd hit it hard." The knuckler was his savior, the only way he could fool the bigger, stronger kids he was facing. Now he was the bigger, stronger kid. So out went the knuckler. Elston Howard noticed a different Bouton during the season's early going. He was no longer trying to fool hitters, Howard saw. He wasn't trying to be cute or "make with the science. He's got the hard stuff and he just pumps away and throws it."[2]

After spending the season's first five weeks in the bullpen, Houk gave Bouton a start. He dazzled, retiring the first nineteen Orioles he faced, losing his perfect game in the seventh. He finished with a two-hit shutout and followed that with another complete game against the Los Angeles Angels. True to his earlier proclamation, he was sticking with his heat, and it was drawing raves. You could almost see the ball elevate as it made its way from his right arm to Howard's mitt, Jacobson remembered. The hop on his fastball was noticeable and dangerous. Nobody was going to hit it, provided Bouton could put it where he wanted it to go. When they did hit it, it was even more dangerous. A couple of weeks later, in another start against Baltimore, a fastball came off Jackie Brandt's bat and hit him square in the face. He dropped like a stone and lay motionless long enough for the training staff to run onto the field with a stretcher. He eventually got up, waved the stretcher away, and left the field on his own.[3] He didn't miss a start, returning four days later and giving up only five hits and one run in a 1–0 loss to the Senators. By the All-Star break he had eleven wins and seemed only to be getting stronger as the season wore on. In late August he took a no-hitter into the ninth before settling for a 5–0 shutout of the Red Sox for his eighteenth victory of the season. It was his fifth shutout of the season, something nobody could have predicted, given that he hadn't thrown a single one in his entire Minor League career and only the one in his '62 debut as a starter.

Although he was dominant on the field, in the locker room Bouton remained a man apart. He may have been on his way to twenty wins, but when reporters gathered around his locker he'd tell them that baseball was only a temporary way of life for him, that he was already working on life after baseball. A life where he would make his living selling his artwork and costume jewelry. He had fifty to seventy-five paintings back at his house in Ridgewood, he'd tell them; if anybody was interested, he'd be happy to negotiate a fair price for whatever they wanted. He could also fashion a necklace or bracelet for their wives if they preferred something like that. "What I'm trying to do now," he told a writer, "is build up a small clientele interested enough in my jewelry designing to become a paying customer. Little by little, maybe, I'll be pretty well established in this by the time I have to call it quits in baseball."[4] There was no other interview in baseball quite like him. Who else went out and blew away hitters and then hawked his jewelry to the beat writers afterward? He fascinated them; they struggled to figure out which box to place him in. In truth, there was no such box, which frustrated some but only further fascinated the Chipmunks.

No other player was as attuned to the financial limitations of professional baseball as was Jim Bouton. This was only enhanced during his star-making 1963 season when he was the toast of the nation's most glamorous team in the richest city in the world yet lived as a relative pauper. He still drove a beat-up 1953 green Mercury with a dragging rear end that operated "on a prayer," as Bobbie put it at the time, and couldn't afford a new one.[5] He was able to scrape together enough to buy a new home, but that stretched him to his financial limit; he couldn't afford to purchase a television set to put in the living room. Whenever Bobbie couldn't make it to the stadium, she traveled to Jim's parents' house nearby to watch the game on their set.

Bobbie, as well, felt the divide. When she'd sit with the other wives at the stadium, she'd be the only one with a scorecard; the other wives would barely watch the game, let alone score it. Some of the wives would parade around in mink stoles and engage in conversation that might as well have been in Turkish for all Bobbie could make of it. Mantle's and Ford's wives, in particular, seemed to her to be from another world altogether—a wealthy and sophisticated one that the small-town girl from Allegan just could not broach. After the games the wives would sometimes retreat to Toots Shor's and order drinks Bobbie had never heard of and speak on topics to which she could add nothing. As much as she tried to fit in, these interactions left her feeling socially awkward and apart. The disparity in their husbands' salaries was perpetually on display. Sitting next to a wife draped in mink might be one who made her own clothes. Negotiating restaurant politics was often dicey: the wealthier wives would order with impunity off the menu, while the poorer ones would order small salads and resign themselves to table water. When the bill came the wealthier ones would think nothing of simply splitting it evenly among them. Eventually, Bobbie spoke up and suggested that, going forward, each of them should be responsible for the cost of their meal only.

But all of this distance disappeared once the Bulldog stepped on the mound, where he formed a bond with Yankee fans like none they'd ever experienced. They loved to count the number of times he'd lose his hat during the course of a start and relished a player who just seemed to be having so much fun out there, like they imagined they would if only they were as fortunate as he. In a game infected with stoicism, here was its antidote—a player who thought nothing of riling up rival crowds like a professional wrestler might, such as when he'd mimic Red Sox pitcher Dick "the Monster" Radatz's habit of stalking off the mound with raised fists, to a chorus of boos in Fenway Park.[6] Or tease Rocky Colavito by pointing back at him in response to Colavito's habit of pointing his bat at the pitcher as he settled into his stance. Here was also a pitcher who would sometimes duck into the clubhouse for a quick shower when he was pulled from a start midgame and then finish the day by watching the remainder of the game from the grandstand.[7] That guy passing your hot dog down the row? That's the guy who was on the mound twenty minutes earlier.

Young fans might have arrived at the stadium early, hoping to catch a glimpse of their favorite player, undoubtedly Mantle. But after he brushed by them, ignoring their pleas and refusing to even make eye contact with them, they'd come upon Jim Bouton, who would not only look at them but also start up a conversation and even ask *them* a question or two. "Bouton was as nice to kids as Mantle was shitty," Lipsyte recalled. "My favorite player growing up was Mickey Mantle, of course," said Al Gornie, who would regularly hang out by the players' entrance before ball games, ogling them as they made their way into the stadium. He and his friend fellow thirteen-year-old George Saviano were starstruck by Mantle, but that was about as close as they could get to him. "He would never talk to anybody. He would just push everyone aside and walk right in." Most of the players were like that—running from their cars into the stadium, maybe stopping briefly to silently sign a few autographs along the way. They were all too busy to stop and chat.

Except Bouton. "Nobody would really talk to us except Jim Bouton," Gornie recalled. "He had a bubbly personality." Soon they developed a rapport. What if we started a Jim Bouton fan club? Gornie asked Bouton one afternoon. Sure, go ahead, said Bouton. Shortly thereafter, their fan club was off the ground, complete with a newsletter, *All 'Bout Bouton*, printed up by Saviano's father. Fifty cents got you a membership card signed by the man himself, a photostat of his lifetime record, and a subscription to the newsletter whenever Al and George managed to put one together. Each issue of *All 'Bout Bouton* updated members on their hero's doings on the mound since the last issue and provided "spotlights" on individual members of the club. For a time membership was exclusive—there were only fifteen members, mostly Al and George's neighborhood friends. But the benefits were outsize. Bouton would regularly leave tickets for Al and George in the family section, sometimes calling their homes before games to personally invite them. Before games he'd come by and chat them up, asking how they were doing in school, how their parents were. He sometimes got them postgame passes to the family waiting area outside the clubhouse, where they'd stand around with the wives while the players showered and spoke to the press. Then he'd emerge and chat them up again.

Things changed after Whitey Ford taped an edition of *All 'Bout Bouton* to his locker. Shecter took notice and devoted a column to it, providing the contact information for anyone interested in joining the club.[8] Immediately, Al and George were deluged with letters. "I can still see the taped quarters stuck on a piece of paper," Gornie says. Some of the quarters came from children, but many came from women. And from all over the country. "We were overwhelmed by it," he remembered. "Tons and tons of money was coming in. At least thirty to forty dollars." Eventually, the club mushroomed to about ninety members. "We were big players on the block." And all of it was chronicled by Shecter, who kept tabs on the club, periodically updating readers of the *New York Post* on the comings and goings of a fan club for a second-year pitcher run by two thirteen-year-old boys.

With their coffers overflowing, Al and George decided to hold a testimonial dinner at the end of the season in honor of their hero. They took the proceeds from the fan club to purchase a watch for Bouton and rented out the Chateau Alexander on Allerton Avenue in the Bronx for the occasion. Seventy members of the fan club RSVP'd, indicating that they'd come. The evening began at the Savianos' apartment, where George's mother laid out cookies, candies, and nuts for the guest of honor, who arrived with Bobbie and his parents. Soon the cocktail franks made their way around the room, along with scotch sours for the adults and milk for Al and George. After Al and George took their glasses, Bouton asked for a glass of milk as well.

Then it was off to the restaurant, where they arrived to a rendition of "For He's a Jolly Good Fellow" from those in the cordoned-off room. A few local politicos arrived, looking to capitalize on the evening; George spotted one glad-handing seemingly everyone in the room and cornered him, asking him if he could address the crowd. "If you could say something about my mother's cookies. She worked very hard until real late last night." After Bouton pitched popcorn balls to the kids and dinner was served, the testimonials began. A gaggle of teenage girls presented him with a large stuffed bulldog, and then Al stepped up to present him with the watch, stumbling through his planned speech as the glare of the spotlight overwhelmed him. All the while Shecter was in the back of the room, taking all of it in, including the moment when Bouton pulled two quarters of his own out of his pocket to become a charter member of one young fan's nascent Don Rudolph fan club. By the end of the evening, noted Shecter, Bouton had made a connection in one way or another with nearly everybody in the room. The politico never mentioned the cookies.[9]

For those who preferred their connections to take place on the field, Bouton didn't disappoint here, either. He appeared to only be getting stronger as the season wore on, earning his twentieth win and fifth shutout in the Yankees' pennant clincher over the Twins. It seemed that the younger generation had finally grabbed the reins as the Yanks won, despite subpar seasons from both Mantle and Maris, who when they weren't struggling were on the disabled list. Mantle hit only fifteen home runs while making it to the plate only 213 times all season; Maris managed only 351 plate appearances of his own. Pepitone and Tresh, meanwhile, seemed primed to unseat them as anchors of the offense, while Bouton and Al Downing looked to be joining Whitey Ford as the foundation of the pitching staff (with Ford's twenty-four wins, he and Bouton became the first pair of Yankee twenty-game winners since 1951). This was their time.

So when the final out was recorded and the Yanks were officially returning to the Series for the fourth consecutive year, the youngsters refused to hold back while the veterans once again toasted one another before retiring upstairs for steaks. This year, led by Bouton and Pepitone, they doused nearly everyone with pink champagne, even teetotaler Bobby Richardson and Mantle, which no youngster had dared to do before. They flung egg salad and sliced tomatoes across the clubhouse before hoisting a container of potato salad over Houk's head and then dumping it on him. Then Bouton led a contingent over to Pepitone, where they cornered him, carried him to the trainer's room, and cut off his hair.[10] Through it all Bouton made a point to include Shecter in the celebration, breaking the wall between the players and the press by dousing him along with everyone else. It was the first time anyone had ever thought to include him. Through it all Berra and Crosetti stewed. "You'd think these bums never won a pennant before," Berra said, before ducking to avoid a gob of potato salad coming his way. Crosetti shook his head in disgust the entire time. Soon, the last remnants of the old guard disappeared into the shower room.[11]

For the next couple of weeks the Yankees watched as the Dodgers battled the Cardinals for the National League (NL) pennant. The Yankee players were decidedly rooting for Los Angeles, given that Dodger Stadium seated nearly twenty thousand more fans than Sportsman's

Park; the larger take would result in a larger World Series share for each of them.[12] Bobbie envisioned a new car coming from Jim's share.[13] Maybe even a TV for the living room. When it became apparent that the Dodgers would be the opponent, Houk set his Series rotation, naming Bouton the starter twice—in Game Three at Dodger Stadium and Game Six back home. As soon as the rotation was finalized, Bouton arranged to leave tickets for Al and George to his Game Six start. The boys were ecstatic; each informed their teachers they would be leaving school early on Wednesday, October 9, in order to make it to the stadium in time to see their hero throw the first pitch of the game. The higher-ups at PS 127 had no problem with Al's request. The dean at Mount Saint Michaels said absolutely not to George's. Bouton called the dean, trying to reason with him, to no avail. He then enlisted Shecter, who devoted an entire column to the matter.[14] The dean stood firm. Pressure mounted by the day, however, and eventually the school administration buckled. George would be able to attend Bouton's start after all, provided the Series went that far. In the end it was all for naught. There would be no Game Six.

Regardless, the World Series gave Bouton the opportunity to become a professional writer for the first time. Now, rather than appearing under other writers' bylines who called it a day after stringing a series of his quotes together, he had his own column in the *Kalamazoo Gazette*.[15] "Series Sidelights by Jim Bouton" was hardly breakthrough journalism—it was the typical jock column one would expect to see during the World Series—but unlike those penned by Mantle and others, Bouton actually wrote his himself. "Sidelights" was an appropriate title, as there were few insights contained within; peripheral information dominated his column, much as it did Mantle's and the rest's. Bouton informed readers that Houk would be using three starters (Ford, Downing, and himself) and that the Yanks "feel we can win." And that was about as deep as it got.

After the Yanks lost the first two games at home, they faced a reckoning in Game Three. Lose and they were all but officially done; win and at least they at least had a chance. Knowing that the fate of the Series was on his shoulders, Bouton didn't get much sleep in the nights leading up to the game. Walking down Hollywood Boulevard with Phil Linz the day before his big game, he stopped in a gift shop that specialized in creating customized novelty newspaper headlines. They had one made up dated the day after the game with the head-line: "Bouton Shuts Out Dodgers, Linz Hits Two Home Runs." They unfurled it on the team bus the following morning in an effort to relieve the tension. It got some laughs but not from Crosetti.[16] Another breach of Yankee protocol.

No matter. The game itself was a classic. Up against Don Drysdale, Bouton hung with him all the way. Drysdale was dominating, strik-ing out nine and giving up only three hits (all singles) in shutting out the Yankees. Bouton was Bouton—working himself in and out of trouble all game. He walked Junior Gilliam in the first, and then a wild pitch sent Gilliam to second. He got Tommy Davis to ground sharply back to the mound, to Bouton's left, the ball ricocheting off the pitching rubber and hitting Richardson at second in the shin rather than the glove. As it rolled into right field Gilliam rounded third and scored easily.[17] And that was the end of the scoring for the day. Bou-ton would throw another wild pitch, tying a World Series record in the process, but didn't give up any more runs. He wound up pitch-ing seven innings and giving up only three more hits, but two hours and five minutes after the game started, the Yanks had lost again, 1–0, and were now one loss away from elimination. They had managed to score all of three runs in the first three games and were now virtu-ally certain to go down in defeat. The only question left was whether they'd be swept. And by the hated Dodgers, of all teams. They would be. Sandy Koufax beat Ford the following afternoon, and the season was over. Still, for Bouton, the Series was a success—he pitched the best game on the staff of the Series and continued to charm; now a national audience got to see him lose his hat on nearly every pitch and tough out a game against an opponent who clearly had more natural ability. And almost beat him. A few weeks earlier, in the haze of the pennant celebration, Shecter asked him if, going into the '64 season, he was going to double-down on his trademark by getting a smaller hat or a bigger head. "Bigger head, I guess" was his reply.[18] To some in the clubhouse, and to the front office in its entirety, this remark would prove prophetic.

8   A Threat, Not a Fine

The postscripts to the '63 Series were not kind to the Yankees. All of the good feelings generated by the youth movement were replaced with skepticism and foreboding. "This Yankee team is not the brilliant, almost incomparable squad that many baseball writers claimed it was," wrote Roger Angell. "There is something wrong here—too little day-to-day opposition, perhaps a tiny lack of pride, perhaps a trace of moneyed smugness."[1] Change would have to come to the Yankees was the general consensus, more than simply promoting the kids and phasing out the vets. Although pitching was the least of their problems, Johnny Sain was eased out the door.[2] Bouton watched as management made Sain the scapegoat for their other, deeper, ills. Managers and coaches keep their jobs, Shecter once wrote, by doing everything "by the book." Go against the mythical "book," and you'd better win, because the moment you don't, you'll be gone.[3] Sain had just become living proof of that maxim. But the changes didn't stop there. Houk was booted upstairs to become the club's new general manager, and Yogi Berra was anointed his replacement in the dugout. All of these moves would affect Bouton directly.

Although on the surface it might seem as if the fun-loving Yogi Berra would get along well with the fun-loving Jim Bouton, the reality of Berra was much different from his image. Shecter considered him "a narrow, suspicious man, jealous of the man other people supposed him to be and which he knew he was not." In 1961 he had his autobiography, *Yogi*, ghostwritten for him, and Shecter called him out on it. "It was a typical baseball autobiography," Shecter wrote later, "all shiny and bright for the kiddies, naturally written by somebody else, a man who could have done better. But by the time the world was ready for a book about Berra, the Berras were not interested in reality. They wanted the book to be about Berra as they would have liked him to be. So it turned out to be a terrible book, cheap and phony and transparent." Berra crossed paths with Shecter the following spring in St. Petersburg. "You son of a bitch," Berra said to him. "You cocksucker." He never said anything like that in *Yogi*, said Shecter, later.[4] Maybe if he had the book would have been worth reading.

The players never respected Yogi as a voice of authority, even as he became more of a de facto coach in his final years as an active player. "He was always 'good old Yog,'" Bouton recalled. His first moves as the manager did little to rally the troops behind him. His inaugural spring training address was a withering tirade, seemingly designed to instill a sense of authority where he knew there was none. "He tossed around one 'don't' after another," said one player in the aftermath. Don't do this. Don't do that. Everybody had to be in bed by midnight. And everyone was going to do gymnastics every day throughout spring training.[5] It was as if he were managing in a time warp, taking the Yankees back to 1946, when he broke in as a player. It was an odd debut, a desperate grasp. And it was only February.

The biggest change, though, was the promotion of Houk, which Bouton later recalled as "a classic example of the Peter Principle in operation." In so doing, the Yankees took a man who was both respected and loved within the clubhouse and promoted him to his level of incompetence. Houk was a players' manager, but one who knew how and where to draw the line over which his players would not step. He was in many ways simply an older version of the guys he managed—a tobacco-chewing, beer-drinking, late-night carouser. Bouton once wrote that perhaps the reason Houk never had a curfew was because that would mean he'd have to abide by it also.[6] Anticipating his upcoming contract negotiations, Bouton understood that things would be different than they had been with Houk's predecessor, Roy Hamey: "With Mr. Hamey it was a business deal. With Ralph it's like arguing with your brother."[7]

Without question Houk realized this as well. Management expected him to act like management, not one of the boys. If he was going to earn the respect of those above him, he'd have to demonstrate his independence from the locker room as quickly as possible. He did it by announcing salary cuts in early January: Maris was cut $12,000, while Ford was given a small raise but only because he was now doing double duty as both the stalwart of the pitching staff and Sain's replacement as pitching coach.[8] Mantle's salary would not be cut, but he would not be receiving the annual raise to which he had grown accustomed. Elston Howard won the AL Most Valuable Player (MVP) Award in '63, so he got a raise. But what about Jim Bouton? A twenty-one-game winner could not have his salary cut, that was for sure, but to how much of a raise was a second-year pitcher entitled? Houk thought a moderate one. Bouton thought a major one. Quickly, they were in a standoff.

By early February there were ten unsigned Yankees; Bouton, who was looking to double his '63 salary to $21,000, was one of them. While the other nine kept quiet about it, Bouton made his opinion of Houk's offer known. "Right now I wouldn't say we were even in the same neighborhood," he told the *New York Times*. "He made me an offer and I turned it down."[9] He was, he said, awaiting a new offer from Houk. By the beginning of March the other nine had signed. Only Bouton was left. Although Houk knew that his offer and Bouton's resided in distant zip codes, he did what general managers had done for generations—he fed the media a fiction that all was well and that there really was nothing to report.[10] For a few weeks he had the benefit of cover, as Bouton was called back to Fort Dix for another stint in the Reserve and was unable to contradict him. When the stint ended a few days later, Houk could no longer pretend otherwise—in his first months as general manager, he had on his hands the first Yankee holdout since Joe DiMaggio a quarter century earlier.

Berra was perturbed and let anyone and everyone know it. Houk understood that this was a direct challenge to his authority, a test of his mettle as a higher-up, so he went to the papers to explain why he wouldn't budge on his contract offer of $18,500 for 1964—an $8,000 raise from Bouton's '63 salary. "I had a long talk with Bouton over the phone," he told the writers. "I explained to him that his demands were unreasonable for a player with the club only two years. . . . When he turned down my top offer I told him I couldn't go any further."[11] This was not an unusual tactic—management using the press to curry favor with the public. What was unusual was what Bouton was doing, which was the exact same thing. Later, he explained his rationale: "Whether I should have said anything or not, I think I'm entitled to a certain defense of my position. If it gets to the point where it becomes a public matter, and if it looks like I might be being portrayed as greedy, or whatnot, I certainly want to make clear why I'm taking the position I do, and why I feel a certain treatment is necessary. After all, I want to come out of this thing looking okay, too. I'm sure if I didn't say anything, people might draw other conclusions."[12] Every time Houk used the press to make his point, Bouton responded in kind.

If Houk was looking for an opportunity to establish his bona fides as a front-office type, as a man beholden to the suits and not his former players, Bouton had presented him with a golden one. He had had a great season in '63, but before that he was hardly a prospect. Nobody thought he would become anything more than a fringe player before his breakout year; maybe he'd become one anyway. He was not a traditional Yankee in any respect; in fact, he had already rubbed more than a few people in the clubhouse and upstairs raw by being, in their eyes at least, a big mouth, a guy who didn't know his place and showed little respect for Yankee tradition. His insistence on negotiating in the media was just further confirmation of all of this. If ever there was a player Houk could feel comfortable staring down, it was Jim Bouton.

So he did.

On March 8—Bouton's twenty-sixth birthday—Houk called the writers over and announced that he had given his pitcher an ultimatum: either sign by the following evening at Houk's price or face the consequences. "If he fails to come to terms by then, I told him I would reduce that offer $100 for each day he remains absent and unsigned. Since the training season has a month to go after Wednesday, this would cost him $3,000 by opening day." Houk was adamant that his threat was not a fine. Rather, it was merely a daily reduction of his contract offer. He then reiterated, once again, that his offer was more than fair. On top of that, he said, he was taking this step for Bouton's benefit: "I want him here for this training period. He already has set himself back some 12 days." That was twelve days of Berra's gymnastics, Houk pointed out. "The later he starts, the greater the risk he runs of straining his arm or suffering some other kind of injury."[13] Bouton's response was not contrition but shock and anger. Speaking with Til Ferdenzi of the *New York Journal-American*, he first questioned the legality of such a tactic. After noting that his lifetime earnings from baseball to that point were such that he could not possibly afford to sit home while the daily salary reductions accumulated, he said, "I just don't see how these tactics are fair. If they did that stuff in business . . . why, they just wouldn't get away with it." He then pointed out the absurdity of it all: "It's ridiculous. Why, if I sat out up here long enough I might wind up owing them money. Isn't that a laugh."[14]

Houk wasn't laughing. He called Tommy Holmes of the *Herald Tribune* over and threatened Bouton again. "We can't go below the minimum salary limit of $7,000," he told Holmes, "but if this thing ever went that far, the Richmond club [the Yankees' AAA affiliate] would be more interested in Bouton than we would."[15] The Chipmunks wanted to know how Bouton would respond. Would he stick to his guns? Phil Pepe asked him. "What gun?" he replied. "I don't have one. They took it away. I'm trying to find out if what they're doing is legal. If it is, then I have no choice."[16] He knew that Houk knew he had him over a barrel. The tactic *was* legal, provided the Yankees weren't stupid enough to call the tactic what it obviously was—a fine. And Houk knew that pressure to sign wasn't coming only from him and the Yankees but from the realities of Bouton's personal life—he had a young wife and a five-month-old son (Michael) to support, a mortgage on a new home to pay, and a beat-up Mercury to replace before it left the three of them stranded in the middle of nowhere one day. Bouton had no choice but to sign, and at the Yankees' price, not his.

Within a day or so Bouton came to the conclusion that he was going to sign the contract. Still, he was going to get his shots in. He told Pepe that the time-honored management tactic of disarming young players by assuring them that they'd receive any money they failed to get now on the back end of their careers was garbage. "They know I give 100 percent on every pitch I make for them. The way I throw, I don't figure to have a long career. I can hurt my arm at any time. Will they give me the difference if I don't have a great career?"[17] He said that management's tactic of publicizing the percentage raise of a player's salary they were offering (the Yankees were offering an 80 percent raise to Bouton, Houk told reporters over and over) was likewise dishonest because all young players were underpaid; practically any raise at all would constitute a significant percentage increase in that player's salary. Why, he wondered, were the clubs so interested in publicizing the percentage raises of young players but not older ones with larger salaries, where to dole out a similarly large percentage raise would cost them some real money? And he drove home his ultimate point: that given the imbalance in bargaining power, a holdout was the only tactic a player had at his disposal to fight for his rights. Threatening a player with a daily reduction in salary for merely arguing his position is "taking my bargaining rights away from me."[18] In the end he'd sign the contract because he had no choice, but he wanted readers to know that he wasn't happy about it. And that the process was crooked. And that the Yankees were ogres.

When DiMaggio staged his holdout in 1938, the press, to a man, turned against him, turning the public against him as well. This time, however, Bouton had some writers in his corner. The old-timers and house men spit-roasted him, as to be expected—Jim Ogle, a columnist for the *Newark Star Ledger* who never met a story he didn't see through the eyes of his beloved Yankees (the Yankees would later repay the favor by hiring him to run their alumni association and organize their Old-Timers' Days), wrote a column suggesting that Bouton's holdout might possibly affect his attitude and performance, thereby jeopardizing the club's chances in '64.[19] But a smattering of others took Bouton's side.

There's something wrong with the economics of baseball when a guy who wins twenty-one games for a club that makes the World Series isn't worth $20,000, one wrote.[20] Johnny Sain also chimed in, through a Phil Pepe column, expressing his sympathy with his protégé and his position. Houston's general manager, Paul Richards, remarked to him during the '63 season that the Yankees had developed a half-million dollars' worth of pitchers in Jim Bouton and Al Downing, Sain told Pepe. That's $250,000 apiece. Why, Sain wondered, were the Yankees keeping nearly all of that?[21]

Bouton called Houk and accepted the $18,500 offer before the deadline, thereby avoiding any of the threatened reductions. His signing was reported breathlessly: "Bouton OK's Yank Offer" blared the March 11 edition of the *Daily News*.[22] "The Bulldog gave up the fight quickly," the house men wrote. Bouton "capitulated."[23] He was returning to the Yankees "chastened" and "smashed."[24] Houk "won."[25] The language used to describe the end of Bouton's holdout most assuredly flowed over Houk like healing waters. For Houk was now, in management's eyes, undoubtedly one of *them*.

The issue had been resolved, except that it hadn't. The attention Bouton brought to the issue compelled other holdouts to speak publicly for the first time. Kansas City's Moe Drabowsky, who had just ended a two-week holdout of his own, said, "When you consider that Jim Bouton won 21 games and had to settle for $18,000, I guess you could say I came out all right. But I still feel the contract I had to sign wasn't fair."[26] Sandy Koufax charged that he signed his contract under duress. He said he was told by Dodger management not to negotiate in the press and obeyed, only to watch the Dodgers do it and malign his integrity on a daily basis.[27] By the end of March there were rumblings that the players might band together and demand a salary arbitration panel so as to prevent in the future the sort of tactics employed by Houk and the Dodgers.[28] Nothing came of them. Yet.

The holdout effectively changed the narrative as it related to Bouton forever after. He had always been portrayed as something of an odd bird, but writers would often go out of their way to paint him as a safe iconoclast—someone who spoke his mind but who was, ultimately, of the institutions he claimed to be challenging. They made sure to include in their stories descriptions of his crew cut, his devotion to Bobbie, and his skill in changing Michael's diapers.[29] His stints in the Army Reserve were played up in an effort to balance the coverage he was getting as a freethinker and speaker. Bouton was more than happy to play along, suggesting that it was his army stint, along with Sain's advice, that led him to bust out in '63: "In 1962, I had a 7-7 record. After my trick with the Army, I came back fit, refreshed, brimming with vim, vigor and desire." He even suggested that the army taught him the value of following orders, even if they might appear silly at the time. His commanding officers knew better, he suggested. They knew that their orders would benefit him, and everyone, in the long run.[30] After his holdout those stories became more difficult to write. Soon they wouldn't be written at all.

Already, there was a feeling of a movement behind him. The Chipmunks recognized this quickly. Bouton was the sixties before the sixties were "the sixties," noticed George Vecsey. "He was acting out the sixties," before anyone even knew what that meant, he said. In June 1964 liberal-leaning *Sport* magazine ran an editorial comparing Bouton with Jim Brosnan, author in 1960 of what was hyped at the time as the game's first tell-all (more accurately a tell-some) memoir, *The Long Season*. Brosnan, the editorial noted, could not find work in '64 despite a long, solid career, and the editors thought they knew why. He was most likely blacklisted, they believed, as a result of spilling locker-room secrets, benign as they were, in his book. "Fall in line or stay out of baseball" was the message the editors thought club owners were sending through Brosnan. As they were with Jim Bouton. They applied pressure to him until he broke, simply because they could and because he had no other recourse. "The bureaucracy of baseball never ceases to amaze," the editorial began. "Just when you think baseball has put its foot in as deep as it can go, something comes along and the foot sinks deeper into that primeval ooze known as Bunglitis." The game was driven by those seeking to feed their "unenlightened self-interest."[31] And here were the Jims, Brosnan and Bouton, pushing back against that.

Bouton was hardly the first to feel the pinch of management, but when he spoke up about it, he immediately had an audience of fellow players, even those who found him otherwise tiresome. "A lot of ballplayers in that day felt they were underpaid," Larry Merchant recalled. This was particularly true when it came to the New York ballplayers. "You came to the ballpark and it was filled, there was television revenue, and there were a lot of successful people—fans, corporate types—hovering around the scene. And being in that world but not being paid what you thought you were worth . . . really bothered a lot of players." They would never voice it but would act out in other ways, demanding treatment with kid gloves from management if they had the clout, like Mantle and Mays did, or seeking to extract small favors or concessions—ultimately meaningless nods in their direction—if they did not. Being a Yankee meant being surrounded by money but having little of your own. Other than a select few, the players counted on their World Series checks to make it through the winter. Almost to a man they felt perpetually taken advantage of, nickeled-and-dimed while everyone around them lived the good life off their labor. Bouton's holdout gave voice to all they were feeling. It was, in a way, the first shot in a revolution nobody realized had just begun.

He was making more than an academic, theoretical argument, though. One thing he knew that nobody else did was that his arm already was starting to bother him. There was little chance he was going to reap the fruits of a long career; he needed to be paid what he was worth *now*. "I recall going over [to Bouton's] in either the fall of '63 or early '64 before spring training, and he was doing some work on his home—carpentry work. He was pretty good at it," Vecsey said. "And his elbow hurt." It may have been his elbow, it may have been his shoulder, but something wasn't right.[32] He was already damaged goods, and he was barely twenty-six years old.

To Vecsey Bouton didn't look quite right from the get-go in '64. He was throwing with a lesser arm; the fireballing right hander was a memory. The first three months of the season were a struggle—he was 5-7 after losing to the Orioles on June 25 and was being hit particularly hard in the early innings. Then he decided to ditch convention and think his way out of his problems. He decided to use a "double warm-up," where he'd simulate the first inning of a ball game by warming up forty minutes before game time. Then he'd go to the clubhouse, change his shirt, and sit there while the fictional "bottom of the first" was taking place. After fifteen to twenty minutes had gone by, he'd go back out and complete his warm-up, pitching what he told himself was the game's second inning. By game time he had tricked himself into believing he was in the third inning rather than the first. It was a revolutionary approach to pitching, something Johnny Sain would have been proud of. "Just because they've done things a certain way for years and years is no reason why it necessarily should be done that way forever," he said at the time.[33] The results were immediate—he went 9-3 over the next two months.

If Jim Bouton wasn't the same Jim Bouton as he was in 1963, the Yankees were hardly the same Yankees baseball fans had grown accustomed to over the previous four decades. They were in a dogfight with the Orioles and White Sox most of the season and didn't grab hold of first for good until the middle of September. To many they appeared to be yesterday's news. In Flushing Meadows, however, the Mets were new and now, opening their new stadium to raves and outdrawing the Yanks for much of the season. After the public reassessment of the Yanks following the '63 World Series, Bouton was perhaps the only Yankee to have the cachet of the new and now as well. Even though he wasn't throwing as hard, he remained a crowd favorite. Fan mail poured in; Bobbie would presort it and separate out the unusual letters and requests that merited Jim's attention. Everyone who wrote got a response, be it an autographed photo or whatnot, but those who sought a more personal connection got that also. He had postcards made up, and he'd often write personal notes on them, responding to something the fan had written in his letter to him.

Although it wasn't his intent, Bouton was presenting to the public a new face of the Yankees. He liked attention and acclaim, so he volunteered often—to speak at Little League dinners, to be the figurehead of a fund-raising drive for the northern New Jersey chapter of the Cystic Fibrosis Research Foundation—with every move reported on by one Chipmunk or another. He wrangled a few players into joining a touring off-season all-star basketball team where, among other things, he would don a gorilla mask and challenge local teachers to games for charity. That drew some attention and ultimately merited a multipage spread in *Sport*, whose editor, Al Silverman, was likewise enamored of him.[34] He was young but knew how to work the media, how to use it to both curry favor and convey his perspective to the public. Management had been expert at this for decades; clubs hired public relations men to do just that, usually former beat writers. Bouton was perhaps the only player who was better at it than they were, or even understood how the game worked at all.

Which was how and why the image of the Yankees began to change as the decade wore on. In '64 they were still run by the same people who had run them earlier—old-school types such as owner Dan Topping, Houk, Berra, and Crosetti. But the Chipmunks didn't care about any of them. Instead, they focused on Bouton, who always had something interesting to say, or Linz or Pepitone, who might not have been as witty but who were personable and at least didn't run into the shower room as soon as the press arrived. Maybe the early reports on the younger players were overly optimistic, as even the Chipmunks realized by the middle of the '64 season, but at least they seemed like good guys, guys you wanted to root for even if they weren't going to come through as regularly as their predecessors had. All of this was personified in the Phil Linz "Harmonica Incident," which drew a clear line between the old Yankees and the new generation. After being swept by the White Sox in Chicago, the Yanks piled into the team bus on Thursday, August 20. They were now in third place, four and a half games behind the Sox, who looked to be pulling away from them. In the back of the bus, Linz took out his harmonica and started to play "Mary Had a Little Lamb." Up front Berra took offense to the violation of the old-school ethos of absolute silence in the wake of defeat, so he yelled back to Linz to knock it off. If he didn't, Berra warned, he would go back there and shove that harmonica up Linz's ass. Because he was lost in the music Linz asked Mantle what Berra had just said. Mantle told him that Berra wanted him to play it louder. He did. Berra repeated his threat and then appeared intent on making good on it, springing from his seat and heading back to Linz. Linz flipped the harmonica to Berra, who swatted it into Pepitone's knee and onto the floor, where it broke. In the incident's aftermath Berra was red-faced and fined Linz $200 for breaking a baseball protocol, and Crosetti said that in his thirty-three years in the Yankee organization, this was the worst thing he had ever seen.[35] Linz thought it was funny, though, and Bouton thought it hilarious, not so much the incident itself but the way it managed to rile up both Berra and Crosetti.[36] And the Chipmunks understood that these Yankees were forcing them to choose a side, and that they had chosen correctly.

The Yanks got hot after that, winning thirty of their final forty-three games and taking the pennant after all. Berra pitched Bouton a lot, even using him once in relief. By the end of the season Bouton had logged the most innings on the staff—271.1. Over the span of two seasons he had pitched more innings than any other Yankee—520.2. Going into the World Series, this time against the Cardinals, his arm was shot. Nevertheless, Berra started him in Game Three, against Curt Simmons, in Yankee Stadium. Bouton sparkled, going the distance and giving up only one unearned run. By the bottom of the ninth he had thrown 122 pitches and was gassed; he had gotten by on guile, and now he was low on that as well. Nevertheless, with the game tied at one, Berra was going to send him out there to pitch the tenth if they failed to win it here. Bouton grabbed Mantle, who was leading off the bottom of the ninth, in the dugout and pleaded with him to hit a homer; he couldn't go back out there in the tenth. Mantle did, and all that was left by the time he touched home plate was for the writers to provide the flourish to the storybook ending Mantle had just provided them. They did, focusing on the home run itself, the legend of Mickey Mantle, and the quirkiness of Jim Bouton. They wrote about how Bouton was kept up nearly all night by Michael, who was cutting a tooth. When he started screaming again at three thirty in the morning, Bouton told them as they scribbled furiously at his locker after the game, "I put him out in the backyard." They wrote about how he spent the morning of the big game at the New York Athletic Club, watching the world handball championship.[37] And they wrote about how many times his hat flew off during the game—thirty-seven by one count, including ten times in one inning alone. But they didn't write about the fact that the guy who was a dominating fireballer the year before struck out only two Cardinals all day.

Berra had penciled Bouton to be his Game Seven starter should the Series go that far, but after the Cardinals took the next two games to go up three games to two, Berra scratched his scheduled starter, Ford (who pitched poorly in Game One), and moved Bouton up a day to start Game Six. He would again match up with Simmons. The Yankees, from the top down, were not optimistic—traveling secretary Bruce Henry had ordered all of the players' bags into the lobby of their St. Louis hotel in the event they'd need to be shipped back to New York after the game.[38] What kind of confidence is that? Bouton wondered. He was weary but determined. He toughed out eight innings, as first his arm and then his shoulder tightened up on him.[39] Pepitone hit a grand slam in the eighth, and the Yanks broke open what had been a taut affair, winning 8–3. "I guess we can take our bags out of the hotel lobby and back to the rooms now," Bouton said after the game.[40] He had now won two of the three Yankee victories in the Series; they would not win again. The Cardinals, behind Bob Gibson, won Game Seven and took the Series four games to three.

Once again in the aftermath of the World Series the writers rained scorn down on the Yankees. They had embarrassed themselves, they wrote. All except Bouton. And maybe Mel Stottlemyre.[41] But if the writers didn't take note of the other news that emerged from the Series, the Cardinal hitters sure did. The scouting reports were wrong, Lou Brock said afterward. "They said Bouton threw hard and lightning fast. I was expecting the kind of speed you'd expect to see facing Sandy Koufax or Don Drysdale. I never saw anything close to

[that]."[42] Months later Bouton would describe the ache in his arm that had bothered him all season this way: "It's a dull pain. It doesn't get any worse. It's a chronic strain of the bicep. Low grade. It's not very glamorous. A guy has pneumonia, he stays home. A guy with a cold goes to work and does a lousy job. It's like I have a cold."[43] However he chose to analogize it, the simple fact was this: Bouton had thrown his arm out. If he had a cold, it was a chronic one. It would never get any better, no matter what.

9 The Bulldog and the Chipmunks

Of course, he didn't need his arm during the off-season, which he spent in the public eye as much as he could. He made appearances on *The Ed Sullivan Show* and on the rubber-chicken circuit, teaming up with Linz, who now answered to "Harmonica Phil" and who would open their act by tooting out "Swanee River." Bouton would follow with his "Crazy Guggenheim" impression, borrowing Frank Fontaine's act from *The Jackie Gleason Show*. He'd put on a funny hat, roll his eyes, and slur his speech, just like the popular character.[1] It always drew big laughs. On the scale of transgressions from the Yankee Way, this was but a small one, but it was a transgression nonetheless. As Bouton would later expose in *Ball Four*, Mantle, Ford, and the others would engage in activities much more undignified, much more "un-Yankee-like," than his Crazy Guggenheim routine, but those were either behind closed doors or on a hotel rooftop. Bouton's was out in the open, for all to see. The Yankee pinstripes connoted a businesslike formality that clashed with the type of clowning around Bouton preferred. He was making all of them look bad by engaging in it so publicly, some grumbled. He was damaging the brand.

His largest transgression, however, was his chumminess with the Chipmunks. "The Yankees still seem to find it hard to get rid of their stuffed shirts," columnist Bob Addie wrote in *The Sporting News* in early 1965. "They have a ready-made 'character' and refreshing personality in Jim Bouton, but his frankness with the press meets with a big chill from the Yankee front office."[2] Like it or not, he was now one of their stars, so no matter what he had to say, he was guaranteed an audience. And he was not shy in seeking one out. On team flights he would sometimes choose to sit with the writers, where he would opine on nearly anything. "Talking [about the game] after the game in the clubhouse was one thing," Vecsey recalled, "but at some point he began to have opinions on Vietnam, religion, local politics.... Vietnam was an issue in '64–'65, and he was talking about [it] and a lot of stuff." He had an opinion even when he didn't have an opinion, Jacobson remembered, and was perpetually bursting at the seams to express it, however and whenever. Bucking the tradition of mistrust between the writers and the players they covered, Bouton announced in February '65 that "of all the things that have ever been written of me, I've never seen one word that could be called unfair or a misquote."[3] The statement was honest, but it was also tactical: he was gearing up for yet another salary battle with management. Houk may have thought he had neutered him earlier with his threatened daily salary reductions, but Bouton knew that the more writers he could sway, the more power he would have to fight back. Yes, he was very good at this game. A master.

He wouldn't cop to the game, though. Not even a little. "I'm not campaigning in the papers," he said as word spread that he was intent on testing Houk once again. "So many stories have appeared that they [the Yankees] might get the idea I'm calling up the newspapermen. I've never done that.... But anytime a newspaperman calls me up and asks me reasonable questions, I'll answer him as honestly as I know how." He then divulged the one piece of information that was sure to tick Houk off more than any other. "They're offered [*sic*] me $28,500 and I'm asking $30,000," he said. "What's the big secret? If the Yankees are going to announce Mickey Mantle's salary, why not Jim Bouton's?" It wasn't so much the money that was important, he went on to say. "It's the principle." He signed for their price the last two seasons. Now they should sign on for his. He closed his case with what would become his calling card, a philosophy that just a couple of years hence would become the bedrock principle within the counterculture: "I have to be true to myself."[4]

Stan Isaacs recalled that Mantle used to be haunted by a recurring nightmare: he goes to Yankee Stadium and cannot get in; all of the

entryways are locked.[5] By the spring of '65 Yankee management probably would have considered that a viable tactic when it came to dealing
with Jim Bouton. He wanted the money he felt was unfairly denied
him in '64 and was intent on making his case with the public if he
could not make it with Houk directly. "We all get overpaid for what
we do," he said. "I don't think I'm worth $30,000 except I consider [it]
my fair share of the money that's being made. Where does the rest of
the money go? Not to charity. . . . When you consider what others are
getting and the money they're making, $30,000 is the lowest I should
have to settle for."[6] For the most part he was winning the public relations battle. Much as they tried, the Yankees were unable to control
the narrative by pleading poverty and suggesting that their players'
only focus should be on the love of the game and the success of their
team. Bouton was able to put his salary dispute in real-world terms
and offer a perspective to which fans earning far less than $30,000
could relate. It was largely for this reason that he was not torn apart
in the press the way DiMaggio was back in '38.

One of the writers Bouton charmed was none other than the *Daily
News*'s Dick Young, who called him "a delightful holdout." Young
was enamored of him chiefly because he gave Young what he most
desired: access. By mid-February there were two key unsigned Yankees, Jim Bouton and Elston Howard. Howard stuck to tradition by
keeping his mouth shut and refusing to discuss the specifics of his
salary dispute with Young. Bouton, on the other hand, opened up to
Young, telling him precisely what he wanted, why he wanted it, and of
what the back-and-forth between him and Houk consisted. So Young
returned the favor by helping him make his case. Bouton's Game Six
victory in the '64 Series alone put $42,000 in the club's coffers simply
by extending the Series to its limit, he wrote. If for no other reason,
Bouton deserved his $30,000, Young concluded.[7]

This was not an unusual take from Young. For a while he genuinely
liked Bouton (well, as much as he liked anybody) and would toss com-
pliments his way through his column from time to time.[8] By the time
Ball Four was published, he had become Bouton's archnemesis, tak-

ing him down whenever the opportunity arose, and sometimes even when it didn't, but in the early to mid-1960s Young treated him much like the Chipmunks did because he allowed Young to do the type of reporting he loved to do. Young was a generation older than the Chipmunks and never considered himself one of them (and they would have been horrified had anyone tried to lump him in with them), but they approached the job of sports reporting similarly. Young made his bones as a baseball writer in the early 1940s and was, himself, a sharp break from the type of reporting that was in vogue when he arrived on the scene. "He was one of the first to go into clubhouses after a game and interview players," former *New York Times* columnist Ira Berkow recalled. "Before a game, after a game, reporters just didn't go into the clubhouse. He started that." While other writers wrote from the perspective of the fan in the stands (the last wisps of that style can still be found in the writing of the *New Yorker*'s Roger Angell), Young wanted to give his readers more, something they couldn't have known even had they attended the game. In order to do that, however, players had to cooperate and open up. In that sense Jim Bouton was a dream subject for a writer like Young.

Young was an early guiding light for many of the Chipmunks. Both of Vecsey's parents were journalists, and his father admired Young so much that he made a point of educating his young son about him. "At six years old I knew who Dick Young was," Vecsey said. He grew up reading Young's column and eventually got a job as a copy boy at the *Daily News* during the summers of 1956 and '57. Although Young was by that point a star, he would come around and talk baseball with him. A few years later, when Vecsey got a job covering a smattering of Yankee home games for *Newsday*, Young helped him gain access to the players and coaches who might otherwise have ignored such a green reporter. "Young would go up to the manager of the visiting team," Vecsey recounted, "and he'd say, 'Here's a kid from *Newsday*. He's a good kid.'" And the manager would then grant Vecsey an interview he otherwise had no hope of landing. "Dick Young was sort of a friend, sort of a hero," Vecsey remembered. Long before Shecter and Isaacs were pissing off the Yankees, Dick Young was succeeding brilliantly in that department. "He was like Shecter," said Vecsey. "The two of them were separated at birth, outside of politics."

But there were differences. Most immediate were the physical ones. "Lenny looked like a walrus," said Vecsey. "Like Zero Mostel, like a rhinoceros. He was tubby; he was unathletic." Young resembled Sinatra, whom he would often portray at the writers' annual off-season dinner and show. He was stylish in an old Broadway kind of way—handsome, elegant, always well-coiffed. Other differences ran deeper. Although Shecter could be acerbic, he was nothing like Young, whom Jacobson called the General Sherman of sportswriters, with his scorched-earth style, torching anyone and anything in his path. While both Young and the Chipmunks craved access, Young was disdainful of what the Chipmunks were producing with theirs. "Young sportswriters think they're writing literature," he once told *Esquire* as part of a feature on the evolution of sports journalism. "They emphasize fluff to camouflage their lack of knowledge about sports."[9] As he aged he became ever more focused on his idea of morality in sports and how nearly everyone (other than him) seemed to lack it. He was evenhanded in his vitriol—players were abdicating their societal roles as heroes to the young, and management was corrupt in allowing money to dictate how they were running their clubs. As Young increasingly saw the world, everyone was out for themselves, which left him with the job of safeguarding the integrity of the sports he covered.

He was protective of his space and contemptuous of television, which he considered an invasive species. He would often push television reporters out of the way in the clubhouse or stand in front of the cameras to ruin their shots. Sometimes he'd even curse right into their microphones so they couldn't use the audio he believed they were acquiring at his expense. The television guys weren't journalists anyway, he believed. They showed up, turned their cameras on to get their two minutes of tape, then left, and you wouldn't see them again for days. They didn't know what he knew. They were impostors.

He may have been a lodestar for the young Chipmunks, but by the early '60s that had worn off. "Dick Young was probably the best ever baseball writer we knew in New York," Isaacs wrote in his unpublished memoir. "He was colorful, imaginative, courageous. . . . He was an early idol but that wore off as he became an embittered right-winger, disillusioned about athletes, about younger newspaper people, and seemingly, about life."[10] The more Vecsey saw of him, the less he liked him; he was a man angry at the world. He became a twisted individual, Berkow remembered. "In later years especially, in the Bouton period, he would let his political or social proclivities and agendas impinge on his column." In a few years he would viciously pounce on Bouton, whom Young saw as the embodiment of all that was wrong in society—a commie liberal looking to take down the institutions that Young believed made America great, the institution of baseball being first and foremost on that list. But in February 1965 Bouton was giving Young what he wanted, so he was generous toward him.

Bouton's showdown with Houk didn't last long. He had had two solid years under his belt by this point, along with two World Series wins and another stellar effort thwarted by Don Drysdale. He had the Chipmunks and Young making his case for him and political cartoonists weighing in on the tightfistedness of the Yankee organization.[11] He had fans debating the physics of his flying hat and little boys and young women taping quarters to pieces of paper so they could join his fan club. Houk—who still answered to "the Major" two decades after his turn in the army during World War II—knew a lost battle when he saw one. So he gritted his teeth, cried uncle, and signed Bouton for his asking price before the calendar even turned to March.

10 Rebel without a Fastball

"We don't talk baseball around the house much anymore," Bouton told Shecter late in the '65 season. "It's not a pleasant subject."[1] Bobbie, who had been keeping a scrapbook of Jim's clippings since they were dating, had put that to the side also. Just as well. "There's not much about me in print anymore," he continued. "I knew it would be this way some day, but I didn't think it would be so quick." The contract hassle with Houk turned out to be the last major victory he would register that season; everything went downhill after that. He hadn't realized it at the time, but he was at the top of a black-diamond slope in February. The drop would be sudden, steep, and full of bumps along the way. He was unprepared for all that was approaching him at lightning speed.

Later, some would wonder whether the root of his problems lay in his opening-day start in Minnesota. It was a cold and blustery day, and as Bobbie remembers it, it was his pitching an extra-inning game in forty-one-degree weather that no doubt caused the damage to his right arm from which he would never recover. However, he went only five innings in that start, and while he struggled, it was no different from how he'd struggled throughout spring training, in the warm Florida breezes. He had an ERA near 6.00 throughout the exhibition season but didn't think much of it at the time. He was just working himself into shape, he reassured the writers, and perhaps himself, when asked about it in Fort Lauderdale.[2] His control was just a bit off, he said. Nothing to worry about.

It would be.

After three starts the questions returned. He was 1-2, but even his win (a complete-game victory over the Athletics) was less than stellar; the Yanks won 10–4, and he most likely would have been pulled from the game had it been closer. "I'm not worried about the way I've pitched," he told Shecter before his next start. "It's only been three games. With the weather and days off I've only pitched once a week. When it's six I'll start worrying." Then he went out and got bombed by the Orioles, leaving before the third inning was over. Bobbie was in the stands, so he showered, dressed, and went to join her, figuring he'd take in the rest of the game like everyone else in Yankee Stadium. "You only threw fifty pitches," she told him when he got there. So he went back into the clubhouse, put his sweaty uniform back on, and threw in the bullpen until the game ended. It wouldn't help. Nothing would. He, like the Yankees, was not going to recover. As a group the Yanks were floundering, "like a large, fat man in a small, skinny swimming pool," Shecter wrote.[3] And Bouton was flopping around more than anyone.

Whereas most players tend to duck the media when they're struggling, Bouton, if anything, started talking even more, trying to put into words what he was feeling inside his right arm. He had, he told Shecter, a low-grade chronic strain. "I'm able to throw about four-fifths my normal speed. So it doesn't look like I'm that much slower. It's not a bad pain, something like an ache in a tooth that's not bad enough to come out."[4] Whenever a writer would ask, he would describe the sensations he was experiencing, perhaps believing that if he could only find the right words, it would all go away. "I know what's wrong," he insisted to Jimmy Cannon. "I'm too smart a guy to forget how to pitch."[5] For every problem there was a solution, he believed. After maintaining for years the bulk he had developed in the Minors (Cannon remarked now on how he was "fleshy and thick in the body"), he decided that now was the time to drop the extra weight. He began doing forty push-ups and fifty sit-ups every day and remade himself physically. By late June he had had a smattering of encouraging starts but then suffered a pulled muscle in his left leg in a start against the Angels that sent him into a deeper tailspin. By the end of July he was 4-12 with a 5.11 ERA. Dick Young took notice. "Says Jim Bouton: 'Pitching and painting are my two loves,'" Young wrote in early August. "'Ever since I was in school, it seemed I always had one or the other to cheer me up. When I was doing badly in painting, I'd be having a good year in baseball, and then it would be the other way around.'" If that was the case, Young noted, "he must be painting Mona Lisas this season."[6]

He finished the season without another win, ending up 4-15. The Yankees nose-dived into sixth place, finishing below .500 and twenty-five games behind the pennant-winning Twins. Now, he said, it was all those push-ups and sit-ups that were the cause of his problems. "Maybe I exercised so much I tired my arm," he suggested. He'd swim and play a little handball this off-season, he said, but not too much of either.[7] And he'd come back stronger in 1966. Much as he tried to convince himself that he was in charge of the situation, that because he was the one who hurt his arm he was the one who could fix it, he was growing increasingly frustrated that nothing he tried worked. He brushed off suggestions that it was his double warm-up that was to blame, along with, eventually, pretty much everything else. "Frankly," he admitted in November, "I don't know what's wrong with my arm and, furthermore, I don't think anybody else does."[8] He had been through four doctors, an array of pills, drugs, diathermy, and sound treatments, and his arm remained as it had. It ached. Not to the point where it bothered him on a daily basis, but the persistent, dull throb prevented him from doing the one thing he needed to do: throw a fastball by Major League hitters. And that was more bothersome than anything else could have possibly been.

He was only one season removed from his gritty World Series performances, and already he was yesterday's news. In December the Yankees floated the possibility that they'd trade him, perhaps to Cincinnati for their struggling starter, Jim O'Toole. The talks went nowhere, but shortly thereafter the Yanks acquired another starter, Bob Friend, who would essentially replace him the moment he showed signs of struggling again. All of this reinforced in him the notion that a ballplayer's life was a precarious one. At any moment it could disappear. His, in fact, might be vanishing in front of his very eyes. In response, he argued that he didn't need his fastball after all. "If I've got my fastball, I'm a 20-game winner," he said the following February, as spring training hovered over him. "But I was a good pitcher in the minor leagues without a fastball.... I've always had the winning attitude. I've had the guts to hang in there in tough spots. I don't think I have changed even a little in this regard." The sharks were circling, and it wasn't even March. He was doing all he could to fend them off, but he knew he wouldn't be able to do it forever. This was going to be the most important spring training in his professional life. He thought he was ready for it, but after what he went through in 1965, couldn't say so for sure. "Just let's say I'm fearful and optimistic," he said as he pushed off once more for Florida.[9]

The fear took hold that off-season, spurring him to seriously consider other ways to earn a buck. He had decided that he wanted to enter politics eventually, but to do that he would need money. "I figure a fellow is a lot better off getting into politics without financial obligations he may have incurred along the way," he said.[10] So he figured out a way to make that money outside of baseball. Identifying a need, he then went about filling it. Ballplayers required housing, he realized, and few were as lucky as he was, playing for a team located close to their boyhood homes. "It was hard for them to find places to live," Bobbie recalled. "So we started buying houses and fixing them up, furnishing them and then renting them. Originally, we rented them just to ballplayers, but eventually we found out that a lot of businesses would send salesmen or executives to the New York area for a year or two, so we started getting long-term rentals and not so many to the ballplayers."

Turned out he would need the money. Houk threatened him with a 23 percent pay cut for the '66 season, and after the year he'd had in '65, Bouton was in no position to hold out once again. He was able to talk Houk down to a $3,000 cut and even agreed to go along with the club's public relations charade of holding the signing of six players at Phil Linz's (who was now a member of the Phillies) restaurant, Mr. Laffs. The Yanks sold the mass signing as evidence of their largesse, informing the media in attendance that the six contracts totaled $128,000 in salary, but the truth was that there was only one raise within the group—pitcher Jack Cullen received a small raise of $3,000. The rest signed for what they had made in '65, and Bouton's pay cut counterbalanced the raise given to Cullen. Houk hadn't mentioned *that* to the press, although he did go out of his way to announce that Mantle would once again be receiving his $100,000 salary. Bouton quickly threw cold water on the event soon after it began when he suggested that the club was punishing him for speaking his mind: "The club had mentioned that injuries would be considered factors in salary adjustments, so I mentioned my sore arm. But apparently injuries count only if you haven't given them trouble before."[11] After he inked his name on the contract, he passed out business cards hawking his rental service to anyone who would take one. As the cards noted, he was now a licensed real estate broker.

Heading into spring training he once again insisted that he felt great. Each doctor he visited the previous year gave him a different diagnosis, so he developed a treatment plan that touched on each of them, hoping that somewhere in there lay the true cause of, and solution to, the problem. He felt strong, he said. He was sure he had corrected whatever it was that caused the dull ache in his arm. Less than two weeks later his shoulder hurt.

The '66 season opened in turmoil for the Yanks. Johnny Keane, who had replaced Berra after the '64 season, was fired after the Yanks lost sixteen of their first twenty games in April and early May. Houk descended from the front office to return as manager and first tried to send Bouton to the Minors but was unable to after he didn't clear waivers. Houk then parked him in the bullpen and promptly forgot about him—he had pitched only one inning all season by late May. Finally, due to a crunch in the schedule, Houk started him in the second game of a doubleheader against the Senators. He pitched well, losing the game but going seven innings and surrendering only one earned run. Houk started him again six days later in Boston, and he won his first game in nearly a calendar year. He then officially joined the rotation and, for the most part, pitched pretty well. In late August he finally won a game at Yankee Stadium, his first victory there since the last day of the '64 season. He was 2-6 at that point with a respectable 3.06 ERA and was frustrated. One day, on the empty bench at Yankee Stadium, he let it all out to a young Ira Berkow. "One day I sat down and began to talk with him," Berkow remembered of the afternoon, "and he began telling me how he should have won the games he had lost. And he began to describe, in detail, why he should have won those games. So, say he was 3 and 7 [sic] at the time, it sounded like he should have been 10 and 0."

He finished strong, though, nearly throwing a no-hitter against the Twins in September, losing it on a Don Mincher single in the eighth and then the game in the ninth on a comedy of defensive errors by the now last-place Yanks. He finished the season 3-8 but with a 2.69 ERA and, more important, hope. The Chipmunks were firmly in his corner, rationalizing that he was still young (only twenty-seven) and did seem to improve as the season went on. Perhaps there was life in that right arm yet. If there was blame to be laid, the Chipmunks laid it on Houk and the organization, who didn't seem to care about Bouton and used him, they believed, like a rag doll. If he burned himself out, "they let him burn himself out," Jacobson maintains to this day. "After he hurt his arm, Houk didn't have much use for him anymore. He was not Houk's kind of Yankee." He'd give him a start and then sit him for a while, use him in relief, and then start him again. "Bouton thought Houk set him up for failure," Jacobson recalled.

Perhaps, but Houk kept him around nonetheless. He even re-signed him for the '67 season without a pay cut, although he'd placed him on waivers after the season and nobody claimed him. While the Chipmunks were aiming their ire at the organization, the old guard in the press box was wondering why the organization was keeping Bouton around at all. "It is most unusual for the Yankees to hang on to a pitcher with [his] credentials," Jim Ogle wrote.[12] After he struggled again in '67, Ogle mused that "there must be a reason why a pitcher with three straight bad years, including a return to the minors, still retains one of the treasured spots on a club's 40-man roster." It must be because he's a hard worker, Ogle concluded. Because he couldn't see any other reason to keep him around. For his part, Bouton was, again, convinced that he was going to turn the corner in '67. "All I want to do is pick up where I left off last year," he said before heading back down to Florida. "If I do, the only thing that can stop me from having a big year is to get hit by a truck."[13]

His arm, again, felt great, he insisted. "I'm so damned happy you can't believe it," he said on his twenty-eighth birthday in Fort Lauderdale. "I really thought I was washed up. But that's over, baby. It's all over."[14] His arm felt "like I have a big dog on a leash," he said. If anything, he was too strong now, he claimed. On top of this he found a compatriot to replace Linz in pitcher Fritz Peterson, who had just made the team that spring. He took Peterson under his wing, becoming, Peterson said, "the big brother I never had." They became roommates and shared a similar fondness for goofy pranks. They'd spend their free time thinking up elaborate ruses like the one Bouton proposed the time the Yanks shared a Detroit hotel with the Shriners, where they'd stake them out, hose them down, and then disappear into a stairwell before being caught (Peterson backed out at the last moment). He felt so good that he decided to put his political ambitions to the test (he'd spent the off-season campaigning for the liberal Democrat Howard Dressner, who narrowly lost his bid for a seat in the New York State Assembly) by running for the position of Yankee player representative.

The position had just become something more than a ceremonial one—Marvin Miller had taken over the reins of the MLB Players Association (MLBPA) the previous year and in his rounds across the clubhouses had spoken of real change coming at last. This was going to be a real union, Miller promised, not merely a mouthpiece for the players to beg for whatever small conveniences the owners would allow. Clete Boyer decided to step down from the post, and Steve Hamilton was the default choice to replace him. That is, until Bouton announced that he wanted to be considered as well. He wrote up a three-page position paper that he passed out to the players, arguing for his suitability for the job. Many of his points were humorous (he wanted to be player rep, he said, because "I get to write 'Player Rep' on all my underwear and sweatshirts with a marking pencil"), but sprinkled within the comedy were serious points—he was interested in the issues and the welfare of the players who would come after him, and he liked to be part of the decision-making process. He may have been not only the first player to actually want the job but the first to campaign for it with a legitimate platform as well. In the eyes of his teammates, these were disqualifying factors. He was defeated in a landslide.[15]

On the field in '67 things didn't go any better. Houk gave him one start in April, and he bombed, lasting all of an inning and a third. He then became a mop-up man and struggled whenever he made his way onto the field. Houk used him only when he had no other options, and when he did Bouton was rarely effective. After seven appearances his ERA was a frightening 6.27. He was also bickering constantly with pitching coach Jim Turner, who Bouton believed to be retrograde in his thinking—Turner's off-season workout plan for Bouton consisted of nothing more than "throwing 15–20 minutes daily at medium speed and some running." This, Turner advised in his note to Bouton, was all that was needed to fix his arm.[16] The only thing surprising about Turner's advice was that he didn't also recommend rubbing a little dirt on it. He was no Johnny Sain, not by a long shot.

At the end of May Houk sent Bouton down to the club's AAA affiliate in Syracuse, telling the assembled reporters that this was to Bouton's benefit, as he'd finally get the opportunity to pitch on a regular basis there and could work out whatever problems he needed to work out. Bouton didn't disagree with the decision and said that while he'd try to bring his fastball back, if that didn't work he was prepared to go full bore with his knuckler. "I used it against Baltimore and it was effective," he said. "I struck out Frank Robinson with it and got a double play on it, so I feel that if I have to go back to the knuckler, I'll be able to do it."[17]

He would have to. One of the hitters he faced in Syracuse was an infielder for the Rochester Red Wings in the Baltimore organization, Frank Peters. The two would later cross paths again in 1975 when Peters was managing the Portland Mavericks and Bouton was attempting a comeback, but for now Peters was a utility infielder without much of a chance to advance beyond Rochester. Peters was shocked at what he was seeing from the former big leaguer. "My impression of him," Peters recalled, "was 'Oh my god. What a . . .' I don't want to say a tragedy but [what he was throwing] really caught my attention. Here was a twenty-game winner for the Yankees, a guy with a reputation as someone who was really tough and really good, and he's here trying to be a pitcher with nothing on his fastball."[18]

11   The Youth of America Is for Kids

His decline mirrored that of the Yankees as a whole. By the time he was optioned to Syracuse the club was a cellar dweller, the pristine image of baseball's cornerstone franchise having been tarnished as well. Ever since Joe McCarthy took over the reins as manager in 1931, the Yankees were not merely a ball club but something of a brand. Bouton would later write, "Probably more than anybody else, McCarthy was responsible for [the Yankee] image. He made the Yankees win, but he also homogenized the Yankees. He gave the Yankees the Yankee Way. Dress like a Yankee. Act like a Yankee. Be a Yankee. Think Yankee."[1] Jackets and ties were required, no matter what, no matter where. The code was passed down from one generation to the next, enforced by the self-appointed caretakers of the brand, players like Hank Bauer, with a "face like a clenched fist," as Jacobson described him; Moose Skowron, who liked to look the younger players up and down to ensure that they weren't soiling the brand with their clothing choices; and front-office types like Houk, who projected the "strong, silent-type" image everyone was expected to emulate. The code of conduct was far-reaching, seemingly knowing no bounds. "At the end of the season," Peterson wrote years later, "each player used to get a list with everyone's name, address, and phone number on it. . . . Whitey made sure to remind me after my first year that I had to be with the Yankees for five years before I could send any of the players Christmas cards!"[2]

When Casey Stengel was fired in 1960, the old order was on its way out, although it didn't know it yet. The Yankees were undergoing a "youth movement," he said at the time, and "the youth of America is for kids."[3] He was so right. Although the dynasty trudged along over the next few seasons, the clubhouse, as noted earlier, was overtaken by a critical mass of young people who came up all together. "When Bouton arrived in '62, he was not the only young guy around," said Vecsey. "He didn't come into a clubhouse of old farts." While this did imbue the club with a spirit that perhaps helped it win pennants in '62 through '64 as the kids flung egg and potato salad across the locker room, it also removed some of the luster and grandeur from the franchise, which wasn't an issue when they won but began to be when they fell on hard times. Bouton and the kids had overpowered the old guard and turned the Yankees mortal. Pepitone could now tell Mantle to get his own goddammed beer if he wanted one so badly,[4] Pedro Ramos could walk around in a cowboy suit,[5] and Bouton could do his Crazy Guggenheim impression on national television. All of it was now, finally, okay. "The air of efficient, heartless, totalitarianism" as Chipmunk Leonard Koppett once described the atmosphere surrounding the Yankees, was gone.[6] But what would they be once they were no longer atop the standings come every October? They'd be like every other club. No better. No different.

Factors beyond the Yankees, themselves, similarly hastened the decline of their brand. One was money. By the mid-1960s money was flowing into baseball as it never had before. For decades the Yankees had been able to refuel their dynasty through the purchase of players from other organizations who needed to sell them in order to balance their books.[7] The Kansas City Athletics survived the 1950s through this business model, selling or agreeing to thinly veiled one-sided trades of quality players such as Roger Maris, Ralph Terry, Ryne Duren, Clete Boyer, and Bobby Shantz to the Yankees in exchange for cash or marginal prospects (or both) that would at least permit them to shrink their payroll. Television changed all of that, lining the coffers of even the bottom feeders such that they could make it through a season without giving up the future in such sell-offs. Between 1952 and 1962 television money poured into the bank accounts of many clubs, with some of them tripling or even quadrupling their television income. Even the lowly Athletics saw a significant increase, although not as much as other clubs. It was enough, however, such that by the early sixties they were able to put a stop to their "kissing cousins" relationship with the Yankees altogether. In the process they dismantled what many saw as a de facto Yankee Minor League affiliate, leaving the Yanks exposed when they needed a patch. For the first time the Yankees were forced to look primarily within their own system for replacements. This compelled them to overlook perceived personality flaws and promote players primarily on talent. Gone were the days where they could afford to hold a solid prospect like Vic Power down on the farm because they didn't like his attitude. Now they had no choice but to promote players they felt were un-Yankee-like. Bouton, himself, was an example of someone slipping through the system when in an earlier era he might have been held back, and Pepitone was another. "I remember, in the minor leagues," Bouton wrote years later, "lots of times our manager would tell us that Pepitone would *never* go up because he never acted like a Yankee." But he did. That opened a lot of eyes: "If Joe Pepitone could be a Yankee, *anything* was possible."[8]

The other systemic factor that led to the decline of the Yankee brand was the arrival of the amateur draft in 1965. This choked off another stream of talent monopolized by the richest team in baseball—top-grade amateur players. For decades there were no rules when it came to signing amateurs; it was whoever found a player and offered the most money that typically signed him. In this Wild West atmosphere, the Yanks were bound to win more of these competitions than they'd lose. Once the draft arrived it no longer mattered how much money the Yanks had relative to, say, the lowly Kansas City Athletics. If potential superstars such as Rick Monday and Reggie Jackson were eligible for the draft, they'd go to the Athletics, which held their draft rights, and not to the Yankees, regardless of how much money they had.

And then there was largest nail in the Yankees' gold-plated coffin—the sale of the club in 1964 from individuals (Del Webb and Dan Topping) to a multinational corporation (CBS). This transformed the Yankees from a treasured entity, whose image was all important, to a corporate asset, one of a multitude that were competing for the attention of the board of directors.[9] People may have had their quibbles with Webb and Topping, but at least they could be assured that the Yankees were front and center in Webb and Topping's vision. There were no such assurances once CBS took over. With the splintering of control came a loosening of the grip on the club's image; there was simply no one person in charge of it all. Very quickly, the Yankees began to look just like every other club. By the time Bouton had debarked for Syracuse, he was leaving a franchise that looked far different from the one he joined only five years earlier.

All of this helped to explain why a guy like Jim Bouton, so un-Yankee-like in so many ways, was able to hang around as long as he did, particularly once he became an ineffective pitcher. It's safe to say that he never would have gotten so long a leash had he played with the club at any other point in its history. There was one more factor, though, one that was particular to Bouton, that most likely helped to extend his stay with the Yankees after 1965. That factor was the Yankees' new president, Mike Burke.

Outside of Bill Veeck, Burke was as close as baseball would ever come to putting a Bouton-like personality in a Major League front office. He was a spy during World War II who befriended Ernest Hemingway and ran Ringling Bros. and Barnum & Bailey Circus for a time simply because he befriended a Ringling descendant during the war and found the idea exciting.[10] In a sport where anything literary was suspect, he not only read but liked to display his Eldridge Cleaver books on his Yankee Stadium office coffee table so that visitors would understand quickly that the individual occupying the space was no ordinary baseball man.[11] Once ensconced with the Yankees he gained a reputation as an "executive hipster" who saw baseball as fans did—as entertainment. He tried to connect with the younger fans who were turning away from baseball by having Paul Simon throw out a first ball and by draping a large banner asking "Where Have You Gone, Joe DiMaggio?" over the Major Deegan Expressway in an attempt to tie the staid Yankee image with youth culture.[12] He even invited the poet Marianne Moore to throw out the first ball of the 1967 season because, what the hell, nobody had ever done anything like that before.[13] If anyone was going to appreciate Jim Bouton, it was Mike Burke.

The admiration was mutual. A few years later, in an interview with *High Times* magazine, Bouton said that he thought Burke was an excellent team president who would probably make a great commissioner.[14] In the end, none of this would insulate Bouton forever from the realities of the waiver wire, but, for a time at least, he brought to the Yankees something Burke believed the club desperately needed—a touch of cool, a touch of hip, a touch of fun. Which might explain to the old-school types like Jim Ogle just why a guy who had clearly lost his stuff remained on the roster year after year. They saw baseball as wins and losses only, and from that perspective keeping Bouton around made no sense whatsoever. But Burke and Bouton saw it as more than that. And through that lens Bouton remained a key contributor, even if his fastball was a memory.

In the clubhouse Mantle appreciated Bouton's presence even if he couldn't pitch anymore. If nothing else, Bouton kept the Chipmunks away from him, enamored as they were with the struggling pitcher who couldn't seem to stop talking. By 1967 Mantle was the last remaining holdover from the club's glory days and would have been inundated by the press even more than he was had Bouton not been in the clubhouse as well. The club "was not laden with stars," remembered Marty Appel, the club's young public relations man during that era. "It was really just journeymen ballplayers coming through. My fondest memory of all of that was seeing Mickey look around the clubhouse and saying, 'Who are these guys?'" In that atmosphere another go-to guy in uniform was welcome no matter what he was doing on the field.

Along with Bouton was Pepitone, who likewise deflected some of the heat from Mantle. Although Mantle's skills had clearly diminished by this point, he enjoyed his waning days nonetheless by having fun with both Bouton and Pepitone. He couldn't figure Bouton out, Jacobson remembered, but found him amusing nonetheless. Bouton understood Mantle, however, as would become clear within the pages of *Ball Four*. Mantle *did* understand Pepitone, though, and enjoyed pranking him by repeatedly encouraging him to humiliate himself for his pleasure one way or another. "He was a hero worshipper," Jacobson said of Pepitone. "The greatest thing that could happen to Joe Pepitone would be to talk to Mickey Mantle during the course of the day." "He was often his own worst enemy," Vecsey recalled. "Mantle . . . didn't do him any favors by encouraging him." "He was one of those guys who was easily swayed," said Fritz Peterson. "He was always looking over his shoulder to see who was approving of him. He didn't want the old guys to not like him." Mantle understood this and used it to his advantage. If the Yanks weren't going to be celebrating pennants anymore, at least they'd have fun watching Bouton and Pepitone do whatever it was they were doing in the clubhouse from day to day. This kept the club at least somewhat cohesive during a time when the organization itself was falling apart.

The 1967 Yankees were in many ways a fascinating cultural stew. Many different ingredients were thrown into the mix, and while they didn't blend naturally, what emerged was interesting nevertheless. On the field they were terrible (they'd finish in ninth place with ninety losses), but off the field and in the clubhouse they were awash in polarities, with Bouton at one end, Houk at the other, and Pepitone straddling the middle as a member of the new breed but one who revered Mantle and the Yankee brand regardless. Which would be why, when Bouton released *Ball Four*, Pepitone would feel a sharp sense of betrayal when his friend and compatriot unmasked Mantle and the organization within its pages. In all the '67 Yankees found themselves in a position shared by most institutions of the day: once revered and unquestioned, now largely hamstrung and struggling to adapt to the new world into which they had just been thrown. Just another piece of the establishment trying to make sense of it all.

12   The End of the Line

It wasn't exactly true that the writers had stopped writing about Jim Bouton once he began to decline, although that was certainly how he perceived it at the time. The old-school guys *did* devote less ink to him, and what they did write was mostly critical in nature. But they were only a faction of the New York baseball press by the late '60s. "The old-guard guys were much more performance oriented," Vecsey said. "If Bouton had three straight bad starts and couldn't throw hard anymore, they'd be pointing that out and saying, 'besides which, he was a loudmouth anyway.'" And then they'd move on to the players who *were* performing on the field. "That was the old Yankee team coverage that you'd expect." The Chipmunks never stopped writing about him, though, finding him, if anything, even more fascinating now that he was struggling—he was a human story now, not just a baseball one. But more than that, they needed him. They considered themselves on the vanguard of sports journalism, and they weren't wrong about that. "New Journalism" had exploded onto the scene along with them, and they saw themselves as part of that movement. And Bouton was a key component of all of that. Without him their ability to join the movement would have been much more difficult.

Like the Chipmunks, the New Journalists saw themselves as seekers of a certain type of truth, one that traditional journalism couldn't reach. In order to find it they sought out the sort of subject matter that could reflect back upon them a sense of authority that mere reportage from the shadows couldn't hope to do. Although it was the style of the New Journalists that caught most people's attention (quick, witty, at times profane), it was their subject matter that really set them apart and allowed them to become arbiters of a certain kind of taste. What they truly wanted above all else was to be arbiters of sixties cool. Style, alone, wouldn't get them there. They needed the right subject matter to take them to the places they could never get to on their own.

Gay Talese published "Frank Sinatra Has a Cold" in the April 1966 edition of *Esquire*; Joan Didion infiltrated the Haight Ashbury hippie mecca in 1967 and published "Slouching towards Bethlehem" in the September 23, 1967, edition of the *Saturday Evening Post*; and Tom Wolfe hung with Ken Kesey and the Merry Pranksters and published *The Electric Kool-Aid Acid Test* a few months after that. Each of these pieces reflected back upon the writers who authored them, giving them not merely a seat at the cool-kids table but the one at the head. The Chipmunks saw Bouton as their Sinatra, their Merry Prankster—an increasingly rogue free spirit with a singular style. They could ride him as Wolfe did Kesey, perhaps to unimaginable heights. If nothing else, he would help them establish their bona fides within the larger New Journalism movement.

In his study of postwar cool, Joel Dinerstein wrote: "There is one constant of cool across generations: *You don't own me. You're never gonna own me.* Cool is an honorific bestowed upon radical, rogue, free agents who walk the line of the law—that is to say, mavericks with a signature style. They transgress social norms and a generation loves them for it. In postwar [America], cool functioned as *an alternative success system* dependent on generational needs."[1] Bouton was never, technically, a beneficiary of the free agent system as it is defined in MLB's Basic Agreement. But he may very well have been the game's first true free agent in how he carried himself in defiance of the game's structure. It was this the Chipmunks were infatuated with and that they documented, regardless of whether his fastball was humming or flaccid. Because by doing so, they were demonstrating their own defiance and cool detachment from the structure of traditional sports reportage.

Leonard Shecter repeatedly liked to highlight the ways Bouton was different from other players. He wasn't obsessed with money and inwardly focused, as most others in baseball were. In a game drowning in jock culture Jim Bouton was a man apart, he'd write.[2] He was constantly swimming upstream. Merchant parroted Didion and Wolfe by inserting himself into a piece he was writing on him. "I had a catch with him before spring training," he recalled. They went to a YMCA on the Upper West Side "as a stunt. I warmed him up in the gym to get the feel of what it was like to catch a major leaguer." Embedded journalism was the rage outside of the sports pages. Now, through the vessel of Jim Bouton, it had reached inside of them as well.

His brother Pete always considered Jim part of the countercultural movement. "Jim was 'do it if it feels good,' the hippie, sixties sort of thing," he said. Whenever the Yanks were in Oakland he and Fritz Peterson would rent a car and head off to the Haight, where he liked to mix it up with the street preachers, Satanists, and whoever else was proselytizing from the street corner. "Here we are in Haight Ashbury," Peterson recalled, "and he's taking off on that devil stuff [with a Satanist], and a crowd of those real liberal students would gather around him. Finally, I'd say, 'Jim, we gotta go.'" Eventually, "it became a ritual. We'd rent a car, blast Mexican music, and head to Haight Ashbury and watch the funny people. They scared me, but they didn't scare Jim."

Bouton never considered himself countercultural, though. "There was a cultural revolution going on then," explains Paula Kurman, Bouton's wife since 1982, "and people said that Jim was countercultural. I don't think he was. I think he was on the leading edge of what was happening.... Those who dared to question. And more and more people were questioning. Questioning became the cultural norm. Let's see what we can upset next. Let's look around and see what trouble we can cause. I remember saying to him shortly after we started going together [in 1978], 'You know, you're really an old-fashioned, conservative guy.' And he said, 'Don't tell anybody.'"

Regardless of the emerging cultural norms, baseball was most certainly not on the forefront of them. So as Bouton became more of an insider within the emerging culture of questioning authority, he increasingly became an outsider within his own clubhouse and baseball overall. He was aware of the shift as it was occurring. Shortly after

Ball Four was published, Marty Appel approached him about this. "I asked him, 'Do you ever have any regrets about being on the outside because of the book and never being embraced or invited to be part of the baseball community?' And his answer was: 'Oh, I was never going to be part of the baseball community anyway.'" Astros pitcher Larry Dierker saw this right away once Bouton joined the club in 1969 "He wasn't one of those old-school, chewing-tobacco, cussing-up-a-storm kind of guys. He wasn't old-school at all," he remembered. To the players who barely survived high school, he was "an intellectual," which is how Peterson thought of him, even though Bouton, like pretty much everyone in the locker room, never graduated college. Occasionally, he would try to fit in but would only succeed in sticking out even further. "He wasn't much of a drinker," Dierker said, "but every once in a while he'd try to go out and chum it up with some of the guys." By the time the drink orders were taken, he was already standing apart: "His drink of choice was scotch and milk."

By 1966 his buzz cut was gone. In its place was a shaggy mop that identified him as an agitator to those who put stock in that sort of thing. He also stopped partaking from the clubhouse spread, concluding that the unhealthy options weren't doing him any favors. He began bringing his own meals to the ballpark, which only further marked him as an oddball and subversive. Within a year pitching coach Jim Turner was advising his pitchers to steer clear of him. He was a communist, Turner told them.[3] Eventually, Turner succeeded in separating Fritz Peterson from Bouton, convincing Houk that Bouton should room alone on the road so as to not infect the rest of the club with his ideas. Soon he would wear his "[Eugene] McCarthy for President" button on his lapel, which sealed the deal for anyone looking for evidence that the Bulldog was a Red. He'd only wear the button, though, after he pitched well, Lipsyte noted.[4]

A growing subset of players did in fact begin to keep themselves at a measured distance from Bouton, but not because they thought he was a communist. Rather, despite how much they might have found him amusing or interesting, they were wary of him because they started to see him as more of a writer than a ballplayer and one of their teammates. He seemed, to them, to be transforming himself into the "other" in the bunker mentality of the big-league clubhouse. "The guys never understood him," Peterson said. "They thought he was feeding the writers all kinds of rumors and facts that shouldn't be told. He was more like the writers," he went on. "Those were more his friends than the players were. . . . He'd go out to dinner with them on the road trips." The players would typically eat together; the writers would typically eat together. Bouton chose his side, and his teammates took notice. Bouton, himself, felt the transformation; the more he hung around with the writers, the more he felt like one of them. Very soon, he would in fact be one of them.

As it turned out, being demoted to Syracuse would be his big break in the writing world. Al Silverman, who had been following his every move, approached him and asked if he would be interested in penning an article about his demotion for *Sport*. This would be real journalism, not another puffy sidebar column like the one he wrote during the '64 World Series. Bouton agreed and immediately began taking notes, just as he would later do for *Ball Four*. He made it his goal to notice everything and to report on all of it. After the season he took a creative writing course at Farleigh Dickinson to help him hone his writing skills and put it all together.[5] When the piece appeared in the April 1968 edition of *Sport*, it would be his first published piece of real writing and send him on the road to *Ball Four*.[6] It contained the seeds of many of the elements he'd later expand upon as the piece brought the reader inside the clubhouse, named names, and focused on the failures and struggles of the professional ballplayer. In just a few thousand words it exposed the underbelly of the game like nobody had done before and provided the blueprint for the work that would in a couple years make him famous beyond the gates of the stadium.

The piece didn't waste its time; it brought the reader into the Yankee clubhouse in the first sentence. Clubhouse man Pete Sheehy whispered that Houk wanted to see him in his office, Bouton wrote, immediately putting the reader where he'd never been before and in a moment about which he most likely had never even thought. By the end of the opening paragraph readers knew how players learned they hadn't made the big club out of spring training—they'd arrive one day to find everybody's equipment bag packed for the upcoming road trip but theirs. Having been transported to the Minors, readers learned how and why players hide injuries from the coaches, how the game's salary structure left all players powerless but none more so than the Minor Leaguers, and how players dealt with the rednecks sprinkled on every roster throughout professional baseball. They also got a taste of the type of gallows humor that would later make *Ball Four* a cult favorite. "Hey gang, good news," he wrote, relaying a popular joke, "the Yankee charter just crashed and we'll be landing in Boston instead of Toledo."

Quick on the heels of that piece Bouton took a deeper dive into his style of investigative journalism, again for *Sport*. In early 1968 Jackie Robinson spearheaded an effort to pressure the United States Olympic Committee (USOC) to support a ban on South Africa from the upcoming Games in Mexico City due to its system of apartheid. South Africa had, in fact, been banned from the '64 Games but was readmitted for '68 after some fancy maneuvering on its part that gave it the appearance of an integrated squad but remained fundamentally segregated and in de facto violation of the Olympic Charter. Robinson and K. C. Jones of the Boston Celtics enlisted the aid of the American Committee on Africa (ACOA) to issue a statement denouncing the policies of South Africa and calling for American athletes to protest its participation in the '68 Olympics.[7] Several athletes signed on to the statement upon its release, most of them track stars (most notably, John Carlos and Tommie Smith, who would later compete in the Games and protest again on the medal stand). There were also some basketball players, tennis star Arthur Ashe, and a few baseball players (Bob Gibson, Donn Clendenon, and Ruben Amaro). The only white signatory was Jim Bouton. As for how he got involved, it all started with a form letter. "I was in the clubhouse," he recalled, "and I was going through the pile of mail. And I get this letter. It's appealing to professional baseball players—everybody in the clubhouse got this letter—

and it wanted to know if I would be willing to sign [the] statement." He did and sent it back. In a couple of months sixty-five athletes had signed on, most of them black.

Then another letter arrived. "They wanted professional athletes from any sport to show up at a press conference to point out that the South Africans were fielding all-white teams in the Olympics. As a fellow athlete, particularly a professional athlete, they wanted me to do what any sportsman would do," which was to point out that that was just fundamentally wrong and a violation of basic sportsmanship, which was what the Olympics were supposedly all about. "I said, 'Well, that surely makes sense to me. I'll join that team.'" Then they asked him to *speak* at the press conference. He initially demurred. "I said, 'We've got better guys than that.' [They] said, 'We didn't get any other guys.' They weren't able to get any players from the other [New York] teams to show up to the press conference." So he agreed to speak at the press conference, held at the United Nations Church Center, along with a Columbia University basketball player, a track star from Ghana, a South African soccer player, and teammate Ruben Amaro.[8] He, along with Robinson, was now the face of the movement.

In October 1968, shortly before the commencement of the Games, the ACOA sent Bouton to Mexico City to lobby for the exclusion of South Africa from the Games. He was accompanied by South African soccer player Steve Mokone. Once there they were joined by Dennis Brutus, a former South African cricket player who by this point was a well-known activist who had been repeatedly jailed in South Africa and who, for a time, occupied the cell next to Nelson Mandela. He and Bouton eventually became close friends. "It was really interesting having Dennis Brutus stay at your home," Bobbie recalled. "He was thrilled that Jim was doing what he was doing." Knowing that he was going to write it all up for publication later, Bouton brought a tape recorder with him to Mexico City. At the end of every day, "while everyone slept, I'd take my tape recorder into the bathroom and whisper into it to preserve the day's events."[9]

Their goal was to apply pressure to the various Olympic delegates on the scene and to educate both them "and the public from all over the world," as Bouton wrote in his report to the ACOA after he returned from the trip, as to "the apartheid that exists in South Africa and the ways in which they should contribute to the solution of those problems as they affect athletics."[10] It was heady stuff. "We felt," he wrote in the report, "that if we could get the IOC [International Olympic Committee] and the world sports federations to adhere to their own charters they would then have to suspend South Africa from international competition." They failed. In a way, however, at least he believed that they hadn't. While acknowledging that their arguments largely fell on deaf ears, something bigger had been accomplished. "Probably our most significant impact," he wrote, "was simply our presence which had the effect of making every delegate aware that their days of operating in secrecy are over. The combination of this awareness on the part of the delegates and a more informed and concerned public will, I believe, force the changes necessary in South Africa. A lot of groundwork has been laid for the future." As it would in the wake of *Ball Four*.

He wrote all of this up in *Sport*. His article appeared in the August 1969 edition and read very much like something that could have been included in *Ball Four*.[11] It was New Journalism in every way—he inserted himself into the story, relying heavily on perspective and humor to make his points and highlight the hypocrisy of what he experienced in Mexico City. Describing his introduction to Douglas Roby, the president of the USOC, he wrote, "'Mr. Roby, I'm Jim Bouton, the ballplayer from the United States. . . .' With a handshake, he replied, 'Oh, yes, and what team are you with?' 'The Seattle Pilots,' I told him, since by now I was out of the Yankee organization. 'Is that in the major leagues?'"

From there he took the reader through his misadventures in the hotel lobby, tracking down Olympic dignitaries and futilely trying to convince them that they were making a mockery of the high-minded principles they were always boasting about upholding. "'Are you mixed up with the Commies[?],'" he reported Roby's reply to his suggestion that Roby simply offer a resolution that South Africa adhere to the tenets of the Olympic Charter. "'Are they paying your way down here?'" At one point he eavesdropped on a Swimming Federation meeting and reported on the "Olympian display of pomposity" he overheard. The piece was funny and incisive and pushed the boundaries of journalistic ethics in places; it was *Ball Four* in miniature. In a way it brought to mind J. D. Salinger's Holden Caulfield in his dueling cynicism and wide-eyed innocence as the world around him exposed itself for what it really was. A pitcher in the wry.

In the wake of his involvement with the ACOA, and particularly after his piece ran in *Sport*, Bouton became a go-to guy for those who felt they were being persecuted by the system in one way or another. He received letters asking for his help, or name, in support of this cause or that one. Not all of them were on the level. "There was a guy in prison, at Rikers Island," he recalled, "and he sent me a letter saying that 'I've been persecuted in connection with South Africa.'" He wanted Bouton to bring attention to his case. "I said 'Okay. When is visiting day?' So I went down to Rikers Island. . . . The smell of imprisoned men is something you will never forget." He met with the inmate and heard his story. "He had a long story—about persecution, and killing, and this and that. I took notes and said, 'Thank you.'" When he returned home he checked the story with the ACOA, "and they said that this guy was a crazy man, a killer. Be careful and don't go near him." He continued to correspond with him for a while nevertheless, then stopped.

By this point his life could not have been more different from that of the typical ballplayer's. Hanging in the Haight, lobbying against apartheid, engaging in thoughtful, witty, cutting-edge journalism—each of these on their own would have branded him a misfit within the cloistered world of the big-league ballplayer. Taken together they made him what the U.S. press chief for the Olympics described him as when Bouton introduced himself in Mexico City. "Oh yes. I know you, you're the un-American ballplayer I've heard about." The one who went around confusing everybody with his All-American looks and discordant left-wing worldview.[12] He was in so many ways the antijock. But one who not only lived within that habitat, but who loved so much of it anyway. He had a perspective on the confluence of sports and the world that nobody else who sat where he sat had. Which was why his mother's words to him at the dinner table back in 1960 came back to him upon his return from Mexico City: you should keep notes and write a book about what it's like to be a professional baseball player. With his career on the downswing, and with even his baseball life in 1969 uncertain, to say nothing of what potentially lay in wait for him beyond that, he realized he had reached a turning point. "I thought, if I'm ever gonna write this book," he remembered, "if I'm gonna keep these notes like my mom said, I better do it now. Because this is the end of the line."

PART TWO The Author

13 Beginnings

Events on the field during the 1968 season only further served to drive home the idea within him that he was closer to the end of something than the beginning. He had arrived in Fort Lauderdale as he always had—full of optimism. Again, he was bursting with theories explaining his loss of velocity, convinced that, this time, he had solved the problem, even if he had no idea what the problem even was. "Ever since I hurt my arm in 1965 I haven't been throwing normally," he told the masses gathered around his locker looking for ways to fill their notebooks during an otherwise dreary spring training covering what was now a sure-fire second-division club. "I used to get a lot of body into my pitches, but for the past three years I was unable to do that. I feel that took a lot off my fastball." As for the culprit, it had to be his decision to lighten up on his off-season training, he said. "I noticed the last three years it took me too long to build up my arm each spring."[1] This, he said, set him up for failure. Now that he was back to his old ways and working out hard during the off-season, his smoldering fastball would be there for him. It would be, but only long enough to remind everybody just how far he had fallen over the past few years. He pitched well in spring training, while his arm was still fresh and strong, compiling a 1.04 ERA and headed for New York as the top pitcher on the staff. It wouldn't, it couldn't, last.

Nobody knew this better than the Chipmunks. George Vecsey by this point had crossed the divide and by now counted himself as one of Jim and Bobbie's personal friends. So much so that he drove in a small convoy with them up to Richmond after the Yanks broke camp for an exhibition game before opening day. Jim, Bobbie, and their growing family (which now included two-year-old Laurie along with Michael) in one car and Vecsey, along with Bill Robinson's very pregnant wife, Mary, and her child, in the other. On April 4 Martin Luther King Jr. was assassinated, and cities across the nation erupted. "We heard that bad stuff was going on in some cities," Vecsey remembered, so they decided to pull off the road and regroup. "We pulled into some Holiday Inn in Brunswick, Georgia, and they see this multiracial group coming at them, and they were in a sweat because there was an unusual situation coming in." First, the heavily bearded Vecsey walked in, followed by Bobbie, Mary Robinson, and a gaggle of kids of all hues. It wasn't the sort of procession the folks in Brunswick, Georgia, saw every day. "I think the people thought we were a Mormon family," said Bobbie. They talked about what had just happened and how to navigate the rest of the trip through the South as all eyes studied them nervously, unsure of what, if anything, was going to happen next.

A few days later it was King's funeral, and on that day not only was the country shut down, but Yankee Stadium was as well. Bouton called Vecsey, concerned that the downtime was going to cause him to lose his groove. "'I haven't had the opportunity to throw in several days, and nobody is coming in," he told him. "Would you be interested in letting me air it out in the stadium? I'll meet you there." When Vecsey arrived the place was empty save for a lone watchman. Not even "Big Pete" Sheehy was there. "I have no memory of anybody being in the clubhouse," said Vecsey. "It was just empty." There were no uniforms; Bouton was in street clothes. "I remember his advice to me: use [bullpen catcher Jim] Hegan's glove, and make sure you put the 'falsie' in there so your hand won't get smoked from catching my stuff." They walked out to the field, Bouton to the mound, Vecsey behind the plate, in as much of a crouch as he could manage. For fifteen minutes or so they had a silent catch in an eerily empty Yankee Stadium, the popping of the ball in the glove echoing in the gloomy, cavernous space. Vecsey never put the falsie in. He didn't need it. "I remember thinking, 'He didn't throw very hard.'"

As quickly as it arrived, the fastball was gone. Returning to the guile he had developed in its absence, Bouton succeeded for a time, so much so that a whispering campaign suggested that he had now developed a spitball to go along with the knuckler.[2] In late May he earned his first start in Yankee Stadium in nearly two years but left after five innings with a stiff shoulder.[3] He returned a few days later and pitched well, even throwing a complete game two weeks later in what would be his only win of the season, a 6–1 victory over the Senators. Still, Houk didn't trust him enough to give him the ball every four days, even considering the sad state of the Yankees' rotation. He spotted him here and there for the next few weeks before giving up on him completely. Bouton was frustrated. To the point that one day, after five innings of anonymous middle relief in Cleveland, he made a proposition to Fritz Peterson. "Jim said, 'Hey, you wanna take a freight train? We'll get on a boxcar and go to Chicago. Your dad can pick us up and bring us back.' I chickened out, but Jim would have done it."

The end came shortly thereafter. He was sold to the expansion Seattle Pilots organization at the June trading deadline for $20,000, or, as Bouton preferred to say it, "a bag of batting practice balls." Not only did the Yanks not receive any players in return, but they also had to agree to pay the balance of Bouton's 1968 salary ($8,678) in order to convince the Pilots to make the deal.[4] Bouton was shocked. "I thought I had pitched better than three or four of the other pitchers and didn't think I would be the one to go," he said at the time. "I guess they had their reasons for using me so sparingly and for making this deal."[5] He vowed to go to the Pacific Coast League (PCL) (which was where the Seattle club was playing as it geared up for its entry into the American League in '69) and "surprise a lot of people."

There would be no shortage of surprises. Not only was he heading off into what might very well become a baseball abyss and doing so staring down his thirtieth birthday, but he and Bobbie had decided to adopt an "unadoptable" child to go with five-year-old Michael and three-year-old Laurie. "It was something I had wanted to do for a long time," said Bobbie, "I guess because I was in social work. In school I had read a lot about 'unadoptables,' and I liked the idea of adopting an unadoptable child. Jim was very open to it." "Once you've satisfied your own ego," he said at the time, you realize that "there are enough kids who don't have homes."[6]

They visited "Welcome House," in Bucks County, Pennsylvania— Pearl Buck's foundation for pairing multiracial, needy children with interested couples—several times before settling on the right child for them. "We turned down the first possibility [they suggested] because he would have been too young," Bobbie remembered. "We didn't want anyone younger than Laurie. We wanted Laurie to be able to be the baby and Michael to be the oldest." They considered an African American child, but, as Jim later said, "In the end, we just didn't have the courage."[7] They were concerned that the child wouldn't accept them as parents, that other black families would resent them and reject their child, that, given what was going on the country at the time, they were perhaps dooming him to a life as a perpetual outsider. Eventually, they were steered toward Korean children. One child's situation caught their eye—a four-year-old boy of mixed race named Kyong Jo. He was in a particularly difficult situation given his parentage. "Because his father was American, his life in Korea would have been very difficult," Bobbie said. They agreed to take him when he was made available to them shortly after they had arrived in Seattle. It would not be easy.

Looking back on it, Bobbie is clear-eyed: "We were very lucky, but it was tough." They met him at the Seattle airport, where he came off the plane with a tag attached reading "Kyong Jo—for Boutons." His teeth were black and rotting, causing him unbearable pain. "When we got him to a dentist they couldn't believe his mouth and how he could have suffered so much and not shown it for all those years." He could barely eat, and, on top of that, there was a language barrier. "Jim and I took a crash course in Korean from a woman, just to learn basic things such as 'Do you hurt?' 'Do you have to go to the bathroom?'— those kind of things." None of it worked. That first night Jim had a game, so Bobbie tried to situate him. She made him rice, beans sprouts, and vegetables for lunch and chow mein for dinner. He refused all of it. Instead, he cried and called out for his mother: "Oma, Oma, Oma." Afterward, he refused a bath as well as pajamas. Eventually, he fell asleep but then woke up. When Bobbie went to see what was the matter, she found him on the davenport, crying.[8]

For three straight days he cried. As Shecter later described it, "It wasn't just an infant crying, demanding comfort, or food. It was a helpless, hopeless *wail*, a terrible howl against life itself." Jim was starting to wonder if they'd made a horrible mistake, if this was going to tear the family apart. "There was so much tension," he said. "Just that crying and sobbing. You couldn't get away from it. And while I agonized with him, I was afraid I had done a terrible thing."[9] Unable to soothe him, they called their Korean tutor to come and speak with him for them. She did and relayed to them all that was bothering Kyong Jo. He was angry, she said, at his mother for giving him away. And he thought the Boutons weren't all that bright because all they'd say whenever he spoke was that they didn't understand him. He also thought they talked too much and wondered why he wasn't living in America, like he was promised. He was told that America was full of toys and a place where every child had his own television set. This was not what he encountered in the Bouton house. Once, he said, they took him to America, and he saw it all: aisles of toys, clothes, televisions. But then they walked out of it, got into their car, and headed back to their home, which wasn't America at all. Why weren't they living there all of the time?

After the season ended the family took a train east. "He started running a temperature on the train," Bobbie remembered. He had developed an abscess in his mouth that had become infected. "He was really ill. They finally had to stop the train somewhere in Montana, and a doctor came out to look at [him]. He gave him a shot [of penicillin]. The doctor refused to take any money, and it was in a way so moving that everyone was so helpful but also so scary. We felt so helpless."

Slowly, he adjusted. For a time he insisted on wiping his feet before entering the house and hoarded food in the couch until he was confident that there would always be some whenever he was hungry. He'd hide his toys when he wasn't playing with them and pushed Laurie away whenever she would try to hug him. But the thaw came. Jim and Bobbie made some connections with Korean families so as to not sever him from his culture, "but [he] didn't want to have anything to do with anything Korean," Bobbie said. "Right away, boom-boom, he wanted everything American." He wanted to be called David and eat hamburgers. Soon, just like Michael and Laurie, and to Bobbie's resigned chagrin, he even stopped wiping his feet.

It had crept up on him, but by now Bouton was something of a baseball vagabond. New York, Syracuse, back to New York, and now Seattle, all within the last twelve months. And before long he received the message from Seattle's management that he was somewhat less than welcome there also. When he sat down with general manager Marvin Milkes prior to the '69 season, he was grilled as to his activities down in Mexico City. Milkes let him know that he was aware of his activities down there and of his rabble-rousing at the Games. "This was another way of [his] saying: 'This is how we're going to keep your salary very low,'" Bouton remembered. "'Because you're on thin ice.'" He was unfazed. "I just brushed it off because I was either going to be a good enough player, or I wasn't," and he'd been in baseball long enough to know that his being a problem off the field wouldn't stop him from making the club if he could pitch. And as for his salary, he was prepared to dig in for what he thought he deserved, regardless of Mexico City and Milkes's veiled threat. "Guys just didn't know how to negotiate," Bouton said, reflecting back on the era. "They just wanted to get on the field and play ball." Most of them would have grimaced and taken whatever Milkes offered them after a threat like that, but Bouton let it roll off his back. In the end he signed for the same salary he made in '68—$22,000. Not bad, considering, but rather than creeping upward as he aged, as general managers promised young players they would, his salary was cratering in lockstep with his career.

By this point he had been cleansed of any illusion that his old fast-ball was ever returning. "When I left the Yankees I was confident I was going to tear [the PCL] up," he told Lipsyte. Instead, he struggled against the Minor Leaguers. "After 50 innings of terrible pitching . . . I realized I just didn't have it anymore. The fastball was gone. There was no point in kidding myself. I could reach all the way back and it just wasn't there." With the Pilots he'd be primarily a knuckleballer. He started working with weights designed to strengthen his fingers, began downing copious amounts of Knox gelatin to strengthen his fingernails, and experimented with letting the nails grow to see how that might affect his grip.[10] The odds of him ever becoming a success-ful big-league pitcher again were longer than his fingernails, but he didn't care. "It's not money," he said when Lipsyte asked him why he was so intent on remaking himself as a pitcher at this point in his life. "I won't make all that much in the next few years as a marginal ball-player." And it certainly wasn't fame, hidden as he'd be in the upper Northwest, on an expansion team few would ever see play. "Well, maybe it's just me enjoying the idea of being a big league ballplayer. The thrill of competition." There was also the idea of the book. If he quit now, he'd never get to write it.

He had been putting it off, but the idea had rattled around in his head for the entirety of his career, ever since his mother suggested it. He had kept it there as long as he could, waiting until he reached a level of fame that would justify his writing it. Now he realized he would never get there. So he decided to down his gelatin and see if he could hang on for one more season and write it anyway. The book he had in mind now was much different from anything he would have written just a few years earlier. After his World Series heroics in '64 he sat down with a writer from *Sport* and told him that even though he had a reputation for being outspoken, there were limits. He said, "I don't think you should criticize another player in public." And as for the off-field habits of his fellow ballplayers? "The personal lives of our teammates and our associates—has definitely got to be taboo."[11] He was older now, though, and had seen too much. And read too much about the game that was just pure nonsense. "I've seen so many half-truths in books about baseball," he said when the book was released.[12] If he was going to write a book, his would be the truth, the whole truth, and nothing but the truth.

It didn't hurt that he had very little to lose at this point in his career. It was, for all practical purposes, over. He was old, in baseball terms, and would most likely be out of the game completely very soon, with little chance that he'd be able to land a coaching position with any-body, given his reputation. He was still the irreverent, fun-loving guy he'd always been, but he was also more worldly and, therefore, more detached from the game than ever. He'd gone through the trauma of adopting David, involved himself in demonstrations to stop the bombing in Hanoi, testified before a congressional committee on racial problems in athletics, and served on a committee to study the game's reserve clause, where he experienced firsthand the hypocrisy of the self-proclaimed "capitalist" owners who were insistent that their sport's anticompetitive exemption remain in perpetuity.[13] He had a lot to say. And now he was going to say it.

14 From Tell-Some to Tell-All

The fact that he was writing a book was not, itself, heretical. By the end of the '60s there was a growing canon of "insider" sports books, and his didn't promise to be all that different from what had come before. Jim Brosnan jump-started the genre when he released *The Long Season* in 1960. It was like Bouton's book would be—a diary recounting a year in the life of a Major League ballplayer. It resonated because it showed fans what the game looked like from the inside—the personal struggles, the doubts, the pettiness of management, and the quirks of his teammates. After reading it fans understood a little more about what it was like to spend an entire game in the bullpen, attend a meeting with a pitching coach, and take a road trip to Chicago. Leonard Shecter loved it, calling it "probably the best look ever at baseball as seen through a mature mind." He saw the blowback it generated, though. He saw how other players began looking at Brosnan with suspicion, particularly after he released his follow-up, *Pennant Chase*, the next year. He also saw how management began to give Brosnan the stink eye. With two books, popularly referred to as "tell-alls" on the market, Shecter understood that Brosnan had made himself a marked man. He'd better be a top-level performer on the field if he wanted to stay in baseball after that. He wasn't, and he was out of the game by the end of the '63 season. Brosnan had always been something of an outsider in baseball: he loved to read; fantasized about becoming a doctor, not a ballplayer, when he was a child; and admitted to a fondness for martinis. But it was his breaking of the clubhouse wall that marked him for the rest of his life, at least among those on the inside. He had committed the cardinal sin. Shecter knew this. As he wrote in the books' wake: "Jim Brosnan will always be an outsider."[1]

While players and management might have grumbled, the public, along with the literati—sporting and otherwise—embraced the books. They received glowing reviews, sold well, and made Brosnan something of a minor celebrity. Few, if any, of them saw Brosnan as having violated any sort of ethical norm by writing his "insider" books. They just found them fascinating and funny. As for why, it was most likely because while they were billed as "tell-alls," they were more accurately "tell-somes." "Brosnan had to pull his punches," says John Thorn, MLB's official historian. "I'm not sure if it was because of club dictates or self-censorship or personal leanings—Jim Brosnan was a pretty straight-laced guy." And his books reflected that. Bouton understood that as well. While he enjoyed them, he found them "too detached" to be true insider accounts. "[Brosnan] was the guy sitting over in the corner sipping a martini," he said shortly before his own book was released.[2] He was in no position to truly tell it like it was. He would refer to Brosnan's bourgeois habits often in dismissing the book, referring to him repeatedly as "a martini drinker." "I'm a beer drinker, sloshing along with the other guys," he liked to say.[3] Larry Dierker would no doubt take issue with that self-characterization.

In 1968 another "insider" sports book hit the market to great acclaim—Jerry Kramer's *Instant Replay*. This was a locker-room and from-the-field account of the Green Bay Packers' 1967 season from the perspective of one of their offensive linemen. In many ways it was the football equivalent of *The Long Season* in that it seemed to tell it like it was without fully telling it like it was. Still, it was a clear-eyed account of a National Football League (NFL) season that was rightly lauded; in 2002 *Sports Illustrated* ranked it as the twentieth best sports book of all time, right behind *The Long Season*, which came in at nineteenth.[4] Although it wasn't much of a break from Brosnan's books, it would be a significant step on the road to the ultimate publication of *Ball Four* because of its publisher, World Publishing, which would later publish Bouton's book. Had *Instant Replay* been a flop, it's not clear who, if anyone, would have published *Ball Four*.

World was a Cleveland-based publisher known primarily for its Bibles and dictionaries. Later it created its Signet imprint, which focused on dime novels and inexpensive editions of classic literature. In short, it was hardly considered a major player in the New York publishing industry, although it sold boatloads of books. In 1962, however, the Times-Mirror Company purchased it and moved its headquarters to Manhattan.[5] With that it began searching for its niche, its foothold, in the competitive world of publishing. The new brass took note of the success of Brosnan's books as well as the ascension of the NFL and, in 1967, approached the writer Dick Schaap, inquiring as to whether he'd be interested in working with a player to pen a football version of *The Long Season*. Schaap had become intrigued with Kramer while working on a piece on his roommate, running back Jim Taylor, so he suggested him. Given that Kramer was a relative nobody—an offensive lineman—playing on a team in Green Bay, World's editors crossed their fingers and hoped the book would sell ten thousand or, if everything broke perfectly, twenty thousand copies. Instead, it sold some two hundred thousand hardback and two million paperbacks and put World on best-seller lists for almost an entire year.

World had found its niche.

Part of the reason for the book's success was that it revealed a bit more than Brosnan's books did. Brosnan touched on the frustrations involved in contract negotiations, but Kramer and Schaap were more open about it, writing about how the coaching staff would seek petty retribution from recalcitrant players by denying them small perks, such as when Kramer's offensive-line coach forbade him from playing quarterback in a meaningless intrasquad match between the linemen, merely because Kramer was at the time engaged in a money squabble with the Packers. They also wrote about the abundance of "pep pills" in the locker room and hinted that there was much more going on behind the scenes than what Kramer was willing to write about: "Max [McGee] has been insisting that only a bachelor can write the full story of what it's like to be a professional football player." As for his "tell-all"? McGee told Kramer that an appropriate title for his forthcoming book would be "Half of It." Kramer and Schaap, while telling more, made it clear that they were still holding back, satisfied to give the reader merely a taste of the life. And they covered their tracks, alleging that the "pep pills" were a feature of a bygone era, having miraculously vanished a half decade earlier. They provided just enough to whet the appetite (aiming some barbs at Kramer's teammates), without risking a full-blown scandal (singling out for ridicule only those players who eventually were cut or who became minor contributors at best). In the end the portrait that emerged from *Instant Replay* was a reverent one of Kramer's coach Vince Lombardi. Despite Kramer's pointed frustrations with Lombardi, by the end he emerges as the book's hero. And his teammates were, ultimately, lovable and all well-meaning. Under cover of a salacious unmasking, the book was actually a paean to the establishment. If there were any doubts as to where Kramer stood, those were erased within the book's numerous asides where he promoted his side businesses and spoke of how his ultimate goal with his archery business was "to sell out and show some capital gains."[6] The hero-making machine of the NFL had nothing to worry about from Schaap and Kramer.

Now looking to create a cottage industry of these "inside the locker room" books, World turned to baseball; it had been nearly a decade since Brosnan's books, so perhaps enough time had passed such that the public would take to more of the same. World's editor in chief, Ed Kuhn, along with editor Bob Gutwillig (who had worked together with Kramer and Schaap on *Instant Replay*), approached Shecter, inquiring as to whether he'd be interested in following in Schaap's footsteps and, if so, if he had anybody in mind with whom he'd be willing to work. Shecter was underwhelmed by the offer. He'd gone down that road before, working with Roger Maris on a slapdash book years earlier, one that hoped to capitalize on Maris's assault on Babe Ruth's single-season home run record in 1961. The collaboration didn't go well, although the book turned out to be better than a book titled *Roger*

Maris: Home Run Hero had any right to be. Maris was a sour guy, and much of the book focused on his surliness. Although Shecter claimed to like Maris well enough when they started their collaboration, by the end they weren't speaking to each other and Shecter spent the next several years damning Maris with faint praise, such as: "Given his limitations, intellectually and as a man, he did his best." More to the point, by this time in his life, Shecter had come to the conclusion that not only did he prefer the game's outsiders to its insiders, he wasn't sure anymore that he even liked sports.[7] In fact, he had recently penned an article for *Esquire*, taking apart the man Schaap and Kramer had just mythologized—Lombardi—unmasking him as, in the words of Stan Isaacs, "the bully and despot he was."[8] An "insider's" book like *Instant Replay* was the last thing he wanted to spend his time on.

There was one player, though, who might make it worth the effort: Jim Bouton. If Shecter was going to do this, it would have to be with him. He was the only player he knew who wouldn't hold back, who might allow him to paint a realistic picture of professional sports. Shecter had made one go of it already, his angry exposé *The Jocks*, which he'd just completed and provided him with the opportunity to vent his frustrations in what read as a 268-page rant. It was a sharp and insightful book, but Shecter was merely a sportswriter, so the book's reach was limited. If he could team up with a ballplayer—and a free-thinking one at that—together they might be able to cast a wider net. So he approached Bouton with the idea and was pleased to learn that Bouton was having his own thoughts about writing a book. Not only that, but he had already begun taking notes. After he assured Shecter that he wouldn't clam up now, that he wouldn't insist on excising the naughty bits, as Maris had earlier, Shecter was ready to sign on with Kuhn and Gutwillig.[9] Now the question was, given who Shecter was insisting on working with, whether Kuhn and Gutwillig were ready to sign on with them.

If Shecter was less than enthusiastic with Kuhn and Gutwillig's offer, Kuhn and Gutwillig were similarly less than thrilled about the pairing of Shecter and Bouton. Although Kramer was hardly a household name, he was at least in the NFL, and on a world championship club to boot. Bouton wasn't even in the Majors heading into the '69 season. Worse, the best-case scenario would be that he spent the season on an expansion club in the invisible Pacific Northwest. And there wasn't a Lombardi figure in sight. This was who Shecter insisted upon, however. So they went along with it, but most likely only because Schaap had by now decided to create a cottage industry of his own—in the space of a few months after the success of *Instant Replay* he had signed on with the golfer Frank Beard to do an insider's look at the PGA Tour, Dave DeBusschere to do a diary of a season with the New York Knicks, and Joe Namath to keep a diary chronicling a season with the Jets. And he had more ideas in the hopper. So many that he had created his own publishing company, Maddick Manuscripts, to churn them out one on top of another.[10] In some cases Schaap subcontracted the writing out to his sportswriter friends, allowing his company to work on several books simultaneously. Quality was a secondary concern at Maddick; it was quantity that drove the company. In his effort to cover himself, Kuhn reached out to Schaap and offered to distribute a baseball diary his literary meat grinder was working on. This one would be authored by Detroit Tigers catcher and Bouton's near teammate at Western Michigan Bill Freehan.

Freehan was the type of player Kuhn and Gutwillig had in mind when they reached out to Shecter. Freehan was essentially Jerry Kramer with a catcher's mitt. He played a grunt position, for a club that had just won a title, and was generally considered to be one of his sports' top players, although he was largely invisible to those who didn't follow baseball closely, hidden as he was behind the plate and encrusted in his mask, chest protector, and shin guards. The Tigers seemed primed to repeat in '69, and Freehan, the AL's MVP runner-up in '68, would no doubt be in the middle of all of it. Barring injury, he would at least be on a big-league roster all season, something that couldn't be said for Jim Bouton. So Kuhn let Shecter have his collaboration with Bouton, confident as he was that even if Shecter's book came to nothing, he would have at least one "inside baseball" book on the shelves come 1970. Maybe two.

With that, Bouton and Shecter went to work. In late February Shecter laid out for Bouton some topics to ponder as he headed toward spring training with the expansion Pilots, pressing him to think beyond the clubhouse. He should think about baseball salaries, Shecter suggested, and how they compare with those of teachers. He should think about baseball's emerging labor movement and how the players feel about Marvin Miller, who was just starting to assert his influence as executive director of the MLB Players Association. As well he should look inside himself: Did he ever regret playing baseball? Did he ever think if he might have been better off—financially, personally, emotionally—had he chosen another line of work? But he should also focus on the fun of the game—the funny nicknames, amusing anecdotes, clubhouse meetings, conversations on the mound. "We ought to try to keep the tone fairly light," Shecter advised.[11]

Whenever they could they met at what was essentially Shecter's second home—the Lion's Head Bar on Christopher Street in Greenwich Village—to talk things out, particularly during the editing process after the season had ended and the difficult work of turning Bouton's notes into a narrative had begun in earnest. The Head (as the regulars called it) was where Shecter liked to unwind; it would play as much of a role in shaping the book that would emerge as nearly anything else.

The Head was not a sports bar, nor was it a bar where athletes hung out. Many of the older Yankees still frequented Toots Shor's, while the younger generation gravitated to Phil Linz's bar, "Mr. Laffs," on First Avenue, which would close in a few years because, as Bouton liked to say, "it wasn't funny enough." Given its proximity to the offices of the *Village Voice*, the Head was a writers' bar, one amenable to the ink-stained crowd no matter what their shift, because it stayed open until 4:00 a.m. Within a few years writers on the night shift at the *New York Post* began hanging out there as well. Along with the writers, old lefties such as union organizers, veterans of the Abraham Lincoln Brigade from the Spanish Civil War (or so they claimed), and self-taught, broken-down, beer-fueled philosophers made the Head their home. It was a place where words mattered but not one that cared a whit about pedigree—the Head was blue-collar right down to the floorboards. Two ethnicities dominated the Head, Irishmen such as Pete Hamill, Frank McCourt, and Joe Flaherty, and Jews like Shecter, Merchant, Jack Newfield, and David Markson. It was the bar, said co-owner Al Koblin, where the Jews drink like the Irish and the Irish think like the Jews.

You couldn't be a dope in the Lion's Head, recalled longtime regular Dermot McEvoy. "Guys would go at you. It was words, words, words.... You were always challenged. You had to be quick, and you couldn't be dumb." There was a jukebox, but its volume was muted so that it would not overwhelm the chatter and debate. In the basement was an old black-and-white television, but Koblin had a rule—it came up only if the World Series was on or the president had been shot. There was a touch of glamour to the place—Hamill might walk in with Shirley MacLaine on his arm, or a prebreakout Jessica Lange might be your waitress—but really it was the writers who were the stars. By the late '60s it had become a "thing" and drew its share of tourists, dropping in to see if Norman Mailer or Frederick Exley might be there. "It was the only place where the people came to see the writers," Merchant recalled. The Head's priorities were clear and for all to see: if you were a regular who had "made it" in Koblin's eyes, he would Scotch Tape your book jacket on the wall. Soon, swiping the jackets also became a "thing" at the Head, so Koblin eventually had to spring for frames and glass encasements for them before they could be hung.

Koblin's television mandate hinted at another priority at the Head— baseball. The four things Head regulars were interested in, according to McEvoy, were "writing, drinking, baseball, and girls." Along with the sportswriters such as Shecter and Merchant, literary writers who dabbled in baseball to a greater or lesser degree also hung out at the Head. One of them was Larry Ritter, who in 1966 published *The Glory of Their Times*, an oral history of early-twentieth-century baseball that was notable for, among other things, being the first book to use the language of the players themselves to tell their stories. Rather than cleaning up their diction or mythologizing them, Ritter essentially turned his tape recorder on and let it go, transcribing the players' stories as they told them. What emerged was something very different from the baseball stories Grantland Rice had written. These were salt-of-the-earth stories told by salt-of-the-earth guys. The book was a hit because it opened the door on the cloistered world of the professional ballplayer just a bit, allowing fans to experience the game as these old-timers did.

The Head begat the Bobo Newsom Memorial Society, which would also play a vital role in the formation of what would become *Ball Four*. The seeds of the society were planted by Philip Roth, of all people, who was thinking about writing a baseball-themed novel and who admired the grittiness of *The Glory of Their Times*. Roth approached Ritter seeking advice on how to make his characters ring authentic, leading Ritter to approach his fellow baseball-loving friends, most of whom frequented the Head. What emerged was the Bobo Newsom Memorial Society, a literary baseball roundtable where, after dispensing with their advice to Roth, Ritter and his friends began to meet and argue about the game on a regular basis.[12]

Ritter chose Newsom to be the group's lodestar because Newsom was eccentric and offbeat, just as Ritter hoped his roundtable would be. Newsom was traded five times, was one of only two pitchers to win two hundred games yet still finish his career with a losing record, and was famous for not knowing anybody's name, referring to nearly everyone he met as "Bobo." Casual fans wouldn't get the joke, if they knew who Newsom was at all. This was as Ritter wanted it. Red Smith soon called himself a member of the society, as did the *New Yorker*'s Joe Mitchell, along with poet Joel Oppenheimer and Donald Honig, who pressed Ritter at nearly every gathering to write a sequel to *The Glory of Their Times*. Ritter refused but told Honig to go ahead and write it himself, which he did, eventually publishing *Baseball When the Grass Was Real*. Vic Ziegel (a sportswriter for the *Post*), Merchant, and Shecter also had seats at the table. The discussions were freewheeling, lively, and, above all else, informed. These were people who knew what they were talking about but who also understood that the object of their fascination was still just a game. They were serious but not self-serious, and their baseball writing reflected that—smart without being preachy or devolving into treacle.

There was no shortage of cross-pollination within the society. Book topics were debated, and ideas were hatched, buried, and resurrected, sometimes within the course of a single evening. Ritter's agent, Theron Raines, soon became Shecter's agent, and he, too, contributed to the process of creating what would eventually become *Ball Four*. Raines's literary agency was known around town as the writer's writer's agency. It was where you hoped to land if you valued words above all else. Raines represented James Dickey, who was at the time the poet laureate of the United States, and who would go on to pen the novel *Deliverance*. Raines would take on baseball writers but only ones like Ritter, Shecter, or Lipsyte who were writing smart. He was not interested in peddling pabulum. He was a gentle, soft-spoken man from Pine Bluff, Arkansas, with a southern intonation who, Lipsyte remembered, "looked like Jimmy Carter with a beard." But above all else, he was a straight shooter. If he didn't think your book met his standards, he'd let you know. After Shecter introduced him to Bouton, he agreed to represent him, too.

All of this represented the primordial ooze out of which *Ball Four* emerged. Smart, funny writing, serious but not overly so, told largely through the language of the men who played the game. All of this rubbed off on Shecter and eventually Bouton as well, who was soon loitering around the Head and who attended meetings of the Bobo Newsom Memorial Society whenever he could. "I thought it was fun," he recalled of those times. "I'd go down [to the Head], have dinner with Shecter and a bunch of the guys. I liked hanging around with them. They were very smart people. I was interested in how they were thinking about the war and what could be done. I enjoyed being in their company."

The members of the Bobo Newsom Memorial Society embraced him, but, still, within the Head itself, he remained at something of a remove. Outside of the society, Head regulars saw Bouton first and foremost as a ballplayer, not a writer. That was the case before *Ball Four* was published and remained so even after it became a nationwide sensation. In the quarter century that passed between the release of the book and the Head's closing, Koblin never hung the jacket on the wall.

15 Take Your Pants Off, Bouton

Hi Len. What I thought I'd do is try to record every single night. Before I start talking I'll put whatever the date is. I'll talk about what happened that particular day, and then when I'm done I'll have a cut off period. Then I'll go into some background things on what other Spring Trainings have been like and that sort of thing. Today is the 28th. I didn't cut a tape on the 26th and 27th, but I made notes on the 26th.

First day. I got to the ballpark and went to Marvin Milke's [*sic*] office and shook hands and he asked me if I had a nice flight down. He said, there's been a lot of things said about the strike and I know you've said some things about the strike, but we are going to forget all that and start fresh. Everybody starts new down here. We have a new team and everyone is going to start with a clean slate. As far as I'm concerned, let bygones be bygones and whatever has been said in the past, I know I've said a lot of things, we'll forget all that and start fresh.

I felt like a former alcoholic who has been given another chance.

So began what would become *Ball Four*.[1] The first words on the first of the fifteen cassette tapes Bouton would fill throughout the 1969 season and ship off to Elizabeth Rehm, a typist for Lighthouse for the Blind, a nonprofit created to help train the visually impaired to become self-reliant. It operated a transcription service at reduced rates—something that appealed to Shecter, given the paucity of the advance he and Bouton received from World. World had offered $10,000 for the book, something no other publisher would top after their literary agent Raines tried to shop the book around. After Raines took his 10 percent cut, Bouton and Shecter split the remaining money evenly, as they had agreed, leaving each of them with a cool $4,500 to work with.[2] Shecter wasn't looking to get rich off this project, but he wasn't looking to lose money, either. So he arranged for Bouton to send the tapes to Rehm in Jamaica, New York, for transcription. She would then send the transcriptions to Shecter's apartment on West Twenty-Fourth Street in New York. The transcriptions would ultimately total 1,091 pages and looked like what you'd expect transcriptions from the Lighthouse for the Blind to look like—accurate but replete with typos, little punctuation, and few paragraph breaks. In places the pages read like a filibuster and might recall Jack Kerouac's stream-of-consciousness scroll that eventually became *On the Road*.

Bouton, with a sharp assist from Shecter, was clear from the beginning what his approach to the book would be. He would take it all down, not editing himself, and then pray that he both made the team out of spring training and had something that could eventually become a book. Shecter pushed him in this and other ways. "Don't try to save any tape," he advised Bouton. "Pour it on." More to the point, describe what you're thinking, what you're feeling, Shecter urged him. "We don't want you to be George Plimpton," Shecter wrote to Bouton early in the spring of '69, "but when you first go out on the mound to pitch your first ten minutes of batting practice, you're thinking *something*. Let's try to keep that in mind as you progress this spring." Bouton did, scribbling down anything and everything he saw and felt. "I didn't know what I was doing," he recalled. "I was just trying to remember what [Gene] Brabender said yesterday, and I don't know whether it's good or bad or anything." After a few weeks, once Shecter had an opportunity to review the first four tapes, he wrote Bouton an encouraging note. "I like what we have so far," he wrote, although he urged him to be more internal. Think a step beyond, Shecter told him; analyze why you feel the way you do. Also, focus on the odd values of baseball: "Why is there so much conservatism and why are players, who used to be so conservative themselves, reacting against restrictions about hair, etc.? Something is changing, but I'm not sure what," Shecter wrote. Tackle that, if possible. And keep an eye on Frank Crosetti, the old Yankee who was now a Pilot coach. "I think people might be interested in more about [him]."[3]

As was apparent from the first few tapes, Bouton had stumbled upon the mother lode in the expansion Pilots. "I got a stroke of luck here," he recalled. He had managed to find himself on a club full of rejects—guys who had all been tossed aside by other teams and who nobody else wanted. "It turned out they were a much more interesting group of characters because they were all just hanging on. They all came from other teams, and now they were together and on the first day of spring training were all introducing [themselves to] each other, telling funny stories about this game or that game. And cruel stories and difficult stories. Stories of abuse of players, [stories about] salaries and those kinds of things. I said to myself, this is a gold mine. All of these people, all thrown together on one team, sitting there on the bus, the dugout, the clubhouse. And telling stories. There was always something going on."

His roommate, pitcher Gary Bell, likewise recognized that this was a special group right away. "When you throw together a team of people nobody else wants, you're going to get some pretty crazy characters in there." For these guys every day was a battle just to stay in the big leagues. It was enormously stressful, so they released the tension however they could, often in the form of pranks and gallows humor. Tommy Davis recognized the dynamic. "I don't know how they put this team together, but it was unusual," he said. "We didn't win a lot of games, but we had a lot of fun. . . . All these guys were funny. . . . We laughed a lot." While they laughed and talked and traded tales of personal and baseball woe, Bouton took it all down, writing this or that on whatever he had available so that he'd remember it that night when he would record the day's events into his tape recorder. In all he'd accumulate 978 separate sheets of notes—on hotel stationery, envelopes, toilet paper, whatever he could find.

The 978 sheets became the bones of what would become *Ball Four*. They were crammed with anything and everything Bouton saw, heard, thought, or felt. Some of them contained writing tips to himself: "When writing a critical piece, start gradually with the weakest stuff and build a case—then come with the big stuff at the end"; some contained his predictions as to who would make the Pilots once the season started or his pitching strategies when facing this or that team; some contained his musings on Dick Allen, who engaged in an undeclared midseason strike against the Phillies: "This might just be a man trying to be one around people who expect something less and used to something less." Still others were attempts to figure himself out along with his place on the club: "I don't want to be just average or appear to be so. I want to be hip and be considered intelligent and aware—creative, funny, fun to be around." But most of them were his attempts to catch baseball lightning in a bottle—the banter between teammates, the odd logic of old-school baseball wisdom, the wiseass remarks, the unintentional humor, the deep cruelties. His goal was to capture as much of this as he could, and he used nearly every inch of available scrap paper to do so.[4]

What he was capturing, he later realized, was the end of an era. "One of the great things about baseball in those days," he later said, "was there were very few college-educated players. Everybody was marginally educated. Little more than a high school education and not sophisticated at all." This was the last generation of the sort of player Ritter captured in *The Glory of Their Times*. "It was kids who were right off the farm, right out of the mills and small towns, and everybody came together with their regional biases and prejudices and now they're thrown together in this cauldron and they're funny as hell because they've got these slang words and these accents. When you got a guy from Mississippi, you got Mississippi. When you got a guy from Brooklyn, you got Brooklyn. So, here's Brooklyn and here's Mississippi, and they're sitting there in the bullpen vying for an opportunity to get in the game." After a while he began to see his teammates differently. "I began to appreciate [them], not as ballplayers but as characters in the

book. . . . I began to really appreciate the humanity of these guys. . . .
I had such good feelings about them and [became] so fond of them
as characters."[5]

The largest character wasn't even a player. It was manager Joe Schultz,
of whom Bouton later wrote: "The great thing about Joe Schultz was
that he had things in perspective. Either that or he didn't give a damn."[6]
"Joe Schultz was just a character," said Pilots play-by-play announcer
Bill Schonely. "And he *loved* his Budweiser. I can remember him many,
many times saying 'Schonz, the Bud's gonna taste good tonight!' if the
Pilots won." As Bouton portrayed him in the book, Schultz was funny,
but he was significant in a larger way. "We love him," said John Thorn,
"because he represents what we think baseball was in the '20s, '30s,
'40s. He's the kind of guy who would have tossed Buds back with the
Babe." He was the stand-in for one side of the culture clash that was
taking place at that very moment outside the walls of ballparks everywhere. Thorn continued, "1969 was a great year, and the Seattle Pilots
are the least of the stories. But that becomes the canvas backdrop for
Bouton to touch upon, overtly or covertly, issues that were resonat-
ing with everybody who was alive in that decade." Bouton recognized
Schultz as the counterpoint to the issues he was so passionate about;
there was little doubt he would have a prominent role in the book,
albeit one that Schultz believed cruelly diminished him.

Although tossed in with the castoffs, Bouton again became a man
apart. He found a compatriot in pitcher Mike Marshall, another player
considered an odd bird by many within the game. Marshall was one
of the few who were college educated; he would eventually go on to
earn a PhD in kinesiology in 1978. He was also a chess player, and he
and Bouton would engage in a moveable game that traveled along
with them; onlookers would sometimes see one of them balancing the
board on their fingertips as they made their way through the airport
in order to resume the game on the team bus.[7] "We would put them
in a different category because they played chess against each other,"
said Davis. "[Jim] was a very intelligent young man, so you could see
how most of the players would look at him a little strangely."

Rather than try to fit in, Bouton again preferred to announce his otherness, heading off to hang with the hippies and protesters in Pershing Square whenever the Pilots were in Los Angeles and asking who wanted to come along with him. "He was always kind of a rabble-rouser," Bell remembered. "Always stirring up crap, but that's okay, that was him." He was far from the most popular player in the clubhouse. "He was just different," said Bell. "He did stuff that went against the establishment, saying stuff that people didn't say, talking about salaries. No one knew what each other made, but Jim didn't care—he'd tell anybody." For some reason here again he felt he could be elected the Pilots' player representative. And here again he lost, this time to Bell, who won largely because he was the longest-tenured player in the game. While he did have friends on the club, most of the players were wary of his outspokenness and liberal leanings, preferring instead the comfort of the old-school Schultz.

He felt lonely and documented that, too: "I play around guys [who] think I'm a flake," one of his contemporaneous notes reads. "There are only a few individuals I feel close to."[8] Despite the national generation gap, more players gravitated toward old-world Joe Schultz than the hipster Jim Bouton. "We loved Joe Schultz," Gary Bell said. "He was a players' guy. He'd say crazy stuff like, 'All right, boys, let's go out and kick their ass and get back in here and pound that Budweiser.' He didn't have to tell us twice."

It didn't help that even on a team of castoffs Bouton was struggling. The Seattle beat writers couldn't help but take notice of what was gone whenever he pitched rather than what remained. His hat no longer flew off his head with nearly every pitch, they'd write.[9] This was not the same Jim Bouton who smoked the American League just a few years earlier, they'd remark. Every once in a while his hat would come off, Schonely remembered, and when it did the crowd would go wild, triggering, as it did, memories of the man who no longer stood before them on the field. He was primarily a knuckleballer now, but even there he had trouble keeping it under control. He had just an "okay knuckleball," Bell remembered. "I don't know how the hell he threw it over the plate, to be honest with you." At this point in his career it turned out that what he was best at was taking notes. Even he knew this—one of his scribbles acknowledged that he was now more of a writer than a ballplayer: "Suddenly baseball didn't matter—suddenly the book became all important."[10]

Once *Ball Four* came out a controversy arose over whether his team-mates knew he was observing them for a book, calling into question the ethics of the entire endeavor. His most vocal critic was his Astros teammate Joe Morgan, who claimed to have been blindsided by the revelation that Bouton was observing him as a subject in a project of which he had no knowledge. "I always thought he was a teammate, not an author. I told him some things I would never tell a sports writer," he said upon the book's release.[11] Many of the book's critics—often old-guard sportswriters—likewise assumed that Bouton kept his team-mates in the dark, a tactic they believed rendered the book morally suspect. Even Bobbie believed that Jim's note taking had been done in secret.[12] To this day even many supporters of the book believe this, giving the alleged ethical lapse a pass because the end product was just so damn good. However, there isn't much support for the idea that Pilot and Astro players did not know that their teammate was writing a book. Instead, it was the frankness of the book that startled them. So much so that when asked about it, they claimed ignorance of the entire thing.

"When we first started rooming together," Bell recalled, "he told me right up front. He said, 'Hey, roomie, I just want you to know I'm writing a book, and I'd appreciate it if you just didn't say anything and let me do my thing.'" But he quickly abandoned any idea of keep-ing what he was doing a secret. "He'd be writing notes on the bus," Bell remembered, "and people would say, 'Hey, Bouton, what are you doing, writing a book?'" Schonely, who traveled with the Pilots, said that Bouton's note taking was hardly a secret. "I'd see him every single day and on long trips and out on the field, and he always had a note-pad in his hip pocket." Schonely occasionally observed him writing notes, so one time he asked him about it. "It was an extra-long flight, and a few of us went to the back of the plane to just shoot the breeze. I said, 'Jimmy, what are you gonna do, write a book? You're always putting something down [in his notebook].' And he said, 'Yeah, I am. But don't tell anybody.'" But many of them knew anyway and kidded him about it. When he was traded to Houston in August of the '69 season, his notepad went with him, and Bouton did little to nothing to hide it. "He walked around with his little note thing and every once in a while would write notes," remembered Norm Miller, his roommate with the Astros. He had told Miller as well he was writing a book, and if it was a secret, Miller recalled, it was an open one. Astro players would often joke with him, "Hey, Bouton, don't put that in the book," whenever they did something embarrassing. "You heard that a lot," Miller said. "He always had a reporter's pad and a pen in the back pocket of his uniform," Astros teammate Larry Dierker remembered. This caused some of his teammates to become suspicious of him and irritated, according to Dierker, because seemingly every time they turned around, there he was, jotting something down.

The truth of it was that while most players realized on some level that he was writing a book, they had no idea what kind of book it would be. "They knew I was writing something," he said later. "I'm not sure what they thought I was writing. But I was constantly taking notes. I was taking notes in the bullpen, taking notes during team meetings."[13] They simply assumed that his book would be no different from the ones that had preceded it. "Tell-somes" as Brosnan's and Kramer's books turned out to be. Miller captured it best: "I knew he was writing a book from day one because he told me. But there had never been anything like that. That's like saying, 'Hey, roomie, I'm going to wear a new suit tomorrow,' and he shows up in a Nehru. I'd say, 'Holy shit. That's not a new suit. That's a new everything.'"

By midseason he knew he had something that was going to rock the baseball world. "I know some people are not going to like what I have to say," he once confided to Schonely during the season. Some of those people might even be members of his family—one of his notes contains a quote from one of his brothers, who knew what was coming:

"This is a great book Jim but what's mom gonna think?"[14] Unbowed, he soldiered on, his incessant note taking making him even more of an outsider than he already was. "Back then," said Norm Miller, "if you were writing a book on anything—gardening—you would have been under suspicion. Because you were supposed to be a ballplayer. 'We don't need any authors'" was the mantra, Miller said.

Players were singularly focused. Doubly at best: "We didn't worry about anything other than getting a hit and having a beer," according to Miller. Everything else was a distraction. And Bouton's note taking was a distraction that separated him from his teammates. Even though Miller counted himself as one of Bouton's friends, he admitted that had he known what Bouton was going to write about Mantle, he never would have agreed to be his roommate. "I didn't want any of the shrapnel to hit me," he said. To him the book was simply a disruption he didn't need. Written by a teammate who insisted upon disrupting everybody every day of the season with his note taking. Far from being shocked that he had written a book when it appeared in 1970, it was the very fact that he was so up front about it that bothered them while they were teammates throughout the 1969 season. So as for Joe Morgan's allegation of Jim's ethical breach? "I'd call him on that," Dierker said. "Everybody knew he was pulling that notebook out of his back pocket and writing things down. How could he be blind and not see that?"

Whenever the Pilots landed in New York, he would arrange to meet Shecter at the Head or Shecter's un-air-conditioned apartment on Twenty-Fourth Street to go over the transcriptions. "He had a hot, sticky apartment," Bouton remembered, "and he'd say, 'Take your pants off, Bouton. We've got a long night ahead of us.'" He would. Shecter would. And there they'd be—two men, in their underwear, shaping the raw material that in less than a year's time would become *Ball Four*.

The Bouton-Shecter collaboration would prove to be the sports-writing equivalent of Lennon and McCartney. They were two iconoclasts who complemented each other perfectly. "Jim was a strong personality," said Vecsey, "and it took another strong personality to work with him to make the book what it became. Lenny was that person." Indeed, he was probably the only person who could have made it work. "Lenny was a great interviewer," Jacobson remembered, "and Bouton was full of stuff, and Lenny could draw it out of him. He could say, 'We need more of that' or 'Tell me what you see. What was this guy like? Describe that circumstance....' He was just the guy to work with him." "I could see where Bouton was sending stuff to Shecter, saying, 'Is this any good?' and Shecter loving it," said Ira Berkow.

Shecter would mark up the transcriptions and let him know what was working and what wasn't. "He was effectively taking the pages and editing them [while I was writing]," Bouton remembered. "About halfway through the summer, I started to begin to see, 'Oh, *this* [topic or section] is good,' because Shecter would say, 'Great! Keep going, keep going.' And I'd say, 'Oh, I see. He likes that; he doesn't like that; don't work with that. So it was a nice editing [relationship]." Shecter wouldn't rewrite; instead, he'd guide Bouton by letting him know what was good, what was essential, and what was peripheral. Shecter's markings on his copy of the transcriptions confirm Bouton's recollection: a lot of underlining, plenty of cross-outs, and many one-word notes in the margins: Yes! Why? Good. OK. Silly. Great. Or, if something particularly caught his fancy, a string of exclamation marks.[15] After Bouton was traded to Houston, Shecter wrote him one of the few letters they exchanged (neither was a letter writer), hoping to guide him through what would become the final section of the book and offering a perspective on what his observations thus far seemed to indicate, even if Bouton himself didn't recognize it. "I think we ought to speculate about why you were traded," he wrote. "My feeling is that you became a rather disliked fellow, always bugging the GM [general manager] and the players.... It seems to me we should somehow explain why the players—many of them—came to dislike you even though you were trying to be one of the boys. Nailing your shoes to the floor is hardly a sign of love, you know. It may well be that you simply can't get along with [the] majority of baseball player types and, obviously, your practical jokes don't help any. You've got a month to alienate the Astros. Let's keep track of how you do."[16]

Shecter had an eye for what would make the book stand apart from the factory of presumed tell-alls Schaap was now in the process of churning out. He was not only well aware of how far those books had gone in their revelations but of where they stopped. He was determined to lift the veil that stubbornly remained over professional sports, despite the "insider" status of those books, which appeared to him to be compacts between the athletes whose names appeared on the covers and the sportswriters who were actually doing the writing to keep the public at arm's length as to the real lives of the American professional athlete. The only compact he and Bouton had was to tell the whole, unexcised truth. To that end Shecter reminded him in his letter of the topics he had promised to write about but, as of yet, hadn't. Such topics included: "1. Difference between major league and minor league pussy . . . 3. Hawaii transvestites . . . 4. [player] homosexual incident."[17]

Shecter sent the first hundred pages of the draft he and Jim had cobbled together to that point off to Ed Kuhn at World for his thoughts. Kuhn responded (in a letter to Raines) that it was the personal rather than the lurid he found most affecting: "I like the family stuff a lot, touches like his son's ability to keep straight what team he's on." Still, Kuhn was on board with the book as Bouton and Shecter were putting it together, although he cautioned that at times the tone could veer toward bitterness. "Jim should not sound too sour grapes," Kuhn wrote. "Occasionally he does. He gets awfully mean about Mantle and despises Houk. This is o.k. if his tone doesn't get sour grapesy."[18] A couple of months later, both Kuhn and Gutwillig left World, and then everything changed. Kuhn was replaced by Peter Ritner, who was less enthusiastic about a book that, at last, would be a true insider's book. The relationship between Bouton, Shecter, and World would deteriorate from that point on.

Once the season ended the real hard work began. Bouton and Shecter's understanding with World was that the book would be released early in the 1970 season—Father's Day at the latest—for maximum exposure. This meant that they had to get the whole thing in final form and off to Ritner within a few months. This was when Shecter effectively moved into Bouton's house on Charnwood Avenue in Wyckoff. "In the house we had an office that also had a hide-a-bed," Bobbie remembered. Shecter would arrive in the evenings, after the children had gone to sleep, and sit down with Jim to go over what they had. "He was fun," said Bobbie. "He had a wry sense of humor. Sort of a curmudgeon." Even though the season was over, they kept a ballplayer's schedule, working at night and well into the morning. The house was in a development on a dead-end road; three houses down was a farm. Occasionally, when the time got away from them, they'd be jolted back into reality by the mooing of the cows in the early morning. If he knew he would be staying over, Shecter would ask Bobbie for some soap so he could wash out his socks so that he'd feel fresh before returning to his day job.

By the time they had finished it was winter, and they had a 617-page manuscript to turn in to Ritner. Ritner then assigned it to a succession of editors who, unlike Gutwillig, showed little to no interest in the book; one of them was a woman who claimed to not know much about baseball at all. Realizing they were on their own, they decided to edit and copyedit the book themselves. Bouton sent a copy to his father, who knew where the soul of the book lay—he told Jim that "the stuff you want to cut is better than the game details," and another copy to Mike Marshall, who had some specific advice here and there of his own.[19] "He did a wonderful job critiquing it," Bobbie remembered of Marshall's advice. Marshall pressed him to remove some of the snarkiness in the book. "Someone was always making a smart remark," he recalled of the draft he read. A lot of that needed to go, he believed. "I told him, 'This story is serious,'" and the smart remarks were undercutting the important points he was trying to make. But it was supposed to be a fun book, also. In the end Bouton compromised, removing some of the wisecracks but keeping the rest so as not to deprive readers once again of the fun that was the authentic voice of the midcentury Major League ballplayer.

When Ritner read the manuscript he was so alarmed that he sent it off to World's outside counsel at Weil, Gotshal & Manges to assess the book's potential liability. In mid-February Arthur Abelman from Weil returned a five-page letter to Ritner, detailing the forty-two potentially libelous statements contained within the manuscript.[20] "Under normal circumstances there would be very few problems because ball players, managers and coaches are public figures and there is a constitutional privilege to libel such persons in the absence of actual malice," Abelman wrote. "However, your author has been frequently quoted in the press and makes remarks, albeit flippant, which may be interpreted as disliking certain persons appearing in the book, all of which may be evidence of malice." Abelman then identified each potential legal land mine, such as:

> "The statement that Joe Pepitone 'stole an elevator' may be libelous"
> "The statement that Mickey Mantle closed a bus window on a child's finger is libelous. The further statement that Mantle should have spent more time sleeping and less at the bar is also libelous"
> "The statement that the author hated the Yankees is evidence of malice and must be deleted"
> "The statement that Steve Barber and Bud Daley are deformed is libelous"
> The discussion of Ray Oyler's aroused condition is an invasion of privacy"
> "The statement that the whole Baltimore team and most of the Tigers and the author's team take 'greenies' is libelous as is the statement that O'Donoghue had a season's supply"
> "The incident of two named ball players staggering into a hotel after curfew and being fined for drunkenness is libelous"
> "The statement that Farrell attacked a maid is libelous"

Abelman took pains, though, to demonstrate that he was open to reasonable compromise: "The statement that the author's wife is a nut may be libelous. If they are happily married you could consider allowing the statement to remain."[21]

Ritner forwarded Abelman's letter to Shecter, suggesting that he and Bouton cooperate and make the proposed changes. He also forwarded on to Shecter his suggested edits to the manuscript, striking out seventy-four mentions of sex, drinking, greenies, cursing, carousing, and pretty much everything else that set the book apart from the ones Brosnan and Kramer had written. Ritner acknowledged that Abelman had performed a "surgery" on the manuscript but claimed that there was little to be done about it; any changes Bouton and Shecter wanted to make from here on out "will have to be done with the cooperation and approval of Mr. Abelman."[22] Shecter was having none of it; he responded by restoring all seventy-four edits.[23] He and Bouton would be more accommodating when it came to Abelman's parsing of the manuscript, though. They'd agree to remove five of the forty-two potentially problematic passages. The other thirty-seven were going to remain in the book.[24] "Many of the stories that Major League Baseball and World attempted to muffle or excise were the very ones that would get [Bouton] in trouble with Bowie Kuhn," Thorn said. To some degree Bouton and Shecter had to understand this, although Bouton would claim surprise over all the furor later. But really, that, at least in part, was the point. To create something that would entertain, yes, but would also slap the sleepy sports world awake. "With rebellion, awareness is born," Camus wrote. As would, through the vessel of their manuscript, Bouton and Shecter. Their book would be published as they intended it or would not be published at all, they insisted.

Ritner took a deep breath. He would publish it.

16 Fuck You, Shakespeare

By March 1970 talk of the book had already begun to swirl, even though it was not scheduled to be released for months. George Vecsey wrote that "it could very well be the most provocative ever written by an athlete," although he hadn't claimed to have seen it.[1] He knew there would be trouble, though, because he knew both Bouton and Shecter. Bouton had better get off to a solid start, Vecsey wrote, because the Astros were perhaps the most Puritan organization in all of baseball. They forbade players from talking to women in their hotel lobby and went so far as to not only require all single players to live in the club's barracks during spring training—far from the nightlife of Cocoa Beach—but also lock the barrack doors at night so as to prevent any of them from sneaking out. While no club would likely take kindly to a true "insider" book, the Astros seemed primed to react more harshly than most.

But Bouton was hardly writing *Ball Four* to please the Astros. He was writing for the fans, he said over and over. Fans were more sophisticated than the club owners gave them credit for being, he claimed. They wanted to know more than just the score; they also wanted to know what the players were like once the stadium lights were turned off and the beat writers went home. Several years later he expanded on this. If the players were merely cardboard cutouts and an amalgamation of their statistics, he said, who would care about them? "It would be like sitting there doing a Strat-o-Matic game. You don't know the players, but this is what the numbers show you and this is who wins the games when they roll the dice. That's fun for people, and kids did that, but after a while, you want to know a little more about the players. . . . There are people who have good feelings about a player who might not be that good a player, but they like him personally. That's part of the fun of sports—rooting. You're not just rooting for a number, rooting for a team. You're rooting for these guys you have come to like, and in some cases love."[2]

His goal was to paint a portrait of baseball as it existed circa 1969. He wanted, he said shortly after the book's release, to create a record that could be referred to for generations. "I want it to be the book that's recommended 25 years from now when someone asks 'What was baseball like way back then?'"[3] So he took care to paint the Seattle Pilots and Houston Astros in Technicolor, like the mythical world of Oz. "Dorothy has the family members," he said, "and they're interesting, but she needs to get away, and when she finds this other world, she comes back and has a whole new appreciation of where she was in the beginning because she's come to see them in Technicolor."[4] His Yankee teammates were great, he said, but they were in black and white. The Pilots and Astros were and will always be in vibrant hues, and through them, he believed, fans would be able to appreciate the whole shebang that was baseball back when he played the game.

In order to provide the effervescent color, he followed Ritter's lead by letting the players speak for themselves. "All I had to do was keep my ears open," he said later. "Half the book is quotes."[5] True, but there was more to it than simply transcribing what he heard. There was a gap between Bouton and his teammates that was larger than he realized. Shecter saw it. Vecsey saw it. All the Chipmunks saw it. Bouton, on his own, didn't. Probably because he was trying so hard to fit in. "I'd get drunk so I could feel like part of the team," he recalled. To no avail. It would only make him sick. As would chewing tobacco. So those became halfhearted attempts at best that he had no choice but to abandon. As Vecsey noted, outwardly Bouton was very much like his teammates in that he cursed and teased and contributed more than his share of clubhouse pranks. But he remained apart from them in deeper, more substantial ways.[6] It was a vibe Bouton returned to again and again in his notes. He felt apart; he felt separate; he felt alone.[7] A book that explored that idea of loneliness beneath the mask of manliness couldn't help but be different from anything that had come before. And that's what the book became—a book about people, not merely characters. About high jinks and pep pills and booze and broads but, lurking underneath all of that, a book about the one thing no sports book had ever touched before—the third rail of men's feelings. This, along with the funny quotes, was what would give the book the depth of color he so badly wanted to paint. This was what enabled the amateur artist to finally paint a masterpiece.

In writing about the players as people, he revealed the gap and, in so doing, revealed the chasm between the assumptions fans—him included—had about the professional game and the realities of it. "I realized there was a tremendous difference between what I had always imagined baseball would be like and what I actually found it to be like," he told Red Barber upon the book's release.[8] The game was hardly glamorous when one peered out from the inside, he found. Instead, it was work and nerves and anxiety, tempered by the crude humor of young, largely uneducated men, most of whom hadn't reached a psychological age beyond fifteen, he believed.[9] This was also what made it so much fun, despite everything else. In terms of what was great and what was horrible about the game, he thought that most baseball people had everything upside down. "Some of the things that the Commissioner and the baseball people think are bad, I happen to think are quite humorous and reveal the fact that baseball players are human and interesting people."[10]

In writing his book about people, he made sure to keep his prose at ground level. The writing "is not the product of an MA [master of arts] in English composition," says Thorn. "It's not highfalutin language; it's not fancy language. It's a people's work. . . . The best writing is not elevated speech, but, rather, portraying people as they are." There is a poetry to good prose, Thorn believes, "and that poetry is in its rhythm." Jack Kerouac followed that dictate as well when he was penning *On the Road*. "It ain't watcha write but the way thatcha write it," he said of his writing philosophy, stressing that the style of one's prose can oftentimes carry ideas more effectively than formal eloquence. In *Ball Four* style and substance combined to produce something uniquely new, resonant, and relatable. "Lenny Shecter was a journalist, and Jim Bouton had never written a book," Thorn continued. Somehow, "the two of them combined to make something of enduring value on a literary, cultural, social, and political basis."

George Gopen, a professor of rhetoric at Duke who analyzed the book for this biography, concurred that it was Bouton's ear for language that causes *Ball Four* to sing. "Mr. Bouton writes musically," he concluded. "He makes his choices not only of which words to use, but—more importantly—*where* they should arrive in the sentence to have certain effects." Bouton, he believed, had an intuitive sense of the proper placement of words in order to provide maximum impact. His ability to do so "makes his prose immediately available for comprehension; and it also makes it forward flowing. No re-reading is necessary for the reader to reach full comprehension. This is a [major] reason [why] *Ball Four* is such a page-turner."[11] It also didn't hurt that the book reads like a conversation between the players or between Bouton and the reader. "If you feel as if the person who is writing might as well be standing beside you, speaking to you, now that's good writing," Thorn adds.

It was a personal work that invited the public in. Because it was at all times written for publication, it can't be technically classified as a diary, but it has the feel of one. And despite his knowledge that he was writing for an audience, Bouton managed to be both profane and confessional, laying bare his vulnerabilities as well as his love for a game that nevertheless frustrated and pissed him off on a regular basis. In the process both his cynicism and his charming innocence are sometimes displayed all at once, recalling a Holden Caulfield–like character who is both attracted to and repelled by the adult world simultaneously. Even his prose at time recalled Salinger's Caulfield:

> The meeting before the game was marvelous. When we went over
> the hitters, Gary Bell had the same comment on each one: "Smoke

him inside" (fastball inside). Frank Howard, McMullen, Brinkman, Epstein—every hitter. "Smoke him inside," said Bell.

It got to be funny as hell after a while, because not only did he get no opposition, but he was taken seriously. According to the gospel of Gary Bell you pitch to the entire Washington team by smoking them inside.[12]

Or:

In the clubhouse Joe [Schultz] delivered his usual speech: "Attaway to stomp 'em. Stomp the piss out of 'em. Stomp 'em when they're down. Kick 'em and stomp 'em." And "Attaway to go boys. Pound that ol' Budweiser into you and go get them tomorrow."
This stuff really lays us in the aisles.[13]

Because of all of this *Ball Four* managed to sear itself into the souls of the millions who read it, unlike any of its predecessors. *The Long Season* and *Instant Replay* were fine books and are still good reads, but they didn't enter the consciousness of the nation like *Ball Four* did. "If the literary detective Don Foster is right," David Kipen wrote upon the release of the final update of the book in 2001, "and the books we read early imprint themselves on our writing styles for life, here's betting that there are a lot of middle-aged writers out there with at least a fragment of Bouton's DNA in their prose."[14]

The writing was so good, in fact, that for varying reasons various factions claimed, upon the book's release and still today, that *Ball Four* was really the work of Shecter, the professional writer, rather than Bouton, the wiseass ballplayer.

These allegations began flying before the book was even released, and they originated where most of the controversy surrounding the book emanated—from baseball commissioner Bowie Kuhn's office. Kuhn was hardly offering his take on the quality of the book's writing; he simply wanted Bouton to disassociate himself from it as a way to shield him from any criticism of it (much of it coming from Kuhn). It was all Shecter's fault, Kuhn wanted him to say. The critique of the game was coming from the outside—from a sportswriter who was already on record stating that he wasn't a fan of sports anyway—and not from a fan favorite and former Yankee World Series hero who was unfortunately duped by the cynical scribe. Although Bouton refused to acquiesce to Kuhn's request, some of his present and former teammates nevertheless found that the best way to reconcile a book they were primed to hate with the man they, at least on occasion, loved as a teammate was to simply tell themselves that their friend would never write a book like that. Fritz Peterson alleged that the book was driven not by his buddy but by Shecter, who was simply looking to make a buck at his friend's expense. "I remember some people thinking, really out of kindness, that this wasn't really Bouton, this was all Shecter," Marty Appel recalled. "They were trying to exonerate Jim that way."

The fact that the book was tough, like Shecter, added to the speculation as to whose fingerprints were more prominent in the text. "[People] think that because Len has a reputation of being a tough writer that it's his book, that he did it," Bouton told Barber. "But that's not the truth." Once the book morphed from scandalous sensation to part of the American literary canon, the jabs not only increased but also became more venomous. "People say, 'Oh, he can't write. He's just a ballplayer,'" says Paula Kurman. It was a way to demean him, to belittle his accomplishment, she believes. "Shecter did not write; he edited," she continued. "There aren't any editors around like that anymore. He really knew how to take something and put it into shape."

Upon the book's release Bouton described their relationship similarly: "Where he was a tremendous help was in the editing. I sent him 450,000 words which had to be cut down to about 200,000 words and he did a great job sifting through all that material and picking out what was useful and helping to arrange everything. . . . Shecter did a tremendous job."[15] Indeed, as noted earlier, the typed transcriptions of the tapes are replete with Shecter's blue pen markings in the margins, remarking in a word or two on what was working and what wasn't, what should go where and what needed to be cut, along with suggestions for future conversations between them to flesh out a particular idea.[16] Certain of Shecter's longer annotations were aimed at drawing out an idea Bouton had introduced and that Shecter found intriguing. When Bouton described a scene from 1962 where he "felt like a big shot" when Mantle and Whitey Ford spotted him eating by himself and summoned him to join them, Shecter prodded him to reflect more deeply on the incident: "Why—and is it lonely" he wanted to know. When Bouton remarked that "I really have mixed feelings about Mickey [Mantle]," Shecter's note in the margin was simple: "Can we expand this?"[17] To the extent Shecter rewrote anything that appeared in the transcripts, mostly it was to ease the transition between the spoken and written word: "I've had to make more adjustments in the writing than I thought I would," Shecter wrote to Bouton about halfway through the season. "What happens is that the spoken word is great for certain anecdotes, but they need rebuilding in print. I think you'll see what I mean very quickly."[18]

Roger Kahn, the lyrical sportswriter who at the time penned a column in *Esquire*, took *Ball Four* as a personal affront, trodding as it did upon both his turf and his beliefs as to how the game should be written. His commentary on the book further fueled the speculation that the book was really Shecter's, particularly when he insisted upon calling Shecter the book's "mustachioed ghost" and attributed all of his pull quotes to "Bouton-Shecter."[19] Kahn approached Mantle one day and asked him the loaded question: "Do you think maybe the book ought to read: by Shecter, edited by Bouton?" Mantle's reply ("For lots of it, sure") was just what all the constituencies fuming over the book wanted to hear.[20]

On the flip side Vecsey initially stood up for Bouton as the author of the book, writing in the July 1970 edition of *Sport* that while Shecter helped to edit the book, he "in no way tampered with Bouton's words or meanings. Nobody tampers with Bouton."[21] However, after Jim and Bobbie's messy breakup in the '70s, Vecsey modified his position, siding with Bobbie in the divorce and approaching Kahn's position in matters more literary. "Lenny really wrote that book," he says today. "Jim may have been taking notes, and he was [maybe] going to do it himself, but that book is a true collaboration. . . . Jim lived the book and talked the book; Lenny wrote the book." What particularly irked Vecsey was that as the years passed, Bouton's reputation grew, while Shecter, who died young a few years after the book's publication, faded into obscurity: "Sometimes when I [see or read] about *Ball Four*, I don't see [Shecter's] name mentioned. . . . I always feel for the writers who collaborate."

Another criticism of the book went something like this: no matter who wrote it, anybody who ever spent any time in a big-league locker room could have penned something just like it if only they had wanted to. "We all could have written a book like that," Jim Kaat still maintains, "but why would we want to expose ourselves to that kind of ridicule from our colleagues and our teammates?" As for the book itself, Kaat found it "entertaining . . . but there was a confidence broken there, and [anyway], it was something any of us could have done." The way Kaat saw it, a clubhouse guy like Big Pete Sheehy, who had been in the Yankee clubhouse for generations beginning with Babe Ruth, could have written a book that would have put *Ball Four* to shame if only he had no qualms about violating the unwritten rule regarding the sanctity of the clubhouse.

Not really. "It was a combination of the time he lived in, the kind of person he was, the kind of upbringing he had, and this unique perspective he has," notes Paula. "He sees through the scrim that everybody else has on life. Always. He just has a way of looking at things. Like the little kid who saw that the emperor was naked. He just sees it. And he can't understand why nobody else sees it. It's so clear to him. And he finds it funny." Perhaps Big Pete could have told some lurid stories, but because he was an organization man through and through, there was no way he was going to write a book that even faintly resembled *Ball Four*. "What runs under all of the stories," Paula believes, "is that sense of trying desperately to get a foot onto the next rung of the ladder, that this is the end of the line. This adds to Jim's sense of struggle— all these guys were struggling. Where do you ever get a story about men's feelings? Because that's what it's about—men's feelings. Well, that's gotta be sotto voce because you're not supposed to talk about that, so it's dressed up as humor, dressed up as something else, but you can feel it. You don't have to talk about it, but you can feel it. And that's the difference. I can't think of another book like that."

The ability of the book to resonate unlike any sports book that had come before led to the swift and furious response to it as soon as excerpted sections hit the newsstands in the June 2, 1970, edition of *Look* magazine. Even before. The book's title itself—*Ball Four*—cued readers into the idea that this would be a baseball book like no other. "Sports books always had these upbeat titles, '*Running to Daylight*,'" Bouton said a few years later. "You never heard of a sports book called '*Running to Darkness*.'"[22] During the season he experimented with various titles: "There's More to Baseball than the Score," "Take Me Out of the Ballgame," "View from the Pitcher's Mound," "Bullpens I Have Known," "Hiya Baseball," "How's Your Old Tomato?" and a direct reference to Kramer and Schaap's book—*Constant Replay*—were a few of the dozens he contemplated but never settled on.[23] But when a drunk woman at the Lion's Head overheard Bouton and Shecter debating possible downbeat titles (the working title for the book as described in the publication agreement with World was "Baseball Journal"), she slurred her way to literary gold by suggesting a title that evoked failure rather than success: "Whyyyyy don't you caaaauull it *Baaaaaallllll Foooouuuuuurrrrrr?*" After rejecting it out of hand, they realized she was on to something.[24]

A swift and furious response was hardly what Peter Ritner at World was expecting. Or even wanted. He had effectively buried the book, ditching the agreed-upon spring release date and pushing it off into the quiet of November—death to any baseball-themed book. When word of the revised release date reached Bouton and Shecter, they exploded. Ritner never wanted the book and was saddled with it when he replaced Ed Kuhn. Bouton and Shecter understood as much and requested to be let out of their contract. Ritner not only refused but also tried to placate them by adding an additional $10,000 to their advance, which he then never delivered. After much heated back-and-forth—Ritner once referred to Bouton as "an angry Spanish Inquisitor"—Ritner offered to release the book in the spring if Bouton and Shecter would agree to accept only half of the additional $10,000 he had offered earlier. Their relationship deteriorated only further from there. "You have told me on several occasions how difficult it is to be responsible for publishing a best seller," Shecter wrote to him at one point. "I sympathized."[25]

Realizing they weren't going to get much help at all from Ritner, they knew that if the book was going to succeed, they would have to promote it themselves. Fortunately, Shecter was by this time a senior editor at *Look* and had the ability to green-light sports-themed excerpts for the magazine. He arranged for excerpts to run in consecutive issues—the second one would appear in the June 16 edition. They would receive $13,000 for the excerpts—more than World had paid them for the entire book at that point.[26] World, meanwhile, was planning only a modest run for the book—ten thousand copies, a typical order for one of their trade titles. Shecter worried that Ritner would abandon them—"As far as we could tell," he wrote Ritner, "you had invested no faith in us at all"—so he began talking up the book even before the initial excerpt hit the newsstands, telling his fellow scribes that the book would blow the lid off the game.[27] After Jerome Holtzman wrote in *The Sporting News* on May 23 that Shecter told him that the book contained a "homosexual scene at 30,000 feet," World upped its print run to thirty-five thousand copies.[28] Shecter kept talking, and soon World had upped the run to fifty thousand copies.[29] And the excerpt hadn't even hit the stands yet.

In selecting the sections of the book to feature in the excerpts, Shecter fixated on the salacious: a hungover Mickey Mantle hitting a home run; an aging Whitey Ford, aided by Elston Howard, doctoring the ball in the hopes of hanging on just a few years longer; beaver shooting; marital infidelity; greenies; and the drunken kisses between players on the team bus and plane.[30] And that was just the first excerpt. The magazine hit the stands on Friday, May 29, when Bouton's Astros just happened to be in New York to play the Mets. It was as if a bomb had been dropped. The shock waves rippled throughout the baseball world and right into Bouton and Norm Miller's room at the Roosevelt Hotel, where his phone would not stop ringing and Howard Cosell was banging on his door. This was by design. Shecter knew that he and Bouton were on their own now, working against not only the baseball establishment but their own publisher as well. "The fact is," Shecter told Ritner, "you didn't know we had a good book. But I knew we had a good book and we proved it with the furor raised by the publication in *Look*. Now I knew it was a good book and *Look* knew it was a good book and the whole country was mashing its teeth."[31]

A few months earlier World's safety net, Freehan's *Behind the Mask*, was excerpted in *Sports Illustrated*, and while Freehan caught some heat, it was nothing like this.[32] Like *Ball Four* Freehan's title provided a hint of what was inside. "Right there that was a tip-off that you were going to get something you never got before," Bouton remembered. Freehan's book fixated on his displeasure with pitcher Denny McLain, and when his excerpt hit the stands the blowback was strong. Freehan wasn't prepared for it. "Freehan was one of those guys who were happy just to have a book written with their name on it," Bouton said. When he realized he had crossed a line, he stopped talking about the book at all, hoping it would go away. He'd get his wish a few months thence. "Poor Freehan," Bouton said a half century later. "He got the heat but none of the credit. He got lost in the shuffle" once the first *Look* excerpt hit the stands. The moment word spread about what was inside that week's edition of *Look*, nobody outside of Detroit cared one whit of what Freehan had to say about Denny McLain.

Inside Yankee Stadium Appel, who had just been named the club's assistant public relations director that January, recalled that "the reaction was furious from the first day. There were so many points in the book [and highlighted in the excerpt] that were just horrifying to traditional Yankees." The front office never met to determine how to manage the fallout, Appel recalled—a failure that only exacerbated it. "The response was fast and furious," he remembered, "because people were asking the parties directly, 'What did you think of the book?'" This led to an avalanche of quotes and angry denunciations of both Bouton and the book within days of the publication of the first *Look* excerpt. Many within the organization were most offended by Bouton's exposure of Elston Howard helping Whitey Ford doctor baseballs. "Everybody really loved [Howard]," Appel recalled. "More than criticizing Mickey Mantle, it was picking on Ellie Howard that really upset people greatly.... He was a beloved figure in the clubhouse, and he became sort of a focal point of, 'Oh, on top of everything, how can you pick on Elston Howard?'"

Very quickly the book became a political statement. "You were either for it or against it," Norm Miller recalled, which made it different from any sports book that had preceded it. While Bouton knew the book would be controversial, he was unprepared for the degree of disruption it would cause. "He was just a fun guy doing what he thought everybody would like," Miller said. "I think he had a disjointed view of what was gonna happen. He thought he was doing a service to the world," but quickly realized that not everyone saw it that way. "He became a hot potato in the baseball industry," Larry Dierker remembered, "and he wouldn't have to do anything but have a mild slump and somebody would want to get rid of him." That fast, Dierker said, "he was a pariah. It was amusing to me how sensitive people were over little things that to me were nothing."

The day after the excerpt hit the stands Bouton received word that Bowie Kuhn wanted to meet with him in his New York office two days thence on Monday afternoon. "Maybe he has read it and just wants to tell me how much he enjoyed it," Bouton joked with a reporter at the time.[33] Inside, however, he was being torn apart by the potential damage he had caused. "My mom was in tears," he remembered. "There was a tremendous wave of fury," and she thought he had sabotaged his career. At one point she tearfully approached Caroline Bouton, Pete's wife, wondering if she should change her name and whether her friends would ever have anything to do with her again given what was in the excerpt.

Ever since Shecter began talking up the salacious aspects of the book, Bouton received the blowback. "Fuck you, Shakespeare!" Pete

Rose yelled from the Cincinnati dugout after Holtzman's *Sporting News* column circulated through the Reds clubhouse.[34] Other players made their displeasure known less eloquently. Some 47,193 fans at Shea booed him lustily and in unison when he entered the game in the seventh inning of the first game of a doubleheader that Sunday (they cheered lustily as well after he gave up three hits and three runs in one-third miserable inning of a 14–4 pasting by the Mets). Dick Young devoted three columns to the excerpt and how Bouton would be marginalized once the book itself hit the shelves, famously calling him a "social leper."[35] Now Kuhn was demanding an audience. Bouton knew that, technically, there was little Kuhn could do about the book (that became clear in the aftermath of Freehan's book, which Kuhn found similarly distasteful), but, still, the weight of the baseball world was now heavy upon him.

Until he went to the newsstand himself, to pick up the early edition of the next morning's *New York Times*. In it was a column by Lipsyte that was the antidote for everything Young had written. "If the excerpts in Look are indicative of the book's content and style," Lipsyte wrote, "Bouton should be given baseball's most valuable salesman of the year award. His anecdotes and insights are enlightening, hilarious and, most important, unavailable elsewhere. They breathe new life into a game choked by pontificating statisticians, image-conscious officials and scared ballplayers."[36] Bouton then ran down to the Lion's Head, to meet up with Shecter and toast to their relief that there were people out there who *got it*. Lipsyte's column was testament to the reality that the whole world wasn't made up of Dick Youngs and Pete Roses. Only baseball's insular one was—the one that knew nothing of life outside of the stadium walls and cared even less about anything not concerned with batting and earned run averages. This was the world Bouton and Shecter were hoping to puncture. Lipsyte's column showed them that they had succeeded. His meeting was scheduled for 5:00 p.m. the next day. He would now attend it not as a beaten man, but as a conqueror.

17   Protectors of the Holy Flame

According to Lou Hoynes, who was an attorney working in the commissioner's office at the time, Bowie Kuhn was "a stiff-necked . . . strict Dutch moralist" with a Kenesaw Mountain Landis complex. He saw his job as primarily being one of protecting the "holy flame of the game" and was furious over what he believed was Bouton's attempt to snuff it out. "The idea that someone would be a part of the family and then tell stories about that family was offensive to him," said Hoynes. More than that, he was a stuffed shirt whose ego oftentimes got the better of him. "The Chicago Public Library had a baseball speakers [series]," Ira Berkow recalled, featuring among others, Berkow and Kuhn. "I ran into Bowie Kuhn in Cooperstown some time after that, and the first thing he said to me was, 'I had a bigger crowd than you did.' I just thought that was an odd thing to say."

More concretely, he viewed the players as the product and, said Hoynes, saw *Ball Four* as damaging the product. He was determined to fight back in order to protect it. Sandy Hadden, Kuhn's number two, and Hoynes counseled him repeatedly to let it go, to let the book run its course without comment from the commissioner's office, but Kuhn refused their counsel. "Bowie felt there was a wrongness there," Hoynes continued, "and felt compelled to speak out about it." Hadden and Hoynes told him what would happen if he did—he'd most likely make a big deal even bigger. Kuhn didn't care. "Bowie wasn't dumb, but he was what he was," Hoynes said. "He knew he was selling books [by initiating a confrontation with Bouton and Shecter], but he wanted to speak out for what he thought was right." On an intellectual level he knew he should hold his tongue, but on a visceral level it bothered him and he was determined to speak his mind.

According to Hoynes, who was tasked with taking the temperature of the club owners in the aftermath of the *Look* excerpts, aside from the fury in the Bronx, most of them weren't all that upset. They'd mention a vignette they'd read or heard about here or there but for the most part weren't offended or even concerned all that much. "Only the commissioner's office was offended," said Hoynes, "and in the commissioner's office, only Kuhn" was so aggrieved. He was determined to meet with Bouton and not only dress him down but do so publicly. Hoynes knew this showdown was destined to be a mismatch. "Jim was a standout person," said Hoynes. "Most ballplayers were just ballplayers, but there were a few, like Bouton, [Tom] Seaver, and [Joe] Torre who had depth." A guy like Bouton would take Kuhn apart if Kuhn was determined to engage him. Hoynes knew this the way he knew the sun rose every morning.

The battle took place on Monday afternoon, June 1. It had all the trappings of a prizefight—pitched crowds outside the Office of the Commissioner, the press pushing and shoving for the best views, trash talk, and entourages. Bouton and Shecter were accompanied by Marvin Miller and counsel for the Players Association Dick Moss, Kuhn by his staff, who were with him in body if not in spirit. From the opening bell, it was clear that Kuhn was overmatched. He told Bouton he was upset that he wrote about greenies in the locker rooms and offended by the kissing incident, which Kuhn did not believe occurred. He ticked off a list of things he found distasteful and summed up by accusing Bouton of writing a book that was bad for baseball. Bouton's response clarified for Kuhn the reality that there wasn't much he could hope to accomplish in the meeting. "I let him know that that wasn't even in my mind, whether it was bad for baseball or whether it was good for baseball. I did it not to please the baseball people but I did it for the fans. I wanted to share with them the fun I had in the game and to let them know what baseball was really like, both the good and the bad. I felt if I just wrote all the good things, that would be deceptive and wouldn't be a true picture."[1]

Besides, he said, he believed that the stories within the book humanized the players and, as such, were ultimately good for the game.[2] Although Miller had counseled Bouton to keep quiet during the meeting, his retort succeeded in backing Kuhn into a corner. After Bouton refused to issue a statement declaring the book to be, essentially, fiction, and refused to stand silently while Kuhn issued a public "warning" to him ("A warning against what?" Miller wanted to know), Kuhn had little choice but to release a vague and meaningless statement that said little and meant less: "I advised Mr. Bouton of my displeasure with these writings and have warned him against future writings of this character. Under all the circumstances, I have concluded that no other action was necessary." There was one action, though, that at least World thought necessary: it upped its press run once again—this time from 50,000 to 135,000 copies.[3]

Given the tenor of the times, there was no way Kuhn's attempted coercive gesture would do anything other than transform *Ball Four* from a baseball book to something of a cultural manifesto. A few days after the meeting, New York congressman Richard Ottinger released his own statement, calling Kuhn's attempted strong-arming an act of "repression and intimidation." He said he would call for congressional hearings on baseball's antitrust exemption "to determine whether current antitrust laws are adequate to assure that the conduct of professional baseball in America is consistent with the public interest and the interest of those individuals who have made it a great sport."[4] Kuhn was surely stunned to read that, at least in this congressman's eyes, it was players like Bouton who made baseball great, not management types like himself.

Thanks to Kuhn, the personal had become political. College students had the Port Huron Statement as their call to action. Now baseball fans had *Ball Four*.

Kuhn wasn't the only one who found *Ball Four* offensive. The old guard of the media viewed themselves as Kuhn did—protectors of the holy flame of the game. They were convinced that they knew what was good for baseball and what was bad for it, and *Ball Four* was clearly bad for it. "How can you attack the sanctity of Mickey Mantle?" Norm Miller recalled the tenor of the questions the old guard regularly posed to him in the wake of the *Look* excerpts. "Mickey Mantle was a drunk," said Miller, "and was a great ballplayer. I think the real question was how good would he have been if he didn't drink so much." But the old guard would never broach such a question because to do so would be to acknowledge the frailties of the men they worked so hard to portray as cartoonish heroes. Because they saw their job to be protecting the players from themselves in order to promote a fanciful image of the game, they saw *Ball Four* as a personal affront in that it took a sledgehammer to the wall they had spent decades erecting around the game and smashed it to bits. They were determined to hit back at the man who hurt them so gravely. They wanted to hurt him, too.

The disconnect between the old men writing about the game and the young fans watching it was brought out into the open like never before. After longtime St. Louis columnist Bob Burnes dismissed the book as one "filled with half-truths,"[5] a reader responded that Bouton was merely painting the part of the picture writers like Burnes had been ignoring for decades: "Actually, what these books present is a balance to the general half-truths perpetrated by writers such as Burnes who imply that if a youngster works hard 'in the finest tradition of the Horatio Alger theme' he, too, will succeed. Such an implication is a falsehood which hero-worshipping writers inflict upon the hero-worshipping public."[6]

Some of the writers seemed to have self-preservation in mind in their criticisms of the book. "I'd hate to think of someone in our sports department writing a book about what goes on in our office without the guys knowing it," wrote Detroit columnist Joe Falls.[7] The road makes bums of us all, *New York Herald Tribune* sportswriter Harold Rosenthal once said. This was as true of the men writing about the game as the ones playing it, and all of them were on edge in the aftermath of the release of the book. Wells Twombly was concerned that, now, players would clam up in the locker room, making his job more difficult. "In the clubhouse of the future, all athletes will enter separately, wearing long black masks to hide their identity from snoopy colleagues. No one will utter a sound all season." In short, although Twombly considered himself part of the new order of sportswriters, he concluded that "too much is too damn much.... Better you should buy a copy of *Portnoy's Complaint*. It is less sordid than *Ball Four*, which is Bouton's contribution to Sweat-and-Snitch journalism."[8]

But it was Roger Kahn's pointed criticism that had the most tangible and lasting impact, albeit in the most unexpected and profound way. Aside from alleging that Shecter was the true author, Kahn objected to the tone of the book, which he felt was superior, leering, and mocking. While acknowledging the talents of both Bouton and Shecter, and applauding their effort to break from tradition and produce a baseball book about people rather than caricatures, he believed they ultimately didn't respect the dignity of their subjects: "Ballplayers, and even their wives, are people; prick them and they bleed." Although agreeing with them that "the puritanism of sport is dangerous nonsense," Kahn thought they went so far as to "give anti-Puritanism a bad name."[9]

Ball Four rubbed Kahn raw. So raw that he was determined to do something about it. "Judging *Ball Four* against other pseudo-diaries, one finds remarkable merits," Kahn wrote in *Esquire*. However, "anyone presuming to write seriously about sport had better recognize the existence of *To an Athlete Dying Young*." More to the point, Kahn closed his column with this: "It is something to cry about, being an athlete who does not die young, and a hero's tears are the profound unbridgeable current between the best-seller *Ball Four*, and a major, or even serious book."[10] Two years later Kahn's ode to all of those Brooklyn Dodgers who didn't die young was released. *The Boys of Summer* and *Ball Four* would forever after be the first two books mentioned in any conversation of the most important baseball books of all time.

But it was Dick Young who was the book's most fervent critic. Young, neither the old-timer nor the Chipmunk, found ways to be aggrieved by Bouton wherever he looked. "You'd kill for my access," he liked to say to his sportswriter colleagues. In *Ball Four* he was forced to confront the reality that there were others who had a type of access he couldn't hope to have—access to the deepest, darkest thoughts of the men who played the game. Players might speak to Young and tell him what they wanted him to hear, but Young could never get any deeper than that. He may never have even considered the limits of his access before *Ball Four* was released. But now he had to know that an entire world existed beyond the one he saw as a sportswriter in the locker room, and he could never reach it the way a player with a literary bent like Jim Bouton could. And he was furious about it.

In the immediate aftermath of the book's release, Young couldn't stop writing about it. Bouton was a social leper. Shecter was a social leper. Mantle drank only to help dull the pain in his knee. As such his drinking *helped* his ball club rather than hurt it, unlike *Ball Four*, which could only tear the Astros apart. Young twisted and rationalized, contorted and demonized. And the columns kept on coming. The book was, at best, "interesting trash," he wrote, but trash nonetheless.[11] As for what he preferred when it came to journalism by the non-professionals, he used one column to first rip Bouton and then praise the San Francisco Giants' yearbook, which, he wrote, "has a delicious feature, recipes by players' wives of their husband's favorite dish."[12]

In his zeal to expose Bouton, Young only exposed himself as hopelessly out of touch with what was going on in the country at the time. When he wrote that the book "reflects the deplorable disregard among some of our young people for the meaning of the word honor,"[13] actual young people wrote back, informing him that, at age thirty-one, Bouton wasn't even part of their generation. "Most people would consider him an adult," one fan wrote in to *The Sporting News*.[14] In truth all of Young's bluster was cover for his pique that the man who considered himself the game's ultimate insider was scooped. Bouton "masqueraded," he wrote. "His label said ballplayer, teammate, friend, and he was not. . . . He betrayed the trust."[15] Perhaps, but that's not what really bothered Young. For years Young told his readers that nobody could get closer to the game than he could. Turned out he was wrong about that. He could no longer make such a claim with any credibility. So he lashed out instead, hoping to soil Bouton's image in the faint hope of restoring his own.

The Chipmunks, on the other hand, loved the book because it represented the logical extension of what they had been doing for the past decade—focusing on the personalities more than the final scores. And besides, it was the work of both their spiritual leader, Shecter, and the one player they had always considered to be an honorary member of their fraternity. In many ways the book was a triumph for their worldview. Leading the charge was Lipsyte. His column on *Ball Four* "opened people's eyes. Opened my eyes," Ira Berkow recalled. "It was really important, what Bob did." After his column defenders of the book became more vocal. The Chipmunks were always going to write what they were going to write, but Lipsyte, writing under the banner of the *New York Times*, legitimized their takes in a way nobody else could. Even the rightward-leaning *Sporting News*, which ran Young's blistering columns every week, ran columns praising *Ball Four* in the aftermath of Lipsyte's column. "Maybe it's the statistician in me," wrote Jerome Holtzman, "but I've just finished the Jim Bouton book and I'm only sorry about one thing. I wish I had kept count every time I laughed. I must have laughed 50 or 100 times. To me, it's the funniest baseball since Ring Lardner."[16]

No matter what the sportswriters said publicly about the book, they all knew it to be dead-on, so even if they publicly trashed it, privately they acknowledged its merit. Among the trove of letters Bouton received in the aftermath of the book's release was an anonymous one that summed up the firestorm of reaction from all sides: "I have been connected with a sportswriting family all my life and that half of the family probably won't like your book—but so far husband and I think it's great. . . . Thanks for having the courage. Not many people can go for that old fairy-tale world any more. When all the big deals are screaming at you, remember—we care and we're for you. Can't sign name—would be disinherited."[17]

If praise for the book seeped into the baseball, God, and country bible that was *The Sporting News*, it flowed like a river in its liberal counterpart, *Sport*, which couldn't seem to find enough good things to say about it. In its August 1970 edition Al Silverman and his editorial staff devoted a full page to their endorsement of both the book and the perspective on sports it championed. After reminding critics of the book that "there is a new morality in the land—in books, movies and public life," they wrote that it was "ridiculous to think that there is some kind of a reserve clause that exempts sports from the trends of our times." Moreover, "We strongly believe that the athlete has as much of a right to express his opinions and observations as anyone else in the public eye." Finally, in direct opposition to both Kuhn and Young, they declared: "We believe that anyone who tells the athlete to desist because it is bad for the game or whatever the reason, is wrong."[18]

18 Against the Unwritten Rules of Baseball

The players, or most of them at least, didn't care about the morality of the book, although they claimed as much whenever the subject was brought up. Rather, they were upset that Bouton had outed them and their lifestyles. "Most of them were fearful," Berkow recalled. "A lot of the married guys, they had their own lives on the road, and if they were going to be exposed, this scared the shit out of them." Bouton realized this as well, saying later that most of the pushback he received was not in the form of allegations that he made anything up. Instead, it was in the form of allegations that he told too much of the truth. Nobody with any knowledge of the Yankee locker room could tell him that what he wrote about Mantle wasn't true. "Not even Mantle would say that," he said. It was the exposure of the illusion as illusion that bothered them. "A good majority of the ballplayers were opposed to *Ball Four*," said Berkow. "But they all knew it was true."

In the aftermath of the book's release there were reports of all sorts of sundry responses by players. One had the San Diego Padres burning copies of the book in their clubhouse in Dodger Stadium and leaving the ashes for Bouton and the Astros, who were due in town later that afternoon.[1] Another, promulgated breathlessly by New York sportscaster Bill Mazer, was that the Yankee players "took Bouton's uniform, threw it into the toilet and defecated on it."[2] Given that Bouton had been gone from the club for two seasons by the time the book was released, and that his old uniform was most likely not easily accessible, if it was accessible at all, and that Marty Appel has no memory of such an event taking place, it's doubtful that Mazer's story is true. Regardless, both his and the Padres' book burning (which likewise could not be confirmed) ring true, and so they live on. Besides, even if these particular events never happened, they do effectively convey the level of disdain most players had for both Jim Bouton and his book.

In the immediate aftermath of the book's release, the players on the Pilots and the Astros were hounded for their takes on *Ball Four*. Most of them trashed it, while going to great lengths to let everyone know that they hadn't read it. After issuing that disclaimer, Pilots outfielder Wayne Comer said, "Bouton never gave a damn for the ballclub. All he cared about was himself. . . . And his notes—he kept taking notes. Sneaking a little pad and a pen out of his pocket and jotting things down every so often. . . . Maybe one or two guys knew he was planning to write a book, but most of us didn't." Pilot first baseman Don Mincher said he thought the book "stinks" and said that he would have socked Bouton had he known what he was doing. Outfielder Mike Hegan likewise claimed to have not read it but, still, objected to the book's takedown of Mantle. "I stood in awe of Mantle," he said. "Still do," although the book indelibly muddied the image in his eyes. Pitcher Fred Talbot, who was a main character in the book, called his former teammate a liar and claimed that many of the book's stories centered around him simply didn't happen. Pitcher Gene Brabender, on the other hand, said he still liked Bouton but thought he had used bad judgment in writing the book. "A guy making his living at it has no right to knock the game," he said.[3] Without the benefit of time, none of the marginal Pilot players could have realized that by making them human, *Ball Four* had made them immortal.

Many members of the Astros were somewhere on the continuum of the opinions of the Pilots. "The people who were saying it was terrible," Astros pitcher Larry Dierker recalled, "most of them hadn't even read it." Still, whenever they were asked throughout the 1970 season, Dierker remembered, many of the Astros called the book "bush," "uncalled-for," or "against the unwritten rules of baseball."

Over at the House That Ruth Built, tempers were only becoming more inflamed as the months wore on in the wake of the *Look* excerpts. Clete Boyer made a public display of folding his arms and refusing to shake Bouton's hand when the Astros met Boyer's Braves in late July.[4] Elston Howard issued a stinging rebuke in the *New York Times*, calling Bouton "a very self-centered and selfish man," claiming that Bouton had held a grudge against him for years, ever since an incident that took place in spring training in 1963, when Howard decked him in a pickup boxing match. "Bob Gibson says Bouton's just knifing us for blood money," Howard said. "You can picture him all you want as a daring guy who told all. But he's just frustrated."[5] Although Mantle liked to limit his public response to the book by saying, "Jim who?" he was unquestionably furious and hurt by it, opening up at one point and admitting that it bothered him that it was selling so well.[6] Of all the outposts in baseball upset about the book, the uproar within the Yankees was the loudest, Bouton recalled. Big Pete Sheehy went so far as to unofficially, and unceremoniously, retire his number, 56, refusing to issue it for years, so badly had Bouton sullied it in his eyes.

In the Minors and elsewhere in the world of the ballplayer, the reaction to the book was far different. Larry Colton, a pitcher who had had little more than a shot of espresso in the Majors (one game with the Phils in 1968) but who was now back in the Minors, recalled he and his teammates enjoying the book when it came out. If anything, they thought, "it didn't go far enough. It was just scratching the surface.... As a ballplayer, it was, 'Yeah, that's right, so what?'" Rick Wolff, who was playing college ball at Harvard at the time, and who would later enter the publishing world and edit an update of *Ball Four*, loved it as well but knew that its author was in for trouble. "No question that baseball had a conservative bent to it," he said. This reached down into the collegiate level. "I remember one off-season wanting to work out with the Dartmouth baseball team," he said. The Dartmouth coach sized him up and let him know that if he wanted to work out on his field, he needed to get a haircut. "So I trimmed all my long locks off and went back." This time the coach let him on the field but then pulled him aside. "He grabbed me and said, 'Rick, you've got to go get a haircut.'" If you wanted the scouts to take you seriously, you needed not merely short hair but a buzz cut.

"You needed to show the scouts you were part of the silent majority, were all about supporting the Vietnam War, were not going to cause problems like those hippies who grew their hair long." While Wolff and his Harvard teammates howled with laughter over the book and pined for an opportunity to join the big-league fun, their coaching staff admonished them for doing so, drilling into them the values of their parents as a way to demonize the book. Through *Ball Four* the generation gap had finally come to baseball.

To Bowie Kuhn's great surprise (and most likely horror), fans overwhelmingly loved the book. Fan mail poured in to Jim and Bobbie's house, and it was running five to one on the positive side. It would continue to arrive for the next half century, for as long as he would live. "Baseball was never, NEVER interesting to me until I read your book," one letter read. "Then it became very crucial in my life to follow baseball whenever it is played."[7] Another fan wrote a few years after the book came out:

> I was drawn to you by a major family crisis that lasted almost a year. It was during those days when I was struggling every minute that I turned to you. The attraction was that your baseball career parallels my life.... Life had been fine (your '63 and '64). Things began to deteriorate fast (your arm suddenly went). Then came the family crisis and my day-to-day living became a great struggle (your critical '69 season that's illustrated in the book). Reading each page five times was not escapism. You gave sensible advice about people and conflicts that I encountered every day.... Besides, *Ball Four* is the funniest book ever written, and it never fails to cheer me up.[8]

Reams of letters. Many of them with similar stories. "Over the years," said Appel, "I can't tell you how many people have told me that they fell in love with baseball because of that book."

The book tapped into the inchoate feelings of fans who were looking for "hip" in baseball and coming up empty until the *Look* excerpts hit the stands. In an important way it saved the game in a way those on the inside never could. "This was a time," Appel said, "late '60s, early '70s, when baseball was not really in fashion. It was not cool. Football, and even basketball, was making enormous headway with the American public. Baseball was going through a very bad period, and this book turned out to be like a breath of fresh air.... A lot of people in their teens, who had sort of turned away from baseball or who weren't interested in finding out about the fascination of baseball, read this book and came away loving baseball."

Teenage boys fell for it as if it were their first love. "As a fourteen-year-old," said Lou Charlip, who read it upon its release and later worked with Bouton at wcbs, "you picked up this book, which was a sports book, and there was a lot of cursing in it. Me and my friends used to sing the Astros song [the hard R-rated version of "Proud to Be an Astro" as related within the book] all the time. Probably because it had curse words in it." Another fan remembered: "I went to a Catholic elementary school, and we were allowed to bring in our own books to read so I brought in *Ball Four*. Once sister saw what I had, she took it from me and underlined all the 'dirty' parts. She then told me to take it home and have [my] parents sign the pages. I took it home and returned it with a note from my dad, which simply read, 'Can't we just be happy he's reading?' and 'You will give him $1.75 so he can buy a new copy.' She did."

Kuhn was convinced that fans were drawn to the game for the hero myth it had sold them for decades. To his stunned amazement he found out that the overwhelming majority of *Ball Four*'s readers concluded that, if anything, they found the gritty world Bouton revealed within infinitely more enticing and intoxicating than the musty fairy tales they had been force-fed and that by now had bored them nearly to the point of abandoning baseball altogether. One "baseball Annie" acknowledged this reality in her letter to Bouton: "From the time I was 19 until last year (a span of five years) I went out with baseball players.... I, for one, applaud you for writing this book.... I know that many players feel hostile about anyone telling what goes on after they leave the field but it really is about time someone knocked them off their pedestals and revealed the truth (that they're not heroes off of Wheaties boxes but just men—horny men at that!)."[9] This was what made *Ball Four* a runaway best seller. This was what made a new generation of fans fall in love with the game anew.

Not everyone loved it. Some of the older ones didn't like the way the book bucked the system; anybody who would write a book like that must be a communist, they figured. "I think you're a disgrace to the Houston Astros," one fan wrote, "one of the finest teams in the National League."[10] "I am at a loss to reconcile your reasoning in writing this rubbish," another fan wrote. "It serves no constructive purpose, only to tear down established values for the sake of destruction. You have done no service to the youth of America, believe me. . . . Apparently your literary skills are on a par with your pitching prowess; or better still, with your batting ability. The baseball guides give your height as six feet, but believe me, Jim Bouton is a much smaller man."[11] To these fans, "Mickey Mantle was someone who went home after a ball game and drank milk and spent time with his wife and kids," said Wolff. Anybody who suggested otherwise was a dangerous subversive. Toots Shor, whose living depended upon the good graces of the athletes he catered to and worshiped, hated the Chipmunks—particularly Merchant—and Bouton most of all for the way he chipped the statue of Mantle Shor genuflected to regularly. His worldview was summed up in a Joe Flaherty piece that ran in *Esquire* a few years later: "He speaks of Ruth and [boxer Jack] Dempsey as if their records shouldn't be in the books, but on the Sistine Ceiling. To him, athletes are the ones who have graced this planet. 'People in sports,' he tells you, 'are the greatest people in the world.'"[12] He despised *Ball Four* not because it spread lies but because it did not.

But Bouton didn't write the book to please Toots Shor. That became clear on the afternoon he met with Kuhn in his office. Waiting for him outside the glass doors of the Office of the Commissioner on Park Avenue was Woodstock, the antiwar movement, the free-speech movement, and the civil rights movement all wrapped up in the form of two long-haired college-aged protesters waving signs and chanting for the unshackling of one Jim Bouton. "I was eighteen when [*Ball Four*] came out, and I thought, 'This is funny,'" said Richard Feuer, one of the long hairs. He had been a Bouton devotee since childhood, when he was a member of the *All 'Bout Bouton* fan club and a regular attendee of the testimonial dinners held in the Bronx at the end of each season in the early '60s. The stakes were higher now, he believed, so he made his way toward Midtown with his friend Steve Bergen to make their voices heard. Bouton, he felt, was one of *them*.

Although he had recently strayed from baseball, Feuer followed Bouton through Shecter's columns, reading about his participation in demonstrations and his outspokenness on issues other ballplayers kept quiet about and saw a lot of himself in his boyhood idol. "One day Richard was incensed to find out that Bowie Kuhn was going to reprimand Jim Bouton," recalled Lynne Schalman, Bergen's widow and Feuer's friend, who helped to prepare for their protest. "This was the sixties and all of us were involved in the protest movement, and Richard decided we needed to protest this as well to restore the First Amendment rights of Jim Bouton." They painted a collection of signs, saying things such as "Bouton's a Real Hero," "No Punishment for Bouton," "Jim Bouton Must Not Be Repressed," and "Kuhn: Stop Repression and Harassment." Because Schalman couldn't get the afternoon off from her job at a dry cleaner in Nyack, she headed off to work while Feuer and Bergen headed into the city. Although Schalman was a die-hard Mantle fan, she nevertheless loved the book. "I wasn't offended by it because we were all inclined to be questioning and protesting and antiauthority, so [the book] fit in with our idea of 'Let's expose the truth,' so we all thought it was pretty cool. We were all impressed with Jim's courage to tell these truths about Mickey Mantle."

Bergen and Feuer walked right into the building and up the elevator. There was no visible security. When they reached the floor occupied by Kuhn's office, they got as far as the glass outer doors and set up shop there, directing their signs to the gaggle of execs and reporters on the other side of the divide. At one point Shecter came out and chatted them up. Kuhn's secretary wouldn't go so far; instead, she warily looked them up and down, later remarking to Dick Young that she wasn't sure if they were men or women. Young immediately inserted that nugget into his next column. After a while Bouton emerged from Kuhn's office, saw the two men, and flashed the peace sign. He then invited them to take the elevator down with himself, Shecter, and Marvin Miller. They all emerged from the elevator together into the golden sunshine of late afternoon to the soft cacophony of camera shutters clicking like cicadas, one on top of another. Pictures at a revolution.

19 Not Enough Sex

The reviews came in shortly thereafter and were overwhelmingly gushing, showing that while there might have been a sharp divide among sportswriters with regard to the book, there was no such rift among the larger literati. Bouton's reporting wasn't stepping on *their* toes or exposing *their* secrets. Christopher Lehmann-Haupt wrote in the daily *New York Times* review that *Ball Four* "is a people book, not just a baseball book," that "has actually gotten me interested in baseball again, and I didn't think that was possible."[1] In the *Times'* "Sunday Book Review," Rex Lardner wrote that "Bouton has written the funniest, frankest book yet about the species *ballplayer satyriaticus* and his numerous bosses, most of whom come out pretty stuffy.... For the baseball fan, in an era of sophisticated reappraisal, it is a gem of honest, good-naturedly biased reporting. I hope he makes a million bucks."[2] In the *Washington Post* Bobo Newsom Memorial Society member David Markson heralded it as well, writing, "No one who reads *Ball Four* will ever again cheer on his heroes with quite the old naïve enthusiasm." In short, he wrote, the book was "a wry, understated, honest and memorable piece of Americana, by a good man they will clobber because of it."[3] The *Wall Street Journal* wrote that "Bouton writes better than he pitches.... The book has more sting than Bouton's fastball ever had" and that "if baseball is in trouble today, it's not because of people like Bouton."[4]

In the black press the *Baltimore Afro-American* drew its readers' attention to the passages within *Ball Four* that focused on how white umpires had isolated the game's first black umpire, Emmett Ashford, going out of their way to embarrass him on the field at times.[5] It was the first time many had heard such an allegation. A few months later Sam Lacy of the *Afro-American* would declare Bouton a friend even though he barely knew him. "I call him a friend," he wrote, "because he is for me, for us. . . . Since his days as a pitcher with the Yankees, Bouton has espoused our call for equal rights—in educational opportunity, in job consideration, fringe benefits like commercial endorsements and what-have-you. . . . He appeared on picket lines, showed up at demonstrations . . . made financial contributions to causes . . . at a time when many of our own athletes were finding it inexpedient."[6]

All of the positive press for the book made Dick Young physically ill. "How can literary editors and book critics be so gullible as to assume that a sports book, because it professes to be 'inside,' tells the true story?" he wrote.[7] He was outraged that so many people were buying what Bouton and Shecter were selling—an insider's guide to baseball authored by someone other than Dick Young. The book rocketed up the *New York Times* best-seller list, remaining there for seventeen weeks. Even in conservative Houston the book was ranked second, trailing only *Everything You Ever Wanted to Know about Sex*, suggesting that perhaps Houston wasn't quite as conservative as its reputation.[8] Turned out that sex, raw truth, and confessional honesty were what people across America were looking for at the time. Philip Roth's *Portnoy's Complaint* demonstrated as much, dominating the national conversation for months and topping the *Times'* fiction best-seller list for fourteen weeks in 1969 on its way to becoming the best-selling book in Random House's history up to that point. Bowie Kuhn's version of baseball offered up none of that; *Ball Four* provided it in spades. In retrospect, perhaps there wasn't quite *enough* sex in *Ball Four*—it never made it to number one on the bestseller list, blocked from the top spot all summer by both *Everything You Ever Wanted to Know about Sex* and *The Sensuous Woman*.

The book made Bouton into a celebrity that transcended the sports world. When he appeared on *The Dick Cavett Show* to hawk the book, he was the first guest of the evening; Charlton Heston had to wait in the wings through two commercial breaks until Cavett finally got to him. It wasn't long before writers like Roth himself were stopping him in the street, genuflecting like dewy fanboys and telling him how much the book meant to them, Bobbie recalled. He became a countercultural icon despite his protestations that he had never intended for anything like that to happen. "I never meant to make an investigation of a subculture," he said years later. "I just wanted to share the nonsense."[9] Too late. Before the book went into its second printing he was being hailed as a revolutionary truth teller and demythologist. The fact that he was soon out of baseball, possibly blackballed, the word spread, as a result of his daring exposé, only added to his countercultural bona fides. He may not have planned any of this, but, in retrospect, his timing could not have been better.

"It's not only the uniqueness of *Ball Four* in being the first to tell the story," says Jeremy Schaap, "but being the first to tell the story at a time when there would have been a certain amount of receptivity to that kind of storytelling." If Joseph Heller's *Catch-22* presaged an era, *Ball Four* helped to define it as it was occurring. "If you publish *Ball Four* in 1950 or 1960, it would have been more revolutionary, but it probably couldn't have gotten published, and even if it had, it would have turned people off rather than fascinate them," Schaap believes. It fitted into the zeitgeist as satisfyingly as the last piece of a puzzle. There was a shock factor to the book that couldn't help but draw you to it initially, says sportswriter John Feinstein, but you quickly understood that there was so much more there once you sat down with it. He read it when it came out and fell in love with it because it clarified for him a particular outlook on the world, giving shape to what he was already feeling. He thought he was the only one who felt that way. Now he understood that he wasn't. "It was the era of the antihero," says Jeff Neuman, an editor specializing in sports books who worked with both Bouton and Feinstein. "*Ball Four* was seminal, but it also came along at a time that was right for it."

It's hard to overstate how seismically it rocked the baseball world, flipping it on its head and showing newly enraptured baseball fans the game from a dramatically different perspective. This much at least was clear to Bouton the moment his meeting with Kuhn ended, and he said so outside of Kuhn's office: "I honestly think it'll be an important book. I had something to say and I won't apologize for any of it."[10] It would turn out to be the first monumental step in altering public opinion on how the business of baseball was conducted, forever after changing the narrative on who, between the owners and the players, was taking advantage of whom. It showed fans that baseball "wasn't this sacrosanct, Elysian Fields, misty, historical pastime," says sportswriter Stefan Fatsis. "It was a game played by guys that cursed and laughed, and who simultaneously took their careers both seriously and not so seriously."

In so doing, Fatsis says, "it subverted the norms of the business of the game. It exposed the owners as being cruel and power hungry and uncompassionate toward the players. [As a fan] how could you live through the owners anymore? Who were you going to side with—some guy in a suit or Jim Bouton?" It was for this reason that Lipsyte included Bouton's in his assessment of the five essential stories one needed to know in order to understand the various ups, downs, twists, and turns of the roller coaster that was twentieth-century baseball. Each of the stories were of Yankees—the team of the century. The first three were obvious: iconic Hall of Famers Babe Ruth, Joe DiMaggio, and Mickey Mantle. The fourth was the story of perhaps the most infamous owner in the history of the game: George Steinbrenner. The fifth was the tale of Jim Bouton.[11] He had upended the game that much.

The book presented the players as real people, not plastic figurines, says Hoynes. After its publication it would be hard for anyone, be they a fan in the stands or an arbitrator at a grievance arbitration hearing, to look at their plight the way they had before. Marvin Miller had been the executive director of the Players Association for four years by the time *Ball Four* was released, but despite all of his efforts the players were still wary of what he was preaching. "The players were generally behind the union," Dierker recalled, "but they weren't that actively involved.... They weren't activists or anything." That changed in the aftermath of everything that surrounded the release of the book.

According to Hoynes, *Ball Four* helped Miller make his case to the players as well as to the public and, ultimately, independent arbitrator Peter Seitz in the 1975 arbitration hearing that dismantled the game's century-old reserve clause. Everybody could now see the game—all facets of it—through the eyes of the men who played it and not just those of the men who profited off it. And a growing number of them preferred to see it that way. It was so much more fun. Tectonic change in baseball was inevitable, but without *Ball Four* it most likely would have been a bit longer in coming. Thousands of people have been connected with Major League Baseball since its inception in 1876, but few, according to John Thorn, became as vital to the telling of the game's story as Jim Bouton, through *Ball Four*. He might not have been the most talented player ever to don a uniform, but, says Thorn, when it comes to understanding the history of the game, "he's more important than [Willie] Mays."

20 The Leni Riefenstahl of the National Football League

A few weeks after the book was released the Old World met the New once again, this time in the form of baseball's forty-first All-Star Game. It, too, was a culture clash in ways both obvious and subtle. The game was played in Cincinnati, home of baseball's first openly professional team just over a century earlier and now home to the old-school Reds, they of the strict uniform code prohibiting the high stirrups that were then the rage among a growing subset of players and any color other than polished black on the spikes. As sideburns trellised down the cheeks of more and more players—the Cards' Dick Allen even sneaked an actual mustache onto the field a few times that summer— the Reds checked the faces of every player before game time, sending those with even a brush of whisker back to the showers for a quick shave before first pitch. Their leader was the patron saint of the old school—Pete Rose. Rose ran full-speed to first base even on walks, just like they did it back when they were kids, old-timers would tell their grandchildren whenever they could, and sported a crew cut that could slice diamonds. In so many ways he was a stand-in for the traditional values of the game and of the nation, fictional as they may have been, to those on the right wing of the culture war.

The venue in which the game was played, though, served as a counterpoint to all of that. Just two weeks earlier the Reds had abandoned their longtime home, Crosley Field, for Riverfront Stadium, a multipurpose concrete bagel that Bowie Kuhn was so proud of he awarded the Reds the game before it was even completed, setting off a frantic scramble to finish it after a series of construction delays forced the

Reds to open the season at Crosley and unexpectedly play the first half of the 1970 season in the old ballpark. It was a heralding of the new, of baseball's progress and influence, Kuhn believed, and he wanted a national television audience for it all. The truth was, however, that the stadium was just the latest piece of evidence that baseball was losing its grip on the national consciousness.

For years the Reds had wanted out of Crosley but had gotten nowhere until the Cincinnati Bengals came to town in 1968 as an expansion franchise in the American Football League. With the merger of the AFL and NFL and with football exploding in popularity (as evidenced by the sales of *Instant Replay*), the city pooh-bahs promised the Reds that they'd finally get their stadium but only if they agreed to a multipurpose venue that would also house the nascent Bengals—an everything bagel if ever there was one. Thus, it was football that built Riverfront, not baseball, a fact that was evident in the stadium's sightlines, which were friendlier to fans when the stadium was configured for an NFL game. When Rose decked Cleveland catcher Ray Fosse in the bottom of the twelfth of the All-Star Game, separating both the ball from Fosse's mitt and Fosse's shoulder from its socket, fans roared. A victory for the old school. But the opening of Riverfront was more of a defeat, as were the openings of similar multipurpose venues built largely to accommodate football, such as Busch Stadium in St. Louis, Atlanta's Fulton County Stadium, the Vet in Philadelphia, and Three Rivers Stadium in Pittsburgh. The Chipmunks had taken a scalpel to the pedestal upon which baseball stood, and then *Ball Four* dynamited what was left of it. Baseball's grip on the culture was loosening, not tightening. By July 1970 the aura that had surrounded the game was gone, and a void was created. Into it stepped the NFL, which readily supplied the heroes now absent from baseball to the millions who needed them. In the process the marginalization of baseball accelerated, unabated.

Outside of the exciting All-Star Game, the 1970 season was lackluster. Each of the four divisions was wrapped up early and won by a small-market club without a national following (Baltimore and Minnesota in the AL, Cincinnati and Pittsburgh in the NL), the playoffs were ho-hum, and the World Series was a five-game affair won easily by the Orioles, 4–1. When the subject of baseball came up during that season, *Ball Four* found its way into the conversation more often than not, in one way or another. Which was great for those who found the book to be a tonic but went down like battery acid for fans who came to the game for escape and found that they could no longer find it there. And despite the phenomenal sales of the book, these still represented the overwhelming majority. During the Series a group of writers acknowledged just how quickly the antihero had come to dominate the baseball conversation by bantering about who would man a club consisting entirely of the game's needlers. They came up with a player for each position outside of shortstop and third base, including Allen, Curt Flood, and Bill Freehan. The starting pitcher, of course, would be Jim Bouton.[1]

If unhappy is the land that needs a hero, as Bertolt Brecht wrote, then in 1970 America was one unhappy place. As everything was seemingly coming apart, heroes were being dismantled everywhere, to the horror of the old order, in government, the military, parents, teachers. In March Hollywood presented the nation with a war movie in *M*A*S*H* that served as a middle finger to the glorification of battle it had served up for decades beforehand. The next month the gay-, drug-, and prostitution-themed *Midnight Cowboy* became the first X-rated film to win the Academy Award for Best Picture. It was the month after that when the *Look* excerpts hit the stands. *Ball Four* may have been an artistic and literary success, but to those who were already woozy from gut punches by the counterculture, it was too much. They would have to look elsewhere for escape, for heroes. They would have to look toward the NFL, which was not only willing to provide them but equipped to do so like never before. All of the things critics praised in *Ball Four*—its humanity, its honesty, its juvenile fun—were the things that repelled the millions who were looking for none of that in their heroes. And on top of everything else was the book's casual acknowledgment of the widespread use of amphetamines—greenies—in big-league clubhouses, which set off a confused, confusing national conversation on drug use in society and the national pastime that only further married the book to the counterculture, causing many fans to sour on the game months and even years after *Ball Four*'s release.

Although *Ball Four* was not the first sports book to mention greenies, its allegation that over half of all big leaguers were taking them was startling to the point of shaking entire newsrooms awake.[2] For the first time writers acknowledged in print what they had observed for years—players engaging in the same pregame activities Bouton wrote about in the book. By the end of 1970 *The Sporting News* took an official position on the issue, admitting that the game it had promoted for decades as pure and emblematic of all that was right with the nation was actually riddled with pill poppers. Crediting "peeping-Tom" books like *Ball Four* with exposing the reality of the game, the editorial noted that while few team physicians would publicly state it, behind the scenes they were admitting to each other that drug use was a problem in the game and that something needed to be done about it. All of this, wrote the paper's editor and publisher, C. C. Johnson Spink, was "a sad commentary on the state of American sports—and our national moral, mental and physical health."[3]

The following spring Kuhn presided over a drug-abuse seminar for player representatives in Phoenix. Chuck Dobson of the A's said he'd go but challenged Kuhn's position that greenies were bad for baseball. "I don't see anything wrong with it," he said. "A lot of guys use them and I've used them.... If he says we can't use them, well, I'd just want him to put on a uniform for 162 games in 180 days and see what he says then." Dobson then made sure to let everyone in earshot know what he thought of *Ball Four* in case they were wondering: "Bouton is like a little kid who learned the facts of life for the first time and can't wait to tell everyone what he knows."[4]

That fall the *New York Times Sunday Magazine* contained an exposé of the issue with a lengthy article titled "It's Not How You Play the Game, but What Pill You Take."[5] By that point the image of sports, and baseball most particularly given that it was *Ball Four* that brought the issue to the forefront, couldn't be further removed from what it had been just a decade earlier. Although players like Dobson, and even *The Sporting News*, tried to make the point that the drug issue in baseball was different from the recreational drug-use debate then raging in the larger culture, the nuance was missed by those in charge of delivering the message. Both Kuhn and Pete Rozelle of the NFL initiated community-action programs that involved players going into classrooms and youth centers to preach the dangers of drug use to children, thereby inadvertently tying professional athletes in with the hippies and Deadheads—invariably the first student question at these events was one asking if everything in *Ball Four* was true. To these students the confluence of baseball and popular culture through these community-action programs must have made it seem as if each big-league clubhouse was a miniaturized Woodstock. One such visit involved Mets catcher Duffy Dyer, who on the one hand lectured students at Long Island City High School on the dangers of narcotics and on the other denied nearly everything Bouton alleged in *Ball Four*, contending that baseball did not have a drug problem after all.[6] The message was muddled and confusing.

Once the real world seeped into baseball there was no way to drain it out. Through *Ball Four*, Bouton connected the game to the world outside of the stadium walls, and for some that was simply more than they could take. Beyond the drugs there was the issue of individuality, expressed on the streets and now, via the book's celebration of it, in baseball as well. The ugliness of labor and employment issues also took center stage, with Curt Flood's antitrust suit against Kuhn being filed in January 1970 and *Ball Four* offering up to readers a few months later an avalanche of anecdotal evidence suggesting that everything Flood was alleging against the owners was true, and then some. It got so that discussing baseball, simply as baseball, became, if not impossible, at least silly given all of the issues that surrounded it. For this reason Vecsey left the sports department that year and became a national correspondent for the *Times*. "Sports [as sports] ceased to intrigue me very much," he said. "I was tired of it." With everything else that was going on, "it seemed like child's play." Shecter, too, announced that he was getting out of the sportswriting business.

In 1970 baseball was adrift. It had been heading toward the wilderness for several years by that point, but to some *Ball Four* announced its arrival. The game on the field seemed boring, with pitchers dominating like they hadn't in years, making runs nearly impossible to come by. The game off the field seemed tawdry and insignificant all at once. For decades compliant writers dutifully assisted the owners in propagating the game's apple-pie image, but after the Chipmunks steamrollered them the game had no championing voice other than a commissioner whom Bouton had just succeeded in unmasking as an out-of-touch empty suit. Baseball's image was now shaped primarily by *Ball Four*, which celebrated the game in a way that made traditional fans gag. To Kuhn's horror *Ball Four*'s narrative became baseball's narrative. By the end of 1970 baseball and *Ball Four* were one and the same. Virtual synonyms. If ever the national pastime was vulnerable, it was right now.

Enter NFL Films.

Created in 1964, NFL Films quickly became, in the words of *Sports Illustrated*, "perhaps the most effective propaganda organ in the history of corporate America."[7] Its guiding light was Steve Sabol, who proved himself a mythmaker from the start, having created his own fictional biography in college in order to garner attention for himself, where he was largely a benchwarmer on the football team. Although born in New Jersey, he created the legend of "Sudden Death Steve Sabol— the Fearless Tot from Possum Trot [Mississippi]." He took out ads in the local paper in the name of the Chamber of Commerce wishing "Sudden Death Sabol" luck in an upcoming game, passed out buttons and other paraphernalia in his honor, and succeeded in making himself something of a local celebrity.[8] Many of his newfound fans were unaware that they were being duped, and Sabol saw it as little more than good fun. He also saw that people loved a story and didn't mind so much if parts, or even all, of it were fabricated. If the story told them what they wanted to hear, they would come back for more.

At NFL Films Sabol carried this ethos into the professional game. The tiny film company (founded as Blair Motion Pictures by his father, Ed) won the rights to film the 1962 NFL Championship Game and in 1964 was bought out by the NFL, becoming its official documentarian. Sabol described his band of filmmakers as historians, yes, but also "storytellers [and] mythmakers." In order to effectively challenge Major League Baseball's stranglehold on the national consciousness, NFL commissioner Pete Rozelle and the league's club owners recognized that football's story had to be more compelling than baseball's. Once the league had bought out NFL Films, it controlled its narrative. "The history of football [will] forever be preserved on film and not by the written word a la baseball," Chicago Bears owner George Halas said.[9] While the Chipmunks were tearing into the myth of baseball with the league powerless to stop them, the NFL now had a powerful weapon to counter any presentations of their game it found to be unseemly or unheroic. By the end of the sixties the Sabols had become, in effect, the Leni Riefenstahl of the NFL, serving up one film after another glorifying the league and its players.

To be sure, there was no shortage of press and books critical of the NFL. The drug exposés often focused extensively on football players shooting up this or that in the locker room in order to mask the pain the game inflicted as a matter of course. And Dave Meggyesy, a linebacker for the football Cardinals, published his tell-all, *Out of Their League*, in 1970, which was much more critical of the business and mores of the NFL than anything Bouton had written about baseball in *Ball Four*. *Out of Their League* caused a stir, but the league had an answer for it in the movies coming out of the NFL Films studios on a weekly basis and shown on televisions around the country, portraying the grace of the game at half speed, backed by a swelling orchestral soundtrack and the booming "Voice of God" that was John Facenda, who could make the pregame coin toss feel like a pitched battle of wills. People read the articles, people read *Out of Their League*, but then they sat down and watched the films and pushed all of the bad news to the side as they bathed in the sun-drenched glory of the game as presented to them by Ed and Steve Sabol. Baseball had nothing like it.

Writers covering NFL games would often complain that the depictions of them conveyed by NFL Films bore little resemblance to the actual happenings on the field, but their critical voices were drowned out by the color, music, and sheer power of the visual medium.[10] Many football writers had likewise taken their cues from the Chipmunks and were seeking to present the truth of the players and the games to their readers, but Halas was quickly proved correct in that the history of the game was being written by NFL Films, which was more interested in presenting football as the league would have it rather than as it actually was. So while *Ball Four* succeeded in making baseball players smaller and more human, NFL Films played Pete Rose to baseball's Ray Fosse, barreling over it by making football players heroic, larger-than-life figures and presenting them to the public as men of honor and traditional American values—not unlike how the old-school baseball writers presented players like Babe Ruth and Joe DiMaggio once upon a time. In the process baseball itself shrunk and the NFL became a behemoth.

On September 21, 1970, as baseball's season was limping to the finish line and *Ball Four* was still on the best-seller list, ABC debuted *Monday Night Football*, which was its attempt to bring the power of the NFL's storytelling machine to a larger, more diverse audience than ever before. The game itself was to be only part of the spectacle as the commentators in the booth—Keith Jackson, Don Meredith, and Howard Cosell—were charged with conveying compelling, dramatic story lines to their audience, not unlike the prime-time dramas that were being shown on the competing networks. Cosell liked to say that he would always "tell it like it is," but in truth he was something of a propagandist like the Sabols, hyping the games and the star players to the max. At halftime NFL Films presented "Halftime Highlights," narrated by Cosell, which made all of the previous day's games seem like epic battles. To fans who had had enough of truth in sports, of the dismantling of the ideals and heroes they grew up with, NFL Films, and now *Monday Night Football*, provided them with precisely what they had been looking for.

Ball Four was praised, appropriately, for vanquishing the heroes, for finishing the job the Chipmunks had started. But into the void stepped NFL Films, which created new ones for fans to worship on Sunday afternoons and Monday nights. In the end baseball, through *Ball Four*, and football, through NFL Films, presented competing narratives to sports fans in 1970—baseball's steeped in fact, football's steeped in legend. The difference was that the Sabols and Cosell all understood that when it came to the preferences of the masses, *The Man Who Shot Liberty Valence* had it right: when the legend becomes fact, print the legend.

21 Taking It Personally

The 1970 season wasn't just rough in the aggregate; it smacked Bouton in the face as the release of the book painted a can't-miss bull's-eye on him whenever he took the mound. You can't write an exposé titled *Ball Four* and not expect to hear about it every time you put a man on base in a crucial situation. "Bouton's 'Ball Four' Authors Astros' Loss" was typical, albeit more creative than most headlines that followed one poor outing after another.[1] His ERA swelled above five, his knuckler wasn't knuckling, and he quickly found his options dwindling as everything was closing in on him. Although he always claimed that baseball was the ultimate democracy in that the only thing that mattered was what you did between the lines—he once said that even Charles Manson would be a big-league third baseman if he could hit .310—the truth was that Manson would have to have been a helluva hitter to make him worth the distraction.[2] All else being equal, clubs would always take the conformist over the rabble-rouser simply to avoid the headache. And once *Ball Four* came out, Bouton was a headache to the Astros.

Whenever he was asked he said that Astros manager Harry Walker's response to the book was fine and that while many of his teammates found one thing or another in it disturbing, they hadn't shunned him: "I'd say probably half of them think, 'well, it's interesting and funny and not mean or anything, [but] I still wish he hadn't have said this or hadn't have said that.'"[3] But, as Dick Young had predicted in his "social leper" column back in May, Bouton didn't last the season. Always an outsider, he was now even more of one, with one writer opining that if the Yankees had their way, Bouton would be pitching not for the Astros but the Egyptian Army baseball team.[4] They'd soon get at least half of their wish.

At the end of July the Astros demoted Bouton, sending him to AAA Oklahoma City. They were able to do so because they had offered him up on waivers shortly after the first *Look* excerpt hit the stands, with all twenty-three other clubs passing on the game's hottest potato.[5] As one account described it, Bouton "was sent down for writing a book and not pitching well, possibly in that order."[6] Ten days and two miserable Minor League starts later—he lasted a total of six innings, surrendering fourteen hits and eleven runs—he retired from baseball. After admitting that he "can't get anybody out," he said that he didn't need baseball anymore, anyway. He had made twice his baseball salary in royalties from *Ball Four* and was working on a sequel, which would most likely add to his coffers. "I'm independent now," he told reporters, "and I can make a decision on what I want to do rather than on what I have to do." He wanted to write, and he didn't want to drag his family from one Minor League town to another, in search of his elusive knuckleball. He could, so he would, walk away.[7]

A few days later Robert Lipsyte wrote his baseball eulogy, noting that now that he was through with professional baseball, Bouton would wake up smiling every day. "As a player," Bouton told him, "you can't allow yourself the luxury of that kind of feeling. You'd never stay tough." In the professional game it turned out that "the cool of the evening," as Johnny Sain liked to refer to the satisfying feeling a pitcher experiences in the aftermath of a solid start, was alarmingly fleeting—a few days at best. "But a book lasts longer, there's more of a glow, and people aren't expecting another one too soon. Besides, if you write a book big enough you can smile the rest of your life."[8]

As Norm Miller said, "[Jim] could throw. He had a good curveball. But once he lost it he had nothing. Like the rest of us. When it leaves it's 'Good-bye. Time to get a job.'" Fortunately for him, he already had one.

Even before *Ball Four* was released Bouton and Shecter were bandying about the idea of a sequel. Something that would focus on the swirl of attention generated by their first book. Shecter confided as much to Richard Feuer, the hippie protester, as they waited outside Kuhn's office back in June. He was there, Shecter told Feuer, primarily to document the meeting and the surrounding circus for the follow-up. First, though, there would be additional headaches with World. Bouton and Shecter were unhappy with the advertising campaign from the outset, and said so. World promoted the book, to a degree, but not the way one would expect a publisher to hawk a title that was in the process of shaking the earth the way *Ball Four* was—the book did not appear in World's spring 1970 catalog until several pages in, where it was wedged onto the bottom of the page, tucked below *Cooking with Astrology*.[9] A few months later Bouton and Shecter alleged that World had breached its contract with them in its sale of the paperback rights to Dell. Litigation ensued, Bouton and Shecter were able to get a preliminary injunction preventing the agreement with Dell from taking effect, and a few months later Bouton and Shecter were finally free of World for good—the settlement agreement gave them half ($100,000) of the proceeds from the sale of the paperback rights, reinstated the agreement with Dell, and freed them from any further entanglement with World.[10]

Focusing now on the sequel, Bouton and Shecter quickly worked out a deal, this time with William Morrow, for $40,000, which they would share equally after Raines took his 10 percent.[11] His baseball career may have been over, but life was good for Jim Bouton—he finally had enough money to take his family to Europe, where he splurged on a suede suit in Paris and tailored shirts in London. He was well aware that it was writing that had afforded him these luxuries, not baseball, and was anxious to do more of it. "Thank God for Ball Four," Bobbie embroidered on a throw pillow that now resided in their living room.[12] There was no matching pillow similarly lionizing Ralph Houk.

Because he had spoken openly about writing a sequel, clubhouses across baseball were bracing for what would be in it this time. "I'd kiss [Willie] Mays," Giants manager Charlie Fox said after a Giants victory one afternoon, "if Jim Bouton wouldn't put it in his next book."[13] Old-guard writers, as well, geared up for another dose of baseball reality served up by Jim Bouton. "The Fink Returns" read one headline in advance of the sequel's release.[14] And Dick Young drew perverse pleasure after learning that the book, *I'm Glad You Didn't Take It Personally*, was not only titled from a quote of his (said to Bouton in the Astros locker room the day after his "social leper" column) but dedicated to him. "I understand Jim Bouton dedicates his new book to me," he wrote. "The only reason I can think of is he doesn't have any other friends."[15]

Hoping for lightning to strike twice, Bouton and Shecter would have to settle for a gentle shower. Released in the spring of '71, the book received significant attention—primarily for a scene in which Doug Rader squatted over Joe Pepitone's birthday cake—but failed to top the craziness generated by its predecessor. Nothing could. *Ball Four* had not only raised the bar for what a sports book should be, but also dulled the shock value of anything that would come after it. People either laughed or were disgusted by the birthday cake depiction, but nobody could say they were surprised to have read it. In that way *I'm Glad* became one of the first victims of the success of *Ball Four*.

The reviews were mixed. Sam Lacy of the *Baltimore Afro-American* wrote positively of it but primarily for Bouton's racial politics, not the book's literary value. Other writers had some nice things to say, but nothing *too* nice. Frank Deford called it "self-centered" and occasionally "horribly provincial" (in its focus on Bouton's foray into the local New York television news scene as a sports reporter) but essentially threw up his arms and said so what. The book "is going to be read almost exclusively by those people who read and loved *Ball Four*," and for them, the book served its purpose. Jerome Holtzman wrote that "it's not bad, I guess, but doesn't compare with the original," and the *Washington Post*'s review was glowing until the final paragraph, where the reviewer lamented the inclusion of the birthday cake incident. "Oh well, no one's perfect, and that's what Bouton was saying all along."[16]

The *New York Times* gave the book only a paragraph of its time, writing that the book "resembles a 15th inning—everyone's exhausted, no end in sight," and chided Bouton for "trying too hard" to shock and amuse his audience. Its year-end sports-book round-up column delivered another blow, alleging that it felt like a cash grab that had "a faint aroma of cheap shot." The *Christian Science Monitor* concurred, calling the book "a tragedy" due to the amount of "gross verbiage" that marred an otherwise "thoroughly amusing book." It also detected a whiff of arrogance in the prose that was off-putting: "One ... gets the impression at times that everybody in baseball is wrong except Bouton, including the commissioner, league officials, the press, and most of the uniformed personnel." Bob Markus of the *Chicago Tribune* wrote that he ignored *Ball Four* because of its perceived ethical breach but read it along with *I'm Glad* and was glad he did. Both books were enjoyable, he wrote, and *I'm Glad* was "fast-paced and good reading." Still, he was bothered by the tone of both books but particularly *I'm Glad*: "The former pitcher, of course, is the guy who provides the keyhole for us. Well and good. But the thing that bothers me is that he's so proud of it." While defending Bouton's right to tell clubhouse secrets, he found *I'm Glad* to be both defensive and sanctimonious all at once. "You have an unquestioned right to write about anything you chose. But please don't be so piously righteous about it."[17]

The harshest review, though, had to be the one that stung the most. Writing in the *Los Angeles Times*, writer John Gregory Dunne pronounced himself a devotee of *Ball Four* who was eagerly awaiting the next offering from Bouton and Shecter. *Ball Four* was, he wrote, "if not the best baseball book ever written then at least the best I ever read." "From one of the best books of 1970 they are now trashing us with one of the worst of 1971." Dunne wrote that *I'm Glad* "reeks of self-congratulation" and "pettiness." He also wondered if Bouton was out of material, given that in *I'm Glad*, "Bouton has gone to the scissors and paste to put together what amounts to a scrapbook on the fame that has visited him since his literary success."[18] To Bouton, who was increasingly thinking of himself as a writer and not a ballplayer, Dunne's review was both a takedown and a message—Dunne made it clear that, to those within the literati, Bouton was little more than a mere visitor. Despite the success of *Ball Four* serious literary types still considered him a ballplayer. And because of the success of *Ball Four* ballplayers considered him a serious literary type. He was forever on the outside, no matter where he stood.

Shortly thereafter, *Playboy*, which had recently launched a literary imprint, Playboy Press, contacted Raines to see if his client might be interested in curating an anthology of essays on baseball managers. It would be a way for the press to bring some quick attention to itself by touting its affiliation with the bad boy of baseball without taxing Bouton all that much; he would only have to write the introduction and be nominally responsible for selecting the essays that would follow. The press would also supply him with the researcher of his choice, who would actually be the one to cull the thicket of manager-themed essays that had accumulated over the decades. It was easy money even if there wasn't all that much of it—a small advance, and then everybody would cross their fingers and hope that people cared enough to buy it.

A few weeks later Bouton ran into a second-generation Chipmunk at Bloomingdales. Neil Offen covered the Yankees and Mets for the *Post* starting in 1967, befriending Shecter shortly before Shecter left the paper. Four years later Offen left as well, to become a freelancer. By the time he met up with Bouton at Bloomingdales he was in serious need of not only a pair of jeans but a job as well. He walked out of the store that day with both. "We agreed that I would do all the work," Offen remembered. "We agreed that my name would be on the book with his and that I would find the stories; arrange them; get the permissions, which turned out to be the hardest thing; and we'd split the profits fifty-fifty." The book would contain not only the essays and the introduction but also commentaries alongside the essays, putting them in historical perspective and providing Bouton's memories or opinions on this manager or that one.

As for who wrote the comments, "the majority of the material was Jim's ideas," Offen says. "I shaped them, did the editorial work. I offered bits and pieces of my own experiences, historical context. Obviously, the book was being sold on the basis of Jim's name, not mine, and the idea was that the comments reflected his personality." Which they did. The book, for example, contained two essays on Leo Durocher, a gentle one by Roger Kahn and a tougher one by William Furlong, who was given his assignment by his editor at *Look* at the time—Len Shecter. Bouton couldn't help but highlight the difference in perspective between the two and offer a dig, just a little, at the man who found *Ball Four* so distasteful. "It's always Roger's style to emphasize the good in his sports heroes, to make everything seem sweetly nostalgic," the comment notes. Furlong, as mentored by Shecter, knew better, wrote Bouton: "It wouldn't have been unlike Len to tell Furlong he didn't want sweet nostalgia."[19]

Offen remembers the collaboration as enjoyable until it was anything but. "We'd go and work on ideas at a pizza place near where I lived in Kips Bay. . . . The place had a boxing motif, so it had punching bags hanging from the ceiling, and Jim could never resist punching the bags. I think they were only supposed to be decorative, but he couldn't resist punching the crap out of them." He was easy to work with, "but he could drive you nuts when he would change his mind on things or not follow up on things." Offen found him to be disorganized and frustrating to work with, as he would regularly miss the deadlines Offen would set, but, outweighing all of that, "he was fun, very outgoing, and very open to ideas."

Occasionally, they'd meet at Bouton's old haunt, the Lion's Head, where Offen would try to keep his attention amid the phalanx of women who by now noticed him and drew his attention. "If we were at the pizza place, or the bar, any kind of public place, he would flirt a lot, with, I was going to say any attractive woman, but, really, any woman." Offen realized that he wasn't working with any old exballplayer. He was in the presence of a cultural icon. *Ball Four* might not have bought Bouton a lifetime pass into the literary world and it might have excommunicated him from the baseball world, but as Offen observed from the reaction to him wherever they went, he now occupied a space unto himself. He was one-of-a-kind and radiated the aura that went with that. What's more, he knew it. And he loved it. "I love being a medium celebrity," he always liked to say. "It's a boost to the ego. But not enough to interfere with life." Offen saw a man who, in *Ball Four*'s wake, was much more than a medium celebrity. And who loved it. "He really, really enjoyed being famous in New York," Offen said. But more than that, "he reveled in being Jim Bouton."

The book was scheduled to be released midsummer 1973. A few months before that, "Reflections on Managing a Baseball Team" appeared in *Esquire*.[20] The essay was, with a few tweaks here and there, essentially the introduction to the book Bouton and Offen were working on and that would appear under both their names. The *Esquire* piece ran under Bouton's name only, though. What's more, Offen had no idea his partner had sold the piece on his own and, in his mind at least, sold him out. "We had a contract, Jim and I, where we had agreed to [equally share] the profits." By selling the introduction to *Esquire*, Bouton pocketed a few thousand dollars that, to Offen, represented "a breaking of the contract. In addition to just being the wrong thing to do. I was angry." Offen considered hiring a lawyer and suing, but "Jim, ultimately, sometime later, apologized, said he was wrong, said that when it comes to money, he just sometimes does things that he shouldn't do." Offen never hired the lawyer, but "there was a lot of really bad, hard feelings between me and him" after that.

Years later the incident still vexes Offen. "He didn't need the money. He had a lot of other irons in the fire at the time. But he just did it. It was a really disappointing end for me to what really was a nice experience. I considered him a friend. . . . This was a dumb thing. It wasn't a lot of money. He didn't need it. Even I didn't need it that much. He just did it because he could." To Bouton the old ballplayer mind-set perhaps kicked in. "When [ballplayers of Bouton's era] got involved in outside projects," Larry Merchant said, "they wanted to make sure they were paid what they were worth." They were so weary of being taken advantage of by their general managers that when it came to financial issues they had more control over, they sometimes pushed the pendulum as far as possible in the other direction. Bouton was hardly the only one. "The feeling was, 'Hey, this is about me,'" Merchant continued. "'This is my idea. I should get paid x or y, or x *and* y, percentage of this.' I don't know Jim's particular situation, but perhaps some of that was involved." Some of it also may have been the unintended consequences of his singular focus. "Jim can be selfish at times," Paula admits, "but this is because he can become so fixated on whatever it is he's working on at the time. It's all he sees. He can't see what's on this side of him, that side of him, or behind him." He could unwittingly stampede over anything and everything in his unrelenting zeal to accomplish whatever it was he had set his mind to.

The book, *I Managed Good, but Boy Did They Play Bad*, came and went, despite the publicity the piece in *Esquire* generated, which largely consisted of mild disdain over an accompanying photo of the former pitcher in a gray Yankee uniform dousing himself with champagne. To those who found *Ball Four* to be an affront to the image of the Yankees, the photo was yet another slap in the face. David Condon in the *Chicago Tribune* wrote that the book's title was longer than Bouton's career but enjoyed the reprinted essays, remarking that in them, the authors showed that "once again, a strong bullpen is Bouton's best asset."[21] In *The Sporting News*, Art Spander focused instead on the *Esquire* excerpt, reminding his readers that it appeared in an issue that featured porn-star Linda Lovelace on the cover. The culture was coarsening, Spander was saying, and because of Jim Bouton baseball was no longer immune to it. Because of this, Spander, wrote, nobody in baseball "wants to lounge around . . . with Bouton. Unless Jim orders hemlock."[22]

22 Bad Stuff 'bout the Mets

Ball Four's humanity may be the reason it has endured for a half century, but in the immediate aftermath of its release it was the notion that it was somewhat depraved that generated such heat around it: "What he has to say is irreverent, iconoclastic, perverse" read a typical magazine piece of the era about the book. "He makes some laugh. He makes others angry."[1] Dell knew where its bread was buttered—its advertising campaign homed in on the book's debauchery: "The whole boozing, feuding, throat-cutting, making-out scene you never read about on sports pages."[2] Thus was launched a revolution in sports literature, as one player after another signed book deals in *Ball Four*'s wake, competing to dish dirt in print, hoping to elicit the sorts of extreme reactions *Ball Four* did. Most succeeded only in boring whatever small readership they could muster and filling remainder bins in bookstores across America.

Ball Four was deceptive in that it was so well written it made it seem like anybody could do it. Nobody else could. But if the players who inked these book deals and their ghostwriters couldn't hope to write something that matched it, they could at least put something out there that approximated the parts of it that garnered the most attention. Editor Jeff Neuman says that *Ball Four* "changed the expectation of an athlete's book; changed what we want from an athlete because we think we want candor, but then of course we punish them for it." In the wake of the book's extended stay on the best-seller list, athletes lined up to tell whatever secrets they could in the hopes that they'd receive enough attention so as to be punished just like Bouton was. "One of the things that Bouton did," Neuman believes, "was to show

that there was a best-seller-level audience for first-person sports books."
Because of this, a "tell-all" book became part of an athlete's marketing portfolio. Whereas for decades the assumption was that fans were
drawn to athletes because of their mythic, God-like facades, now the
idea was that it was their frailties that connected them to the people
in the stands. "Athletes are symbols more than they're people," says
Neuman. "And their job is to do things we think are heroic, but heroes
are only interesting when they have flaws. This goes back to Aristotle."
It's a perilous line between revealing frailties and simply dishing dirt
and complaining, though, and few of the books that followed were
able to successfully navigate it.

In football Johnny Sample and Izzy Lang announced they were
going to hold nothing back in their forthcoming books.[3] In baseball Jim "Mudcat" Grant proclaimed that his book was going to
focus on the sex life of a ballplayer: "I've got lots of experiences. All
I need is a publisher."[4] Bo Belinsky, who had already garnered a reputation as a playboy, inked a deal as well and quickly threw together
his own tell-all. His book, *Bo: Pitching and Wooing*, was ghosted by
another Chipmunk, Maury Allen, but dropped like an anvil upon its
release. "Jim Bouton's wry account of life in the bigs made baseball
players seem more interesting than they ever had," read one review.
"'Bo,' on the other hand, makes sex seem drearier than I would have
thought possible."[5] The books kept coming, one on top of the other,
each more lurid than the next. Before long *Ball Four* seemed tame
by comparison.

All of these books were promoted as the next *Ball Four*. All of them
failed. Still, they kept coming, moving the locus of action within them
further and further from the playing field. In the midst of this flurry,
old-school quarterback Earl Morrall (with the crew cut to prove it in
case there were any doubts) put out an old-school sports book, *In the
Pocket*, that would have been of its time a decade earlier but that by
this point reeked of an outdated relic. The contrast threw the current
wave of tell-alls into relief. Morrall's book "was a modest story of a
modest average man with a name too clean," wrote Furman Bisher in

The Sporting News. "It sold like athletes foot." As for why, Bisher laid the blame at Bouton's doorstep: "Jim Bouton set the pace with not one but two peepshow books," he wrote.[6] And now there was no escape from them. In 1975 Joe Pepitone published his tell-all, hoping to even the score with Bouton by dishing on the Bulldog's sexual habits.[7] It caused a sensation. Then it disappeared.

The only other tell-all from that era that would endure was Yankee pitcher Sparky Lyle's 1979 collaboration with Peter Golenbock, *The Bronx Zoo*. The book was a diary of the Yankees' 1978 World Series championship season, but what sold it were the scandalous stories of Reggie Jackson, Thurman Munson, and, most of all, owner George Steinbrenner. The book was a fun read and was a direct descendent of *Ball Four*. "I did with Sparky Lyle what Lenny Shecter did with Jim," Golenbock recalled. "I'd go over to Sparky's house three, four times a week, and we would yak about what the hell happened the day before. *Ball Four* was the prototype for *The Bronx Zoo*, for sure." But it came from a very different place than *Ball Four*. "[Lyle] had been the Cy Young Award winner in 1977, making $140,000 a year. When George Steinbrenner went out and got Goose Gossage and paid Gossage $2 million, they took Sparky's job away," said Golenbock. Lyle was angry, "and I think that was some of the motivation for him to be truthful about what happened to him." *The Bronx Zoo* was a rollicking ride, but it hardly reinforced the idea of a love of the game.

A few years later Golenbock teamed up with Yankee third baseman Graig Nettles to compile another diary. Their collaboration, *Balls*, read like an angry screed. *Sports Illustrated* wrote that "Bawls" would have been a more appropriate title, as "the book is an almost unrelieved flood of bitching by Nettles," replete with "numerous lapses of taste and judgment."[8] The cavalcade of tell-all books that jammed bookstore shelves throughout the 1970s and '80s were unquestionably the offspring of *Ball Four*, but they hardly resembled it in spirit. The descent of the sports tell-all was perhaps best captured by *Saturday Night Live*, whose fictional baseball player, Chico Escuela, announced during a 1979 edition of "Weekend Update" that he, too, had written a clubhouse exposé, *Bad Stuff 'bout the Mets*. Its most damning allegation? "Ed Kranepool: borrow Chico's soap and never give it back."

A mere decade after *Ball Four* revolutionized the genre, it was dying. By the mid-1980s and '90s too much had changed. Players were treating the books as pro forma exercises, unwilling to reveal deeper truths and settling instead for personal gripes and locker-room tales that by that point no longer had the power to shock or, in most cases, even amuse. What's more, the players, themselves, had changed. There was no chance to recapture the magic of the original. "It's probably never going to get written again," Bouton became convinced years later, "for the simple reason that most baseball players today have played college baseball. Colleges are now replacing the Minor Leagues. And so [today's players] are a different kind of character." Players were now entering professional baseball armed with both agents and a greater level of sophistication than ever before. In the process the raw cultural diversity of the clubhouse diminished. The Fred Talbots and Gene Brabenders were largely scrubbed from the game. With them went the humanity of their stories.

The genre had to shift if it was going to survive. Since athletes were now either unwilling or unable to take a deep dive into their sports, they ceded this ground back to the sportswriters, who themselves had learned from Bouton and applied his lessons to produce sports books that navigated this new landscape in ways that resembled *Ball Four* more than the hagiographies their forbears had written decades earlier. When the young journalist John Feinstein thought about the book he had loved since he was a kid, he realized that, like him, Bouton was something of an outsider and an intellectual. While this made Bouton a suspicious character in the clubhouse, it also permitted him the freedom to write the ultimate insider's book. Maybe, thought Feinstein, he could write an insider's book, too. As an outsider, Feinstein realized, "there's no reason to pull any punches." In 1985, using *Ball Four* as the template for the proposal that would eventually sell his book, he began work on what would become his exposé on Indiana basketball coach Bobby Knight, *A Season on the Brink*. Bouton may have been viewed with suspicion by his teammates, but because he was there every day he nevertheless became invisible, a fly on the wall. Feinstein realized that so long as he showed up to basketball practice every day, Knight and the Indiana players would likewise soon forget he was there. "I didn't want to be any kind of presence," Feinstein recalled. "I wanted it to be as if I wasn't there." In the process he produced a book that some refer to as the *Ball Four* of basketball.

Feinstein also understood that, just like Bouton, he could scoop the beat writers, the ones who had for so long crowed that only they could provide readers with the real inside story. "The only person who knew any of the stuff that I knew was Bob Hammel, who was the local Bloomington writer," Feinstein recalled. Hammel became Feinstein's Dick Young, trashing the book once it was released. "I think he felt that what I wrote was what he should have written," said Feinstein. "But he couldn't. Because if he had, he couldn't have covered Indiana anymore.... He figured out early on [in his career] that he could either write the truth and have no access to Bobby Knight, or play the game and have access to Knight." He chose access. It was a Faustian bargain. "[Hammel's] nickname was 'the Shadow,'" said Feinstein, "because he was always tracing around behind Bob, but it didn't do him any good as a writer." Access was one thing. The need for perpetual access was another. Hammel, like Young before him, never understood the shackles that bound him.

A Season on the Brink unleashed its own wave of copycat tell-alls, these by journalists but all of them in the spirit of *Ball Four*. In 2008 *Wall Street Journal* reporter Stefan Fatsis released *A Few Seconds of Panic*, his deep dive into the Denver Broncos' locker room as he managed to convince Broncos management to allow him to parachute in for a preseason, as a faux kicker. Inevitably, it was often referred to as the *Ball Four* of football. "*Ball Four* made me believe that the best way, the truest way, to understand a subculture is to be part of it," Fatsis says. What you get is "a mix of memoir and expertise." The truth couldn't come from a Dick Young, who had too much to lose. It could only come from a player unafraid to tell the truth or a writer with the ability to immerse himself in the environment and then leave it forever. "I think you can argue that *Ball Four* completely reshaped journalism," Fatsis believes. "I know I'm not the only writer who grew up in the '70s that was influenced by reading that book."

The final word on the impact of *Ball Four*, though, belongs to Rick Wolff, a longtime sports book editor at Macmillan, Grand Central Publishing, and Houghton Mifflin:

> In the world of book publishing and literature, there are only a small, small, small percentage of books that continue to sell and sell and sell. People use the word *classic* all the time, but this is the real meaning of the word—a book that speaks not just to the original readership but to a readership over the course of many generations. . . . [*Ball Four*] changed the landscape of sports reporting and sports writing. I think that if you talk to any sportswriter over the course of the last fifty years, they'll say the same thing. It's just extraordinary that Jim was able to pull this off.

1. Jim Bouton at fifteen, 1954. Courtesy of
Bobbie Bouton-Goldberg.

2. (*right*) Bouton and Bloom Township High School coach Fred Jacobeit holding the 110% Award trophy. Courtesy of Fred and Barbara Jacobeit.

3. (*bottom*) Jim and Bobbie cut the cake at their wedding, December 23, 1962. Courtesy of Bobbie Bouton-Goldberg.

4. (*left*) The Bouton boys, (from left) Pete, Jim, and Bob, December 23, 1962. Courtesy of Bobbie Bouton-Goldberg.

5. (*bottom*) Jim's parents' home in Ridgewood. From left: Bobbie, Jim, and Jim's mother, Trudy, 1962. Courtesy of Bobbie Bouton-Goldberg.

6. (*above*) At the Jim Bouton Fan Club Testimonial Dinner, 1963. From left: Al Gornie, Jim Bouton, and George Saviano. Courtesy of Al Gornie.

7. (*bottom*) At the Jim Bouton Fan Club Testimonial Dinner, 1963. Bobbie is seated at left, Jim standing at center, with Al Gornie and George Saviano in front. Courtesy of Al Gornie.

8. (*left*) At spring training with the Yankees. Courtesy of Bobbie Bouton-Goldberg.

9. (*bottom*) Al Downing (left) and Bouton (right) clown with the Yankee batboy during spring training. Courtesy of Bobbie Bouton-Goldberg.

10. Michael takes batting practice as Dad catches,
1968. Courtesy of Bobbie Bouton-Goldberg.

11. (*right*) Jim Bouton with the Pilots, 1969. Courtesy of the Digital Archive Group.

12. (*below*) The *Ball Four* tapes. Courtesy of the author.

13. One of the 978 sheets of paper in the butter-yellow
box. Courtesy of the author.

14. Bouton's advice on pitching to Frank Robinson. Courtesy of the author.

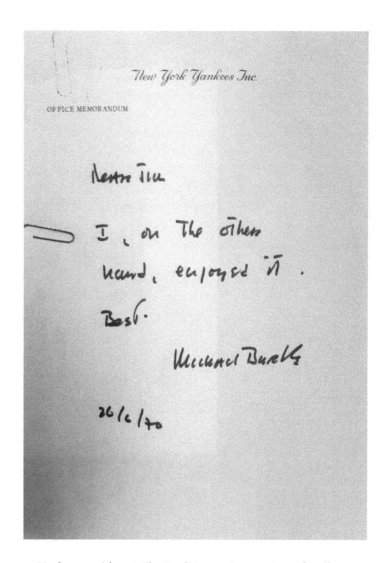

15. Yankee president Mike Burke's succinct review of *Ball Four*.
Courtesy of the author.

16. Electricity in the air around Portland's Civic Stadium, 1975.
© Bob Peterson.

17. Mavericks owner Bing Russell shakes Bouton's hand after his successful debut with the Portland Mavericks, 1975. © Bob Peterson.

18. The Bulldog in motion on the mound during his comeback debut with the Portland Mavericks, 1975. © Bob Peterson.

19. Relaxing on the bench between innings of his comeback
debut with the Portland Mavericks, 1975. © Bob Peterson.

20. (*right*) Michael and Jim in Sarasota during spring training with the White Sox, 1977. Courtesy of Bobbie Bouton-Goldberg.

21. (*below*) Sightseeing in Mexico during Jim's comeback attempt in Durango. Clockwise from left: Michael, Bobbie, Jim, David, and Laurie, 1977. Courtesy of Bobbie Bouton-Goldberg.

22. (*above*) John Thorn and Jim at SABR 47 in New York City, July 1, 2017. Courtesy of Jacob Pomrenke/ Society for American Baseball Research.

23. (*left*) Old-Timers' Day, 2018. Courtesy of Edwin Castro.

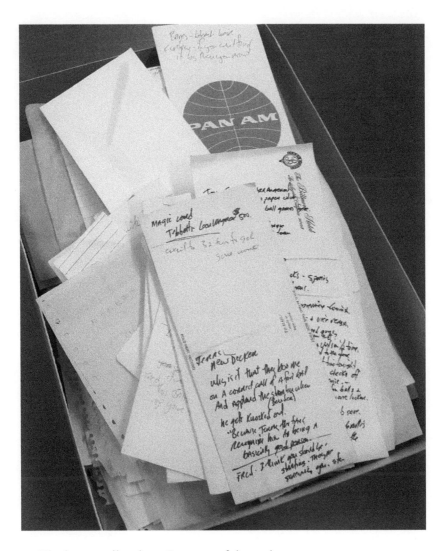

24. The butter-yellow box. Courtesy of the author.

PART THREE The Iconoclast

23   Not Selling Refrigerators

Who would've guessed that the man who burst into Bouton's hotel room the day the first *Look* excerpt hit the stands would also be the man to usher him into the next phase of his life? Howard Cosell was armed with an ego that matched his intellect, so it was somewhat of a surprise that it would be he who would inform his bosses at WABC Channel 7 news in New York, where he was the 6:00 p.m. sports anchor, that the now-notorious Bouton might make a worthy coworker. The intellect in Cosell told him this must be so. "Once upon a time, the legend had it," began a *New York Times* op-ed he wrote in April 1971, "there was a world that remained separate and apart from all the others, a privileged sanctuary from real life. It was the wonderful world of sport, where every competition was endowed with an inherent purity, every athlete was a shining example of noble young manhood, and every owner was motivated by his love of the game and his concern for the public interest."[1] That fictional world was gone, he realized, so the coverage of it needed to be as rooted in truth as any other reporting. Young fans in particular, he wrote, "will only be turned off—not on—by simplistic parodies tied to the past. Their quest is for truth everywhere, and in that quest they do not carefully exclude sports." Bouton, he believed, was the sort of man television sports journalism required as it headed into this new world.

Along with himself, of course. Cosell was widely acknowledged for having changed television sports journalism by actually instilling some actual journalism into the gig. Not content to simply read off the scores of that day's games, Cosell would interview controversial figures such as Jim Brown and Muhammad Ali, ask difficult questions, and focus on the personalities in the game—all things the Chipmunks had introduced a decade earlier in print but that had somehow eluded television until Cosell arrived. Why he wanted to share the spotlight with somebody else, particularly someone who found the spotlight as easily and often as Jim Bouton, was anybody's guess. Al Primo, WABC-TV's news director at the time, thinks his guess is on the mark, though. "Howard was always looking out for number one," Primo remembers, "and at that time, Bouton was a pariah with the players." Cosell, who fashioned himself a journalist and resented the stardom of the athletes he covered, most likely believed, Primo thinks, that Bouton would ultimately fail as a broadcaster, given the cold shoulders he was likely to receive on his beat. "Howard was of the opinion that one did not really need to have a live sports report on the 11:00 o'clock news. He wanted to keep that spot open for himself but really didn't want to come in. I think he was really not looking for someone to succeed as mightily as Jim did because Howard basically wanted to do a taped commentary after the 6:00 o'clock news that we would use at 11:00."

On Cosell's recommendation Primo brought Bouton in for a screen test. Primo knew that hiring him would be controversial, but he was funny and unique, if raw, so Primo thought it was worth the gamble. And a little controversy didn't hurt, either. When you're struggling for ratings in the competitive world of broadcast news, "you bring to bear as many innovations as you can possibly think of," Primo said. He had recently pioneered the "Eyewitness News" format, which stressed personality and "happy talk" between the news anchors and thought Bouton would score high on both counts. Primo had had success with an earlier jock sportscaster, Frank Gifford, and hoped he could repeat that magic.

"I was more interested in having fun with the whole thing than anything else," Bouton recalled. "There's always some way to look at sports other than simply reading off the scores," and he was determined to find it on a nightly basis. He struggled at first, slurring his S's, but he hired a voice coach to help him smooth out his delivery. His pitch would rise when he got nervous, so he worked on both his nerves as well as his timbre to keep his voice as deep as possible.[2] Within a few months he was better, but not polished. He didn't want to be polished. He wanted to be real and funny, witty and different from anything viewers had ever seen in a sportscast. An artificial sheen was the last thing he was looking for. In the process he revolutionized the role of the television sportscaster, just as he had the jock memoir a few months earlier. "The same kind of thing [that happened with *Ball Four*], maybe even more starkly, happened in local sportscasting," says Keith Olbermann, who grew up in the New York area and couldn't believe what he was seeing with his eleven-year-old eyes when he saw Bouton on TV for the first time. There was nobody who had ever done what he was doing on a nightly basis. "This was a strategy to use humor for insight and for criticism, and I remember seeing it and saying, 'That's what I want to do when I grow up.'"

He won quick praise for having a definite point of view. An early review in the *New York Times* remarked that he was very much a work in progress but that his perspective outweighed his surface flaws. The fact that he was bold enough to not only read the news but take a position on it "immediately puts him giant steps ahead of the other ex-jocks who read scores on television these days."[3] He told everyone he wanted to be the television version of the Chipmunks, doing for local TV news what Stan Isaacs, George Vecsey, and Larry Merchant did for print. And he succeeded. He soon felt secure enough in his position as the 11:00 p.m. sports anchor to taunt Cosell as "just another pretty face."[4] In rapid succession Cosell's taped commentaries disappeared from the 11:00 p.m. newscast, and then, within months, Cosell himself was gone. Bouton was now the unchallenged star of Eyewitness Sports.

Primo's humanistic approach to local news proved to be a success also, vaulting past the competition to number one in the New York market. And Bouton's 11:00 p.m. sportscasts were widely admired as being funny, unawed, clear-eyed, and must-watch TV. He focused, whenever he could, on offbeat topics. "By the 11:00 o'clock news, everybody knew what the score was," he said, "so I was always trying to find some interesting way of looking at the games." Much of the time he'd ignore the Yankees or Mets completely, choosing instead to focus the entirety of his airtime on topics sportscasts typically overlooked, like New York's legendary summer basketball Rucker League. He not only talked about it from the comfort of his news desk, but also took his camera crew up to Harlem to film it and interview some of the players.[5]

He loved visiting playgrounds and finding stories there. "They love you in places like that," he said. "I don't go for the usual interview," he said at the time. "To me, that's like a carnival show—the same old questions, the same obvious answers."[6] Focusing on the stars, he realized, led to a distance between the fans and the games they were watching. "For the average fan, life is not going down to work and knocking off fifty or sixty thousand dollars a year," he told the *New Yorker*. "Life is not all two-hitters and touchdowns. A fan might relate more to an offbeat story—a guy coming off the bench after an injury, or a marginal player with a more human story to tell."[7]

He had contempt for his fellow jock talking heads. Frank Gifford was, in his opinion, nothing more than a "refrigerator salesman."[8] Ira Berkow recalled a time he and Bouton were waiting to interview Kareem Abdul-Jabbar, who had just been named NBA MVP and was at a press event to discuss it. Berkow and Bouton watched as the other local ex-jock sportscasters, Kyle Rote and Frank Gifford, approached Abdul-Jabbar and asked him the same questions in succession. "Bouton was third in line. So Kyle Rote (from the local NBC station) asks his questions, then Gifford (at the local CBS station at the time) goes in and asks his questions on camera. I turned to Jim and said, 'Jim, these two guys asked exactly the same questions.'" Bouton shrugged and said, "Same muse." He had his own muse, and she resided in a zip code miles away.

He was insistent on taking a stand and on making his perspective known. When Russian weight lifters were disqualified from a championship event for taking greenies, he expressed sympathy for them and talked about the realities of big-time sports that led athletes to take them.[9] He was determined to take viewers as far as possible from the bright lights of the stadiums they were used to seeing. "I remember he did an exposé on the cruelty of the dog racing he saw when he was in Florida during spring training," Steve Jacobson remembered. "He talked about the way the dogs were treated, and he made it his cause." Just as he had in *Ball Four*, he touched off a wave of no-holds-barred honesty in local news reporting. "People stopped stopping themselves from saying in public what they said in private," said Olbermann. It was the era of truth telling that spurred this interest, but Bouton's sportscasts showed television journalists how to get there. "How do I say 'This guy's an idiot' without him coming over and wanting to punch me in the head?" Olbermann continued. After watching Bouton, they knew how: "I'll find a way to do it using humor."

Sometimes, his insistence on driving toward uncomfortable truths drove Primo nuts, particularly when Bouton touched on sensitive topics. "He was more interested in developing his commentaries," Primo recalled, and less so with informing viewers of the result of that night's Yankee game. "I'd bring him in and tell him the facts of life," Primo said. "I'd say 'Look, [if] you want to work in this business, you can't do that. There are powers-that-be and lines that you just can't cross.'" Cut the commentaries, Primo told him; cut the jokes. "'You're a handsome guy. You deliver the news excellently. Just deliver it straight. You don't have to reach out to be funny or unique or different. You *are* unique and different. You're an athlete. A twenty-game winner. A baseball player delivering the news. Nobody else does that.'" Not a chance. He was not going to be another Frank Gifford. He did not get into this to sell refrigerators. When Primo admonished him to read the scores he did. But that's all he did: 3–1, 4–2, 6–0, he told his viewers. If they wanted to know who scored what, or who even played that evening, they could open up their newspapers and find out for themselves.

He prided himself on his irreverence and took no prisoners. When his former Astros teammate Jim Wynn was stabbed by his wife on his wedding anniversary, Bouton looked straight into the camera that evening and told his viewers that he knew Wynn's wife and was surprised by her act. Because, he said, he thought she knew that on your seventh wedding anniversary, you give copper, not steel. It was his balancing of humor, attitude, and perspective that caught the eye of the young Olbermann, who later patterned his sportscasting on the model provided by Bouton's *Eyewitness News* broadcasts. "I'd seen Kyle Rote and Frank Gifford and Phil Rizzuto and all these straight-arrow, pray-to-the-establishment guys," Olbermann recalled. Bouton's sportscasts were nothing like any of them. "Wow! I mean, highlights *and* jokes *and* substantive commentary."[10] All wrapped together, one after the other. "There was an edge" to his broadcasts, he remembered, "but most importantly for me, what he showed on top of that humor was where the line was." He was watching the night of the Jim Wynn stabbing story, "and I was just like, 'Wow! That's perfect!" The Wynn story was a potentially tragic one that really wasn't—Wynn suffered only a flesh wound and wasn't going to press charges. What Olbermann learned about sportscasting that night was this: "If *they're* not treating it like it was the end of the world, then *you* can treat it like it's not the end of the world. You don't have to get more sober or self-circumscribing than the people whose lives are actually described by the event. That's always in the back my mind when I ask myself, 'Should I make this joke? Where is it relative to the line?' To me Jim Wynn is the line." Olbermann later developed a friendship with Bouton, broadcasting iconoclasts spanning the last four decades of the twentieth century. "Jim, I learned all I know about sportscasting watching you!" read one of his Christmas cards.[11]

Capitalizing on his irreverence, Primo started getting Bouton out of the studio on a regular basis, turning him into something of a participatory journalist. Sort of a poor man's George Plimpton. For a sports reporter who liked to say, "To be honest, there's nothing in sports today worth reporting," the opportunity to ignore the Mets and Yankees in toto was too much to pass up.[12] "They wanted to liven up the segments," he recalled. "So they would say to me: 'You know, the rodeo is in town. Wouldn't it be fun to go down to Madison Square Garden and get into the barrel when the bulls are in the ring? Normally, they have a clown in that role. For that, I was the clown."

There were no special effects or simulations. Just Jim Bouton in a barrel, hoping to avoid being gored to death, with the cameras rolling. "This bull—with real horns—has banged me up, and now I'm rolling around, trying to hold myself inside the barrel. I don't want to get flipped out of the barrel, so I'm holding onto the hand grips." Soon, the clowns entered the ring to lure the bull away from him, rolling him to the side of the ring, to no effect. "The bull puts his face in the barrel, and there I am, nose to nose with this sloppy, slobbering, drooling, snot-wielding thing. And I said—I was miked up—'Please! Stop doing this! I don't want any more in the barrel! I want to go home!' I enjoyed doing that. After the fact." A year earlier he had ridden a Brahman bull for a segment, gotten thrown, and broke a rib. He wasn't going to do that again. This time, his producer assured him, he'd be protected. "I was going to be in a safe place," his producer assured him. "Inside the barrel."

The Plimpton-esque acts became his signature. Bobbie would sew Ping-Pong balls on an old jersey, and he'd go out and experience what it was like to play the reigning world champion; he'd skate with Peggy Fleming; he'd spend an afternoon with the women of the Roller Derby, who would whip him out of the ring and into a pile of folding chairs. "It was 'Let's see if we can knock the sportscaster on his ass,'" he remembered. "Everybody seems to enjoy that."

Bouton took a measure of revenge against Primo by giving him the Joe Schultz treatment in *I'm Glad You Didn't Take It Personally*. Primo "is a man who can hear a $5 bill hit the snow," he wrote, who was more concerned that the news team wear their Channel 7 blazers properly than just about anything else.[13] He made Primo look small, petty, dictatorial, silly. "It really didn't bother me," Primo said. "When you do what I do for a living, you have to take a shot every once in a while." Bouton's portrait "wasn't as flattering as it should be, didn't show me the proper respect, but that was okay. . . . I think he thought I would be pissed off about it, but I wasn't."

Not everyone took Bouton's barbs as well as Primo. In 1971 Sal Marchiano joined the sports team from WCBS, and the two clashed almost immediately. Primo hired Marchiano to replace another jock, Rick Barry, on weekends. Although Marchiano had worked with ex-jocks before (he was paired with Gifford at WCBS for four years), he wasn't prepared for life with Jim Bouton. "I got along very well with Frank [Gifford]," Marchiano said. When Primo hired Gifford to replace Cosell at 6:00 PM, Gifford brought Marchiano with him to continue on as his field reporter, to go along with Marchiano's weekend desk duties. Occasionally, Bouton would use some of Marchiano's stories on his 11:00 PM sportscast. His ethos of not taking sports too seriously rubbed up against Marchiano's ethos of approaching every story with the same seriousness, no matter when it appeared on the newscast. "[Frank] gave me my start at Channel 2," Marchiano said. "And Frank was so much a part of CBS—the Tiffany Network. Truth was the biggest issue there. Frank said to me when I was starting out, 'You have to be sure when you're reporting something because the phone will ring, and it might be Bill Paley, Walter Cronkite. This is where they all live.' So I had that background." Going from that to the happy-talk format of Eyewitness News was a culture shock for him. "At Al Primo's Eyewitness News, it was anything goes. . . . As a matter of fact, when Primo hired me he said, 'Listen, I don't want you to be so straightforward. I want some character. I want you to laugh. If you miss a word, mock yourself, whatever. We want characters here.'" Bouton was the prototype for what Primo was looking for. It was too much personality for Marchiano.

From Marchiano's perspective, Bouton was little more than a show-boat. "He was there to entertain. At that moment in time he was different than the rest of us in that we did it straight. What he was doing was drawing attention to himself, which was clever," but it demeaned what the straight journalists were doing, Marchiano believed. Worse, Marchiano felt that Bouton viewed him with contempt. "I disliked him and he disliked me," Marchiano remembered. "He would make remarks about me. He called me an 'ordinary reporter.'" Ratcheting up the tension was the fact that Marchiano's and Bouton's news-room desks were in the same room, facing each other. Every day the one would look up and in the other be face-to-face with the visage of everything they disdained about the business they were in. "I give him credit for trying to be different. He did a piece on the NYU [New York University] fencing team that was hilarious. That kind of thing, he was good at doing. But he found the reportage of the night's events—scores—to be mundane to him. He was more interested in promoting himself. That's the bottom line, to me, about his broadcasting career. It was about him."

Clearly, Bouton was enamored with the adulation that a New York news gig brought him. Wherever he went a trove of young women followed, sometimes right up into the newsroom. Marchiano was taken aback. "I have no idea why they were there," he said. "I mean, he was married." Young women would vie for his attention whenever he was in public, pushing people out of the way to get next to him. Bobbie couldn't help but notice this but, at the time, wasn't concerned. "I wasn't thinking at the time that anything negative was going on," Bobbie remembered. "Maybe I was naive."

It was more than just the teenyboppers, though. "When Jim became a broadcaster," brother Bob remembered, "he was in the company of professional women." This opened his eyes. Bobbie was midwestern to the bone, Steve Jacobson said, and now he was exposed to something else entirely. "In his house Bobbie was making American cheese sandwiches with mayonnaise, tuna, meatloaf, that sort of thing," said Marvin Kitman, the television critic and family friend who later worked with Bouton on the *Ball Four* TV show. The more time he spent in the professional world of New York, the more constrained his life with Bobbie felt to him.

His new life reporting on fun and games was not always fun and games, though. As much as he might have wanted to avoid them, he couldn't be a New York sportscaster without covering the Yankees at least occasionally. With the wounds from *Ball Four* still fresh, many of them were determined to make things as difficult as possible for him. As soon as he got his job with Channel 7, Elston Howard, who by this point was a Yankee coach, organized a boycott. When Bouton took his microphone onto the Yankee Stadium turf to conduct some interviews near the end of the 1970 season, Fritz Peterson reluctantly brushed him away. "I can't talk to you" was all he was permitted to say. "All I wanted to do," Bouton said afterward, "was a friendly television piece on the Yankees. But a couple of guys on the team intimidated the others and, finally, nobody would talk to me."[14] Marchiano later spoke to Howard, who told him that "if I ever get [Bouton] alone, I'm going to beat the shit out of him." Marty Appel, who was the club's public relations (PR) director at the time, had a front-row seat for all of this. "I remember seeing Jim at spring training, peering through the fence with his microphone, and hearing players say, not within earshot of him but within earshot of me, 'Fuck him.' That was pretty standard at the time." The Yanks, as official policy, barred him from their spring-training complex in Fort Lauderdale, forcing him to stick his microphone through the fence if he hoped to land any interviews. "Of course," Appel remembers, "nobody went to him."

Nobody besides Peterson. The clubhouse, Peterson recalls, "was like a big fraternity—'Ya gotta stay away from him,' 'There's Bouton—don't talk to him.' I was kind of on the other side because Bouton was my friend." So he approached Bouton, who was standing outside of the right-field fence, and spoke to him. "I thought it was pretty funny. It kind of depicted what they thought about Jim." Although he knew he'd hear about it from his teammates when he finished the interview, "by that time I didn't care."

The Yankee reaction was on the extreme end, but, for the most part, many players on all teams were at least somewhat reluctant to speak with him. "The very fact that he had exposed inside information on the Yankees made him persona non grata with teams," Marchiano said. He did better with athletes in individual sports. "A guy like Al Oerter [the Olympian discus thrower] was fine, but when he did team sports there was a problem." When he did an Eyewitness News publicity photo shoot at Yankee Stadium that required him to sit atop the goalpost crossbar decked out in his Channel 7 blazer, New York Giant football players interrupted it by zinging footballs at him, several at a time. "I saw [Tigers manager] Billy Martin throw Jim out of Yankee

Stadium on opening day," Marchiano recalled. Before the Yanks' 1971 home opener, Martin "walked out of his office and told Jim to get out of the clubhouse. He said, 'As long as I'm manager here, you're not welcome here because of that book.'" The next spring, when the Tigers' bus pulled up in Bradenton, Florida, for an exhibition game with the Pirates, Martin spotted Bouton on the field, interviewing Pirate players at the batting cage. He turned to his third base coach, former Pilots skipper Joe Schultz, and said: "Schultzie, get out there real quick when we dress and get that man off the field. I don't want Bouton around my players. I wouldn't go on his show for $25,000. I didn't read his book, but he's a Benedict Arnold." Schultz gleefully carried out the order. "Get the hell out," Schultz yelled. Later, he admitted that "I had waited a long time to get a crack at Bouton."[15]

If Bouton was going to get close to the Yankees, he'd have to do it undercover. Which, in August 1973, he did. Having learned that the club was holding open tryouts at Yankee Stadium, he contacted the Yankees under the pseudonym "Andy Lawson," requesting permission to attend so he could give professional baseball a shot. Separately, his producer contacted the Yankees, asking if they could send a film crew to the tryout, reassuring them that Bouton would not be tagging along. The Yankees said yes to both requests.[16] On the appointed day Bouton showed up covered in a wild black afro and glued-on mustache, claiming to speak only badly broken English. "Jim spoke Spanish," brother Pete recalled. "He learned it in high school, and when he was in [Amarillo] Texas, he used to go across the border to help the guys negotiate to buy Mexican goods." He took the mound, "and he's throwing heat. So he's getting questions from these Yankee scouts: 'Hey, kid, where you from? Where did you play?' And Jim would respond in Spanglish, telling them stories of where he played in the Mexican League and Venezuela. It was absolutely bizarre."

It was just a stunt, but, to the Yankees, it was beyond the pale because once again, Bouton had undressed them publicly. "Every couple of weeks he'd do something on the air that really exposed a fault line somewhere," Olbermann remembered, "and that made him very dangerous." With his Andy Lawson prank, "he showed that if you could throw a ball at a certain speed, they really wouldn't check to see who you were. You could be Charles Manson having escaped, and if you could put a ball over the plate at ninety-four miles per hour, they'd give you a second look." The Lawson prank was funny as slapstick, but it demonstrated that the revered "Yankee Way" was a farce and a fiction. As Olbermann saw it, "there was a humorous aspect to it, and you could sense a kind of personal revenge aspect to it as well. But it was also insurrectionist." At the time Bouton claimed that he harbored no hopes of returning to the bigs for real. And anyway, when he left the house that morning, Bobbie made it clear that baseball was over for her, too. "I'm not going to the Rookie League again," she told him.[17] They laughed. It was the second best prank he would pull while at WABC. The best would ultimately cost him his job.

24   The Most Famous Vasectomy in New York

Post–*Ball Four*, Bouton dipped his toes in many waters, more empowered than ever to cause ripples. Although it hadn't appeared at the time that the clubhouse walls muffled his voice in any way, now that they were gone he felt completely unfettered. He wasn't the first ballplayer to have a vasectomy (he had his shortly after he and Bobbie adopted David), but he was the first to announce it publicly and make a political statement out of it. In the process it became, one reporter said, "the most famous vasectomy in New York." The April 10, 1972, edition of *New York* magazine contained a piece penned by Bouton describing the procedure, as well as a painstaking account of the complication that caused his scrotum to balloon due to a hematoma, along with his thoughts on population control.[1] He tied the issue of vasectomies with that of adoption and wrote that he thought the federal tax code should be revised to encourage families to consider vasectomies and to adopt nonwhite or handicapped children. He became a charter member of the National Organization for Non-Parents and spoke out about how he believed too many families were having children for the wrong reasons and that couples without children were being unfairly shamed. He liked to attend and speak at the organization's "Non-Parent of the Year" award ceremonies, one time quipping that when it came to sex with Bobbie, "We take a big bag of jelly beans and throw it out into the backyard. That gives us about a half an hour."[2] The award ceremonies could become contentious, with shouting matches between people with many children and those with none not uncommon. Bouton's humor-laden speeches could cool the room while at the same time get his point across.

He also considered turning the tables on baseball by becoming part of management, toying with the idea of purchasing the Waterbury, Connecticut, Minor League franchise that had become available in 1972. He had an ulterior motive, though. At a New Year's Eve party he mentioned that he wouldn't mind getting back into the game and making a comeback. Surrounded by his Chipmunk friends, they wondered who on earth would sign him. "I dunno," he said. "Maybe we ought to buy a club." So they decided to try. He rounded up twenty investors—mostly Chipmunks—who contributed $2,000 each, and made a play for the franchise, announcing that he'd run it in the style of Bill Veeck, "where everybody has a lot of fun." Rather than sell to Bouton's syndicate, the Eastern League relocated the franchise to Sherbrook, Quebec, and sold it to a local there instead. The Bouton group then set their eyes on another seemingly available Eastern League club, in Manchester, New Hampshire, but there again the league decided it was wiser to relocate the club to West Haven, Connecticut—a half hour from Waterbury—and sell it to a local.[3]

Thwarted, he turned his attention more directly toward politics and threw himself headfirst into it. He had been drifting in that direction ever since the South Africa Olympic boycott effort in 1968, and his widening contacts afterward pulled him in even further. He organized a Planned Parenthood event with Paul Newman, met Elliott Gould during an anti-Vietnam protest they both were speaking at, and joined the army of Hollywood stars and folk singers who became enamored with and eventually campaigned for the civil rights, antiwar congressional candidate Allard Lowenstein. He began attending Democratic National Committee (DNC) fundraisers—first for Lowenstein and later for others—and eventually began holding some in his home. At one he met Alice Twombly, who was living in Englewood, New Jersey, and head of the local Democratic Party chapter there. He and Bobbie became friendly with the Twomblys, who convinced them to move from lily-white Wyckoff to the more integrated Englewood. "They convinced us that Englewood was a much more interesting, diverse, and dynamic town," Bobbie said. David particularly loved the change. "He said in Wyckoff everyone's the same; in Englewood everyone's different." When he said that, Jim and Bobbie knew they had done the right thing: "David was the only non-Caucasian in the school in Wyckoff. Just before we moved, the first Jewish family moved into the neighborhood; Wyckoff was very homogeneous. That's not what we wanted."

Pete had a less sanguine view of his brother's move from an upper-middle-class neighborhood to one further down the ladder. "Jim had some social engineering ideas that just didn't pan out," Pete believed. "Wyckoff wasn't diverse enough; it was too white bread. He wanted [his kids] to have a more diverse opportunity, to see what the world was like, so he wanted to move to where there was a mix of races and cultures and stuff like that." By the mid-1970s, Englewood got tougher, succumbing to many of the ills that were devastating large and small cities alike. Most of the white liberals who flocked to the town a few years earlier left or at least put their kids in private school. Jim and Bobbie refused to do either, and their children bore the brunt of those decisions.[4]

Once entrenched in politically active Englewood, he became a leading figure on the scene. He joined Shirley MacLaine in stumping for presidential candidate George McGovern in the summer of '72 and later became a Bergen County delegate for the DNC, ultimately being elected vice chairman of the New Jersey delegation.[5] The Democratic Party was in the process of being upended and overrun by politically active newcomers who threw out the party bosses and were determined to run things their own way, and Bouton was emblematic of the revolution. Many of the newly elected delegates had no political experience, just a raw passion for whatever their issue happened to be. As a group the New Jersey delegates were younger, more diverse, and more radical than their predecessors were just four years earlier. As an indicator of just how frustrated and angry voters had become with the Vietnam War, Bouton won the vice chairmanship by beating out a former Marine veteran political operative.[6] By the fall of 1972 he had become so active in the campaign, hosting fundraisers, knocking on doors, and speaking at rallies, that he took a leave of absence from WABC to campaign for McGovern full-time. His decision freed

Al Primo from the sticky situation caused by a news personality so freely aligning himself with a specific candidate.

Now free to devote the bulk of his time toward campaigning for McGovern, he threw himself into it. He rang doorbells, handed out fliers, spoke at rallies. He did the things that all of the other McGovern volunteers did, but there was no escaping the fact that none of the others was Jim Bouton. "He was our rock star," remembers New Jersey state senator Loretta Weinberg, who, like Bouton, was a young delegate on the McGovern bandwagon. As a group they were idealistic. Maybe too much so. "It was a pretty heady time," she recalled. "We thought we were completely reworking the world." She worked closely with him and witnessed the power of his presence. "Because of his name he helped us raise money," she said. "If we had a fundraiser, it was 'Come and meet Jim Bouton,' which was much more interesting than 'Come and meet Loretta Weinberg.'" As always Bouton slipped into the role of the prankster. "He kept us all laughing," Weinberg said.

The Democratic National Convention was held in Miami, and it soon descended into chaos. The political bosses had all been defeated and weren't there, and while this led to the broadening of the party's platform (the Vietnam War, women's rights, and civil rights were the largest priorities), there wasn't anybody there to instill any sort of order. "We didn't do things exactly to the best of our advantage," Weinberg said. Still, they had fun. "There was a bus that would take us back and forth from the convention center to our hotel," Weinberg remembered. "We'd be riding back on the bus, everybody bleary-eyed, and Jim would pull one of the billboard ads for a venereal disease treatment center off the wall, run to the bus driver, show him the ad, and tell him he had to pull over because he had to make a quick call. Everybody would break up at that."

The convention itself was another matter. *Rolling Stone* sent Hunter S. Thompson down to cover it, and he returned with a nightmarish story that let readers know that based on what he saw there, America was most likely stuck with four more years of Richard Nixon. He chronicled the chaos and infighting that caused the Democratic Party to squander its prime-time television moment, wasting it on pointless nominations for vice president. "The nightmare dragged on for four hours," he wrote, "and after the first 40 minutes there was not one delegate in 50, on the floor, who either knew or cared who was speaking." With the VP nomination sown up hours earlier, Tom Eagleton waited offstage all night as, in Thompson's words, "these brainless bastards persisted ... using up half the night and all the prime time on TV, debasing the whole convention with a blizzard of self-serving gibberish that drove whatever was left of the national TV audience to bed or the *Late Late Show*." By three on the night the delegates should have nominated McGovern hours earlier, Thompson sensed a crowd "bordering on rebellion. All over the floor I saw people caving in to the lure of booze, and in the crowded aisle between the California and Wisconsin delegations a smiling freak with a bottle of liquid THC was giving free hits to anybody who still had the strength to stick her tongue out."[7]

After the last pointless nomination had been made, it was finally Bouton's turn to speak and announce that the New Jersey delegation was nominating George McGovern for president of the United States. Nobody was watching. "It was a tremendous amount of fun, and it was very exciting," he remembered. "But it was a very unorganized affair. By the time I got up to speak, everybody'd gone to sleep. I had a list of things [the other New Jersey delegates] wanted me to say before I nominated McGovern. They wanted to say we wanted to ban non-union grapes, so I had to say something nice about union grapes."

"We were completely unaware that it was two or three o'clock in the morning," Weinberg said, "and nobody was watching on TV anymore. Nobody planned this to be a television spectacle. So we did things that would not be considered good for your candidate." After the debacle the DNC altered the delegate process to introduce the concept of superdelegates, ensuring that the establishment would never again be forced to the sidelines during the national convention and that somebody like Jim Bouton would never again have to stand up at three in the morning and prattle on about union grapes while the nation slept.

25   Are We Rolling?

At an antiwar rally in Central Park, Bouton ran into Elliott Gould, who asked him afterward if he wanted to shoot some baskets. "He said, 'I've got a movie thing I've gotta do when I get back to California, and I'll give you call and we'll get together.'" Four days later Gould called. "It's three o'clock in the morning," Bouton remembered. "He said [Stacy Keach] got sick, and we need to have you here tomorrow morning. Altman's with me. You'll be perfect for this. Get on a plane. Just throw some clothes on and pack a toothbrush and get out here." He did, and that's how he came to play Terry Lennox in Robert Altman's *The Long Goodbye*.

This was not his first acting gig. He had taken a drama course in high school and played Bob Cratchit in *A Christmas Carol*. "I was terrible but convincing," as he remembered it.[1] In 1967 he was an extra in the movie version of George Plimpton's *Paper Lion*, pocketing fifty dollars for the day's work. But that was about it, although he did show Robert De Niro how to act like a baseball player when De Niro was preparing to film *Bang the Drum Slowly*. "Into my office [at WABC in 1972] walks a very young, thin, good-looking guy in a short-sleeved plaid shirt," he recalled years later. "He asked me how he should go about learning how to play a ballplayer from the South. I told him to contact the president of the Southern League and spend a couple of weeks down there, riding a bus and learning how to spit tobacco juice."[2] Bouton later reviewed the movie in the *New York Times*. For the most part he liked it, he wrote, although he found it hokey in places and chided the screenwriters for putting the word *mustn't* in the mouth of a player. "No ballplayer in the history of baseball ever said 'mustn't.'"[3]

For a brief moment there was talk that *Ball Four* might become a movie, too, but although Shecter produced a rough screenplay, it went nowhere.[4] That didn't stop Bouton from casting it anyway. "If Selma Diamond were a man," he said, "she would be a good Harry Walker." He had his dream cast all picked out. His friend Elliott Gould would play Steve Hovley. Donald Sutherland would play Gene Brabender. Ernest Borgnine would play Sal Maglie. And, of course, Paul Newman would play Jim Bouton. If not Newman, he said, then he just as well would play himself.[5] Now he had a real chance to act on the big screen. So he packed his toothbrush and took off for Hollywood. Or Malibu, to be precise.

Eventually, the whole Bouton crew packed up and headed west for the shoot. It wasn't at all what they were expecting. There was no screen test, no memorization, nothing. "Altman took one look at me and said, 'You'll be fine,'" he recalled later. "I never even had to say hello. I couldn't believe being discovered was that easy. Just think of all the time I would have wasted sitting at a drugstore soda fountain in a tight-fitting sweater."[6] Although he was given a script, once on set he was told to chuck it and just say what came to mind. "We're just going to have a conversation," Altman told him. "'Say whatever you feel like saying.' Which is a terrifying thing when you have no clue what you're doing." He didn't even realize the cameras were rolling. Gould arrived, started to put out some cat food, and engaged him in a discussion. Partway through, Jim asked, "Are we rolling?" Altman called "Cut." That was take number one. After a while Altman strung enough of these offhand conversations together to constitute his scenes. Bouton enjoyed the process and the week or so he spent with the cast and crew in Malibu but didn't come away unscathed. During the filming of his death scene, when Gould's Philip Marlowe shoots Bouton's Terry Lennox dead in a pond, he was required to spend a long time in the muddy water. That led to a lung infection that bothered him for months afterward. Otherwise, the experience was a good one. "Acting was a whole other world," he said, "and I couldn't quite figure it out. But evidently I wasn't bad enough that they had to switch actors again."

The movie, itself, was in so many ways the embodiment of his life up to that point. Raymond Chandler's Marlowe was a tough loner, seemingly out of his element, thought by those around him to be socially immature but who was ultimately revealed to be more knowing than any of them. Chandler once wrote that as he envisioned him, Marlowe "was not only an uncommon common man, but a man who wore his job like a cross." As one critic described him, Marlowe "functions as a cultural symbol of secularized righteousness."[7] Bouton didn't play Marlowe in the movie, but the movie was very much an artistic expression of his essence. As Chandler once wrote, "I see him always in a lonely street, in a lonely room, puzzled but never quite defeated."[8]

As Altman interpreted him, the Marlowe of the early 1970s would be the ultimate antihero. His goal in all of his movies was to search for the real, the unscrubbed, truth—of a situation as well as a character. In *The Long Goodbye* Altman set out to do with gumshoes what Bouton had done with ballplayers. "The lone-wolf private-eye was, in its time—from the heyday of pulp magazines in the 1920s and 1930s through the film-noir era of the '40s and '50s—a pretty unbeatable archetype of modern masculine heroism," film critic Terrence Rafferty wrote in a retrospective on the film.[9] They were independent, unshakable, sexy, and virile. "It was a myth for an urban society" that no longer fitted, Rafferty wrote. Altman blew the myth to bits in a movie that suffered the barbs of the critics for his having done so. Over time, though, the movie became thought of as a genre bending, timeless, classic. Made by a director who was marginalized by mainstream Hollywood for being, in the eyes of his critics and summarized by film historian David Thomson as "wayward, inconsistent, a maverick (tricky, difficult and evasive, as the moment calls for) and not an industry person."[10]

The film struggled to find an audience because it was just so different from what had come before. Still, Vincent Canby of the *New York Times* gushed over it when it came out, remarking that Bouton, in particular, was surprisingly good. In summarizing Altman's Marlowe, he could just have well been talking about Jim Bouton: "He's a bright, conscientious but rather solemn nut, a guy who hopes for the best but expects the worst, having experienced the social upheavals, the assassinations and the undeclared war of the sixties."[11] And at the end of the film Marlowe dances off into the sunset. Despite it all he gets—as Marlowe always gets—the last laugh.

Bouton was now unquestionably a star and a sex symbol. Soon the women's adult magazine *Viva* came calling, offering him $5,000 for a nude layout. *Viva* was the brainchild of Bob Guccione, who envisioned it as the female equivalent of his *Penthouse* franchise. Bouton passed the opportunity on to his friend Shep Messing, the goalkeeper of the New York Cosmos, for whom, Messing liked to joke, $5,000 was more than he was making in professional soccer. Messing did the shoot and was then released by the Cosmos for violating the morals clause in his contract.[12]

Through it all Bouton's confidence continued to grow. At least it appeared this way from the outside. His accomplishments were mounting, one on top of the other. "He doesn't just have a part in a movie, he has a part in a Robert Altman movie," says Paula. "He doesn't just go on TV, he becomes a major anchor in the New York market. He doesn't just play baseball, he plays for the Yankees. He doesn't just write a book, he writes *Ball Four*." If he appeared cocky at times, it wasn't without reason. "It's not based on nothing," she said. "He's not deluding himself." Some called him arrogant for his willingness to so often go it alone, to not listen to others tell him how things "should" be done, but so be it, was how he looked at it. He had his vision and his dreams, and only he knew how to turn those into reality. And nobody was going to tell him otherwise.

At times it was hard to tell if he was so sure of himself because he so often prevailed or if he needed to prevail in order to maintain what was, underneath it all, a fragile sense of self-worth. Nearly anything and everything could be, for him, a test of his mettle, ability, value. Even jigsaw puzzles at home with Bobbie could become at times something else altogether as an internal drive to "win" the puzzle would overtake him and manifest itself in fiercely competitive ways. Jim and

Bobbie enjoyed their quiet time together, working on the puzzles, but occasionally, when they were close to completing one on the eve of one of his road trips, Jim made sure Bobbie was unable to complete it without him. "He'd take kind of a unique piece," Bobbie recalled, "one that might have a person's face on it, or a dog or something, a piece that you'd look for, and take it with him. Then when he'd come back, he'd stick it in there." It was a Bouton family trait. Card games with his father and brothers brought to the surface the hypercompetitive juices in all of them, leading observers to wonder what the Bouton men were really playing for, as it was clearly not the nickels in the pot. "Sometimes," Bobbie said, "you didn't like to watch them because you worried somebody was going to get hurt." Even highway driving represented a challenge he was determined to conquer. To win. Fritz Peterson recalled the white-knuckle experience of driving to Yankee Stadium in the passenger seat: "Jim would use the safety lane between the left lane of the highway and the cement barriers as his 'private' passing lane. When he used it, dust, Coke cans, and cigarette butts would go flying everywhere, but it worked—for Jim." Later, when working with critic Marvin Kitman on the *Ball Four* television series, Bouton taught him the physics of driving: "The more crowded the space," he'd tell Kitman, "the faster you go. Because the space will open. Miraculously." For him it did, but most likely because the other drivers on the road just wanted to get the hell out of the way of the madman charging up behind him.

On rare occasions he'd ponder the costs of his internal drive, reflecting on his competitive nature and how it could overwhelm his worldview. "Sometimes," he told *Sports Illustrated* in 1975, "I wish I could do something anonymously. You know, like working with wood. I love the smell of freshly cut wood. I'd love to go off with my family someplace and just make things. But I don't think I could. . . . Working with wood sounds nice, but maybe it would smell rotten after a while. Jeez, waking up every morning seeing that same wood. I'd have to enter something in a contest. I'd have to win a prize. And when I did, everything would change."[13]

26 One Smart-Ass and Four Lawyers

His demise at Eyewitness News began relatively early in his tenure, in the late fall of 1971, when he decided to have a little fun at the expense of New York Giants football coach Alex Webster. The Giants were putting the finishing touches on another miserable season (they'd end up 4-10, losing their final five games), and Frank Gifford sent Sal Marchiano out to Yankee Stadium to interview his former backfield mate. "I was supposed to go to a Floyd Patterson press conference," Marchiano recalled, "but he didn't show, so I called Frank at home and said, 'We don't have a story for today.' He said, 'Why don't you go to Yankee Stadium and talk to Alex about what went wrong this season and what do the Giants need to improve next season.'" The interview was pro forma but good enough for Gifford, who played it on the 6:00 o'clock news. When Bouton pondered the possibilities for his sportscast at 11:00, he reviewed the tape and found it boring. It'd be funnier, he thought, if he ran the tape backward and remark on the "gibberish" and double-talk coming from a pro coach trying to explain away a losing season. The problem was, though, that in running the tape backward he unknowingly erased the audio. When he played the tape on the air, Webster's lips moved, but no sound came out at all. Undeterred, he allowed the silence to set in before suggesting that that was about as informative as Alex Webster ever was, saying that in response to the question of what went wrong that season, "I guess Alex doesn't know either."[1]

Marchiano was at home, watching the sportscast with Giants defensive end Fred Dryer, who had come over for dinner. They sat in stunned silence as the piece played. The next morning Marchiano went to Yankee Stadium, where both Webster and Giants owner Wellington Mara were waiting for him. Mara was steaming, telling Marchiano that he was going to sue Bouton and the station for making his coach look like a clown. Primo was pissed as well. "That was the beginning of the end for him," Primo remembered. "What he did was something that was, essentially, not true, not accurate, not journalistically sound." By messing with Webster's words, he was, in Primo's view, "tampering with documentation. So we had to suspend him." "I was being a smart-ass," Bouton recalled. "And then the next day, four lawyers showed up." He figured they were coming, so when his producer asked him what he was going to do, he was ready with his plan. "I told him, 'What we're gonna do is, we're gonna get a camera and we're gonna roll.'" He was going to capture the entire confrontation on film. Which he did. As Mara's and Webster's lawyers tried to confront him, he turned the confrontation into farce when he pivoted toward the camera and provided the play-by-play: "Just to make sure you know what you're looking at here—this is the lawyer for Alex Webster, and he's here today because he feels badly that I played his video backward." He made them look mean and petty. But more than that, he remembered, "I made them look so stupid."

Viewers may have found the whole thing funny, but here again he had rattled the cage of the insiders, shaken the foundation upon which the establishment found its footing. Mara was determined to see his lawsuit to the end, telling Marchiano that while he was going to sue him as well, he was only doing it so he could use him later to testify against Bouton at the trial. "He told me, 'Be prepared to be part of the litigation because we want you to testify that Alex answered your questions honestly.' I said, 'Okay, no problem.' And that's what happened." Later that morning, in their cramped, shared office at WABC, Gifford let Bouton have it for humiliating his friend. "He was screaming at Jim, for what he had done," Marchiano recalled. When he was finished it was Marchiano's turn. "I told him if he wanted to do something like that again, he should have the balls to go do the interview himself." He then relayed to Bouton a message from Alex Webster, which was that there was yet another person who very much wanted to beat the shit out him. This time his Chipmunk friends turned on him as well. Leonard Koppett wrote in the *New York Times* that "to edit out the sound, so that no one can know what exactly Webster said, and then to say the man had nothing to say is not fair commentary. It's not honest. It's not even clever—and it should not go unpunished." He added, "I don't believe Bouton knows the difference between what's fun and what's wrong," and he called on the Federal Communications Commission to investigate the incident.[2]

The case snaked its way through the legal system over the next several years. Finally, in 1976 a judge dismissed it. In so doing, Judge Martin Stecher held that Webster, as the Giants head coach, was a public figure, and, as such, Bouton's sportscast could not be actionable absent malicious intent. While Stecher allowed that a jury might perhaps find that his sportscast was "motivated by a sly malice masquerading as humor," he stressed that "the intent to inflict harm is not itself actionable," as the words that accompanied the intent must likewise be malicious. Here, though, there was mostly an absence of words. What few words there were (Bouton described Webster as "evasive" before playing the clip) were insufficiently actionable, the judge held, because they were directed toward a professional football coach whose position invited questions and criticism from the press.[3] Once again he had approached the line, peered over it, tiptoed on top of it, but did not cross it.

Post-Webster, Primo did what he could to hold his sportscaster in check. "After that we had producers and writers all over him. All the time." In particular, Primo recruited Bouton's producer, Art Browne, to be his spy. "I had Art Browne watching him like a hawk. He was my minder. I told him, 'I don't want another problem with Jim Bouton the rest of my life, so you just watch him.' If there was anything that was questionable, he'd bring it to me and we'd deal with it." Bouton and Browne got along well, mostly because Bouton never knew Browne's secret mission. "I don't think Jim ever realized he had a minder," said Primo, "but that's what he was." Bouton thought Browne was shadowing him merely because he was new and was offering him advice simply as a veteran producer would. When informed nearly a half century later that Browne was in actuality a mole, he laughed. "That doesn't surprise me at all," he said. He always liked Browne, he said, because they shared the same sensibilities. "Very nice guy," he said. "Very funny." Browne may have had his secret orders, but he and Bouton nevertheless bonded over their many commonalities. The most obvious of which was that neither of them thought much of Sal Marchiano.

By this point it was clear that when it came to the understanding of "risk," Bouton and Primo were working with different definitions. Bouton's involved poking sacred cows to see what might happen, while Primo's involved scaring off sponsors or pissing off his bosses. Primo had no problem exposing Bouton to physical risk on a regular basis—putting him in a bullring, allowing the Amazonian women of the Roller Derby to slingshot him into a field of metal folding chairs. In fact, each week he'd try to think up something more dangerous than the week before. "Once they got some huge ratings," Bouton recalled, "now the question was, 'What is this idiot Bouton going to be doing next?'" But when it came to poking the establishment and its values, that was too much.

Irrespective of Art Browne, Bouton continued to make everyone at WABC, along with the network, nervous. Nobody knew which tree he might shake next and what might fall from it when he did. Particularly nervous was Roone Arledge, the head of ABC Sports, which had just started *Monday Night Football*. Arledge wanted nothing to do with Bouton's sportscasts on an ABC-owned and -operated New York affiliate and let Primo know it. Arledge was trying to nurture his fledgling relationship with the NFL and didn't need the fallout from whenever Bouton would poke fun at it. Arledge was also working on securing a Monday-night baseball package (it would finally arrive in 1976) and knew that negotiations with Bowie Kuhn would be smoother if Jim Bouton wasn't an ABC employee.

Although stories abound as to the event that caused his dismissal in the fall of 1973, there was no single incident that led to a "You're fired!" moment. It wasn't when he showed clips of *The Long Goodbye* rather than Olympics highlights (as Marchiano alleges), it wasn't for refusing to read promos on the air or for telling viewers one January not to watch the Super Bowl on ABC the next day (as Bouton has alleged). Rather, it was simply that Roone Arledge and the network didn't want him there anymore. "I don't think I ever revealed this to Jim," Primo says, "but I knew his agent very well, and I told him, 'Go get him another job. We're not going to stand in his way because he's not going to be renewed here.' This was well in advance of the end of his contract." In Primo's eyes he did Bouton a favor. "I gave him a lot of time to get another job. I said to his agent, 'He's not going to survive this. I can't hold Roone Arledge and the National Football League off much longer."

His last day at WABC was in September 1973, when he went on the air and informed viewers that he had been terminated for being too outspoken.[4] Because he had had so much lead time, he already had his next gig lined up—at rival WCBS, channel 2. The deal was finalized less than a week after he signed off at WABC, and a month later he was at the 11:00 p.m. sports desk at WCBS. It didn't take long before WCBS leapfrogged past Eyewitness News to become number one in New York. He had a knack for this; he was preternaturally good at it. Olbermann later ranked him as the second-best local sportscaster of the twentieth century, noting that the only reason he wasn't number one was because he didn't stick with it long enough. But he always exuded the feeling that as a sportscaster, he was merely passing through. He wasn't a lifer. He wasn't Sal Marchiano.

For all the time he spent as a sportscaster, he kept a ballplayer's habits. He liked to dunk his head in the bathroom sink and wet his hair before going on the air because, as a ballplayer, he always showered before taking the mound. "It's a tough habit to break," he said at the time. Showering before a game "made you feel good, freshened you up so that you felt like you were starting the day all over again. It was a shock to discover that people in the real world didn't do that. They showered in the morning and that was it." He loved signing autographs, admitting that doing so reminded him that he wasn't a has-been. Whenever asked he said that he missed the crude humor and refreshing honesty of the locker room and would return to baseball in a heartbeat if the opportunity ever arose. "I still won't admit my career's over," he said around the turn of the new year in 1975. "I know the date and the hour [of the day he walked away from the game], but my mind refuses to accept the fact that I couldn't go back if I tried." In the next breath, though, he'd say: "I'm only 36," as if to cajole himself into wondering whether maybe there was still time left to try anyway.[5]

As a sportscaster he seemed to be on a mission to remind people that what he was now doing wasn't worth their time, scolding viewers that they should go outside, play with their kids, watch less television. From almost the moment he arrived at wcbs, what was most noticeable was how unsettled he seemed to be. By 1975 he had put in two years there and was their star, but he was convinced that there was something else in store for him. "I live from month to month," he said, "doing whatever seems interesting at the time." Local television news was losing its appeal. He missed being a ballplayer. "I hated the travel," he said to a reporter one afternoon in the cbs men's room, "being away from my wife and kids half the year. But there was even something good about that. The time I did spend at home was richer, the hours with the kids more important. Now I see them all the time and things are not the same."[6]

27　You're a Long Time Dead

"You see, you spend a good piece of your life gripping a baseball and in the end it turns out it was the other way around all the time."[1] If there is one line from *Ball Four* remembered above all the rest, it is this one, the final one in the book. So iconic and so true that it is etched across the entirety of a wall at the Hall of Fame museum in Cooperstown. A fitting tribute, in a way—if any aspect of Jim Bouton's baseball life was going to be enshrined and immortalized, it only made sense that it would be his words. They would be more true for Bouton than even he realized.

Although it appeared that he had quickly moved on from baseball, taking his broadcasting gig with WABC within weeks of his retirement, he never really moved on. Two weeks after walking away from Oklahoma City in the American Association, he was pining for a return to the mound, this time with the Ridgewood-Paramus Barons in the Bergen County Metropolitan League. This was, obviously, quite a few rungs lower on the baseball ladder—semipro ball on a team locked in a pennant race not with Boston or San Francisco but with Emerson-Westwood. The Barons' manager, Bob Baron, who was so fond of his surname that he plastered it on the jerseys of all of his players, found his club in a late-season jam, with rescheduled games piled one on top of the other and in dire need of pitching help. Coincidentally, Bouton had a casual relationship with the father of one of the Barons' outfielders, who hailed from Houston. During a conversation the father mentioned the Barons' dilemma. Did they need another pitcher? Bouton wanted to know. Because if they did, he'd fly home immediately to help out, he said. It was really no big deal, he assured him; Bobbie would load the kids in the car and drive home within a few days to join him. It all sounded great to Baron, who had seen Bouton in the stands occasionally whenever he was back in the area and who understood that even a washed-up big-league pitcher was still a big-league pitcher.[2]

Unfortunately, once again there was trouble from the commissioner's office. Not Kuhn's this time but the Met League's, which informed Baron that club rosters had closed on July 27 and that no new player, no matter how well they could pitch or write, could join as ringers for a late-season pennant push. A few days later, though, he was declared eligible to play in an exhibition tournament in the Bridgeton (New Jersey) Invitational Tournament after a phone call from the league to Kuhn's office confirmed that he was truly retired from professional baseball. This time he wore the uniform of the Trenton Pat Pavers and pitched a complete-game 7–5 victory over the Washington DC Black Sox. He gave up thirteen hits over the team that won the tournament the previous year, including a long home run, but survived, in part because the Black Sox catcher got stuck at work and missed most of the game. In the dugout between innings, his new teammates tossed one-liners from *Ball Four* back and forth, admonishing Bouton to "smoke 'em inside" and wondering whether they were going to go beaver shooting after the game.[3] At last he was sitting in a dugout with the very people he had written the book for.

He decided that he needed to play and that he'd suit up in 1971 for the Barons, fitting in as many games as his television schedule would permit. He immediately began working out in his backyard, throwing to Michael and David, who on occasion would wallop one of his hanging knucklers over the tall bushes that separated their yard from the neighbors: Although only semipro he took it seriously, charting pitches just as he did at Yankee Stadium or the Astrodome. Occasionally, he had to correct a curious onlooker that he was only studying a hitter's tendencies, not taking notes for his next tell-all. It was all for fun but also a deadly serious pursuit; every once in a while he'd let his guard down and admit that he could return to the big leagues one day if he could only master his knuckleball. Hell, Hoyt Wilhelm was still pitching, he'd say, and he was in his late forties.[4]

He was a curiosity—the big leaguer come down to earth to play ball with the amateurs. Reporters sniffing for a story would regularly find their way to Veterans Field in Ridgewood to talk to him, ask him why he was still doing this, what the end game was. He loved the attention; loved ranting about Bowie Kuhn, the state of baseball, or the Yankees; and loved going out on the mound to pitch, even if it was in front of just a few hundred fans. It was all so much fun, he'd say. And it was. But one of the first things he did after being granted his leave of absence from WABC in 1972 to campaign for McGovern was to head up to Pittsfield, Massachusetts, to work out for the Texas Rangers' AA affiliate for a week in the hope of being signed for the rest of the season. This was no spur-of-the-moment decision; he'd amped up his workouts by preparing in a Farleigh Dickinson gym for weeks beforehand. In the end he was disappointed the Rangers had declined to sign him. Oh, well, he said, shrugging it off, "my wife wanted to see the Berkshires."[5] Still, he let it drop that he was going to call around to see if any other club might have any interest in working him out.

For the next few years he continued to play semipro ball—for the Barons, the Teaneck Blues, Ridgewood Rangers, Clifton Tigers, whoever would have him. Before leaving for the television studio in the morning, he would go in the backyard and throw hard for twenty minutes from a distance of eighty-one feet. As for how he settled on that distance, he explained that it was "the same principle as swinging the heavy bat." This was all the competition he needed, he'd say, remarking on how in the Metropolitan League, it wasn't so much tobacco juice or Vaseline that slopped up the balls as raspberry sherbet, provided to him between innings courtesy of Laurie. So long as he could find a field that boasted of a porta-potty, he knew that Bobbie would bring the kids and come out to watch him pitch. This was everything he wanted, he liked to say.[6]

Except that it wasn't.

By 1975 the urge to compete—really compete—on a ball field over-flowed like lava, burning through and melting everything in its path. He was now pitching two nights a week in two separate leagues, and even that wasn't enough. The feeling that something was missing was overwhelming. Later he would refer to this period as something of a midlife crisis, but whatever it was, even Bobbie could sense that something was wrong. "Every now and then he would not seem par-ticularly happy or fulfilled or whatever," Bobbie recalled. "I figured it was a midlife-crisis sort of thing. He was so competitive, and playing ball seemed like something he really needed." Reading the sports on TV and playing beer-league ball with the other working stiffs couldn't hope to satisfy him. Taking in his struggle, Bobbie concluded that the cause was all of the competitive steam that was building up inside of him, with nowhere to go. He needed an outlet—a legitimate, high-level outlet—she thought, or he might explode. "I knew he was not happy. I figured it was because he wasn't doing what he really wanted to do." Which was true. Among other things.

For guidance, he turned to his dreams. "I have this crazy dream," he said at the time, "that my knuckleball is going to come round and that I'll be back to the big leagues. I know it sounds nuts, but everyone has a crazy dream and that's mine."[7] He knew that, to others, he might sound foolish by merely contemplating a return to organized baseball after being away from it for so long, but he didn't care. "My friends know what I'm doing," he said. And, anyway, so what? "You're a long time dead."[8] Might as well try. He had some vacation time coming to him from WCBS, so he used it by packing the family up that July and heading off to western Canada, where he joined the Calgary Jimmies for a tournament in the Alberta Major Baseball League. It was a step up from the semipro ball he had been playing; future Houston Astro Terry Puhl was playing for neighboring Saskatchewan at the same time as an eighteen-year-old. This would give him an opportunity to see if he had anything left. He did. Enough, he figured.

When he returned he remembered an ad he had seen in the classi-fied section of *The Sporting News* a couple of months earlier. An independent Class A professional club in the Northwest League—the Portland Mavericks—was advertising for ballplayers in the newspaper, not something you saw every day.[9] Joe Garagiola had also traveled up to Portland with a film crew and shot so much tape that he created two pieces on the Mavericks for his NBC *Monday Night Baseball* pregame shows, which ran on consecutive weeks. Bouton saw them and was intrigued. The more he read up on the Mavs, the more he realized that if ever a ball club had been constructed with him in mind, it was this one.

The Mavericks were the brainchild of Bing Russell, a longtime Hollywood stuntman and action/western actor who was usually shot dead before audiences learned his character's name but who managed to hang on for thirteen seasons of *Bonanza* as Sheriff Clem Foster. In a few years he'd be better known as Kurt Russell's father, but in the early '70s he had a dream just like Bouton did. His involved returning to baseball, a game he played professionally for a short time on an independent club before a beaning caused him to give up the game and head off for Hollywood. Now, with his film career stalled, he focused again on baseball, this time hoping to resurrect the spirit of independent ball in baseball-damaged Portland, Oregon.

The city was for many years the stalwart home of the Portland Beavers of the AAA Pacific Coast League, but attendance faltered in the early '70s, and after the '72 season the club packed up and moved to Spokane. While most people assumed that baseball and Portland just didn't mix anymore, Russell thought otherwise. "You know what killed Coast League baseball in this town?" he asked a reporter before answering himself. "Every time we got somebody the fans loved, that guy was called up to the major leagues by the parent club. What good is that?" He decided to fix things by creating a new way to run a Minor League franchise. His wouldn't be beholden to the big club. Instead, his would be independent and would stock its roster through open tryouts, attracting players who had been kicked aside by organized baseball who just wanted to play professional ball for $300 a month. "There's no plan here to produce players for the major leagues. All we want are some players who will be playing in Portland for a long time. I don't care about developing athletes for folks in Minneapolis or Cleveland or Cincinnati to enjoy. That's stupid."[10] He would make the game fun. He dressed his players in "streetwalker red," he liked to say; painted the bases red, white, and blue; and vowed not to trade any player unless both the player as well as the Portland fans approved of the move.[11]

On the field the Mavericks wowed the locals, stealing bases whenever the spirit moved them (once seven in an inning), fighting with the opposition on a regular basis, and basically poking their collective finger in the eye of the traditionalists. People poured through the turnstiles in record numbers, and, soon, the Mavs were making regular headlines as the upstarts from the Northwest who were bringing fun back to baseball.

Not everyone was a fan. "I recently read your article on the Portland Mavericks," a Northwest League umpire wrote to *The Sporting News*, "and agree that this team has been very successful operating independently." Nevertheless, he wanted them out of the league. "I personally witnessed several games in which their antics were cruelly displayed. From the harassment of fans to altercations with umpires, this team was rightfully named 'the bad boys of the league.'" He then recounted one game where the Portland fans became so rowdy after being encouraged by the Maverick players that he had no choice but to call the game a forfeit. "Following the forfeit, the Portland manager literally stole the first base bag in protest only to return it the following day signed by the entire team." The Mavs, he concluded, were replete with "undesirables," from the manager on down.[12] If Bouton was going to attempt a comeback anywhere, there was no better place than here.

By 1975 the Mavs were managed by Frank Peters, who had taken over after Russell's inaugural choice, Hank Robinson, was thrown out of the league for slugging an umpire.[13] "Hank Robinson was an old-school Marine," Peters remembered, "and he didn't just punch the guy—he knocked the motherfucker out." Without a manager for the foreseeable future, Russell and sportswriter Ken Wheeler retired to

Peters's bar, the Peters Inn, for a few, or many, beers. Peters had been an infielder in the Orioles system, among others, finishing up with the Beavers in 1972 before opening his bar. He devoured *Ball Four* when it came out, relating to much of it. "He was really telling my story," he realized. When Russell and Wheeler walked into his bar that evening, Peters also realized that he missed all of the fun Bouton had recounted within the book. As Russell and Wheeler drank, "they got to talking and, maybe they got drunk, but Wheeler talked Bing into hiring me to manage the Mavericks." Before the tab was paid Peters was back in baseball.

This time he loved it. "My job was to take all these guys who had been rejected, released, not been drafted, and to make them believe in themselves." He didn't have any rules, didn't have any signs; he just let the players showcase themselves in whatever way they felt was most advantageous. Most of his players were pissed that they had been rejected, so it didn't take much to motivate them. Under Peters the fighting continued, only now it was not only between the Mavs and other clubs, but between Peters and some of his players. Eventually, he realized he would need a bodyguard to protect him from his players and vice versa. "The bodyguard wasn't so much for me but to keep me from them," Peters said. "I was beating up my ballplayers." Anyway, "it's always good to have a bodyguard if you're a manager" was Peters's philosophy. "You're not pushing the envelope if you don't need a bodyguard, are you?" Everything about the gig was fun for Peters, after spending the past couple of years dealing with bartenders. "I had two bars and twenty-five bartenders. I know 125 ways a bartender steals. The problem was that they know 150 ways." Managing a bunch of rebel ballplayers was a vacation from what he otherwise had to contend with.

Before Bouton arrived the biggest star on the club was Reggie Thomas, a small-time thief and big-time talent who had spent some time in the Houston, New York, and Cleveland organizations and who was later rumored to have been an informant for the Federal Bureau of Investigation. He was a nightmare to deal with. No other club knew how to handle him, but Peters thought he might. "One of the first things I did with Reggie Thomas was to make sure that we secured the valuables. My speech went like this: 'Okay, if you get your wallet stolen, you're the sonofabitch that's causing our team to have thieves.' I wouldn't blame the thief because it was always Reggie Thomas. If he got kicked out of a game, he'd go into [the locker room] and go through everybody's wallets and steal their money.'

He'd try to swindle his teammates, and if he found a gullible one, he might walk away with $1,500 that was theirs just a moment earlier. He'd also steal bases—seventy-two in only seventy-three games in 1974, sometimes stopping at first after hitting a gapper just so he could swipe second and secure his dinner plans for the evening—the souvlaki shop next to Portland's Civic Stadium offered free souvlakis to each player who stole a base. Sometimes, if he was thinking far enough ahead, he'd swipe third as well: breakfast. "The players only got $300–$400 a month so, you know, you had to supplement your income," said Peters. Even the batboy was on the take, filching a few beers for himself whenever he was given money to go out and buy some for the club. Peters was good with all of it. Whatever it took. Whatever made it fun. Whatever kept fans in the seats and put W's on the scoreboard.

The essence of the Mavs could be found in their annual open tryouts. Anyone with a dream could grab their mitt and take the field, hoping against hope that they might end the day on the roster of a professional baseball club. One year the tryout roster was bookended by a fifty-year-old catcher on one end, who had played beer-league ball for three decades before deciding he was ready for a shot at the big time, and a thirteen-year-old on the other, who concluded that he was ready after being named the MVP of his Little League squad. The Mavs cut the catcher but signed the Little Leaguer to be their batboy.[14] One catcher who did make the squad was an oddball in another way—he was left-handed. For whatever reason, a century of received baseball wisdom dictated that there was no place in the game for a left-handed catcher. But when Jim Swanson showed up on tryout day in 1975, he saw that of the roughly four hundred players there, most of them were outfielders and almost none of them were catchers. He ran home, got his left-handed catcher's mitt, and returned, this time declaring himself a catcher. An excited Russell turned to Peters: "Is that guy a lefthanded catcher? He is a lefthanded catcher! Let him play another game."[15] Soon Swanson found himself on the club as a backup catcher and Peters's unofficial bodyguard. Another guy with a dream was an Ivy League pitcher from Cornell named Rob Nelson who, after college, had taken off for South Africa to spread the gospel of baseball in that country. It was winter in the Southern Hemisphere, so when Nelson's father sent him clippings about the tryout, he flew home to give it a shot. Dreamers all. Each and every one of them.

28 The Battered Bastard of Baseball

There was no bigger dreamer than Jim Bouton. His curiosity piqued, he boarded a plane for Portland, where Peters picked him up at the airport. "He was just a delightful, charming person who was here to give it a go," Peters remembered. Other than the delightful and charming stuff, he was no different from any of the other Mavericks, in Peters's eyes. It didn't take long for Bouton to find out what the Mavs were all about and warm to them. Right away, as he stuck out his hand to welcome him to the Mavericks, Peters told him that he had to correct one misperception about his team—that there weren't any rules. In fact, he said, he did have one rule and wouldn't bend it for anyone—if you were going to smoke dope, you had to do it in the back of the bus.[1] A few hours later, on the mound, Peters ingratiated himself to Bouton even more. "First game," Peters recalled, "he's doing okay. He's in a little trouble about the fifth inning, so I go out to the mound. And he says, 'Don't take me out,' and I said, 'Listen, Jim. You won twenty games for the Yankees; you pitched in the World Series. If you want to come out of this game, you tell *me* when you want to come out. I just came out to say hello.'" A little while later Bouton turned to Peters and said, "You know, this is the first time baseball's really made sense."

He walked off the mound a winner, a 5–3 complete-game victory over Walla Walla in front of a packed house in Civic Stadium. He admitted that he was a little nervous beforehand: "You always have those nightmares," he said. "A walk, a single, an error and then a home run and you're down 4–0 with nobody out."[2] Instead, it was more like the dream he'd dreamed when he decided to give professional baseball another shot. The first hitter he faced whiffed badly, missing his knuckler by four feet and looking like someone taking after a bumblebee with a flyswatter. The crowd roared. Between innings the PA announcer called out the names of those in the stands who had won autographed copies of *Ball Four*. After the final out he flew back to New York, where he stayed only a week before announcing that he was taking another leave, this time to return to Portland to finish out the season with the Mavericks.

His dream ended the dream of at least one Maverick—Larry Colton. Because the Northwest League had a rule that each club could have no more than one player with big-league experience on its roster, Colton, who had appeared in one game with the Phils in 1968, had to be released in order for Russell to sign Bouton. Even though he was the cleanup hitter at the time and was hitting an even .300, his career ended the day Bouton was signed. "Bouton coming to play with the Mavericks turned out to be a defining moment in my life," Colton says, "because I then wrote an article about playing for the Mavericks that the *Oregonian* bannered at the top of the front page." This launched Colton's writing career, which included a nomination for the Pulitzer Prize for Nonfiction. The first interview he ever did was with the man who replaced him on the roster. "When I was doing my story for the Mavericks, I went to interview Bouton," Colton recalled. "I was kind of nervous. Not because it was Jim Bouton but because I'd never done an interview before. About twenty minutes in he looks at me and goes, 'Are you going to take notes or anything?'"

When Bouton returned to Portland the Mavs were on their way to breaking their own single-season attendance record, which they smashed with him on the mound a couple of weeks later in an 8–1 victory over Seattle.[3] Along the way Bouton found a kindred soul in Rob Nelson, the pied piper of South African baseball. They had met before, after Nelson contacted him in 1973 seeking advice as to how to throw a knuckleball. "I was up in Ithaca, going to graduate school," Nelson said. "I contacted Jim because I had one good year in college and I didn't have the goods to be a big-league pitcher and I was working on a knuckleball. I contacted him and told him that I didn't have much of a future in baseball, but maybe the knuckleball was my ticket." Bouton gave Nelson his number at WABC and told him to contact him. Nelson did, and they agreed to meet at Bouton's house where, for a half hour, Jim taught him how to throw the knuckler. "He had nine out of ten that danced like butterflies. I had one out of ten."

They had more than the knuckleball in common. Bouton was fascinated by Nelson's degree in philosophy as well as his time in South Africa, given his own work on the Olympic boycott movement in '68. "He was intrigued that I had played baseball in South Africa," Nelson remembered, "and he was interested in the politics there, along with the quality of the baseball." Jim asked if he knew Dennis Brutus (Nelson didn't) and wanted to know why Nelson would go to South Africa, given the presence of apartheid. "I said I had a chance to teach school, and I wanted to see the world. I was curious about the world and had a team there that was willing to give me the ball every Saturday." It was more than that, though. He had started up the South African Baseball Federation and was putting together a squad of former college players to tour the country and give baseball clinics. The idea behind the federation was for the players to play as a team—the American Eagles—for a series of exhibitions and then to split off in pairs to join local clubs for a year. They would also be required to focus on Little League–aged youngsters—black and white—and act as cultural ambassadors toward a hopefully brighter future. "I wouldn't have gotten involved in this program otherwise," he said at the time.[4]

Rob and Jim didn't just talk about world affairs. "Particularly because Bing Russell was such a breath of fresh air, we would talk about how he was an owner who really understood the players and really understood baseball in the sense that it was entertainment. [He understood] that we were putting on a show and that we were all players on a stage." Bouton liked to refer to Russell's creation as the "Battered Bastards of Baseball"[5] and himself as their patron saint—the baseball lifer who went his own way and wouldn't take no for an answer. After Nelson was cut from the Mavs, he stuck around by creating the "Little Mavericks Baseball School." After a time the Mavs reconsidered and offered Nelson a spot in their bullpen. It was an acknowledgment that while he might not have the talent to play professional ball, by refusing to walk away after being cut he obviously had the heart of a Maverick. It was only right that they make it official.

Now a permanent member of the club, Bouton fitted right in. That didn't mean that the other players weren't just a little in awe of him. "He was a celebrity and a big deal," Nelson said. Not only that, but he had made it and could talk about what it was like in the big leagues, although he didn't hold that over their heads. In the end he was like them—just a guy playing for the love of the game and chasing his dream. Soon he decided that he wanted the left-handed catcher who at the time wasn't doing much beyond protecting Peters from his players—Swanson—to be his personal catcher. "To this day I don't know the answer" as to why Bouton wanted Swanson to be his batterymate, Swanson admits. "He was kind of different, and I was real different," so maybe it wasn't any more than that. "Bouton loved him," Peters remembered. "Whenever Bouton pitched he'd say 'I want to pitch to Swannie,' so, shit, Swannie was Bouton's boy."

Swanson recalled a pitcher who survived more on guile than anything else. "He threw his knuckleball and it wasn't that good, but he was getting people out." As a battery they worked to intimidate the A-ball hitters, most of them teenagers. "All the young guys knew about him and talked about him," Swanson said. "That's Jim Bouton, who played for the Yankees," was the conversation, and now they were digging in against him. Swanson capitalized on that awe whenever he could. When a batter stepped in Swanson would start working on him. "That's Jim Bouton," he'd say. "He used to play for the Yankees. He played with all the big boys, and he really throws hard." Then he would toss a soft knuckler their way, and they'd swing out of their shoes.

He got along with pretty much everybody, even Reggie Thomas. "Reggie Thomas and Jim Bouton—those two players personified the Mavericks," Peters believed. They couldn't have come from more different backgrounds, but on the Mavs, they shared a commonality:

"They had both been rejected." In the end, "one went one way and one went the other." Which was how most things went in life. The Mavs weren't about guarantees and promises but about opportunities and last chances. This created a bond between them that other Northwest League clubs couldn't hope to match.

Bouton finished the season 4-1 with a 2.20 ERA, helping the Mavs to a division title and the Northwest League finals. He then returned to WCBS and resumed his sportscasting gig. A few months later the arbitration hearing that would change the economics of baseball forever got under way, and he was pulled into it via the book that couldn't help but remain in the headlines, *Ball Four*. Dodger pitcher Andy Messersmith and Expos pitcher Dave McNally had played the 1975 season without signing their contracts, which meant that, pursuant to the reserve clause present in every player's contract, their 1974 contracts were automatically renewed "for one year," according to clause 10A of the Uniform Player Contract. The issue Messersmith, McNally, and MLBPA executive director Marvin Miller were pressing was whether "one year" meant what it said—one additional year, nothing more. Kuhn and the owners, on the other hand, insisted that "one year" meant, essentially, "in perpetuity," which was how their reserve clause had operated for nearly a century by that point.

There was more to the case than the contractual language, however, as Miller and the Players Association's attorney Richard Moss were determined to show independent arbitrator Peter Seitz that baseball, itself, had been perpetuating a plantation system for decades, to the detriment of the players and unjust enrichment of the owners. In order to make their case, Moss called Bouton to the stand (he was one of only three witnesses to testify on their behalf) to impress upon Seitz the inequalities inherent in the reserve system and the cruelty management could impose upon the players simply because the reserve system permitted it.[6]

Although Bouton has always maintained that he had no agenda in writing *Ball Four* beyond showing fans the fun of a life in baseball, he

THE BATTERED BASTARD OF BASEBALL 245

would at times admit that, yes, he also wanted to lay bare the meanness and pettiness of management when it came to contract negotiations in an effort to bolster the then nascent Players Association. Now was his chance. "I think the proudest thing I have about *Ball Four* is that [the book] was accepted as evidence at the arbitration hearing," he later said. It wasn't just the book that was so important, but his method in creating it. He had saved all of his notes—the anecdotes, stories, quotes, jotted down on air-sickness bags, hotel stationery, whatever. The 978 sheets. "That was probably the most damning evidence against the owners," he said, those "contemporaneous notes. It wasn't somebody's memory. These were the original notes."[7] They were incriminatory, demonstrating—in real time—the cruelty of a system where owners could act like ogres and players had no choice other than to accept the abuse or walk away from the game.

Walking into the arbitration as one of Kuhn's lawyers, Lou Hoynes knew there was going to be trouble. Two years earlier Seitz had heard Catfish Hunter's grievance against Oakland's petty and vindictive owner, Charlie Finley, and even though the issue was unrelated to the one he was now deciding, Hoynes understood what Moss was doing by calling Bouton to the stand and that things did not bode well because of it. "Charlie Finley was the epitome of a bad owner," Hoynes said, and through his obnoxious behavior throughout the Hunter arbitration hearing, Finley had given Seitz a view of ownership that told him that something had to change. "Finley caused Seitz to come at the system from a different bent" than the one the owners had presented to the public for decades. "And," Hoynes recalled with a laugh, "Finley was bent." Now, with the introduction into evidence of Bouton's notes, along with passages from the book itself, everything Finley had suggested that was typical of the owners two years earlier was now confirmed to Seitz. "*Ball Four* humanized the players on the other side of the table," Hoynes said, finishing the job Finley started by turning the images of the owners and the players upside down.

From the day Marvin Miller assumed the helm of the Players Association in 1966, a top priority of his was to find ways to better articulate the plight of the players to the public. He was hired to guide the Players Association in its labor battles with management but understood that before he could make much headway at the bargaining table, he had to win in the court of public opinion. So long as most fans viewed the players as privileged and pampered, and the owners as benevolent public servants, he would never be able to obtain the leverage necessary to force the owners to concede anything. Slowly, Miller was able to convince the players to take up their own cause, and then, first through *Ball Four* and then through Curt Flood's battle to take down the game's antitrust exemption, he was able to present to the public a different portrait of their heroes than they had ever seen before. Through their work Jim Bouton and Curt Flood made the players human to the fans, showing them that the men they idolized were working stiffs just like they were—guys who struggled to pay their bills, manage their lives, and were bullied by a powerful governing structure that seemed to exist solely to enrich management at the expense of their employees. By 1975 Hoynes realized that Miller had succeeded brilliantly. "By that time," Hoynes remembers, "we [Kuhn and the owners] were just buying time. Just trying to hang on to what we had until the path forward became a little clearer as to how to work things out."

They would not have the luxury of that time. "If we just could have hung on a little longer," Hoynes says, "we probably would have ended up with some sort of a salary cap like the NBA or the NFL has." Too late. "I'm sure the owners wish [now] they had raised that minimum [salary] and meal money" back when the players asked for such minor concessions in the '60s, Bouton would say later. "If they had, they wouldn't have heard a peep out of the players."[8] But they didn't, and now, staring down an energized players union and forced to argue their case in front of an arbitrator who, through the words and deeds of Jim Bouton and Charlie Finley, viewed the players with sympathy and the owners with scorn, they really had no chance. The arbitration was technically about nothing more than a single clause in the Uniform Player Contract, but in truth it was about so much more than that. On Christmas Eve 1975 Seitz announced his decision. Messersmith had won. McNally had won. Marvin Miller had won. Jim Bouton had won. The reserve clause was, for all practical purposes, dead. Once the technicalities were worked out the players would be eligible for free agency at last, free to shop their talents on the open market for the first time in nearly a century. There was no other way to look at it—the owners had been handed a complete and total defeat.

The next morning Kuhn fired Peter Seitz.

29   *Gilligan's Island* in Baseball Suits

Even after it became clear that *Ball Four* was not going to make it to the big screen, Bouton pressed forward, hoping to translate it to another medium. He considered turning it into a musical and unleashing it on Broadway and flirted with the idea for decades, but by the mid-1970s television was king and the sitcom ascendant, with shows such as CBS's *All in the Family* and *M*A*S*H* showing that it was possible to create a program that was funny, sharp, and poignant all at once. *Ball Four* the television show would fit right into that burgeoning oeuvre, he thought. After seeking counsel from his neighbor Hawkeye Pierce himself (Alan Alda was an Englewood resident as well), who thought the idea might very well work,[1] he approached a Chipmunk friend and Lion's Head compatriot, Vic Ziegel of the *Post*, who pitched the idea to Marvin Kitman, the TV critic at *Newsday*. Soon, the three of them were sitting together in a room, scratching their heads and trying to figure out how to turn the book into baseball's answer to *M*A*S*H* and Bouton's character into something resembling Hawkeye Pierce in a jockstrap.

"I knew nothing about baseball," Kitman says, "but I knew about television, the way it worked, about management and how they go about selecting pilots." He wasn't a fan of most local sportscasters, but he liked Bouton from the moment he first caught him on air at WABC. Al Primo's Eyewitness News team seemed, to Kitman, "like an old-age home for professional athletes," he recalled, but Bouton was different. "I don't think I had even read *Ball Four* at the time, but I used to do a lot of columns on Jim because he would do offbeat things. He was unlike the usual jocks they had on television at that time, who were always proestablishment. He was an antiestablishment guy. Howard Cosell would say that he was 'telling it like it is,' but he really wasn't doing it." Bouton was skewering broadcasting *as he was broadcasting*, revealing hidden truths about the medium even as he was reporting through it, all of which intrigued and delighted Kitman. An antiestablishment, subtly subversive show on a major network seemed like something that could be a lot of fun.

Of the three only Kitman had any real knowledge of television, and that was from pressing his nose up against the window. Now they had to put together a treatment that would entice a network executive to green-light a pilot. They had decided that the logical network to focus on was CBS because Bouton already worked at their local affiliate and because the network was having success with smart comedies (they were also currently airing *The Mary Tyler Moore Show* and *The Bob Newhart Show*). Their *Ball Four* program might seem to CBS to be a natural extension of what was currently working for them, the three hoped. Beyond that they had no idea what they were doing. "The usual treatment for a television series was about four pages," Kitman recalled, "because these executives can barely read English, and they certainly didn't want anything long to read." By the time the three of them were finished with their treatment, it ran to eighty-four pages. It went into depth describing each character and meticulously detailed how specific scenes from the book would translate onto the screen. The morning they completed it Kitman had it delivered to CBS's vice president in charge of comedy, Alan Wagner, "a humorless guy," Kitman recalled, who nevertheless was entrusted with the job of determining what was funny to the CBS eye.

At that point tradition dictated that you waited to hear back from the network, perhaps in a week, perhaps in a month. Bouton wasn't one to bow to tradition, though. "By that afternoon Jim was on the phone to Wagner," Kitman remembered, "asking him what he thought of his eighty-four-page treatment. I was astounded by this because it violated all the rules." Then he realized that he hadn't signed on to work with just anybody; he was now working with the Bulldog—a guy whose hat flew off whenever he pitched and who assumed the ready position as soon as he released the ball, seemingly daring it to come his way. He was different. He was tenacious. He wouldn't be content with his dreams; he had to turn them into reality. Network television was perhaps a new medium for him, but his approach wouldn't waver. He would bowl over anybody in front of him until he got where he saw himself going. Alan Wagner didn't stand a chance. "It seemed like, in nanoseconds, the guy had read it and had put it through the works there," Kitman said. "By the end of the week, they had decided to make the pilot."

The treatment didn't hide the fact that there had never been a successful sports-themed show, which should have given the risk-averse network executives pause. But it then argued in its eighty-four pages that this was because none of the previous attempts had made any effort to show the human side of the game. *Ball Four* the television show would do that, they said. On the surface it would be a baseball show, but, really, it would be a human comedy. It would be groundbreaking television in that it would not shy away from sensitive topics such as drugs in sports and women in the locker room—topics that would go on to dominate sports headlines in the following decades but that were at the time verboten. It would also feature a gay player as a regular character, something network television wouldn't touch until 1977, when the ABC show *Soap* broke that barrier.[2] Every week it would offer the audience something to think about once it was finished laughing.

It was a heavy burden to assume and would have been difficult to pull off under even the best of circumstances. Right away, though, it was clear that these were not going to be the best of circumstances. "They wanted the character playing Jim Bouton to be played by Jim Bouton," said Kitman. "And Jim was such an egoist he didn't object. Theoretically, who could better be Jim Bouton than Jim Bouton? Well, now the problems began, because Jim Bouton is not Laurence Olivier or even Jerry Seinfeld. He's Jim Bouton." He had started taking acting lessons with Lee Strasberg in the hope of transforming himself into the next Alan Alda.[3] If anything, the lessons only set him back. As an actor he could be awkward because he was untrained, but, as he showed in *The Long Goodbye*, he had a natural charm that overcame that. Strasberg's instruction scrubbed away the awkwardness but also much of the charm that went with it, replacing it with a woodenness that was hard to watch. "He was a natural," Kitman remembered, "because he was a funny guy, he had been on television, and was really charming in his boyish way. Without the lessons at least he would have been Jim Bouton." With them he was just another bad actor.

On top of that he had simply put too much of the show on his own shoulders. He was working on scripts during the day, going to acting school at night, and rehearsing with the other actors as they were hired whenever he could fit that in. Once shooting started his schedule became only more hectic. He had a finger in every part of the production, recalled Marco St. John, who played the ballplayer Rayford Plunkett on the show. "He wasn't just a sports figure. He was the lead of the series who had written the book upon which the series was based. So he was always talking to this one and that one. . . . Jim was a little different. Most people only do one thing. Jim wanted to do everything. He was an unusual fellow." In the middle of it all Bobbie confronted him when she suspected he might be having an affair. "There were a lot of attractive young women around," she recalled, "and Jim was working with one, and I was a little concerned about that relationship. But he assured me that there was nothing to it, that she had a boyfriend, and they were just friendly."

The whole process was complicated and confusing, with the key players being pulled in multiple directions practically from the start. Kitman decided that even though he was now a television producer, he was going to keep his column as a television critic. "I'm kind of hoping I can do a criticism of the show as well as write it," he said at the time. "I know how great a show it was originally and what CBS has already done to ruin it."[4] Ziegel as well kept his column, which meant that he was constantly being torn away from the writers' room to meet a deadline at the *Post*. And on top of everything else Bouton was still harboring dreams of returning to the big leagues. When he got home after shooting he'd pitch to a friend for an hour or so in order to keep his arm in shape, and on his morning drive in to the studio he would often navigate the George Washington Bridge with his left hand while doing strength exercises by working a steel ball in his right.

In the run-up to the show's premiere everybody said the right things, but they knew they were headed for disaster. Bouton said that he hoped his show would "reach new heights and breakthroughs in terms of grossness" and joked that he hoped the big shots at CBS would pull a Bowie Kuhn by criticizing everything about the show and admonishing viewers not to watch it, thereby guaranteeing huge ratings.[5] But the problems with the show ran deep and, in Bouton's and Kitman's opinions, flowed from the top. Bouton, Kitman, and Ziegel were looking to do something new and different, but, despite the breakout successes of *All in the Family* and *M*A*S*H*, network executives had a mortal fear of originality. They employed producers and scores of minions who failed over and over but who engendered trust simply because they had a track record in network television. It didn't matter that the track record was poor. All that mattered was that this wasn't their first time on a soundstage.

The producer overseeing *Ball Four*, Don Segall, was a case in point. He came to the show with something of a track record but was certainly not a rule breaker, or even bender. Originality was simply not in his wheelhouse. Instead, he could be counted on by the network higher-ups to deliver pretty much what had been delivered before. And they loved and rewarded him for that. "Don was a really sweet, lovely man," remembered Jill Baer, who worked on the show. "But he was a very old-school sitcom guy." He hired some old-school gag writers to fill out his writing staff, a couple of whom wrote for Bob Hope and Milton Berle back in the day. They occupied the same writers' room as younger talent such as Greg Antonacci, who would later work on *The Sopranos* and *Boardwalk Empire*. The younger generation would push for a smarter, edgier show but would repeatedly be overruled by Segall and the older writers, who were convinced they knew best because they knew what had come before.

"Originality was a moon shot," Kitman said. "Every once in a while a show like *All in the Family* would find that opening, and suddenly there was something new and different. But what would happen then was that, instead of building on the idea of expanding the opening, they would all imitate *All in the Family*. They would all then have people in living rooms shouting at each other." *Ball Four* was a big book that broke ground in a major way, but to the network executives, none of that mattered. Instead, they were interested in taking little more than the idea of the book and fitting it into the stale sitcom formula they had been foisting upon the public for years.

Bouton assumed that because he had not only written the book but was the star as well as one of the producers his vision would prevail, but because he was an outsider in the world of network television he was routinely pushed aside. "He may have felt that gave him a lot of leeway to do whatever he wanted," St. John said, but the network honchos didn't see it that way. "In dealing with the networks, you're dealing with executives who know it all," Kitman said. "These are people who probably knew only twenty-five letters of the alphabet and whose only writing experience might be shopping lists. They made themselves the experts. They were editing the scripts we were writing, but the thing with these people is that there were set rules in television comedy—they knew how comedies were supposed to work, ignoring the fact that the airwaves were filled with failures." "There were many vice presidents," Bouton recalled of the activity buzzing in and out of the writers' room every day. "None of whom could write, but they could 'help.'"[6] Most of their help revolved around sanding down every original idea until it resembled the ones they had seen before.

Their script notes in particular drove him nuts. Should the word *tarpaulin* be used because some people might not know what that is? Could they change the locker-room language to something a prime-time audience would be more comfortable with? Could they not use the phrase "pissed off"? Bouton rolled his eyes and suggested "irrigated off" before dropping the idea altogether. For some reason CBS had decided to slot the show at 8:30 p.m. on Wednesdays, between

Good Times and *All in the Family* and opposite *The Bionic Woman* on ABC—right smack in the middle of what was then known as the "family hour." That alone meant that there would be no discussion of greenies, no genuine discussion of the issues surrounding gay ballplayers (Standards and Practices even forbade any explicit acknowledgment that the player was gay), no salty language, nothing controversial. What it meant above all else was that there was no way *Ball Four* the television show would bear any resemblance to *Ball Four* the groundbreaking book.

The pilot was a disaster, and at that point the network execs stopped deferring to Bouton's vision even a little. They swooped in and assumed even firmer control over the process, ignoring the book altogether. They made the show sunnier and, therefore, something closer in spirit to the Chip Hilton books Jim read as a child. Whereas in the book Bouton failed in his attempt to become the club's player representative, in the show his character—Jim Barton—not only is nominated by his teammates but wins the election.[7] Worse, the show was filled with dumb jokes and sloppy sight gags. Rather than work to elevate the show's tone and structure, the network execs were obsessed with finding a put-down phrase that would rival *Welcome Back Kotter*'s "Up your nose with a rubber hose."[8] Writing sessions would last far into the night, to the point where everyone in the room was so tired that even the stupidest things would seem hilarious and end up in the scripts. Quality became a fly ball lost in the sun. The show devolved from a searing social satire to *Gilligan's Island* in baseball suits.[9]

At that point Ziegel quit, Kitman began focusing more on his *Newsday* column, and Bouton was completely ignored.[10] He'd rail against the script changes, upset that an exec had tinkered with his words, to no avail. "He wrote the book," St. John said, "and that's a big deal. They gotta pay some heed to whatever he's saying." But they didn't, and that would piss him off. One aspiring writer witnessed firsthand the extent to which Bouton was being shunted aside. She didn't have much experience but was brought in, Bouton told her, "to rewrite the rotten scripts turned in by writers with credits." He told her to come up with a story on baseball groupies, one that would expose the Jim Barton character's double standard—preaching for women's rights on the one hand but then going off the rails when he learned that his girlfriend was fooling around on him when he wasn't around, just as he was on her. She produced the script, which was then rejected by the show's story editor as being too risqué. Wasn't that precisely what Bouton wanted? she asked him. "Jim goes off on tangents," the editor told her. "You have to learn how to cut through them."[11] In other words, pay no attention to anything he was saying.

Once the network execs tightened their grip on the show, any hope of its becoming anything other than one more lowbrow mid-1970s comedy nightmare was permanently dashed. The execs became a regular presence on the set and would sit in a row in the studio as a type of bizarre network appellate court, passing judgment on pretty much anything and everything they saw. "Executives are not usually creative thinkers," Baer said. "They're corporate thinkers: 'How is this going to affect our sponsors?' They're not thinking, 'Oh, this is great, we need to keep this in there.'" They weren't there to make the show better. They were there to make sure it didn't damage the network brand. "They thought they were regulating our morality," Baer added. "They were probably excited to be around [Bouton] because he was such an important New York personality and was magnetic. But at the same time they probably found him threatening. . . . He was a freethinker. Nobody was going to tell him what to think, and he was going to say what he thought. That's very threatening."

The show was missing many things, but what hurt it the most was the absence of a Lenny Shecter–like figure to take control of the morass of a project and shape it into a cohesive whole. Ziegel and Kitman were, from the outset, too distracted to fight for their vision, and Bouton had his hands in too many pots to be able to step back and see how it all fit together. He had no shortage of stories that would have translated to network television to create a transformative show, but without a fully engaged partner with the skill and power to mold his raw material into a compelling narrative, he was left with the equivalent of his shoe box of funny anecdotes written on air-sickness bags that, when left to the network dullards, were simply piled one on top of the other in numbing succession. Baseball's Lennon missed his McCartney.

The show limped toward the airwaves and then bombed spectacularly. Ziegel knew what was coming, writing to Shecter's widow, Ginny: "I think it's a stinker. Len, I'm sure, would have felt the same." The morning after the show's September premiere, *New York Times* skewered it as "a collection of bare-chested athletic types playing desperately for laughs," noting that, above everything else, Bouton was "a dreadful actor." *Variety* wrote that it was "certainly headed for early replacement" and noted that Bouton's "delivery is as limp as overcooked pasta." The *Washington Post* remarked that even the 1962 Mets had more baseball credibility, and provided more humor, than the *Ball Four* TV show: "Embarrassment should redden [Bouton's] cheeks every Wednesday night when 'Ball Four' flickers onto the TV screen. Because no matter how brave he was to stand up to the Neanderthals of baseball with his book, Bouton is a wimp as an actor." The *Chicago Tribune* concluded that the show was so amateurish that it "makes 'Welcome Back Kotter' look like wry wit by comparison," and in a column syndicated across the country, a United Press International review declared the show a "megaton bomb." Looking back on it, Bouton hated pretty much everything about the process of putting together a show within the constraints of 1970s network television but, even so, was able to find a silver lining: "It was so much fun just to sit there and fail at a very high level."[12]

In all six episodes were shot, with only five airing before CBS pulled the plug. Rather than retool the show on the fly, the network execs panicked and abandoned it. "They threw us away quickly because it was a sports show," St. John believes, "and sports shows didn't have a good record. They weren't as popular as westerns or crime shows." Once this sports show started dragging down the ratings of the shows that bookended it, that was enough for CBS to walk away from it. The irony of it all was that now that he had failed in network television, Bouton probably could have had made this his career now if he so wanted.

"A track record of failure in television was much better than success in other fields," Kitman said. Now that he had a track record—he had been on cbs, with a major show wedged between two bona fide hits—he "could have gone to work in Hollywood, could have had a career in television, doing failure after failure, because that's how television worked." The execs ignored the author of the groundbreaking book, but the more he would have worked in television, the more they would have heeded the words of the multi-time network television failure. Television executives, it turned out, weren't all that different from baseball executives. Bouton wanted no part of either of them.

The writer in him couldn't walk away as easily, though. There was a book in this, a *Ball Four* of television. He and Kitman secured an advance from Doubleday to write it and, in order to enhance the authenticity of the project, stole one of the show's teleprompters with the idea of using it to write the manuscript. They got about halfway through a draft until they became distracted by their real passions— Kitman by his five *Newsday* columns per week and Bouton by his burning desire to return to baseball—and they returned the advance.

Within a few years television would change. By the end of the decade the medium had grown so stale that even a few network execs started to question why they were listening so much to the people who brought them one rotten show after another. Younger talent, lacking track records but not smart, challenging, and fresh ideas, started to gain a foothold, and shows like *Taxi*, *Cheers*, and *Hill Street Blues* began appearing on prime-time schedules. It is tantalizing to imagine what *Ball Four* the tv show would have looked like had it been developed by a visionary like Steven Bochco, who finally brought integrity to television in the 1980s and was writing *Columbo* scripts and producing interesting but little-watched shows while *Ball Four* was drowning in the swamp of sitcom cliché. *Ball Four* the tv show was ultimately a mess, but one could argue that, unlike the book it was based on, it, or at least the idea of it, arrived on the scene too soon. It didn't capture the zeitgeist; it anticipated it, at a time when the networks were run by people too afraid of change to allow it to become for television what the book became for sports literature. In the end, while timing may not be everything, it's a helluva lot, so while the book exploded on the scene at the precise moment its audience was ready for it, the show just smoldered on the side of the road, stalled out, a smoking mess on the shoulder, many miles and a few years ahead of the road crew.

30   Too Old, Too Everything

If hope springs eternal in the ordinary human breast, in Bouton's it is able to leap tall buildings in a single bound. Almost as soon as his show was canceled he was on the phone looking for a place to resume his comeback in 1977. He gave the official word to WCBS that he was through, giving up the $65,000 yearly salary to chase what seemed to be an impossible dream. When asked why he answered simply: "Winning is great, but the next best thing is losing."[1] He always considered himself a warrior, and as he liked to say, warriors don't bow out gracefully. Expecting that they would "is like expecting Spartacus to move on to gardening."[2] This was not the end of something, he liked to say, invoking, as always, Hoyt Wilhelm and his retirement at age forty-nine whenever the opportunity presented itself; it might just be the beginning. Given Wilhelm as a barometer, he could very well have another eleven seasons in him. On the surface it was all very inspiring, but every so often he would allow something else to bubble up that cast a darker shade. "Of course, the minors are not as good as the majors, but the question to me is whether the minors are better than much of the rest of life. And to me, they are."[3]

He didn't find any takers. "He's too old. He's too everything," said the Brewers' director of baseball operations. "We need him like we need a hole in the head."[4] After burning through his Rolodex, he decided to pay his own way to spring training and do the only thing left to do: beg for a tryout. He finally found a sympathetic ear in Chicago White Sox owner Bill Veeck, who had spent his life as a baseball huckster and figured, what the hell, what's another gimmick? He'd signed a three-foot-seven pinch hitter back when he owned the old St. Louis

Browns, so why not a thirty-eight-year-old knuckleballer who'd been out of the big leagues for six seasons? Veeck was impressed enough to offer Bouton a spot on his Knoxville AA roster at $1,500 a month. "I just can't wait for that first bus ride," Bouton said, "the first bowl of chili at a roadside stop. Do you realize how much fun it is again to be putting on the old jockstrap, the sanitary hose, the spikes?"[5]

The older you get, though, the more expensive your dreams become. Without his broadcasting income he could no longer afford the house in Englewood, which was paid for largely through the royalties from *Ball Four*. Now he was, in effect, taking the *Ball Four* money, which hastened his exit from organized baseball, to finance his return to it. The house would have to be sold, something he was fine with but that promised to be hell on Bobbie and the kids. (He had initially tried to hold on to the house by securing a loan to finance his comeback but couldn't find a bank that would take that risk.)[6] They would all be downsizing, but while he would be chasing his dream, the rest of them would just be living in a smaller house. The house sold for $125,000, and they moved into one costing only $75,000.[7] The extra $50,000 would become the sticker price for his dream. When the bills kept on coming and that ran out, he cashed in his children's college funds and sold a lakeside vacation home.[8]

He could get testy when asked about whether it was worth it to put his family through all of this. "Look, it's not like I sold a $20,000 house and put my family in a shack. We went from a $125,000 house to a $75,000 house, and as I keep telling the kids, there's still food in the refrigerator." They may no longer have their stereos, but they still had their bicycles. And it could be beneficial to the kids to see the old man struggle for a change, he said. Not everything in life was easy; they would now see that with their own eyes. "Anyway, I can spend my own money the way I want to." Bobbie reluctantly went along because as she saw it, there was no real alternative. Her husband was miserable, and, fingers and toes crossed, this might bring him out of it. Nothing else seemed to be able to do the trick. It was going to be tough on her, but, as she said the following year, "whether or not what

Jim is doing is fair to me or the children doesn't matter, because for now, he's doing what I want him to do."[9]

He got himself into terrific shape, cutting out sugar and white flour from his diet, and dropped twenty pounds from his old playing weight. He ate mainly fresh fruit and vegetables, whole grains, fish, and chicken. To strengthen his fingernails he began downing *schav*, a staple of Lower East Side Jewish families for aeons, consisting of sorrel, egg yolks, water, radishes, cucumbers, and scallions.[10] It looked like pond scum but came with mythical healing properties, rivaling only chicken soup in many Jewish households. Good enough for him. He wasn't taking any chances.

On May 5 he took the mound as a member of an affiliated Minor League franchise for the first time since Oklahoma City in August 1970 and was impressive. He threw only knuckleballs—ninety-two in a row—and lasted seven innings. Ninety of them danced like Baryshnikov; two flopped over heavy, like watermelons in grocery sacks, and were hit out of the park. He lost the game 3–1. It would be downhill from there. He gave up three more homers in his next start, which he also lost, and then, on Jim Bouton Day in Knoxville, managed to keep the Columbus Clippers in the park while still losing once again. By the end of May he was 0-5, and increasingly it was the short game, not the long ball, that was his undoing—hitters were bunting off of him with regularity, testing the old man's legs. In one start against the Jacksonville Suns, four of their eight hits were bunts, including two squeeze bunts.[11] His knuckler was floating and easy to deaden. After being hammered in his next start, he was knocked from the rotation. A week later, after failing as a reliever, he was released. "When you're throwing a knuckleball," he told a reporter upon his release, "95 out of 100 have to be right. If you get only 85 out of 100, the 15 that miss are going to turn into eight triples, five doubles and a home run or two."[12]

Once again he pulled out the Rolodex and called around. This time, though, he wasn't a curiosity but a thirty-eight-year-old pitcher with an 0-6 record in AA ball. If the reaction to him earlier was tepid, now it was frosty. American baseball seemed to be speaking as one with each hang-up, so Bouton did what would seem logical only to a dreamer—he pivoted south to catch on with a club in the Mexican League. He found a taker in the Durango Alacranes. With that the Boutons packed up and headed off to Mexico.

The logistics of the move, if only for the summer, were complicated. "That was an experience," Bobbie remembered, "getting the visa for the cat, and all. And then Laurie got sick, running a fever." Bobbie snuck Columbus the cat (never was a cat more appropriately named) on the plane in a box wrapped in a pillowcase and then, once in Mexico, found out that there was no such thing as kitty litter there. This necessitated regular scouting visits to construction sites and cigarette ashtrays, where she would swipe sand for Columbus's litter box. "It was tough," she said, "and it was tough getting around. We didn't have a car so we took the buses. Shopping in the grocery store was tricky because I didn't know what the cuts of meat were." She had one year of high school Spanish and remembered little more than a few numbers and colors, so she made sure not to leave the house without her English–Spanish dictionary.

On the day of Bouton's first start in Mexico, there was more than a whiff of despair wafting through the league. John "Blue Moon" Odom, formerly a starting pitcher on the three-time World Champion Oakland A's, was himself trying to find a way back to the bigs in Mexico, starting his initial game in Mexico City. He, too, seemed to be a man attempting to outrun his limitations, having just been released by San Jose in the Pacific Coast League and out of options in American baseball.[13] On this day at least, despair prevailed, as both *desperados* won. Bouton went eight innings and pitched well, giving up seven hits and three runs before tiring.

Despite being in outstanding physical condition, the high altitude of Durango (sixty-two hundred feet—a thousand feet higher than Denver) left him gasping for air; he had trouble making it through his starts. Still, before tiring he was pitching well, although he mostly found himself on the losing side of the ledger. "I've proved to myself that I still can pitch and I know that I can go back to the major leagues as a reliever," he said after another loss.[14] And, aside from a nightmarish evening when, with Jim out of town, Laurie contracted strep throat and ran a high fever, leaving Bobbie at her wit's end without a car, telephone, or facility with the language, the experience was a positive one overall. "The kids got along and played with the kids in the neighborhood," Bobbie remembered. "They did well down there. They adjusted." They particularly loved going to the ballpark to watch their father pitch. The experience was like nothing they'd ever seen. "They'd have a doubleheader," Bobbie recalled, "and between games there'd be a bullfight." The cheering was different; the foods were exotic; the whole experience was immersive and transformative. Despite the inevitable bumps in the road, Bobbie thought that traveling with the kids was beneficial to them. "I always thought [it] was a good educational experience for them, and I didn't worry if I had to take them out of school for a while because I figured they were learning things and it was good for them." She took books along and would read to them, providing the context for what they were experiencing. "Jim would read to them, too. He was good that way." The kids kept journals documenting what they were seeing and experiencing, drawing pictures of the sights. "The kids learned a lot."

Education wasn't the point of the excursion, though. Baseball was, and no matter how good he felt about his performances, he kept losing ball games. After he lost his fourth straight, he was released and found himself out of baseball once again. Before July turned to August the Boutons were packing up and heading back to the States. When they arrived home they were nearly penniless. Bobbie emptied the kids' bank accounts to pay for groceries, while Jim searched around again for a team that would have him.[15]

Faced with the stark choice of abandoning his dream and running back to wcbs for the paycheck that would stabilize things or embracing it to the end, he played his final card. After a phone call he was back on a plane on his way to Portland, to suit up once more for the only professional club on the North American continent that would have him. The Mavericks, says Rob Nelson with a puff of pride, existed just to exist. Just to survive. Everybody associated with the club knew that it was the bottom of the barrel and that the next stop after Portland was a bartending gig. This ignominious reality didn't hang over them like grim death but, rather, was something they wore as a badge of honor. They were here. They were surviving. So fuck off. Now Bouton was here with them again. In a way he was never more at home during this time in his life than when he was at the ballpark in Portland.

If few people could understand his motivation at this point, Bing Russell was one of them. "He's just a boy," he said at the time. "He'll always be a boy."[16] Boys play baseball; they don't put on a sports coat and read the 11:00 p.m. news. This time around, Bouton, along with everyone else on the Mavs, would be receiving $400 a month, a raise that signaled loud and clear that nobody on the club was there for the paycheck. He still enjoyed playing, he said upon his return. But more than that he felt he was on the verge of finding the knuckler and figuring out the magic formula of how and when to use it. "There's always the chance that tomorrow you'll find the right combination. That dream is always there."[17]

The Mavs hadn't changed since his last visit. If anything, they were now even more countercultural, baseball-wise. Right before Bouton arrived the club's "designated sweeper," Joseph Garza, a utility player who was known as "JoGarza" and acted as the team's unofficial mascot—jumping on the dugout with a broom and sweeping away the opposition during a Mavs rally—got a little too into his act, sweeping and riling up the Portland fans while the game was still taking place on the field. He was quickly ejected from the stadium by the league's commissioner, who was on hand and appalled by the lack of decorum. "I warned them last year," he said with a huff. "We're just not going to have that."[18] After Garza was ejected again, Russell grabbed the broom and led a contingent of fans around the warning track in a "victory lap" that was more of a middle finger to the league than anything else.[19]

Bouton's first start was shaky—two wild pitches—but he escaped with a win and a complete game. After winning his next start his third was a disaster. He was shelled for eight runs in the third inning in a game at Eugene that only devolved further after he departed as six Mavs were ejected for "various and sundry reasons," according to *The Sporting News*.[20] Rather than retreat to the clubhouse, he walked off the mound and right into the stands, where he remained, in full uniform, for the remainder of the game. Pete Dreier, a professor at the University of Oregon, who was in the stands that evening with some friends, took this in and wanted to talk to him. His friends laughed at the idea—a former big leaguer just chatting up a local for no reason while the game was on—but he approached Bouton anyway and ended up in a surprisingly deep conversation. "We talked about the players' union, racial segregation in baseball, the war in Vietnam—his opposition to it and how the players weren't all that political and how that made him a fish out of water that way. He was mostly funny, but he had some serious moments," Dreier said. At some point Dreier told him that he was a burgeoning journalist as well and might want to write an article about their in-game conversation, which he thought might shut Bouton down. If anything, it only opened him up more. "He was very up front about stuff," Dreier remembered. "I've done a lot of interviews with politicians and athletes, and they usually censor themselves to make sure they don't say provocative things. In his situation (on a perilous journey back to organized baseball), one would think he might be cautious, but he wasn't and I was quite surprised about that."[21]

He embraced the totality of the Mavericks experience. After surrendering the first professional homer by future big-league slugger Dave Henderson, he waited for Henderson to round the bases and greeted him at home plate. Watching his pitcher extend his hand to Henderson, Swanson, the left-handed catcher, couldn't believe what he was seeing as he was awaiting a new ball from the umpire. "Mr. Henderson," Swanson remembers Bouton saying as a bewildered Henderson tried to absorb what was happening as he touched home plate, "I've played with Mickey Mantle and Roger Maris, and I've never seen a ball hit so hard." Swanson considered decking Bouton on the spot but didn't. Good thing; he didn't give up too many homers after that. He found his groove in Portland, going 5-1 and helping the club to its third straight divisional title. He could still get shelled if his knuckler abandoned him, but when it didn't, he felt as if he could beat anybody, anywhere. "I threw about 20 pitches tonight that no one could have hit," he said after a particularly inspiring effort.[22]

"Following him around was tough," Bobbie recalls. "Man, we were all over. So many different places. Following him around while he was making his comeback was very stressful. At least on me and the kids." Portland was a nice town, but the whole ordeal was hell on the family. Jim tried to ease the financial strain, at least a little, by sublimating his personal beliefs for a moment. He agreed to do a commercial for an Oregon lumber company. "If it's a choice between ravaging the environment and a couple of hundred bucks, I'd take the bucks," he said at the time.[23] Jokingly, but, really, he needed the money and a couple of hundred bucks was a couple of hundred bucks.

31 Magic

After the season Jim and the family returned to New Jersey to await whatever would happen next. What would in fact happen would change all of them for the rest of their lives. The Bloomingdales in Riverside Square in Hackensack, New Jersey, was hosting a hospital fundraiser. "There were a lot of people there with money," Bouton remembered. "Joe DiMaggio was there—heavy hitters, politicians, musicians." And Jim Bouton. Along with Paula Kurman. "I was invited as a courtesy because I had done some seminars there," said Paula. Jim, in his wide-lapeled velvet suit—"It was killer," he remembered—was signing autographs but also scoping out the room. "He was following me from department to department," said Paula. "I was with my wife," said Jim, "and Paula was there with her husband. At some point Paula walks over to me and says, 'I think we're destined to meet.'" "I had never done that in my entire life," she said. "I asked him, 'Why are you signing autographs?' He looked familiar to me," but she couldn't place him. Perhaps they had gone to high school together, she thought. At that point, "my husband [who knew exactly who Jim Bouton was], who was living off my income at the time, said, 'Why don't you introduce yourself because maybe he can help you get into TV?'" With that her soon-to-be ex-husband threw his soon-to-be ex-wife into the arms of her future husband. Robert Lipsyte, who was also at the event and taking in the dynamic, turned to his wife and said, "Uh-oh. Trouble." Jim asked Paula what she was doing at the event, and she told him that she had done some seminars at Bloomingdales on relationship problem solving. After telling Paula that he had a few relationship problems himself that needed solving, he asked for her card. Paula's soon-to-be ex excitedly slapped one of her cards in her hand to give to Jim.

For the next three months Jim would call the number on the card and hang up. "I knew it was him because nobody else was calling that number," Paula recalled. But he was afraid to leave a message. Finally, they spoke, agreeing to meet up for lunch and talk. "We talked about our kids, and then he said he wanted to have an affair," Paula recalls, with a devious smile. "That was too much for me. I said, 'No, I can't do that. But we can be friends.' He said, 'We don't have enough in common to be friends?'" Lunch ended, and each planned to go their separate ways, forever. Before splitting up, "he kissed me on the street corner. And that was it. I was finished. He gets in the cab, and I think it's good-bye because he didn't want my friendship, and now I've changed my mind about the affair." Jim had changed his mind as well, deciding that friendship was better than nothing, so he called Paula and asked her to lunch again. She agreed, but "I didn't tell him on the phone that I had changed my mind, too." After a quick lunch they made plans to meet again, and it was at that third meeting, Paula recalled, "that we really crossed that barrier" from friends into something else.

During these lunches, "one of the first things [Jim] asked me was what was I like as a teenager. Because he wanted to know if I was an outsider also." She was. Always tall for her age, smart and introverted, she was socially behind her classmates because she had been skipped ahead in elementary school. Later, she was a classmate of Suzanne Pleshette at the New York School for the Performing Arts and, like Jim, experienced the sting of not being "good enough" in the eyes of everyone around her. "[Pleshette] was little, she was pretty, she was perky and pert and everything I wasn't. All the boys wanted to date her, and I was tongue-tied all the time." Always on the outside looking in. From there on out they would be on the outside together.

Determined to see his comeback through, Jim plowed ahead, seeking employment for the upcoming 1978 season. There would be one change, though. He would continue his journey alone, something he decided after Bobbie and the kids joined him that February in Florida as he looked for clubs that would give him a tryout. They then turned around and went back to New Jersey. A few months later he admitted to Frank Deford of *Sports Illustrated* that while he felt for Bobbie and the burden he had placed on her to manage the house and the kids while he chased his dream, "I feel a need to be away from my family for a while right now. I need to be by myself at this point in my life."[1] He didn't admit it publicly at the time, but the comeback provided him a measure of cover for his unofficial separation from Bobbie. He could tell the world he was focusing on baseball while using the time to figure things out in his marriage. The cover of an improbable comeback, says Paula, "was his oblique way of describing his unhappy feelings being with her. He wanted to get away from her and the way his life seemed to be going at that time so that he'd be able to think clearly. Baseball and the challenge of a comeback gave him a legitimate way to do that without committing to a decision either to stay or to leave."

He also, and perhaps not coincidentally, had a heightened need for validation, for external affirmation of his worth. "Jim was simply never better as a human being than when he had a uniform on," Chipmunk buddy Vic Ziegel said at the time.[2] He needed the uniform to make him the person he wanted the world to see. The thousands of fans who read the pile of articles written about his comeback, and the millions of viewers who laughed along with him as he charmed the pants off Johnny Carson one evening on *The Tonight Show*, never knew that behind the swagger and the wisecracks stood a man who was utterly adrift.

After being quickly shut down by the expansion Seattle Mariners, whose GM, Lou Gorman, told him that the scouting reports didn't lie and they all said he couldn't pitch anymore, he appeared to be finally out of bullets.[3] Even Portland was no longer a last-ditch option, as the Mavs had been booted from the city and the Northwest League after the AAA Pacific Coast League reclaimed the territory for the 1978 season. There was only one more maverick left in baseball, and that would have to be his last shot. On his own dime he traveled to West Palm Beach to make his case to Ted Turner and the Atlanta Braves.

Turner was appealing for several reasons. First and foremost was the fact that his Braves were terrible; they couldn't afford to look past anybody. They were also one of the few teams in baseball who not only employed a knuckleballer (Phil Niekro), but an aged one at that—Niekro was only three weeks younger than Bouton. Turner himself was only four months older than he was, so if Bouton was old, that would mean that Turner was old, something he would never admit. But most important, Turner hated Bowie Kuhn and was always looking for a way to twist the knife. The two had just gone through a legal battle that arose after Kuhn suspended Turner for a year and took away the Braves' first-round draft choice in 1977 upon a complaint that Turner had perhaps a few too many at an October 1976 cocktail party and bragged to Giants owner Bob Lurie that he would do whatever it took to sign Gary Matthews away from the Giants in the upcoming free-agent signing period. Turner won his case; Kuhn was, as always, righteously indignant about the whole affair, and now here came Jim Bouton—*Ball Four*'s Jim Bouton—looking for a tryout.[4] The opportunity to tweak Kuhn again was too delicious to pass up.

Turner instructed his director of player development, Hank Aaron, to give him a look. Aaron assigned him to their Minor League spring-training camp, where he pitched well. In eleven innings, ten of them were scoreless, and he gave up only five singles in all. Still, Aaron didn't see much need for another thirty-nine-year-old knuckleballer, so he released him. An hour later Bouton was on a plane to Atlanta to plead his case to Turner personally. He told Turner that his eleven innings weren't a fluke, that he had something left, that he was a winner. "He should buy me as a person," he later told a reporter of his meeting.[5] Turner figured, why not? Later, Turner would explain his decision-making process in his own earthy way: "Pitching is like pussy—you can never get enough of it."[6] Turner picked up the phone, called his GM, and ordered him to find a place somewhere in the organization for Jim Bouton.[7] When word got around that Turner had signed him to an unspecified position, reporters wanted to know why. "You never know," Turner told a young Keith Olbermann. "We could be short a guy in the bullpen, or short a guy in the rotation, or short a guy in the broadcast booth."

Eventually, he landed a "job" as a batting-practice pitcher for the Braves' Minor League affiliate in Richmond, Virginia. When Bobbie asked how much the position paid, Jim told her that they hadn't discussed it.[8] Bobbie held her tongue as she continued to drain whatever savings account they had left, as did Aaron—at least for a while, though he privately stewed over being overruled by Turner. Later, Bouton and Aaron would trade barbs, with Aaron calling Bouton a "snake in the grass," after Jim alleged that Aaron didn't put enough time in his job and couldn't even tell one player from another. "I knew he would try to get back at me because I was the one who released him," Aaron said.[9]

He received a warmer reception in Richmond, where the club's GM, Jon Richardson, counted himself a die-hard *Ball Four* fan and a Jim Bouton devotee. Richardson would lend his copy of *I'm Glad You Didn't Take It Personally* to anyone who hadn't read it, considering it, along with *Ball Four*, to be required reading. Better still, Johnny Sain was the Richmond pitching coach. At last, so many of the pieces, at least the baseball ones, seemed to be falling into place. In early May the big-league Braves were scheduled to play an exhibition against Richmond, and Turner, ever the showman, announced that not only would he be coaching third base for the game, but Old Man Bouton would start the game for Richmond. In an instant a meaningless exhibition game transformed into a cultural happening. Ticket sales went through the roof, so much so that it was clear very quickly that rickety Parker Field would not be able to handle the demand. That didn't stop Turner from selling tickets; he just added standing-room space in the outfield. For the game only a rope would partition the playing field from the fans, necessitating a special set of ground rules for balls that rolled into the overflow crowd. The game would draw more than thirteen thousand to a stadium designed to hold ninety-five hundred and that regularly saw less than half that many.[10]

To a person as self- and hyperaware as Jim Bouton, the implications of the game were obvious. As was the pressure. This was it. He was running out of money, running out of chances, running out of opportunities to run out of. He was either going to pitch well and hold on to his dream or pitch poorly and then have to figure out his marriage along with the rest of his life. A writer following him around for the game could tell that behind the jokey front he was putting up, he was plainly scared. (The writer also made note of the fact that his confidence couldn't have been boosted by the fact that Bouton's number that evening—28—happened to be the same as Seymour Baseball's, the Richmond mascot who wandered through the stands seemingly drunkenly, entrapped as he was, and possibly even asphyxiated, by a giant plastic baseball over his head.)[11] "The only way you can really be sure of getting Jim to do something is to tell him it can't be done," Paula says now. This had been true ever since he was a kid. And, scared as he was, he was determined to make sure that this would hold true this night as well.

With Johnny Sain as his cornerman, preparing him for the game of his life, he felt good. He was in better shape than most of the Richmond players, and while he looked older than most of them, he didn't look *that* much older. Still, he was clearly out of place: he wore a Washington Americans jacket and carried a Washington Americans duffel bag, props pilfered from the disastrous *Ball Four* television set—reminders that he didn't always beat the odds. And he was on edge. Bruce Cunningham, who was covering the game for wxex tv-8 in Richmond, remembered that he was like sandpaper. "He wasn't easy to be around," he said. "He wasn't the friendliest fellow, that's for sure. I was waiting to interview him, and there was a pay phone outside of the clubhouse. This very old man came walking by with an Eskimo Pie, and he took the wrapper off and threw it on the ground. Bouton's on the phone, and he slammed down the receiver and was like 'That's why this country looks like a fuckin' pigsty. Because of fuckin' assholes like you!' The old man looked like he was gonna cry." As always Sain was there to stand up for him: "Ya know," he'd say in his southern drawl, "he rubs some people the wrong way, but the kid will always go out there and work hard, and that's why they call him the Bulldog."

As it turned out, the special ground rules were all for naught. Few of the big boys could touch him. He went six innings against the big leaguers and struck out seven of them, giving up only one run. Later, he called the game "my greatest day in a baseball uniform. I never had more pressure because if I didn't come through, I was gone. You lose in a World Series, you'll still be a starter next spring.... That night I was magic. I've had other great moments, but that night I felt I was omnipotent."[12] The thirteen thousand fans there that night cheered, and countless others were wowed when they read the account of the game later in *Sports Illustrated* or saw clips of the game on their local news. But the closer some got to him at that time, the less awed they became. "Having read *Ball Four* when I was fourteen, I wanted to love this guy," Cunningham says. "But he really didn't let you love him.... At [nineteen—Cunningham's age when he covered the Richmond game], you want your heroes to be godlike, and he wasn't. He was very human, very normal, with all the positives and negatives. Bouton was my introduction to the fact that big stars aren't all going to be the way you expect them to be." Cunningham thought he had gotten the point of the book when he first read it, focusing on the wisecracks and the beaver shooting, but meeting Bouton exposed to him its deeper truth: "In Bouton World, that's the kind of the way things work out sometimes. He'll rub people the wrong way, but he'll get them to think."

Turner was sufficiently impressed to sign him to a Minor League contract, assigning him to AA Savannah. His manager was a lifelong busher, Bobby Dews, who himself was considered a nonprospect—first as a player and now as a manager, stuck as he was in the lower rungs of the Braves' system. He was fifteen days younger than Bouton, though, so the signing signaled to him that maybe he, too, was still a prospect. Although initially hesitant to embrace Bouton's comeback because it forced him to cut a younger player, Dews became a believer because to believe in Jim Bouton was to believe in himself: "He makes me think somebody is going to take me up there."[13] Somebody would. The following season Dews was promoted to the Atlanta Braves' coaching staff.

While Bouton never stopped getting fan mail, now it took on a different tinge; older men were writing to thank him for showing them that they should never give up on themselves. "I do wish you well," one letter went. "I've been telling myself I'm not over the hill. This has been doubly difficult for me in that I've got some serious health problems that have messed up my lungs and I don't get around as fast as I once did. Anyway, your life is an inspiration to many of us, including me." A dozen years earlier Gay Talese showed American men in his piece on Frank Sinatra that cool wasn't reserved for the young. Now Bouton was doing the same. "He does not feel old," Talese wrote of Sinatra. "He makes old men feel young, makes them feel that if Frank Sinatra can do it, it can be done."[14] Not that they would. Just that somebody like them could. Twelve years later, every time they picked up the paper to read about Bouton striking out somebody a generation younger, they felt the same way.

32 Dreaming in Baseball

"Jim dreams in baseball," Paula said recently. "It's his metaphor for life.... If he's happy, feeling strong, he will be pitching well in his dreams, or running successfully to catch a ball. If he's down, he struggles in a baseball context while he sleeps." It was the metaphor he returned to over and over in his writing and whenever he was trying to explain some offbeat, otherwise hard-to-explain passion in his life. *Ball Four* itself opens with his dreaming in baseball—standing on the mound in Yankee Stadium, vanquishing his old team with his dancing knuckler and driving in the winning run to boot. "I'm 30 years old and I have these dreams," the book begins.[1] It was always important to him that he think good thoughts; if he didn't, he paid the price for this negativity on the mound in his dreams. Where there was no governor, no way for him to slow the runaway truck as it careened down the side of the mountain. Tough times during waking hours could transform themselves into baseball nightmares. He'd flail in his sleep, slap the bed, looking, looking. What's the matter? Paula would call out. What's wrong? "I'm looking for the ball!" he'd say in the netherworld of consciousness. "There's no ball here!"

His comeback presented him with a confluence of emotions and feelings. He was suddenly succeeding beyond expectations on the field, but his personal life was in complete upheaval. He needed the positive to overshadow the negative; he needed to feel good about himself, or he knew he'd pay for it when he closed his eyes. Although he liked to talk about his comeback as something of a Zen thing—a dog-eared copy of *Zen and the Art of Archery* sat on his nightstand in his cramped Savannah apartment, and he liked to baffle reporters by uttering things like: "I don't want to aim for the target. The way to hit it is not to aim for it"[2]—there was in fact little of it that brought him peace. He needed to make it bigger than it was. And it was big already. He would tell his Savannah teammates that they were bearing witness to a monumental achievement, that he might be *Time*'s Man of the Year, or at least *Sports Illustrated*'s Sportsman of the Year, if he pulled it off and made it back to the big leagues. Marveling at both his sinewy body and his oversize ego, they would shake their heads when asked about their aged teammate and say that the only fat on him was in his head.[3]

Once he made it back to the bigs he had breakfast one morning in Houston with his old roomie Norm Miller, who noticed that the man sitting across from him had a persona that now mimicked his knuckler, in that he had difficulty controlling it. "He really thought this was a big deal. I said something to the effect of 'Are you kidding me? Anybody can throw a knuckleball, Bouton.' Just kidding around. He didn't like that. We didn't talk for years after that." Bobbie as well saw a change. When he would tell her that he thought he should be on more magazine covers or getting more endorsement offers, she remembered thinking, "Oh, dear. This isn't good. I would sometimes try to kid him out of it, but he seemed to think that what he was doing by making a comeback was the biggest sports story ever, which I didn't think was putting things in perspective."

Perspective was hard to come by what with fans, along with copious amounts of media, slavishly following him around as he marched back to the Majors. Writer Terry Pluto approached him about cooperating on a book he wanted to write about the comeback. Bouton demurred, but Pluto trailed after him anyway and wrote it without his input.[4] Future Pulitzer Prize winner Lawrence Wright hung out on his couch for a time as he penned his own piece on the comeback.[5] The ABC newsmagazine 20/20 sent a crew out to film him for a segment that aired later that summer. And fans packed whatever rundown stadium he happened to be pitching in that evening. His debut for Savannah saw Grayson Stadium bulge with 3,182 people jammed inside to see him win his debut 5–3, striking out eight.[6] After losing his next start he rebounded with a shutout, which only brought more attention to what he was doing.

And, no mistake about it, it was a great story. The old-timer making an improbable return to the young man's game and making the kids look like fools as they flailed at his knucklers. A Yankee, no less, from what already seemed to be a bygone era, who had grown accustomed to playing in the shadowy cathedral of Yankee Stadium with Mantle and Ford, now toughing it out in nowhere towns playing in beat-up ballparks. Looking backward, there's a pull toward sentimentalizing those Minor League stadiums beyond all reason, but Grayson, before it was refurbished, was comfortably nestled beyond romance's grasp. Poison ivy crawled up the old light towers, rain poured into the locker and umpires' rooms whenever one of Savannah's torrential downpours occurred, rats roamed the corridors, and mosquitoes dined on who-ever was crazy enough to plunk down a couple of bucks to spend a few hours there. Before a start Bouton would make his way toward the dungeon of an umpires' room to work them a bit, letting them know what he was going to throw, making sure they were prepared for what was coming. To the extent possible he was managing his come-back, working it to ensure that things turned out as he wanted them to. Unlike the television show, he had a measure of control here; he was determined that this time, he wasn't going to humiliate himself.

He was playing with and in front of a new and different generation; huge fans of his would come out just to cheer the guy who wrote *Ball Four*. Occasionally, they'd be working the plate. Sonny Fulks was one of those guys. He kept a beat-up copy of the paperback edition in his trunk and in late July called balls and strikes for Bouton's start against the Charlotte Orioles. He saw a pitcher whose knuckler was slower than Charlie Hough's or Wilbur Wood's, but effective nonetheless. "Theirs was more of an abrupt, quick break. His had a more looping break to it." More like a butterfly, he remembered.

In discussing Bouton's mechanics with Bobby Dews before the Charlotte game, Fulks chuckled when Dews told him that, butterflies notwithstanding, Bouton's delivery reminded him of a rusted metal robot throwing a knuckleball. "It makes me hurt to watch him," Dews said, before chuckling himself—nobody had told him before the season that he'd be managing old-timers' games. Yet the first time through the lineup that evening, nobody could make solid contact. The second time through was a different story; the young hitters were more patient, waiting for the break. Before the next night's game Fulks got his book signed: "Thanks for not laughing at the knuckleball . . . Jim Bouton."

He wound up going 11-9 with Savannah, along with a sparkling 2.82 ERA. Occasionally, the kids would try to test him by bunting for hits, one after another. But he was in better shape now than he had been the year before and was able to handle the action.[7] Although GM Bill Lucas had privately confided to the Atlanta beat writers that there was no way he was promoting Bouton to the big leagues,[8] by early September Turner had seen enough and overruled him, handing Bouton a big-league roster spot along with a place in the club's rotation. Immediately, he found himself right back where he was the last time he was on a Major League roster—in the middle of a roaring controversy.

At the time of his first start—September 10—the Dodgers, Giants, and Reds were in the middle of a heated race for the NL West divisional crown, with only six games separating the three clubs. The Braves, on the other hand, were comfortably in the basement, nearly two dozen games off the pace. That afternoon he was scheduled to take the mound against the Dodgers, and nobody knew what to expect—Vegas was so skittish it took the game off the board.[9] Reds manager Sparky Anderson sensed a sideshow looming in Atlanta while his club was locking horns with the Giants and complained that Turner had called Bouton up solely to boost his gate.[10] To be sure it was somewhat of a sideshow, what with Laurie doing gymnastics on the field before the game, but if Turner was throwing him out there just to massage ticket sales, he miscalculated—only 11,108 fans showed up for the Sunday game, 15,000 less than the night before. The circus atmosphere further receded after

the game's first at-bat when Bouton showed that he belonged, striking out Davey Lopes, who got nowhere near his knuckler. He retired
the side in order to a standing ovation and then, after walking Steve
Garvey, did it again in the second. And once more in the third. The
second time through the lineup, though, the Dodgers got to him, scoring five runs. LA won the game and, afterward, disparaged the whole
affair, calling it a disgrace to baseball. Reggie Smith was so upset that
he got himself thrown out of the game in the fourth inning, blaming the "circus atmosphere" for his pique.[11] Lopes, who later flew out
and then homered off Bouton, said the game "was an injustice to San
Francisco and Cincinnati. He can't pitch and if he's honest with himself, he'd admit that. He has no ability."[12]

For his part Bouton was satisfied. "I think I proved my stuff is good
enough," he said afterward. "It's only a matter of being consistent. I
did it. I came all the way back, and I got out big league hitters." As for
what this meant, he wasn't sure, as he had run out of guideposts. "I'm
in territory nobody's ever been to before."[13]

His next start probably made Sparky feel a bit better; he went out
and beat the Giants 4–1. He went six innings and gave up only three
hits. Afterward, after striking out and flying out against him, Bill Madlock called the whole thing "a disgrace. I hope he's not around next
year. If he is, I'll send my little son to hit him. He was just a plain joke,
gathering material for another book."[14] It was his first big-league victory in eight seasons; only Cactus Johnson, who went fifteen seasons in
the 1920s and '30s, had gone longer between wins. Despite the howls
and protests, Bowie Kuhn had finally learned his lesson; he would be
staying out of this Jim Bouton flap, he announced in late September.[15]

Five days later he went up against his old team the Astros. It would
be the fireballer against the junkballer, as he was matched against
perhaps the hardest-throwing pitcher in the game—J. R. Richard.[16]
They battled to a standstill, each going seven innings and giving up
two runs. His final two starts were against Sparky's Reds, and in his
first one he gave them all they could handle, going eight innings but
losing 2–1. His final start of the season came in Cincinnati after the

Reds had just been eliminated from the race. They knocked him out in the fourth and tagged him for his third loss of the season.

He finished the year with a 1-3 record and a 4.97 big-league ERA. He had two very good starts, one bad one, and one that went well for four of the five innings he pitched. "There are so many shouldn'ts and can'ts in the world that when someone challenges them, as I have, and beats them, as I have, then it has to inspire them," he said.[17] It inspired Turner. "After the season," Bouton remembered, "Ted Turner handed me a check for $10,000. I said, 'What's this?' He said, 'That's for putting fannies in the seats.'" He didn't put that many in them, though. He had only two starts at home, with the second drawing only 12,298—500 fewer than what showed up the night before. His three road starts likewise failed to motivate the masses—only 3,358 came out to see him pitch in San Francisco, and 5,710 Houston fans turned out to see the man who popularized the alternative lyrics to "Proud to Be an Astro" in his book. Some 20,660 did show up in Cincinnati for his late September start, but that was more likely due to their pennant-contending Reds than the prospect of seeing the return of Jim Bouton. In fact, Bouton's start drew the smallest crowd of the three-game series between the clubs that weekend. In the end his return was inspiring in a literary sense more than a baseball one; writers stumbled over themselves trying to capture it on the page, but the multitudes mostly didn't care. Here was more proof that his world was the literary one and not the baseball one. Turner perhaps realized as much; while he was congratulating Jim he was also making a play to pilfer the San Diego Chicken from the Padres.[18] After Padres owner Ray Kroc fended off the attempt by throwing an additional $10,000 the chicken's way, Turner announced that he saw no reason why Bouton couldn't come back and try it again in 1979.[19]

In a way his comeback created the same sort of divide *Ball Four* did: those writers who made their living away from the game applauded it, while those in the trenches either abhorred it or, if they were being generous, called it simply "misguided."[20] He had exposed them again, eight years later, at a time they thought they were finally rid of him.

Nobody can walk away from the big leagues for eight seasons and then come back and be effective. Particularly not at the geriatric base-ball age of thirty-nine. But Jim Bouton just did. Simply by taking the mound and deceiving the likes of Davey Lopes and Bill Madlock with his knuckleball, he made fools and liars out of the beat writers and columnists who pretended once again to know the game inside and out. Which was why Dick Young cheered when Bouton went undrafted in the November 1978 free-agent draft.[21] It was surely an "ego crusher" for the Bulldog, Young wrote, a phrase that reeked of projection more than anything else.

A few weeks later, despite assurances from Turner that he could return to the Braves, he walked away from baseball for the second time. "I think I am too weird, too strange," he said at the time. "Not for Ted, but for the other people in the organization."[22] He was upset that he wasn't considered for the Comeback Player of the Year Award, but, more than that, he felt that he had accomplished what he set out to do. The excitement was in the struggle to make it back, he said, to prove that it could be done. Once he did that everything that came afterward felt like a letdown. "I remember how routine it seemed—almost boring," he said of his post Dodger-game starts.[23] Once the interest died down and he was just another pitcher in the rotation, he felt an overwhelming sense of the familiar. He had been here before, he said. It was all so routine.

There was an additional factor, though. One that he kept to him-self at the time. He had decided that his marriage was over, that he was moving forward with Paula. Which meant that baseball, at least professional baseball, was over. She had children of her own to take care of, she told him, and she wasn't going to uproot them and fol-low Jim from city to city like Bobbie had as he pursued his singular dream. Okay, Jim said, then I'm done. He called WCBS and got his old sportscasting gig back, anchoring himself in northern New Jersey for good. He could continue to dream in baseball all he liked. But when he woke up he was going to have to move on from it.

33 Mask of the Bulldog

In the postmortem of their marriage it was the old trope that was brought out time and again—Jim and Bobbie had simply grown apart. "Jim changed, and I didn't change enough," Bobbie said at one point.[1] New York, fame, and celebrity had made Jim a more worldly person, old friends still say, leaving midwestern Bobbie in the dust of her Allegan, Michigan, upbringing. After meeting Paula, Marvin Kitman said, Jim knew about wines and breads; he wasn't the same guy who sat in the WMU student union during Twirp Week, letting his date do all the talking. "[Bobbie] was a midwestern homebody, and he wanted a harder, tougher, more sophisticated, and earthy woman," Steve Jacobson contends. Bobbie could have tried to change, but it would have never worked, he believes. When their separation and then divorce became public, the media pounced, blaming Jim's ego along with the philandering nature of the professional ballplayer—as popularized by Bouton himself in *Ball Four*—for the dissolution of their marriage. Not so fast, he said. "A lot of guys have been faithful to their wives in baseball. It didn't happen with me, but I don't think you can blame baseball. I don't think I became more egotistical at age 38. I was egotistical in the third grade."[2]

More likely, it was that Jim *didn't* change, at least in a deeper, more fundamental way. On the surface he was different. Underneath the veneer, though, he was still the same boy Bing Russell and everybody else admired so much. Still the kid who wasn't good enough. Who had to transform himself into the Bulldog and single-handedly beat the varsity football team on the streets of Homewood, Illinois, to prove his worth. Outwardly, he projected a cool confidence, but that was mostly a shield. Every once in a while he'd let his guard down and shock people with his naked vulnerability—the most resonant parts of *Ball Four* occur within these moments, although most remember it for the beaver-shooting and bathroom humor. Vic Ziegel once summed up the popular perception of him when he said, "Jim doesn't have doubts. He believes: 'I think it, therefore it must be true,'" but this was only what he was trying to convince himself of, despite everything around him that was screaming otherwise. The writers covering him would occasionally witness this unmasking and be unmoored by it, given that it contradicted everything else they were writing about him. He seemed to enjoy beating himself up, Frank Deford noted near the end of his lengthy *Sports Illustrated* profile of him during his comeback. Success apparently made him uncomfortable, he wrote, although Deford couldn't pinpoint why that was.[3]

"I found in him a self-effacing, shy, not-sure-of-himself individual who was so skilled and brilliant in so many ways that the two pictures of himself didn't match," Paula says. He knew he had achieved great things, "but some part of him was saying, 'Oh, you're not so great. You're not so great.'" In a loop, over and over. No matter what he achieved. She was stunned to hear him say that he was reluctant to meet her friends because he didn't believe there was anything about him they'd find interesting. "The world had this impression of him as a swaggering wise guy, [but] he's never really been like that personally. Ever." Paula saw how his family would at times reinforce this innate feeling. "I noticed when I joined the family that they used Jim as a kind of scapegoat. They revered him, on the one hand, and belittled him continuously, on the other. They were proud of *Ball Four* and of his being a Yankee ballplayer, [but] on the other hand it was, 'You think you're so much better than everybody,' and 'You're just so self-involved.' It was constant, constant criticism. They would pick him apart. . . . It was so pervasive in the family—to pick on him, to diminish him somehow." For a Bouton, divorce wasn't an option, so for years he felt stuck. "There was never a divorce in the history of our family," Jim said. "It was not acceptable." So he endured his marriage for years, leaving the house whenever he could find an excuse and medicating himself with pot occasionally to help him quiet the voices within and without that were barking at him. Until, finally, he decided he had had enough.

Bobbie never realized he was so at war with himself until it was too late. "This was all thrown at me at once," she remembered. "I knew we were having problems, but there was so much stress and strain with the move with the house and the moving around the country, getting the kids in different schools, and what have you, and I was struggling balancing the money because we didn't have an income coming in, to speak of, that I thought things were going to be getting better. Instead, I got hit with [Jim's request for a divorce]. That was a shock." It came as a shock to everyone in the Bouton family. "I really wasn't aware" of the problems Jim and Bobbie were having, or of the depth of Jim's unhappiness, brother Pete admits, when thinking back to that time. "I didn't know what was going on. None of us knew." When she found out about Paula's existence, Bobbie was stunned but, in retrospect, admits that perhaps she shouldn't have been. "There were a lot of plusses [that came with being married to Jim Bouton], and worrying about the women he might meet on the road, that was minor. I really didn't worry about that much. I trusted him. Maybe I shouldn't have. Maybe I should have realized from all the stories of the other guys [in *Ball Four*] that he wasn't that different."

He most assuredly wasn't. Women were drawn to him, and he loved the attention; this dynamic only intensified after his playing career had ended and he became both a bigger celebrity and more unsure of both himself and his marriage. "Jim was very candid with me," Jill Baer remembered of her time with him both on the set of the *Ball Four* television show and afterward. "He was not the most monogamous person during those days. He told me he'd had a couple of flings during the period before we got involved. But that's not really what he wanted anymore, and I don't think he really even knew exactly what it was he wanted. [But] he wanted something else." Baer was the young woman (she was fifteen years younger than Bouton) on the *Ball*

Four set Bobbie was so concerned about, but Jim was honest when he denied her allegation of an affair; at the time the two were simply friends. Baer was an aspiring writer who quickly became enamored of Bouton. She was a baseball fan and a social activist and saw everything she was hoping to become in the more established Jim Bouton. "Jim, like me, was an activist, and we bonded over things like boycotting grapes—I had worked for Cesar Chavez when I was in college—so we had similar ideas."

There were no writing spots available on the show, but eventually Baer finagled a job as Don Segall's secretary. She'd type, make copies, and keep an eye on both Laurie and Segall's daughter, Pamela Adlon— two ten-year-olds who would play together while their fathers worked on the show. Eventually, Bouton got Baer into some writers' meetings, where she pitched the idea of a gay ballplayer (inspired by her uncle, Art Bear, a then-closeted television executive who once had a tryout with the Yankees), which Bouton loved. After the show ended, they deepened their relationship. "He was definitely a very sexual person, but that didn't make him a superficial person," Baer said. "I think he was trying to find whatever it was he needed next in his life."

Baer traveled with Bouton through the South as he began his comeback in 1977, hung out in *The Tonight Show* green room with Gregory Peck when he made his appearance on that show and bore witness to the turmoil that raged inside of him and was hidden from pretty much everyone else, including Bobbie. "He was a little lost at sea," she remembered. "He was searching and he was lost." By the time Jim met Paula at Bloomingdales, Baer was back in California and their yearlong romance had cooled. The timing was fortuitous. "[Jim's] instincts were right for somehow finding his bearings," Baer said. The first time she saw him walking hand in hand with Paula, she realized he had found what he needed. "Just by watching the two of them together, I could see he had found his true North. He needed her."

Paula met Jim's family before they met her. He had been covertly seeing her for several months by the end of the '78 season and had finally decided to make a break from Bobbie. First, though, he invited

Paula to Atlanta to watch his comeback game against the Dodgers and to take in the extended Bouton family from afar, as something of an anthropological exercise. "We were being observed by Paula as his family because we didn't know that she existed," Pete said. Bobbie, the kids, his parents, brothers, friends were all invited to take in the comeback and were seated in one area. Paula sat apart, observing, accompanied by her beard, Jim's friend Peter Golenbock.

"Jim had invited me to come and see him pitch," Golenbock said, and when he got on the plane that would take him to Atlanta, "sitting next to me was a woman—Paula. I didn't know who she was." All he knew was that his friend had asked him beforehand to pretend that he was her boyfriend for the weekend, to make it appear that she was with him rather than Jim, if anybody asked. He had no idea of the depth of their relationship. He figured this was nothing more than another woman on the side for the moment. So he agreed. "I was incredibly loyal to Jim," he remembered. "I loved the guy. I would have done anything for him. So I did it, not knowing what would happen." Later, in the ashes of their divorce, when Bobbie pieced together the events of that weekend, she was furious with Golenbock, who was a longtime family friend. "Bobbie, quite properly, felt betrayed," Golenbock says now. "And I felt awful about it the rest of my life." They never patched it up. Jim finally came clean to Bobbie about Paula before his final start of the year, in Cincinnati. "He told me in a rotten way," Bobbie said. She flew out expecting to watch him pitch, and he told her before the ball game. "Jim had arranged to tell me, and he had made arrangements to take me back to New York. It was not pleasant, to say the least." Expecting to spend some time in Cincinnati with Jim and a friend of hers, she instead went back to the airport and took the flight home.

The divorce that followed was predictably messy. The kids all blamed Jim because he was the instigator, and family friends declared their allegiances to either Jim or Bobbie. Old Lion's Head buddy Larry Ritter not only chose Bobbie but also wrote the foreword to her book a few years later, *Home Games*, which, through an exchange of fictional letters with her friend Nancy Marshall (onetime wife of Jim's Pilot teammate and helpful pair of eyes on the *Ball Four* galley, Mike Marshall), recounted the specifics of their estrangement and divorce. From this point on his life could be neatly separated into his pre-Paula life and his post-Paula life, with very little overlap between the two.

He carried few friends over the threshold. Most felt that he became a different person once he married Paula, someone they no longer recognized. "He used to be the most happy-go-lucky guy one could imagine," Golenbock said. "Neither of us ever drove the speed limit. We wanted to get where we were going, we were fast-paced people, and then, after he married her, he became somebody else. Instead of being this fabulous TV character, this sports person who would ride a Brahma bull, who did some of the craziest things, he left the TV business and became a businessman. It was saddening to me because we had had so much fun together, and all of that went away. He was one person with wife number one and a different person with wife number two." Ritter, Vecsey, and Jacobson, among others, saw a changed Jim they had trouble recognizing. As did his parents, George and Trudy, and brothers, who maintained their close relationships with Bobbie despite the divorce. Even decades later Bobbie spent most holidays with brother Pete and his family and regularly visited Bob as well. For years postdivorce, Jim's parents invited Bobbie to their home for Christmas; she had a better relationship with them than he did. "They used to invite [Bobbie and the kids] to holiday dinners, but not us," Paula remembers.

His parents were shocked and upset over the divorce. "I don't think they liked the fact that I was Jewish, either," Paula says, "so for a couple of years they pushed Jim out of their lives. His mother, although eventually we were able to speak civilly to each other, never accepted me to the day she died." As Pete remembers it, "My parents loved her at first, hated her right after that. They called her a Svengali. Somebody [they would say] has a spell over Jim because he wasn't doing things the way they thought he should do them. He wasn't being logical [in their minds] so therefore she must be a sorceress of some kind." The Jim they knew would have never walked out on his wife and family, it wasn't something a Bouton man did. So he had to be under a spell of some sort. The animosity lasted for years. Eventually, George came around. "At some point," Jim said, "my dad saw that Paula was tremendously helpful and wonderful, that she was helping me and was a great partner," so he accepted Paula and eventually developed a solid relationship with her. "I didn't call him 'Dad,' as the other in-laws did," said Paula, "but we got along very well, which was nice, as he aged."

The idea that Paula had some sort of spell over Jim comes up more often than you'd expect when the subject of Paula is broached with those who missed the old Jim. The suspicion that she somehow knew some mystical way to reach a part of him that triggered the reactions she was looking for, that made him truly feel invincible rather than just playacting as he had before, is one that carries some measure of weight with them. The words *Svengali, sorceress,* and likewise are sometimes tossed into the mix when her name is raised. They miss the mark, though, and likely stem from a misapprehension of her philosophies combined with their struggle to come to grips with the evolution of the man they thought they knew. In her presence Jim grew up and finally began to feel comfortable in his own skin. To those who thought they'd already seen the final product, it was a lot to process.

Unlike many second wives, particularly those in the sports and entertainment worlds, Paula was not only an age-appropriate partner for Jim but, of all things, a Jewish intellectual. She received an undergraduate and then a master's degree from NYU in speech pathology, with her master's thesis focusing on how nonverbal behavior in children impacts the impression others have of their speech. She later went on for her PhD at Columbia, where she studied under the famed cultural anthropologist Margaret Mead. "She lived on top of the Museum of Natural History," Paula remembers, "and that's where I would go to meet with her. It was very cool. I was scared the whole time." After receiving her doctorate in 1975 she taught at Hunter College for a few years; she was teaching there at the time she met Jim, using the skills she learned as a teenager at the School of Performing Arts to hold the attention of the hundreds of students she was now lecturing to. "I've been able to use everything that I've been trained to do," she says. "I find that the lines between disciplines are often artificial and that concepts from one can be applied to another." Like Jim, she's not one for conventional wisdom. Soon, she would leave Hunter and Jim would leave WCBS to be on their own. "Jim and I have always preferred to work for ourselves," she says. "Because, then, nobody thinks of us as bizarre. Except our families."

It was while she was working on her dissertation that she first became enamored of the work of Milton Erickson, a post-Freudian psychiatrist who specialized in Paula's field—nonverbal communication—but who was also a pioneer in the field of medical hypnosis. It was Erickson's belief that the unconscious was not a minefield of neuroses and hostilities that needed to be calmed by the conscious mind (as Freud thought) but rather that it was a positive force of energy that could be tapped and utilized to help in the healing process of the patient. "Through hypnosis," wrote a modern-day family therapist summarizing his work, "the therapist could harness the healing power of the patient's unconscious. The role of the therapist was not to give the patient insight, but to utilize his unconscious to give him a new interpersonal experience that would lead to change."[4] Patient, heal thyself, was essentially his unorthodox approach, and hypnosis was the tool that would facilitate the process. All of this appealed to Paula on both a scholarly level as well as a practical one; she had a tremendously skilled new husband who nevertheless doubted himself at every turn and a blended family that was struggling to coexist. Friedman was well into his dotage by the late '70s, so she reached out to his disciple, Sidney Rosen.

"I would consult him, sometimes, for things," Paula remembered. "I was interested in training myself in self-hypnosis. I was interested in how these signals and observations were used in hypnosis, and all through my life from that point, I have turned to hypnosis as a tool to aid in healing because it really doesn't have any negative secondary effects. If you have the time, it's one of those avenues to explore before you begin to talk about medications or surgery." At the time Jim was suffering through a bout of acute pain associated with kidney stones, so Paula sent him to Rosen. Rosen helped him sublimate the pain such that he didn't need medication and was able to pass them painlessly. After some time seeing Rosen individually and as a couple, Rosen taught Paula how to hypnotize herself. "Jim [was] a good hypnotic subject," Paula says, and at times over the years she worked with him to help him hypnotize himself as a coping mechanism.

When she uses words such as *hypnosis*, or its close cousin *trance*, though, she's referring to something other than the popular perception of creating a sleeping zombie susceptible to nearly anything. "Being in a trance is nothing different than being 'in the zone,'" she explains. The state in which people, particularly elite athletes, are able to clear their minds of everything but the task at hand. She knew about trances, and Jim knew about being in the zone; soon they realized they were talking about the same thing. He would tell her about his ability to hyperfocus on the mound, his ability to eliminate all of the sights and sounds of the ballpark but for his target. The sensation of having the entire world fall away such that only his catcher's mitt remained. And he was also familiar with the idea of training his mind to recall past moments of personal satisfaction to help him battle present-day doubts, which was something else Erickson's method stressed. One of the 978 sheets of *Ball Four* notes documents his frustration in this regard: "Once in a while I'll try and remember exactly how I felt as a kid and then see if I can recapture that feeling I got when I first walked onto the mound at the Stadium. I can't quite do it. It was fun being a name and a star and it's that part I want to find again."[5]

He may not have known Milton Erickson from Milton Bradley, but he was already intimately familiar with so much of his method. Accordingly, Paula realized that he'd probably benefit from diving deeper and working on being able to reach that state of singular concentration when confronted with issues beyond the ball field. But when his family heard the words, they conjured something else entirely. "His family all believed Jim was too dumb to get out of the rain," Paula says. "So they figured he'd be susceptible to [their understanding of] hypnosis," to being manipulated.

Whenever she could, Paula used what Rosen taught her to help Jim battle through his moments of nagging self-doubt. And he had plenty of them. Additional external achievements weren't going to cure what ailed him; he'd had no shortage of those already, to no effect. "No matter what he did, he was the top of everything he tried," says Paula. "Whether it was acting in a movie, or being a sportscaster, or playing for the Yankees. Then he writes a book that turns out to be a best-selling classic. But it didn't convince him." After they'd been together for a while, Paula asked Rosen when, if ever, it would. "Sid used to say, 'Don't worry. He'll find peace. He'll mellow.'" Eventually, he did.

She became his protector, pushing back on the external negativity she believed was reinforcing his internal doubts. "The kids were [no longer] allowed to make fun of him, or use him, or walk all over him, or take advantage of his absentmindedness to get away with murder," she said. She was determined to run a different kind of household than the one Jim and the kids had grown accustomed to. "We made order out of chaos," she said. His family wasn't the cause of his self-doubt—that had been ingrained in him since childhood, when he was never good enough and had to don the mask of the Bulldog to gin up the courage to fight on anyway. But, in Paula's eyes, they reinforced it, confirmed it. Hypnosis, she believes, helped him quiet the noise and arm himself with the skills required to address his internal turmoil at last. And, without question, it worked. As Rob Nelson, one of the few friends who bridged the pre- and post-Paula divide, said, "It's not like she's Yoko Ono or anything. She's a smart woman."

For a long time the extended Bouton family was fractured after Paula's arrival, and she wondered—and wonders still—if the sorcery allegations weren't really just the family's way of protecting the Bouton family mythology. "Like any organization of human beings, a family develops a mythology about itself," she says. "And that mythology is a way of self-definition." The Bouton family mythology was that everybody was happy and content. When Jim announced that he was leaving Bobbie, it couldn't be because the Bouton mythology was a fairy tale; it had to be something else. The work of a sorceress. Except that in the wake of Jim and Bobbie's breakup, other Bouton family breakups followed. Jim's marriage to Bobbie was the loose thread in the garment, Paula believes: "Pull the loose thread, and you sometimes discover that the garment was not well knitted." For years, Paula remembers, "they blamed me for all of it." Jim's divorce devastated the Bouton family the way *Ball Four* devastated baseball—by exposing the mythology, laying it bare, and upsetting everyone on the inside whose protective bubble had just been burst.

Within a few years of meeting Paula, Jim wasn't the sort of guy anymore who drove fast or rode Brahman bulls or who had to win every time. But not because she put a spell on him. Instead, it was because he finally realized that he didn't have to do all these things to prove his worth. He didn't need them anymore. All of those things were fuel required to maintain a fire that no longer burned within him. He had, at last, evolved. If, as Peter Golenbock laments, he was no longer the locus of fun at every event, it was because he no longer required that degree of external validation in order to quiet the demons that threatened to emerge whenever he put his head on the pillow. Where he would invariably drift away to dream in baseball.

34   Hey, New York—Bouton's Back!

It was perhaps his final stint as a sportscaster that convinced him that he had to change, evolve, figure out a way to find peace. In January 1979 he returned to wcbs. It didn't go well. Things started off rocky and then devolved from there. He replaced Steve Albert on the 11:00 p.m. newscast, relegating Albert to the early-evening broadcast, and gave news director Steve Cohen a reason at last to fire the temperamental Ron Swoboda, who celebrated his dismissal by throwing a typewriter out the window. If Cohen was looking for peace, Bouton didn't understand why he had decided to replace Ron Swoboda with Jim Bouton: "It's like firing Frankenstein and hiring Dracula to take his place."[1] But as Cohen saw it the hiring was a no-brainer, despite the risk. Bouton was a star, he reasoned, just like all the other on-air talent at the station at the time. And he was a far bigger star than Ron Swoboda. He would fit in for that reason alone.

His producer Tom Flynn loved him, at least at first. Bouton was smart; smarter than the average sports anchor, Flynn remembered. More interesting to be around, more provocative, yet still a lot of fun. Paula likes to say that he was "childlike without being childish," and that side of him was on display right away. To celebrate his return the promo department put together a quickie commercial that began "Hey, New York—Bouton's Back!" followed by people on the street proclaiming their affection for his outspokenness and crazy stunts. "As a gag," remembered another wcbs producer, Cliff Gelb, "this part obviously didn't air, but at the end of the spot there was a guy, your typical New York City Vinnie Boombotz, right out of central casting— construction worker, hard-hat type—looking straight into the camera with his hard hat and sandwich saying, 'Fuck him. Who needs him?' Like a little kid, for twenty minutes, Jim was hysterical over that, laughing. That was Jim. Like a little kid who never grew up. That was his charm, and that could also be his Achilles' heel, in this kind of world where people have their knives out."

Although he publicly promised to read the scores this time around, he told Cohen that he wouldn't be making a habit of it. That quickly, he became a problem to Cohen. "I said, 'Jim, it's sort of part of the deal. You're a sports anchor. We need to do scores.' He would not relent . . . He would say, '[Scores are] passé, man.' That's the way he would talk." Needing a way to get the scores in despite his new sports anchor's refusal to do them, Cohen developed a technique that over time became standard in sportscasts across the country. "We invented a way for the scores to be seen without him having to talk about them," Cohen remembered. "Today it's called 'over-the-shoulder graphics.' So you see the guy on the screen, but behind him are the scores." This freed Bouton to talk about whatever he wanted to talk about while the scores ran in a loop behind him. "I don't think he ever said a score after that."

He maintained his focus on the offbeat but this time cut back on the daredevil stuff; he wasn't going back in the ring with the Brahman bull or skating in the Roller Derby. Instead, he homed in on the humorous. When in St. Petersburg for spring training, he told Flynn that they were going to cover the annual Kids and Kubs game, which was a softball game pitting a team of eighty-year-olds against a team of ninety-year-olds. It was a fun story, but after the game ended, Bouton saw a better one. "We're packing up our gear in the parking lot," Flynn remembered, "and Jim said, 'Get the camera out! Get it out quick!' It was like bumper cars in the parking lot. All of these eighty- and ninety-year-old softball players were running into each other. They were all terrible drivers. So we shot that and ended up using more of that footage than the softball stuff."

Cohen remembered his time with Bouton as a difficult one. "It was hard for him to focus. Broadcasting requires you to sit down and do the work. You gotta watch the highlights; you gotta write or ad-lib the play-by-play that you're gonna do. There's a certain discipline required to do it. My impression of Jim at that time in his life was that it was just really hard to focus. He had just come off [his comeback]; very clearly, it was the end of his baseball career, and I don't think he had figured out yet whether broadcasting of the type we did was really what he wanted to do." He was high energy all the time; Cohen saw his role as news director as trying to harness all of that energy and transform it into something that worked on the air but felt he wasn't always successful. Bouton still liked to douse his head under the sink right before going on air and then sprint onto the set—the routine reminded Gelb of something out of a Road Runner cartoon—and he preferred to wing it, refusing to settle on a tight, agreed-upon script before going on air. His insistence on being extemporaneous drove the producers nuts, Cohen recalled. They never knew where he was going and how long his segments would run.

Barely two months in, he found himself in scalding hot water. Back in Fort Lauderdale to do a series of Yankees stories over the course of a few days during spring training, he got into a serious tussle with Thurman Munson. Although the two had never played together, Munson deputized himself the keeper of the Yankee flame and, as such, considered *Ball Four* to be a sacrilege. He also believed that Bouton had humiliated his friend and mentor, Elston Howard, in the book and afterward. Spotting Bouton and his producer Flynn on the field one day, Munson walked over to Flynn and told him that there was no way he was going to do an interview with them so not to even ask. Flynn relayed this to Bouton, who said, "We'll see." A few days later, Flynn recalled, "Munson was on the field, and I think we were in the dugout. Jim says to the crew, 'C'mon,' and went scooting across with the crew in tow and put the microphone right in Munson's face. He started asking questions, and Munson was furious. I don't remember him exploding; it was more of a quiet burn. But he was mad." Munson repeated his mantra that he wasn't talking, but Bouton plowed ahead anyway, jamming the microphone in his face. "He was trying to provoke him," Flynn said. "That's what he was trying to do. And he provoked him. He got him. Munson grabbed the microphone, which had a cable on it, and strung it around Bouton's neck and started to squeeze him. Bouton got all this on tape, of course, because that's what he wanted."

That night Phil Pepe called Flynn to confirm the story and then wrote it up for the next day's *Daily News*. Meanwhile, Flynn apologized to Munson along with anybody and everybody connected with the Yankees, saying that none of it was Munson's fault, and could they please allow him back on the field to do the live shot he needed for that evening's sportscast? After the requisite number of mea culpas had been issued, the Yankees said okay but that their player interviews were over. When Bouton found out that Flynn had apologized, he was furious. Upon their return to New York Flynn met with Cohen and told him that he wasn't going to work with Bouton again.

Cohen replaced Flynn with Gelb, who had a reputation of being able to work with anybody. Bouton tested that reputation on their first assignment. It was an April day where both the Yankees and the Mets were off. Bouton told Gelb they were going to a ball field on Fifty-Fourth at Eleventh Avenue to shoot an amateur ball game. It seemed like a harmless-enough piece: they filmed the men playing a boy's game on a decrepit field, Bouton interviewed a few of them as to why they came out to play—and then returned to the station to put it together. Contrary to Cohen's assertion Gelb recalled a man who was meticulous in going through the tape, cutting this and adding that. Gelb was amazed that he was doing all of this for a piece that was intended for the air in just a few hours; it looked more like the type of work one might see for a weekly feature. For the piece's finale Bouton was adamant about including the winning team's victory dance—the turtle. "Some guy screams out, 'Hey, let's do the turtle!'" Gelb remembered. "And he gets on the ground near home plate and starts wiggling around like a turtle. And all of his teammates jump on him and start grinding it out. It almost looked like a gay porn movie, with all these guys humping each other in the middle of Eleventh Avenue on this dingy, rundown playground. It was absolutely hilarious, but it definitely straddled the border of good taste." After the executive producers refused to okay the piece unless Bouton removed the turtle dance (it was still the Tiffany Network, after all, and Bill Paley had an office down the hall), he dug in against them. "He was banging heads with everybody in the room," Gelb recalled. Finally, he said that if they wouldn't approve the version that included the turtle dance, he wouldn't play it at all. That evening he went on the air, said that nobody played that night, and turned it back over to Jim Jensen. "It was a twenty-second sportscast," said Gelb. "Screwed up the whole timing of the show. But that was Jim. He wasn't gonna do it. He was principled to the extreme."

He had no interest in pleasing the brass upstairs. In fact, he took particular delight in making them uncomfortable. He was constantly drawing lines in the sand, Cohen remembered, which made working with him so difficult. Despite the daily challenges, Cohen found working with him invigorating. "He required you to be smart. You had to know what the hell you were doing. You couldn't play with him because he was as smart as anybody." He kept everyone within his orbit on their toes. But over time he could grate. One day Gelb was passing by and heard a flustered Cohen muttering about him in frustration. "He said, 'You know, I like Bouton, but I'm going to be really happy the day I fire him.'"

In the middle of all this Sal Marchiano returned.

Steve Albert was moving on, so Cohen reached out to Marchiano to take over the 6:00 p.m. sportscast. "I made it very clear to him that he was to tell the general manager that I would have nothing to do with Jim Bouton off the air," Marchiano recalled. On air he'd be cordial and professional; off air he and Bouton would exist in separate universes, or they wouldn't exist at all. Cohen and upper management agreed to the condition, one that had practically no chance of being kept, given that Bouton and Marchiano would share the same newsroom.

They wouldn't speak, but that didn't stop Bouton from doing his best to get under Marchiano's skin. Bouton's desk sat at one end of the newsroom, while the Associated Press and United Press International wires sat at the other, tapping away constantly, spewing forth hundreds of feet of paper that piled up on the floor throughout the day. In the middle sat Marchiano, who would prepare for the 6:00 p.m. newscast with one eye on his typewriter and one eye on Bouton. Although the practice in the newsroom was for the person who cleared the wires to roll the paper tightly in a scroll, Bouton, of course, deviated from the protocol. "He would rip the wire, and drag about a hundred feet of wire copy through the newsroom," Gelb remembered. "I'll never forget this one day: Sal is typing and trying to ignore Bouton, and, like a little kid back in third grade, you can see Bouton walk to his end, where he sat, and somehow the entire hundred feet of wire copy was over Sal's head, wrapped around his face, strangling him. He didn't say a word."

The newsroom erupted in laughter, while Marchiano seethed in silence. This was just more evidence to him that Bouton wasn't a journalist but an ex-jock who couldn't graduate beyond a locker-room mentality. Lead anchor Jim Jensen was different, though. He and Bouton got along well, often hanging out together in their free time. After Jensen's son died in a hang-gliding accident, Bouton was there for him, Cohen remembered, and they bonded even more deeply. Marchiano aside, said Cohen, "Bouton was capable of a great inner feeling. I felt that he had an enormous empathy that did come through on the air—for athletes but for other people, too." His camaraderie and on-air rapport with Jensen saved him from the guillotine more than once, according to Cohen. Jensen would cover for him when he screwed up, when his tape wasn't cued up correctly, when he ended his sportscasts abruptly, when one of his segments was particularly rough around the edges. "I think with a more standoffish anchor, it would have been harder for Bouton," said Cohen. "Because of Jensen, Jim was able to hold his job as long as he did."

Jensen could only do so much, though. Bouton could tweak the local brass as much as he wanted, but the network was a different story. In June, CBS was airing the 1979 NBA Finals on tape delay, an abomination to him, a contrived television event. Given that the network would air the games at 11:30 p.m., after the local news, his orders were to hype the upcoming game, which was already over and which he was forbidden to talk about other than to promote it to his viewers. To, in effect, turn his sportscast into a commercial for the network. He refused to play along and hype the game. As soon as his sportscast ended the phone in the newsroom was ringing. It was the network, wanting to know why the sports anchor of their owned and operated New York affiliate had just cut their legs out from under them.

Later that summer there was more hot water. Thurman Munson had died in a plane crash, and while the sportscasters on channels 4, 5, 7, 9, and 11 were in tears as they recalled the Yankee captain, seemingly trying to outdo each other in publicly displaying their grief, Bouton read the story straight, giving the facts of the accident and little else. Angry letters poured in; in the end he received more negative mail in response to his sportscasting (the Munson incident in particular) than anything related to *Ball Four*.

Soon he was gone from sportscasting once again, this time for good. Depending on whom you talk to, it was this incident or that one that was the final straw—take your pick. But really, his departure was inevitable, Cohen believes, simply because the nature of local sportscasting was evolving once again, this time away from guys like Jim Bouton. He arrived in 1970 on the wave in New York of ex-jocks turned sports anchors who were emotionally involved in the sports they covered, whose authority stemmed from the fact that they had been there themselves. In fact, he was so good at it that the ex-jock as sportscaster model exploded across the country in *his* wake. By the end of the decade, and largely because nobody could quite do what he did, that was ending. "A Marchiano, or a Warner Wolf, they see sports as journalists," said Cohen. "This is what's happening on the field. This is who's involved. Let's report on what's happening, just as a journalist would on any other event. Bouton did not see it that way. Bouton was someone *of* it. A part of it. Saw himself as a combatant in the game and could not separate himself from either the relationships of his past or the relationships going forward. We would cover the Yankees and Steinbrenner from afar, while Jim would be emotionally involved in that reportage. And that's a type of reporter involvement that is different than a broadcaster who has a few degrees of separation from what he is reporting on. Those are real differences."

At the dawn of the 1980s local news directors were looking for sportscasters who could stay in the five- to six-minute box they were allotted and deliver the sports facts of the day easily and predictably. Jim Bouton could never be comfortable in such a box. And in any case, by this point there was just too much swirling around and within him to succeed on the air. "He was in no state to work," Paula remembers. His family life was in turmoil; he was unsure of who he was or where he was going; he was, in many ways, lost. And it showed when the camera light turned red.

When Cohen told him his contract was not going to be renewed, he took it in stride. There was some tension in the newsroom that morning when word got around that he was being, in effect, axed; the ex-jocks tended to get emotional about hearing such news and sometimes had to be escorted out of the building. But he didn't pick up a typewriter and heave it out the window. He just packed up his things and left. Warner Wolf, Len Berman—even Sal Marchiano— were the future of local television sports reporting. He was the past. And he knew that.

But in a way he was also the future, although nobody could have known that at the time. A future where cable sports shows dominated and there was room for the insightful, funny, brash stuff Bouton favored and that couldn't be packaged so neatly into a nightly thirty-minute over-the-air newscast. "He was smart," Gelb said. "Maybe not classically educated, but smart. Back at Farleigh Dickinson there was a high jumper named Franklin Jacobs who was about five-foot-six but who was high-jumping over seven feet, and that was Bouton's thing. He loved that type of stuff. He would rather show that for three minutes than show Yankees, Mets, Rangers highlights. That's where his heart was. He would have been better if there had been a sports magazine–type of show back then where he could have traveled around the country and been the Charles Kuralt of sports. He had a perspective on sports that a lot of guys back then didn't have." He just didn't have the right outlet for it. By the '90s, with the explosion of cable and ESPN, he would have.

But that would come too late. After leaving WCBS he would never work for somebody else again.

35   Lightning in a Pouch

One day while still at wcbs he showed up in Steve Cohen's office holding a small aluminum pouch with what looked like shreds of tobacco inside. "Do you know what this is?" he asked Cohen. When Cohen said it looked like chewing tobacco Bouton corrected him. No, it's bubble gum. Try some, he said. As Cohen was chewing, Bouton was nearly quivering with excitement. This is it, he told Cohen. This is the thing. This is gonna set me up for my retirement; this is gonna free me to write, to do whatever I want. "I looked at him like he was out of his mind," Cohen remembered.

He was always on the lookout for the next big thing, always in search of a new and different way to bring in income and have fun while doing it. The urge to find interesting ways to make a buck had never left him, even though most of his ideas ran out of steam before he could fully capitalize on them. In the early '70s he jumped the gun on the analytics movement in baseball by nearly a quarter century when he came up with the Baseball Brain, a neat little sliding chart that, for a buck and a quarter, would show you the hitting tendencies of hitters against various types of pitchers. "Did you know that Rusty Staub hits for a .177 average ... when he tries to pull a certain group of righties?" the promotional pamphlet read. In 1974 almost nobody did and, it turned out, almost nobody cared. Four decades later almost everybody did, and franchises were being run according to what the numbers like these dictated.

In the tradition of the tinkering Boutons, he tried out one idea after another. He had an idea of how to improve multipurpose stadiums, envisioning a domed stadium with easily moving stands that could be repositioned to provide optimal sight lines for fans coming to see a variety of different sports. He applied for a patent and was awarded one in 1976. Although indoor arenas today feature just this sort of mobile seating with great sight lines for basketball, hockey, concerts, or whatever, at the time the idea didn't fly. Still, he kept at it. "I have a whole basement full of stuff," he said recently. And he did. "I was always coming up with some absurd, long-shot possibility."

The biggest and best, though, was what was in that aluminum pouch—what would one day become Big League Chew. Bouton was right that day in Cohen's office. Big League Chew would set him up for the rest of his life. His royalties from *Ball Four*, his income from his television gigs, would be peanuts compared to what he would rake in from those little pouches of shredded bubble gum.

This time, though, the idea wasn't his. It was Rob Nelson's, who loved to chew bubble gum as a kid and whose nickname growing up was Nellie, after his favorite player, Nellie Fox. "Fox's trading card always had a picture of him with this huge lump in his cheek, and of course he was chewing the other stuff. When I was eleven," said Nelson, "I used to chew a log or two of Bazooka bubble gum. It was like a rock. So if I had an 11:00 AM Little League game, I'd start chomping on bubble gum at about nine because I wanted to have *the look*." He used a Nellie Fox bat and tried to imitate him any way he could. When he finally made the Mavs in 1977, he spent a lot of time in the bullpen, where there was a lot of time to chew tobacco or, if you didn't chew, talk. Neither Rob nor Jim chewed, so they talked. "Looking at my Maverick teammates in the bullpen, chewing the other stuff, spitting and dribbling on their uniform, aiming at their teammates' shoes, spitting for distance, it was pretty repulsive," said Nelson. They talked about their experiences trying without success to fit in by chewing tobacco, and then, a couple of innings later, Nelson sprung his idea on Bouton—I have this idea where we would shred gum, put it in a pouch, and I think guys would really dig it. We could look cool but wouldn't make ourselves ill. "Jim's eyes got as big as baseballs," Nelson remembered. As well they should: Nelson's idea was, in its way, a cousin of *Ball Four*—an attempt to bring fans into the inner sanctum of the world of the big-league ballplayer. A point of entry that allowed anybody to experience, just a little, the fun that came with being a Major Leaguer.

They talked a little longer; the idea sounded like a blast to Bouton. What would you call it, he asked Nelson. "I kind of plucked it out of the air and said, 'I don't know, Big League Chew?'" Jim said, "I can sell that idea," although he wasn't sold on the name. Later he would refer to that conversation as the moment they caught lightning in a pouch.

They let the idea marinate for a while, and then Nelson saw an ad in the back of *People* magazine for a do-it-yourself bubble-gum kit. He sent away for it and in February 1979 cooked up a batch in the kitchen of the former Mavs batboy's parents—Nelson's Portland apartment lacked such an amenity. He flavored it with root beer extract and maple syrup and colored it brown so as to mimic the real thing. He then sliced it up with a pizza cutter.[1] He showed it to Jim, who loved it, particularly the realistic look. Later, after test marketing it on kids, they changed the color to pink.

Although Bouton liked to refer to the whole process as lightning in a pouch, the reality of it was nearly three years of work between the germination of the idea and its flowering. In between life got in the way—his comeback, his return to WCBS, a divorce, a new relationship and lifestyle. But through it all he kept the idea of fake chewing tobacco for kids in the mix of everything else that was competing for attention in his brain. Nelson admits that although the idea was his, it was Bouton who made it work. He did the legwork; he paid the legal fees to get the name and packaging style trademarked; he put up an additional $10,000 to see the whole thing through. Nelson had no money so was unable to put up anything. Nobody else did, either. "Jim always broke the mold and went against conventional wisdom," Nelson says, "and it worked for him. Nobody else—not Bing Russell, not Kurt Russell, or anybody else in the city of Portland—put up ten grand on a crazy idea. Jim was the guy who put his money where his mouth was. Jim thinks he can make anything happen, and in many ways he's right."

The decision to trademark the name turned out to be the one that was the game changer. "Someone had already thought of bubble gum in a pouch or shredded bubble gum or something like that," Bouton's patent attorney Steve Pokotilow says, but that wasn't where the value lay. The value was all in the trademark. "The mark, Big League Chew, is one of those quintessential marks that tells you everything you need to know about the product, from the standpoint of not only what it is but the standpoint of the audience—it's all about baseball." Add in the cartoonish drawing of the ballplayer on the pouch—in the style of *Mad Magazine*, which at the time was not only hot but suggested a sly, knowing, off-center approach to the world—and a kid knew everything he needed to know about Big League Chew. It not only told him what it was, but also told him who *he* was, or at least wanted to be. It was brilliant.

Nelson then returned to South Africa to play ball while Bouton shopped the idea to bubble-gum companies, starting with the baseball-focused ones, Topps and Fleer. They passed. After several months of legwork he eventually sold it to a subsidiary of Wrigley—Amurol—who agreed to test market it in a Naperville, Illinois, 7-Eleven to see if there was anything worth investing in long term. In ten minutes the packages were gone. Amurol then signed on and in the spring of 1980 rolled it out nationwide. By the end of the year they had sold $18 million worth of Big League Chew. It was an enormous sum in the abstract, made even more impressive by the fact that Amurol was a relatively small subsidiary, with about eighteen products of mostly sugarless gum that typically generated about $8 million in total sales annually. In two years Amurol had sold about seventy-two million packages of Big League Chew, with Bouton and Nelson splitting their royalties fifty-fifty. It was, by far, more money than he had ever made playing baseball or selling books. For the next decade it would gross about $12 to $14 million a year, with the two ex-Mavs splitting their fat royalties down the middle.

Big League Chew quickly became one of Wrigley's hottest and most lucrative brands. In 1981 the Wrigley family sold the Cubs for $20.5

million, suggesting that in just a little over a year's time their shredded bubble gum–in-a-pouch franchise was worth about the same as
their baseball franchise. And given how the Cubs performed annually,
Big League Chew looked to have a far greater upside. Quickly, Wrigley signed a big three-year contract with Nelson and Bouton, which
paved the way for those large annual royalty checks. "The truth is,"
Nelson says, "if they had offered Jim and [me] a flat sum, and I would
have paid off my student loans and bought a car or something, we
probably would have done it."

Even Amurol didn't quite understand where the value lay in what
they had just purchased. For years afterward they introduced variations
on the theme of Big League Chew, selling Popeye-themed bubble gum
in a pouch and "Hang Time" shredded gum hawked by Michael Jordan, among other ideas. All of them tanked. Only Big League Chew
worked. Bouton understood where the value came from, though, and
continued to fight hard to protect the integrity of the brand, often
running up against the powers in the Amurol and Wrigley executive
suites. His fierceness oftentimes surprised the execs, who had dealt
with athletes and celebrities before and were surprised that Bouton
wouldn't easily sign his rights away like the others had. Rather than
leave the details to his lawyers or, worse, the suits at Wrigley, he insisted
on not only being present for all important negotiations but conduct-
ing them himself. "He had a paranoid sense that these guys would do
the wrong thing by him," Pokotilow said. He was right to have that
sense—it's not paranoia if they're really out if not to get you, then to
screw up whatever it is you worked so hard to create. "Jim was not afraid
to walk away," he continued. "He had great instincts about the value
of his property and a level of integrity about how the product should
be sold." If the suits weren't going to do things the way he wanted,
he would not hesitate to shut things down altogether until they did.

He had a strong sense of right and wrong and did not hesitate to tell
those on the other side of the negotiating table where he was coming
from and why. He was guileless; everything was up front, which could
throw those who were used to hidden agendas and games. "He was

an unusually smart person," said Pokotilow, who found Bouton to be one of his favorite clients. "A smart businessperson and very creative. It's always exciting, when you're an intellectual property lawyer, to see people who can create things and then bring value. The Steve Jobses of the world, who can not only invent things but then really pick up the business side of it. They're rare. When you see those people, it's a lot of fun to represent them."

Not surprisingly, Bouton got into a big tiff with Amurol over the advertising campaign. He was adamant that the focus should be on the cartoon on the package rather than celebrity endorsements, which was what Amurol was pushing. Choose the wrong celebrity, he said, and a scandal surrounding him might capsize the products he's endorsing. The great thing about the characters on the Big League Chew pouch, he argued, was that there was no chance you'll ever find them in bed one day with another woman. Also not surprisingly, he dug in his heels and held firm until Amurol blinked. There would be no celebrity endorsements for Big League Chew.

There were other battles over advertising, including one surrounding the royalties owed Bouton and Nelson based on the amount of advertising Amurol was doing, or not doing, for Big League Chew. It was a complicated issue, but ultimately what it boiled down to was that Bouton believed that he was being shortchanged, so he renegotiated the royalty agreement. The validity of the renegotiated agreement became a thorn that then turned into a lawsuit, with Bouton suing Amurol to enforce what he believed to be a valid amendment to their agreement. He won in the lower court but was reversed on appeal. Pokotilow was distraught—it was the first time in his career that he'd ever had a case reversed on him, where he'd won in the lower court but then lost on appeal.[2] "I was beside myself," he recalled. "I was upset for several weeks." Bouton was less so. Big League Chew was Amurol's best-selling product at the time, and soon the agreement would be up for renewal. Since Amurol had no automatic right of renewal, Bouton knew that Amurol would have to pay top dollar to keep it. And part of that top dollar would include the revenue he was convinced he'd lost as a result of the appellate court ruling. He was right. While it was Pokotilow who drafted the renewal agreement, Bouton was the one who negotiated it. In the end he got his money back and then some. Nelson, as well, was philosophical about the defeat in court. Don't worry about it, he faxed Pokotilow upon being informed of the decision; you threw a strike. The ump just missed the call.

Nelson was more than satisfied by the success of Big League Chew. With the money he was now making he was free to toss the business world aside and concentrate fully on traveling the globe, teaching baseball. Bouton wasn't satisfied at all. He had more windmills to tilt at. Even with all of the Big League Chew money rolling in, he refused to do what most people would and invest it. Instead, he steered clear of the stock market. "We never invested in stocks," Paula says. "We didn't understand it. Neither of us had any background in financial understanding." What they invested in instead was themselves. Jim knew real estate from his time fixing up houses and renting them out years earlier, so he invested in that. And he knew how to create and profit off of his creations, so he invested in those as well. "But the stock market?" Paula asks. "I wouldn't know where to begin, and neither would he."

Years later his basement was still full of the cavalcade of ideas he turned into products. Most failed, but he had some successes along the way. In 1988 he received his second patent, for the Table-to-Go, a small plastic table for your lap to use at a ball game or picnic.[3] It had one major flaw—it couldn't fit in a dishwasher. So it failed. He then riffed on the sensation of the moment, the Rubik's Cube, by creating what he called Rodney's Cube, which mimicked the original except that Rodney's Cube was monochromatic, with six white sides, meaning that the puzzle was solved right out of the box. "The Twentieth Century's Least Amazing Puzzle," read the packaging. "Get Respect. Requires No Intelligence. Impress Your Dog. Saves Energy. Breaks the Ice at Funerals," read the accompanying testimonials. Needless to say, it didn't make anybody forget Big League Chew.

He couldn't be convinced that the lack of enthusiasm over, say, Mudders, his idea for baseball spikes that wouldn't cake mud, was because his idea was less than earth-shattering. He'd push and push until there was absolutely nowhere else to push. "Because Jim believes all his ideas are great, he goes the full distance on each one," says Marty Goldensohn, who worked with Bouton in the late '80s and early '90s. And he does this, Goldensohn says, "precisely because he believes success and failure are right next to each other." His dynamism could be intoxicating for those in his orbit, but also frightening if you were the one who had to deal with the aftermath when things didn't go well and you had no other options. "People would cold-call Jim from Wall Street," Goldensohn said, asking him to invest in this or that. He'd always turn them away. I don't invest my money there, he'd tell them. I invest my money in myself. "As a result, Jim was always coming up with the next entrepreneurial thing to do. Jim was very much of a risk taker. He got high from the risk and the fun and the entrepreneurial part of it. It made him high and happy and optimistic that it would work out and they would find a way." All that stuff tended to scare Paula, although much of it was also what she found so appealing in him. "Maybe she was scared of the same part she was in love with," Goldensohn wonders.

She was the sophisticate—the PhD, academic appointments, interest in ballroom dancing; he was proudly and defiantly not. She could regale a houseguest with an analysis of anthropological theory; he was busting at the seams to tell you which of his teammates knew how to say "fuck" in the most languages. She was measured and intellectual; he was Charlie Parker—all feeling, all emotion. "If you don't live it, it won't come out of your horn," Parker once said. Bouton lived it and emoted all of it, each of his ideas another note from his horn. "Collect-a-Books" (essentially foldout baseball cards), "Big League Ice Cream" (Good Humor bars with player autographs etched on the sticks), "Smart Toys" (computerized toys that could talk to each other), "Big League Cards" (personalized baseball cards for use as business cards): each of these a note from his horn. Some rang true—Big League Ice Cream was a solid seller for Good Humor for a few years—while some sounded dissonant. But they were all distinctly from the instrument of Jim Bouton. They could come from nowhere else.

One of his more intriguing ideas wasn't for a product but a television show. It was the end of the 1980s, the failure of the *Ball Four* show was sufficiently behind him, and television had drastically evolved. Now, at last, one could, if he had the courage, tell the real story of baseball through that medium. "A reality show about a Minor League Baseball team," Bouton recalled of the idea he pitched to Marty Goldensohn one day. Unlike *Ball Four*, the show, tentatively called *Bus League*, would focus not on the fight to stay in the Majors but the fight to get there. "The Minor Leagues were even better [than the bigs]," he said, "because the guys are more candid, funnier; there's less at stake." The concept of reality television was still a few years off—MTV's *The Real World* wouldn't debut until 1992—but here as with most things he saw the future before pretty much anyone else. And here again he was perhaps a bit too far ahead of the curve; he was unable to sell the show.

At the time Goldensohn was producing and hosting a show called *Hour Time* for ABC radio and had hired Bouton to be one of his commentators. Bouton loved the gig because it allowed him to do the sorts of pieces he loved doing on television but with more freedom. And no scores. Goldensohn edited him, and, as with Shecter, Bouton was able to find someone who was interested in making his work sharper, not dulled to the point where it couldn't even cut whipped cream. Eventually, Goldensohn sublet space from Bouton in Teaneck so that even when they weren't working on a piece for Goldensohn's show, they were together—Bouton in his space working on one invention or another, Goldensohn next door cutting together this radio piece or that. They were a good team; both of them realized this.

"Jim, always being ahead of his time, says to me, in 1989, that the next big thing in television is going to be reality television," Goldensohn recalled. "How he knows this I do not know. 'Let's go make a reality TV show about Minor League Baseball,' he says. 'Find me a team.'" Goldensohn made a few calls and settled on the Birmingham Barons. They worked out the details, Goldensohn bought a camera, and they headed down to Alabama to shoot the pilot. They proceeded over the objections of Paula, who hated the idea. As there was no recent reference point for what a reality show could be, she could only envision a repeat of the nightmare that the 1972 PBS show, *An American Family*, turned out to be, with the cameras catching, and possibly even causing, the destruction of a family. "When I was in academia," she remembered, "that was when the Loud family was in the news. The ethical questions that surrounded that kind of stuff were very important to me. I didn't see how they could avoid trouble."

The 1990 Barons were an interesting bunch. Future Hall of Famer Frank Thomas was their first baseman, and the roster was sprinkled with others who would eventually make it but filled with many more who wouldn't. King World underwrote the pilot, and all the players were miked (Thomas later refused to sign the release to use the footage of him; most everyone else acceded). They shot footage of the games, but as they envisioned it, *Bus League* would be much more than that. "There was very little of the baseball being played," Goldensohn said of the pilot. "We'd go to the homes of the players and their wives, [cover] the traveling, and the bus." In one scene Goldensohn's camera panned across a greasy griddle at a proverbial greasy spoon in the middle of the sort of nowhere that defines life in the Minors, the fat popping and hissing under the slick burgers. Later, Bouton overlaid the audio, commenting wryly on the strict dietary habits of the professional athlete. It was tongue-in-cheek funny but also very real—there was footage of players being told they were being released and attention paid to what it was like to be a black ballplayer in Birmingham, Alabama. It was all too real and too different for King World, which passed after viewing the pilot. They then pitched it to other networks, without success. Just a few years later a show like this would be an easy sale, with cable networks salivating to enter the reality market and green-lighting projects that lacked the depth, nuance, and humor of *Bus League*. But in 1990, no way.

36   The Solo Artist

Through his forays in this, that, and the other, Bouton had strayed from the one medium he had unquestionably conquered—books. He had continued to write, of course, penning dozens of articles along with his updates to *Ball Four*, but hadn't undertaken a big project since *I'm Glad You Didn't Take It Personally*, in 1971. He was lured back to book writing by another writer who had strayed, Eliot Asinof. Asinof had made a splash in 1963 with his take on the 1919 Black Sox scandal, *Eight Men Out*, and a few years later hopped on the wave of "inside the locker room" books with *Seven Days to Sunday*, which focused on a week in the life of the New York Football Giants. He'd written some other nonsports books but hadn't written anything in a long while until he had the idea for a novel that explored what it might be like to fix a Major League Baseball game. He was in his seventies, though, and without the energy he once had, so he looked around for a coauthor. In Bouton he found what he thought, at least at first, would be the perfect partner.

He liked the idea of two of baseball literature's heavy hitters collaborating on his idea, with himself and Bouton alternating chapters and perspectives—Jim writing from the perspective of a career Minor League knuckleballer called up to pitch a game that could put his club, the Cubs, into the playoffs, Asinof from the perspective of the umpire who had agreed to throw the game to their opponent, the Phillies, in order to repay a debt. He didn't think there was much money in it, though, so when he pitched the idea to Bouton he told him not to get his hopes up—maybe they'd get a $10,000 advance if they got lucky. Bouton, though, thought it was a great idea that could fetch much more, so he convinced Asinof to let him shop the book. He did, and Bouton sold it to his old friend from *Sport*, Al Silverman, who was now editor and publisher at Viking Press, for a $90,000 advance without even showing him a sample chapter.[1] Asinof was stunned.

He was probably a bit humiliated as well; in so many ways he no longer had his fastball. This was just more proof of that. Always gruff, he bit back even harder now that he felt threatened. Asinof could emit a grandiose view of himself that marginalized those around him—he saw himself as a writer and Bouton as merely a ballplayer who had once written a book—and thought he'd be granted a degree of deference in the writing and editing process of the book that would become *Strike Zone*. As the *real* writer Asinof believed the book should start with his chapter, which would set the tone for the ones that followed. Bouton disagreed. Asinof also insisted on rewriting Bouton's chapters. Bouton objected. He had an outsize ego who found himself up against an ego to match, but one that was younger and more nimble than he was. Before long they had locked horns over nearly every aspect of the book, including whose name should go first on the cover. They fought over everything until they both realized that fighting was futile. By the time they got to chapter 6, the two were no longer on speaking terms.

They both appealed to Silverman, whose role morphed from editor to referee. Asinof assumed his status would cause Silverman to see things his way, but what he didn't factor in was that Silverman had idolized Bouton ever since the '60s, green-lighting one fawning *Sport* profile after another on his favorite athlete. Silverman had a serious man crush on Jim Bouton. And, more to the point, Bouton was most likely more in the right than was Asinof, who simply wasn't the writer he once was and didn't have the editorial or marketing instincts Bouton had. "You make a mistake when you think of Jim as a ballplayer and not a writer," Paula says, and she saw firsthand how badly Asinof had underestimated her husband. Their writing styles were dramatically different—Asinof's was more formal, a whiff of yesteryear in his prose that at times might be considered clunky. Bouton's was as it was in *Ball Four*—conversational, chatty, immediate. A modern audience was expecting the type of writing Bouton was producing, not Asinof. Silverman knew this better than anyone.

When it was released in 1994 the book received some nice reviews but didn't come close to earning its advance back. Asinof distanced himself from it right away, calling it "garbage" and questioning the intelligence of anyone who thought otherwise. He was bitter over pretty much every aspect of the book, including the cover, where he lost his battle and had to suffer the indignity of seeing Bouton's name above his. Bouton, though, liked the book and dutifully went on the stump to promote it. *Strike Zone* would turn out to be a departure for him; it was a nice read, but the only feathers it ruffled were Asinof's. In that sense it was hardly the sort of work one expected to sprout from the mind of Jim Bouton.

He satisfied that urge in other ways. He stood up for the NFL players in their 1987 strike, going so far as joining them on the picket line outside Giants Stadium during a game featuring replacement players.[2] He was so irked at the spectacle of the thing that he followed that up with a letter to the *New York Times* slamming NFL commissioner Pete Rozelle for failing in the primary mission of a league commissioner—to protect the integrity of the game. The games featuring replacement players were a "sham," he wrote, and Rozelle seemed to be indifferent to what was taking place on his league's fields.[3]

He also continued to toss grenades in the direction of the baseball commissioner's office. Although Kuhn had been removed as commissioner in 1984, Bouton continued to single him out for scorn, referring to him as "Ayatollah Kuhn" in a 1989 retrospective on the *Ball Four* Astros in *The Sporting News*.[4] He supported Marv Albert, though, when he became embroiled in a sex scandal in 1997.[5] And, maybe most surprisingly, he distanced himself from the players who were unmasked as steroid users in the early 2000s. If Jose Canseco, who penned a twenty-first-century tell-all focusing on steroid use in baseball and was getting roasted across the board in the aftermath, thought he'd find a sympathetic ear from the man who wrote about greenies decades earlier, he was mistaken. Bouton took pains to put a wall between his drug revelations in *Ball Four* and the ones now splattered across the back pages of sports sections across America in the early 2000s. Asked for his take on Jason Giambi, who was outed as a steroid user in 2005, Bouton said, "I really have no sympathy for the guy.... Guys who take steroids are basically looking to cheat their teammates for the opportunity to play and cheat the opposing team."[6] As was so often the case, whenever you were sure you knew where he was going, he would surprise you and go someplace else.

By the 1990s he was a committed solo artist. WCBS was well behind him, and the following decade saw him become, if anything, even more contemptuous of organizations of pretty much any sort, along with the hierarchies they couldn't help but embrace. He couldn't avoid them altogether, though, needing them to publish the updates to *Ball Four*, which he did once every decade and which he enjoyed putting together, largely because the continuing success of the book allowed him to insulate himself from the corporate scrum of the New York publishing world.

He started working on his first update in 1979, when he was still at WCBS. Shecter was long gone by that point, having died in 1974, so he was looking for an assistant. He reached out to the young publisher of *Baseball Magazine*, Rick Cerrone (not the catcher), asking him to come on over to the station if he was interested, to talk about what he had in mind. World Publishing was long gone as well, and the copyright to the book had just been purchased by Stein and Day, which wanted to put out a ten-year anniversary edition of *Ball Four*. Bouton gave Cerrone the contact information of the old Pilots and Astros, as best he knew them, and instructed him to cold call as many as he could, for a "Where Are They Now?" section he wanted to include in the update. Bouton knew there would be trouble, so he highlighted the names of those former teammates who would most likely be hostile to a call from Cerrone. George Brunet, Wayne Comer, Don Mincher, Ray Oyler, Fred Talbot, and, of course, Joe Schultz "will be hostile," although several others might merely be mildly disagreeable, he noted on the sheet he handed Cerrone.[7] "Those were not pleasant conversations," Cerrone remembered. Bouton also instructed Cerrone to ask his former teammates what they thought of Ball Four now that a decade had passed, but Cerrone rarely got that far before the phone slammed and all that could be heard from the other end was the dial tone. "I was a young kid, and guys were MF'ing me on the phone and hanging up," Cerrone remembers with a laugh. Sometimes they'd simply hang up the moment Cerrone uttered the words Ball Four. "Part of me thinks he was okay with the fact that so-and-so hung up on him," Cerrone says. It let him know that the book was still relevant, still sharp. Even a decade later, the arrow still found its mark.

It was during the discussion over the artwork for the updated edition that Shecter's name disappeared from the cover of the book, much to the chagrin of writers like Vecsey, who considered the act a whitewashing of history. Both the World hardcover and the Dell paperback editions displayed Shecter's name, in small print, on their covers. While reviewing mock-ups for the new cover, Bouton contributed his own thoughts, stressing that he wanted both an uncluttered look and a jacket that let the buyer knew he was getting the original, unaltered classic along with something brand new—"Ball Five"—at the end. As for where to put Shecter's name, he wanted it on the spine. Stein and Day, however, removed it altogether.[8] The omission stung Shecter's former colleagues, who could only see their old friend fading into obscurity and assumed that Bouton was behind the decision.

A decade later Bouton put together a twentieth anniversary edition of Ball Four. In 1989 Stein and Day closed up shop and had a fire sale of their licensed properties, one of which was Ball Four. Rick Wolff was an editor at Macmillan at the time, and when he saw his favorite book from his college days up for sale, he convinced his brass to put in a bid for it. They did and won the rights. Besides being a Ball Four fanboy, Wolff saw that, from a business perspective, acquiring the rights to the book was a no-brainer. It had continued to sell, nearly two decades after it had been released, which was practically unheard of in the publishing world for any book not on high school or college reading lists. It had become a classic, and Wolff wanted to be at least a small part of it. Wolff, who was doing a lot of sports books at the time, immediately went to work on putting together the next update. He and Bouton worked together on updating the preface and on the new afterword, which they would call *Ball Six*. Wolff recalled working with a man who was very particular and precise as to how he wanted the update to read and how things should be done. "This was his life's work," Wolff says, "and he was very eager to make sure it was done the right way." The update was released in 1990 and propelled the book into the last decade of the century on fresh legs, where it continued to outsell most other sports books.

Whenever he was involved in a project, he was adamant that it be done the way he envisioned it. This was particularly the case when it came to anything having to do with *Ball Four*, of which he was especially protective. When the PR director of the Astros asked him to put together a piece on the *Ball Four* Astros for a special anniversary game program, he touched on the scene where his old roomie Norm Miller drilled a hole in the dugout to look up the skirts of the women sitting behind them. Miller, who by this time was in the Astros' front office, ordered that section excised, causing Bouton to explode. "I told [the PR director] to take that out," said Miller. "I'm a grown man now, I've got kids, I'm a fairly respectable guy, and I didn't want to be the brunt of those jokes again. He called me and he was pissed. He said, 'What happened to you? You joined the system.'" Miller told him to go fuck himself and grow up. Bouton refused to allow the piece to run as edited by Miller, so the piece never made it to print. The two spoke only one time after that. Both knew better than to bring up the incident.

He was simply more comfortable being on his own, answering to nobody. When he wasn't pitching for Heflin's Builders, Mama's Restaurant, or the Saugerties Dutchmen in the Albany Twilight League, this time just for kicks, he marketed himself as a motivational speaker for corporate events. He would speak extemporaneously, peppering his talks with funny Yankees and *Ball Four* stories, but making sure to hit on his three main themes—focus on the process rather than the goal, be persistent, and have fun. Like Camus, who once wrote that "we must consider Sisyphus happy," Bouton's speeches turned convention on its head, advocating for abandoning the culture of winning, which he believed was soul crushing and counterproductive in any event. Find the joy in the repetitive and the mundane, he preached. As he told Lipsyte in 1998, the treadmill of life will kill you if you let it, no matter how successful you are. "No one will accept winning the pennant as enough. If they win the World Series, the next day people will say, 'Can they repeat?' The Yankees will never have a night's sleep. They will be expected to start lifting weights for next season during the victory parade."[9] The key to life, as well as success, he believed, was in removing yourself from that mind-set, to enjoy the daily grind and, when victory presents itself, allow yourself to enjoy it. To bask in the Cool of the Evening, as Johnny Sain advised decades ago. It was the message of a man who had at last learned how to be at peace.

He also, at Paula's urging, took up ballroom dancing, not because there was something to be gained by it but simply because it sounded like fun. Years earlier he gave jazz dancing a try but quit because, as he told Paula, "there was no ball to catch or throw and you couldn't win anything."[10] By the mid-1990s he no longer cared so much, at least about the winning. He and Paula had relocated to the Berkshires by this point and began dancing in productions at Jacob's Pillow and elsewhere. He started working with Marge Champion, who in her distant past was a dance model at Walt Disney Studios whose movements were studied and captured by Disney's animators and transformed into Snow White. "I can say without fear of contradiction that I am the best former New York Yankee ballroom dancer," he liked to pronounce whenever his dancing chops were brought up.[11] He was never smooth, but Champion was able to make him a more comfortable dancer, which was all he needed in order to enjoy it, which was the point of the whole thing. He later became involved in the Dancing Classroom, a program teaching public school fifth graders the art of social dance, and learned enough about dance to become a judge in its annual grand finale competitions, scoring the competitors on their mastery of the merengue, fox trot, tango, rumba, and swing. He loved being involved with the Dancing Classroom and here as elsewhere saw things that others didn't. He advised Pierre Dulaine and Yvonne Marceau, who had created the Dancing Classroom, how to market and expand it. "He saw the whole, big picture," Marceau said, "and how you can create attention and hook one thing up with something else so that you start to create this bigger picture."

As someone who radiated within the spotlight as a young Yankee, breathing it in as though it were oxygen, it was perhaps surprising how much he sought out solitude in his fifties, having escaped New York for the middle of nowhere, otherwise known as western Massachusetts. But it made sense; he wasn't the same guy in a lot of ways. He didn't need now what he needed then. Or he did, but he was able to satisfy his cravings from the inside rather than externally. He retained the artistic urge but now expressed it through stone masonry, building complicated, ornate walls in and around his home that nobody other than friends and family would see. He taught himself how to do it when he lived in Teaneck, building a low wall that separated his property from his neighbor's, and practiced at it until he became skilled. He sought out advice from the guys he befriended at the local quarry, construction workers, and studied the work of the stone artists he admired through books and photos. When he and Paula bought their first home in the Berkshires, he did the stone facade work on the exterior. When he was finished the building inspector gave him the ultimate compliment: "You shoulda been Italian," he said. He signed his name on the cornerstone: Jim Bouton, stonemason.

He still felt as if he could do anything, that he could make anything work, that there were no limits. Whenever he had an idea he would go to the so-called experts and ask them how to do it. When they'd shake their heads and tell him that it was a nice idea but it couldn't be done, he'd push back. Okay, he'd say, it can't be done. But if it *could* be done, how would you do it? Then they'd think a little harder and find a way. That was his life in a nutshell—pushing, questioning, finding a way to do that which conventional wisdom dictated could not be done. And then watching as everybody else followed, copying his steps as if they were the most natural thing in the world.

37   Laurie

Although he had escaped New York, he was unable to fully extricate himself from the Yankees. Their pushing him away ever since the release of *Ball Four* served ironically to tie them together. He couldn't seem to escape the inevitable question whenever he was out in public: How does it feel to be excommunicated from the church of the Yankees? He liked to say it didn't bother him, although it sure seemed like it did. As early as 1978 he was ticked that the Yanks had never invited him back to Old-Timers' Day. "They even had Bill Stafford back," he said at the time with an edge in his voice, "and he can't carry my glove."[1]

If he didn't care about his Yankees affiliation, he had an odd way of showing it. When Yankee Stadium was being refurbished in the mid-1970s, he went to the site and walked away with an old turnstile and manager's chair from the clubhouse.[2] When he would conduct baseball clinics up through the '90s he would sometimes do so wearing Yankee pinstripes. When asked why, if he was on the outs with the club, would he still wear the uniform, he'd bristle: "The Yankees don't own the uniform and I earned the right to wear it."[3] He had old Pilots and Astros uniforms at home also; they sat in their boxes up in storage.

He seemed to like it when writers like Vecsey would write that, in its own way, his number 56 was retired by the club, just like Ruth's and Gehrig's: "I hope they never invite me back," he'd say, adding that their refusal to issue his number for a time or their refusal to invite him back for Old-Timers' Day said more about the small-mindedness of baseball than anything about him.[4] Their stance toward him validated everything he wrote about them in the book, he argued. "What kind of crime did I commit?" he would shoot back at reporters whenever an

Old-Timers' Day would roll around without him present. "I think it's terrific," he'd add. "I hope they never invite me back." Sometimes he'd try to rationalize it all. If the book cost him his relationship with the Yankees, it worked out for the best, he'd say. On balance he came out on top. "A lot of guys can throw 95, but not many write a book. When the other guy's fastball is gone, my book will still be in the library."[5]

The August 1997 death of his daughter Laurie, then thirty-one, stripped bare all of the artifice. Laurie had been driving home on Route 21 in Nutley, New Jersey, when she stopped short to avoid an accident in front of her. She was able to stop, but the car behind her didn't, slamming into her two-door red Ford at sixty miles per hour. She died a few hours later in the hospital. "It's all so unbelievable," he said at her funeral, where he gave the eulogy. "Sometimes it's hard to breathe, like there's a big stone on my chest and I can't get it off."[6] Laurie had been the apple of Jim's eye, brother Bob recalled recently. "Laurie was an absolutely free spirit who was Jim all over again, just in female form," Pete said. "Rebellious, would dance to her own tune, did things her way," he added. She and Jim were "peas in a pod." The immediate aftermath of the accident was chaotic and horrible; family members—Jim, Paula, Bobbie, the kids—rushed to the hospital with nobody sure of what to do, what to say, how to act. Nothing in life prepares you for something like this. Years later there remains some rawness of feeling among some members of the blended family over that night, when the two worlds of Jim Bouton were forced together amid the worst of all possible circumstances. Some redirected anger that perhaps helps, at least a little, to mask and manage the overwhelming pain surrounding the horrible fact of the tragedy itself.

Laurie's death robbed him of something other than his daughter. It took from him the optimism that up to then had been a core component of his being. "Jim just fell to his knees when he found out that she had died," Pete remembered. "It was gut wrenching to the point of throwing up. That's the kind of pain that we all felt, Jim obviously more so because it was his daughter." Her death left him in a fog that he had trouble emerging from. "That was the only time when Jim had a window into what it was to not feel positively about life," Marty Goldensohn said. In the aftermath life went on. Only now in a darker hue. He wasn't suicidal, per se, he wasn't looking for a way out of the world, but if that should happen, he thought, it'd be okay.

It was around this time, when he was about as low as he could get, that the Yankees came back into the picture. Contrary to the popular perception, there was never really an organizational feud with him; it was, instead, a couple of smaller, more personal ones, one of which was patched up before Laurie's death. Mantle, of course, had been upset with him for years, refusing to speak with him or about him, to the point of instructing Herb Gluck, the ghostwriter of his 1985 autobiography, not to mention his name anywhere within the book.[7] That relationship had thawed significantly since then, particularly after Mantle's son Billy died in 1991. Bouton wrote him a condolence letter, adding that he hoped Mantle was now okay with *Ball Four*. Several days later he was surprised to find a voice mail from Mantle on his answering machine, saying that he was in fact okay with things now and, in any event, didn't believe that he was the reason Bouton kept getting shunned at Old Timers' Days. I never told anybody not to invite you, he said on the recording. Which might be technically true but nothing more—he never told anybody that they ought to invite him, either, and without the Mick's official blessing there was no way anybody in the Yankee organization would risk upsetting the icon of the franchise.

Still, Bouton took Mantle's voice mail to be such a blessing; by 1997 he had no qualms showing up to a fundraiser for the Mickey Mantle Foundation. Mantle had died two years earlier, and Mantle's son, David, was surprised to see Bouton there. Other ballplayers at the event muttered to each other that Bouton wouldn't have had the nerve to show up had Mantle still been alive, but they, like pretty much everyone else, were unaware that the two had reconciled years earlier.[8]

That hadn't resolved the issue with the Yankees, though. And that was because the primary force behind the organizational blockade of the Bulldog wasn't Mantle or even George Steinbrenner. It was a man few people even knew existed—Jim Ogle. Ogle was a longtime sportswriter for the *Newark Star Ledger* who found himself in Bouton's crosshairs in *Ball Four*. "And now a final word about my favorite baseball writer, Jim Ogle of the Newhouse papers," Bouton wrote in the March 30 entry of the book. "Ogle was a Yankee fan and he reacted to players purely on how much they were helping the Yankees to win. Charm, personality, intelligence—nothing counted. Only winning. Ogle didn't have even the pretense of objectivity. He was the only writer in the press box who would take the seventh-inning stretch in the Yankee half." Ogle, Bouton believed, was the prototypical sportswriter who was a fan first and a journalist last; he was everything that was wrong with the sports pages. He was everything Shecter was not. He was such a fan, Bouton wrote, that "in fact, Ogle's ambition was to work for the Yankees. But they would never give him a job."[9] He was wrong on one count—the Yankees did hire Ogle away from the *Star Ledger* in 1975 to be the director of the club's alumni association. In this position he had two main responsibilities: keeping the Yankees in the good graces of their most iconic alumni and organizing Old Timers' Days. In his mind both responsibilities could be best discharged by blackballing Jim Bouton.

By the late '90s he was still employed by the Yankees but was in his mideighties. In 1997 twenty-six-year-old Joe Schillan had replaced him as the point man for organizing the Old Timers' Day festivities, but Ogle still kept his hand very much in it, essentially dictating to him the list of invitees. Beyond any personal animosity Ogle may have had toward Bouton, as an old-school sportswriter Ogle felt a sort of protectiveness toward the players he wrote about, which repelled people like Shecter but came naturally to sportswriters like Ogle, who not only covered but covered *for* the Yankee players. "Jim Ogle felt a loyalty to Mickey Mantle," said Rick Cerrone, who by this time had graduated from being Bouton's cold caller for the *Ball Four* update to become the club's director of media relations. "Jim Bouton was probably persona non grata to Jim Ogle more so than he might have been to Mickey Mantle."

On Father's Day 1998, after witnessing his father struggle to get to his feet in the months after his sister's death, Bouton's son Michael wrote an open letter to the Yankees in the *New York Times*, urging the club to patch up its differences with his father and invite him back into the Yankee fold. Please have him back for Old Timers' Day, Michael urged in his letter; his dad could use the hugs.[10] That got the ball rolling. Schillan then called Cerrone and asked him to speak to Steinbrenner about it. Cerrone did, and that's when he learned that, in fact, there was no organizational edict to ban Bouton from Yankee events. At least not one that stemmed from the top.

People assumed a lot of things about Steinbrenner, particularly those who worked for him. Oftentimes those assumptions were on the money, but every once in a while they were flat-out wrong. For years the Yankees had a strict rule that once a number was retired nobody else could wear it, not even on Old Timers' Day. What ensued was sheer absurdity: Tony Kubek and Chris Chambliss would take the field wearing different numbers than they had as players because the Yankees had subsequently retired number 10 for Phil Rizzuto. Bobby Richardson and Bobby Murcer had to select different numbers when they were invited back because their number, 1, had been retired for Billy Martin. Graig Nettles would take the field wearing number 45 (four plus five) because his number, 9, had been retired for Roger Maris. All because of an edict from Steinbrenner. At least that's what everybody assumed. When Cerrone finally went to the Boss to ask him about it, Steinbrenner was shocked. It was the first he'd heard of *his* edict. Turned out that it was an edict from the equipment manager, who was the last link in a convoluted whisper-down-the-lane episode that led him to believe that this was what the Boss wanted. Steinbrenner put an end to the silly practice immediately. Same with the alleged organization boycott of Jim Bouton. When Cerrone asked him about it Steinbrenner was surprised to learn that it was supposedly coming from him. It wasn't. "At least not from what I was able to discern from my conversations with him," Cerrone says. When presented with Michael's letter, Steinbrenner ordered Cerrone to invite Bouton back.

Cerrone instructed Schillan to call Bouton with the invitation and then sought out Ogle, to inform him of what was, without a doubt this time, an edict from the Boss. Ogle may not have been thrilled with the news, but there wasn't much he could do about it. And the circumstances were such that even to him it sort of made sense to let bygones be bygones. "If I had called Jim Ogle out of left field and let's say nothing had happened in the Bouton family," Cerrone said. "And I said, 'Hey, we're inviting Jim Bouton this year,' I'm pretty sure Jim Ogle would have given reasons why that was not a good idea. But when I had the conversation with him, he understood."

There wasn't much time before Old Timers' Day 1998, and Schillan had a lot to do to get everything ready. His first job was to convince Bouton that he was serious. "I called him up, and he thought it was a joke. Because his friends had always played jokes on him, calling and saying, 'This is the Yankees. We want to bring you back.' I said to him that this is not a joke." Still, Bouton wasn't convinced. Schillan gave him his name, told him to look him up in the Yankee yearbook and media guide, gave him his number at the stadium, and told him that, if he liked, he could call the Yankees' switchboard and have them connect him to prove that this was not another prank. "This is for real?" Bouton asked. "This is for real," Schillan replied. At one point Schillan thought he heard a catch in Jim's voice when he realized this wasn't just another prank call from one of his friends.

Because there was so little time, the initial plan was just to announce Bouton before the Old Timers' game but not have him in uniform. The story of his return to Yankee Stadium broke so quickly and so wide, though, that Schillan realized that that wouldn't be enough. He had a personalized Yankee uniform, with a large "56" on the back and his name stitched inside, ordered on a rush basis. For the first time in years the Yankees sold out Old Timers' Day.

Still, Bouton wasn't sure what to expect. "We were in touch a lot in those days," Keith Olbermann remembered, "and he said, 'Would you come with me because I don't know what the reaction is going to be, if someone is going to take a swing at me or what.'" Olbermann reassured him that that wouldn't happen but said he'd be happy to chaperone him, as he was going anyway—he would be doing the on-field play-by-play for the Old Timers' game itself and thought he might write up the Bulldog's return in a piece for *Sports Illustrated*. Bouton said fine and they went together. In fact, nobody did take a swing at him or even say anything negative at all; they understood why he was there. Neither Cerrone nor Schillan, who were both in the locker room while the Old Timers were getting dressed and kibitzing, and in the dugout as they were introduced, saw anybody turn their back on Bouton or confront him.

Yet to Olbermann at least (who was in the locker room as well), it didn't feel as if all had been forgiven. There was an absence of overt hostility, but "there was still a kind of a reserve" in the locker room, Olbermann noticed, as the others greeted him, "like, is he writing a book about this, too? Is he going to expose the terrible secrets behind Old Timers' Day?" Even though the years had rendered *Ball Four* tame and even though there was now more controversy in one hour of *SportsCenter* than there was in all of its pages, there was still at least an undertone of caution and a sense of remove by many of the others toward their former teammate. Watch out for him was the mood Olbermann picked up on; that guy might steal your wallet. "'And if he doesn't steal your wallet, he may steal your figurative wallet.' It was very interesting to see it firsthand," Olbermann said. It was "a permanent kind of 'Yeah, you're welcome back and we're very sorry and we're not gonna be mean to you because of this and you have lots of friends here and all that,' but there was still a little of 'Can we trust this guy or not?'"

He might not have been fully welcomed back into the fold that day, but that's not what he was looking for anyway. He was appreciative of Michael's having written the letter and enjoyed returning for the day, but acceptance? From the Yankees? That would be like Lenny Bruce seeking absolution from Merv Griffin. Having built his life as an outsider, acceptance at this point into the inner sanctum of the Yankees would have undermined a lot of not only what others expected of him but what he expected of himself. So, no, not acceptance. A begrudging welcome struck the proper tone.

Most of the stories written the following days and weeks got the tone of the day all wrong. They left the impression that the prodigal son had returned and that the day was a triumphant one. The Yankees, at last, had forgiven Jim Bouton and invited him back into the fold was the common theme. But Bouton not only wasn't looking for forgiveness, but didn't believe he needed to be forgiven for anything. If anything, all he had done was tell the truth too soon. Hardly a crime in his book. And while the sportswriters who covered the day made much of his return, probably because, as writers, it meant so much *to them*, in truth the reaction from the sellout crowd was buoyant but still somewhat muted. The stadium was packed, yes, and the people came, and some were there for no other reason than to witness the return of Jim Bouton, but many more were there to see the return of the '78 world champs on their twentieth anniversary; Graig Nettles got more and louder cheers than "baseball's Bolshevik," as the *Village Voice* called him.[11]

Which was fine. Bouton remembered the day as an emotional but ultimately sad one because of the events that led to his return. Goldensohn, who was there as well, likewise remembers it as anything but a celebratory moment. "Jim never said, 'Oh boy, I've been invited.' He felt understood a little bit. He was still in that post-Laurie softness—there was a softness to Jim; he was a quieter person during that period. There was nothing to celebrate, but it was much appreciated." In a small way the phone call from Schillan and the day at Yankee Stadium helped to bring him out of the fog just a little bit, brother Bob said. Looking up in the stands, at all of the family and friends who were there—including Bobbie, who was surprised when Jim offered her a ticket to the game—he understood that life could and would go on. It was what he needed to know at the precise moment he needed to know it most.

38 Existential Bad Faith

For someone as determined to rattle the status quo as Bouton, he at the same time had a fierce appreciation for the old, for that which new ways of thinking might vanquish. As much as *Ball Four* shook the establishment and changed the way fans related to baseball, it was in large part a love letter to the disappearing landscape of the game—the crusty old managers; the uneducated, salt-of-the-earth ballplayers; the simplicity of the baseball life. He mourned the death of old Yankee Stadium when it was refurbished in the mid-1970s and after he relocated to the Berkshires fell in love with another relic of the past, Pittsfield's Wahconah Park, that was similarly in line to be demolished—if not immediately then surely eventually—and replaced with something new but hardly better. It was still standing, though, and, Bulldog that he was, decided that he could stop the forces itching to level it and focus attention instead on preserving it in amber such that it would last for generations. He couldn't. But he got a helluva book out of trying.

Wahconah Park was in many ways the spiritual birthplace of the men of *Ball Four*. Whether any of them actually ever played there was beside the point. And, anyway, its author, in fact, did: Bouton's 1972 tryout with the Texas Rangers took place there. It might be difficult to imagine the past while standing in one of the myriad twenty-first-century Major League stadiums, which nod perfunctorily to the bygone cathedrals with their faux brick and odd outfield angles but are in actuality glitzy baseball shopping malls disguised as ballparks, but you couldn't help it in Wahconah. If you couldn't feel it the moment you stepped inside one of the nation's last standing wood stadiums, you certainly did the moment the game paused to let the sun set, angled as it was such that the glare shone right in the batter's eye moments before it vanished below the horizon. It was impossible to miss the cues that this was a relic of another era. It was all too apparent to the current tenants of the stadium, the Pittsfield Mets, whose owner announced in May 2000 that he was moving his club to a new stadium being built in Brooklyn, New York. Wahconah was outdated, he said, and not up to modern Minor League ballpark standards.[1]

Technically, the stadium, itself, was never scheduled to be demolished. Instead, it was scheduled to be shunted aside; demolition would then be inevitable once it became abandoned. Pushing the construction of the new stadium was the local newspaper, the *Berkshire Eagle*, itself a relic of another era—the last functioning daily newspaper in the region. It wasn't only pushing it, though. It would be, via its parent company, donating the land for the new stadium along with a couple of million dollars toward construction. In return Pittsfield's mayor granted the *Eagle* naming rights for the stadium.[2] Thus was established an uncomfortably cozy relationship between a local government and its purported watchdog. Their attempt at creating a Pittsfield Civic Authority with eminent domain powers that would construct, own, and operate the new stadium fell through, though, and when it did Bouton stepped into what he thought was the breach, announcing his plan to renovate Wahconah and purchase an independent Minor League team to play in it.

It was an idea that couldn't fail, he believed, because it gave everybody what they wanted. It gave Pittsfield a renovated but preserved Wahconah Park, it gave its baseball fans a new team to root for, and it gave everybody in the struggling town—baseball fan or otherwise— relief in the wallet because his plan wouldn't cost taxpayers a dime; his plan called for private investment, not construction on the public dole. Everyone from the mayor on down to the *Eagle* would cheer this on, he believed. He couldn't have been more wrong. In the process he stepped into something much bigger than he ever expected.

His sidekick in this expedition was Chip Elitzer, a lifelong Republican he met when Elitzer and his wife showed up in his home one day to take ballroom dancing lessons from Paula. "I didn't know it was Jim Bouton's house," Elitzer said. "All I knew was that [my wife] was dragging me to take ballroom dancing lessons with somebody called Paula." Jim wasn't there the first lesson but showed up for the second. During a break Chip introduced himself to Paula's husband, asking him what he did. "He told me he was a motivational speaker. I thought his last name was Kurman, since that's what Paula's was." Eventually, he put the pieces together and realized that he was taking dancing lessons in Jim Bouton's house.

The two couples eventually became friendly—Jim told Paula they ought to get together with that couple with the wife with the really crazy laugh—and Bouton and Elitzer bonded while building a tree house for Elitzer's kids. They didn't know what they were doing but did it anyway and all out—they started off with an idea of building a platform forty-five feet off the ground until their wives made them bring it down by half. They realized that they worked well together— each was an overgrown kid at heart with the enthusiasm of a teenager. They made all sorts of plans while working on the tree house—at one point they contemplated building a zip line between Chip's house and Jim's two miles away. They spent hours up there, talking, thinking, dreaming. "We were building it for my kids, but I think Jim and I spent more time in the trees building it than they ever did using it." Neither of them could do anything halfway, they realized. Once they seized upon something, even something as outlandish as a two-mile zip line, they couldn't seem to let it go. If Bouton was the Bulldog, then Elitzer was at least the Terrier.

Which was how and why they found themselves immersed so quickly and so deeply in the Wahconah Park ordeal shortly thereafter. They dreamed a beautiful dream and then couldn't let it go. They also smelled something rotten and couldn't let that go, either. "It became," Paula says, "without anyone ever intending it, a whistle-blowing experience. . . . It's not as if Jim is a troublemaker, looking for places to explode mines. He's not like that at all. Yes, he has a streak of mischief, but he set out in this project to do something good for our new community. He wanted to take this old ballpark and invest time and energy and money in making it a showplace where exciting things could happen. He had no idea that he was stepping into a cesspool of corruption." Once he saw it, though, he couldn't walk away from it. Once you see it, he believed, you had no choice but to fight it. To say nothing, to walk away, was to become part of it.

Elitzer noticed this about his new partner right away. "He certainly doesn't take himself seriously," he said, but "he takes issues seriously. He cares deeply about doing the right thing. And about the right thing being done in the public arena." To Bouton the Wahconah Park issue was simple and straightforward. The ballpark was a cultural landmark that needed to be preserved, and it was in the public interest to preserve it if at all possible. That public officials were not only not receptive to this idea but actively plotting against it made no sense to him. Until he believed he saw the reasons they were so adamantly opposed to his plan. So he started doing what he had done three decades earlier to capture the truth of baseball as honestly as possible. He started taking notes.

He believed the *Eagle* was so willing to donate the land for the ballpark because the property, which had been until 1987 a General Electric (GE) transformer plant that used PCBs to make its transformers, was hopelessly polluted. By donating it, the paper, or more accurately, its corporate parent, could divest itself of a headache and save itself the environmental cleanup costs.[3] The mayor's office, as well, would welcome the construction, Bouton believed, because it was ethically challenged in its own right and stood to benefit from the project.[4] The entire scheme, at least as he saw it, was a tidy package that reeked of corruption and backroom deals, one that, if nobody stopped it, would pave over and bury a myriad of problems underneath a shiny new ballpark that would not only seep carcinogens but bleed the taxpayers dry. All of it was orchestrated by a consortium of "awful people, just awful people," he said recently. "They don't care." *Functionaries* was a term he ground up and spit out of his mouth whenever referring back to the government and business cronies he clashed with back then, the word arriving across the room like the smack of body odor. He was going to expose them, he decided. The Jim Bouton way. "The only thing you can do is to try to have fun with it. Otherwise, you'll go nuts. At least you can humiliate them every once in a while."

Elitzer saw that he had teamed up with a behavioral purist. "The actions of those people were fairly despicable," he said, and whereas others might have become immune to at least some of it through life experience, "Jim [was] less likely to shrug that stuff off." He could be flexible when it came to ideology but rigid when it came to personal conduct. He could be easygoing and forgiving when it came to almost anything. But ethical failings and downright shitty behavior were something else. David Scribner, an editor at the *Eagle* who became Bouton's nemesis in the fight, used to carry an old baseball glove in his trunk. In the midst of everything he thought he'd try to lighten things up one afternoon by asking Bouton if he wanted to have a catch. Bouton refused, maybe the only time he'd ever refused the offer of a game of catch with someone who, above and beyond the Wahconah issue, was still a fan.

When he saw something rotten, when he smelled it, it wrinkled his nose such that he had to record and expose it. Soon he was writing down nearly everything he heard at meetings and hearings regarding the Wahconah issue. He hadn't told anybody beyond Paula and the Elitzers that he had a book in mind, but everybody in Pittsfield knew of *Ball Four* and how it attacked the entrenched power structure in baseball. When they saw him taking notes in their town, those with something to lose knew that they might soon understand what it must have felt like to be Bowie Kuhn.

What he found in Pittsfield was a story about the decline of America: the death of newspapers and the dangers of corporate conglomerate ownership. All wrapped up in a fight over an old wooden ballpark in the middle of nowhere. There were more than mere wisps of smoke regarding the possibility that Pittsfield's local government was corrupt, just the sort of story a small-town paper would normally tear into and devour. But because there was only one daily left in Pittsfield and it was in the middle of the story, there was nobody left to report on it. Scribner recognized this. "It was really embarrassing," he says now. "There were all these relationships between the publisher of the paper and the mayor, trying to get this stadium done." He knew of some of them at the time but not all. The cozy relationship between their employer and the mayor's office made life in the newsroom difficult, he recalled. "It was really awkward. How can we report on this?" They really couldn't. So Bouton decided that he would. Problem was, he was not a journalist or any sort of investigative reporter, hard realities that would singe him and his book later on.

Within the pages of the *Eagle* Scribner and his colleagues championed the project, shooting arrows at Bouton whenever the opportunity arose. The paper's editorial page became an out-and-out advocate for the new ballpark plan, failing to consistently remind readers that the *Eagle*'s parent company was involved in the deal. Even later, after the dust had settled, editorial page editor Bill Everhart couldn't see the problem with this. "It was a good idea," he told the *American Journalism Review* of the new ballpark plan. "Everyone was very clear that the Berkshire Eagle, or more accurately MediaNews Group, was involved. There was nothing to disclose."[5] He and Scribner (Bouton nicknamed them Ever-Scrib) dismissed Bouton's Wahconah idea as "a fantasy world vision of 'historic' Wahconah Park that is as unrealistic as the field of dreams from the Kevin Costner movie of the same name," contending instead that Wahconah Park was "a proud old lady too long kept on life support."[6] Perhaps. But the new ballpark idea was riddled with problems as well, which Pittsfield residents were kept in the dark about.

As the battle intensified, Bouton threw himself into it. Along with everything else it gave him something to do, something to reignite him in the wake of Laurie's death. He didn't realize it at the time but later, upon reflection, understood that championing the cause of an old ballpark helped him to crawl back to the world of the living.[7] The fire had returned; he was determined to both root out the corruption and make his ballpark plan work. He sought out local investors and found some. "One of the things that really impressed me about Jim and Chip was that they seemed to want all of the stakeholders to get something out of it," says Howard Cronson, who became one of them. "It was not, 'What's in it for me? How much money can we make out of this?' but they seemed to really want to have a great product for the people in the Berkshires. And at no taxpayer expense."

His intentions may have been pure, but he was up against more than he realized. And his methods rankled more than a few. "Pittsfield's one of those places where, if you haven't lived there your entire life, you're an outsider," Cronson says. Many of its residents were skeptical of the *Eagle*'s new ballpark plan but hesitated to rally behind Bouton and Elitzer's alternative. "There was definitely a feeling that Jim and Chip were these two New York guys—outsiders—who were coming in and telling people what they should do with Wahconah Park," said Cronson. Irrespective of the fact that their plan was the best deal they were ever going to get to save the stadium—a tax-free upgrade and a new ball club to play in it—parochialism won out in the end. According to Scribner, Bouton and Elitzer succeeded in alienating the very people they needed to win over. "You could see it happening. Had they played their cards a little differently, it might have worked out differently. They came in as the arrogant South County guys trying to tell the city what to do, and right as they may have been, that was not the approach to take."

As he seemed to do wherever he went, Bouton managed to turn nearly everyone on the establishment side of the battle against him. His plan called for the use of nonunion labor in places to save on construction costs, and that got the labor unions on his case. "We were threatened," Paula recalled. "It was very scary. Some of these people knew where we lived and got extremely hostile. They paraded a union goon in front of us, who showed us all kinds of scars on his chest from knife fights and stuff. We were afraid to be in Pittsfield after dark."

Looking back on it, Scribner has regrets. The best thing to have done, he realizes, was to figure out a way to make the Bouton-Elitzer plan work, to try to come to some sort of agreement that would have resulted in the refurbishment of Wahconah Park. But for so many reasons there was no way that was going to happen. And that, as well, Scribner believes, makes the Wahconah saga a uniquely American story. Pittsfield, he points out, is a typical American town in that it refuses to respect its past. A few miles away sits Stockbridge, home of Norman Rockwell, cradle of the type of Americana people conjure up when thinking about their country, but Stockbridge, really, is a national outlier. More representative is Pittsfield, a town that can trace its roots down hundreds of years that nevertheless remains anonymous and without any sort of identity. In the midst of the Wahconah battle, historian John Thorn uncovered a document that contained the earliest recorded mention of baseball in North America—a 1791 bylaw passed by the Pittsfield Town Council outlawing, among other activities, the playing of baseball within eighty yards of the town meetinghouse in order to protect its windows.[8] Pittsfield, it turned out, could legitimately state its claim as baseball's Garden of Eden, or at least one such garden. More so than Cooperstown, whose creation story came not only without documentation but has also been thoroughly debunked by those who study such things. Baseball, or more specifically the history of baseball, ought to have been Pittsfield's identity, with a refurbished Wahconah Park being the town's jewel. Instead, if it is known for anything, it's known as the place where the Swiffer was test-marketed. "The first mention of baseball was 'Don't do it here,'" Scribner says, "and two hundred years later that's still the operative principle."

Despite all of the obstacles Bouton marched on, undaunted, pissing off nearly every moneyed interest in town. When they threatened to sue he threatened back. He had his notes, he reminded them; he had records of everything. "I'm not even going to need a lawyer," he told them. "It'll be me versus your lawyers," he recalled saying. "I've got all the material. I've got it all." What was more, he told them, he was going to reach back and pull a trick out of his sportscaster hat and get a camera crew to film the whole thing. He'd make a reality television show out of it, he said. That put an end to the lawsuit threats.

At least with regard to the Pittsfield people. Once he sold the book he ran into an entirely new set of problems. Ones that *would* end with lawyers and legal action. But without a television crew.

He quickly sold the book to PublicAffairs, an independent publisher that had a reputation for taking on tough issues and taking principled stands that other publishers wouldn't touch. He had a story that was much more than a baseball tale, one that looked like something resembling investigative journalism. Exactly the sort of thing PublicAffairs published. Acquiring editor Paul Golob thought working with Bouton might be a lot of fun, and publisher and founder Peter Osnos signed off on the deal, buying the book for a $75,000 advance.[9] When Bouton turned in his manuscript, though, Osnos was uneasy. The book contained explosive allegations regarding GE's polluting the area surrounding its former factory site, and Osnos pressed Bouton to do what an investigative reporter would do and dig deeper; among other things, he should interview, or at least try to interview, all sides. But Bouton wasn't an investigative reporter. Why should he speak to GE? he wanted to know. He didn't speak to Bowie Kuhn when he was putting together *Ball Four*.[10] The issue then became muddied when Osnos let it slip that GE's general counsel was not only a good friend of his but an investor in PublicAffairs. The two continued to argue over how Bouton should approach the GE issue, and when Bouton refused to accede to Osnos's demands, Osnos told him drop the GE angle from the book completely.[11] "Basically, it was a request for censorship" was how Elitzer perceived it. "And of course Jim doesn't take kindly to that kind of suggestion." To Osnos, though, it wasn't a request for censorship but a demand for thorough investigative journalism. "He wouldn't prove the conspiracy allegations he was making," Osnos says. "He would not do so, despite the fact that we asked him to do so. So we canceled the contract and sued."

Osnos couldn't understand why Bouton was so upset. "I don't know why he decided to make such a major issue out of it," he says upon reflection. "He takes things very personally. . . . Jim's a gifted but extraordinarily complicated character." Ultimately, it was clear that the two were talking at cross-purposes. Osnos was looking to publish a work of investigative journalism, while Bouton was looking to write a book that felt like *Ball Four* but with a much bigger target. He could get away with ignoring Kuhn's side of things or Mantle's side of things in *Ball Four* because in the end he was writing a baseball book. The stakes just weren't that high. Here, however, the juicy bits involved quite a bit more than whether the Mick was too drunk to hit a fastball. Here, they concerned a multinational Goliath conglomerate with the connections and bankroll that allowed it to get its way almost without fail. He was on the mark when he identified the breach created when the *Eagle* abandoned its journalistic duty but wide of it when he thought that he could fill it by re-creating the technique that worked so winningly with *Ball Four*. There was too much money, too much power, on the receiving end of his arrow.

Bouton and Osnos sparred until both realized they could no longer work together. "He didn't like us," says Osnos, "and in the end it turned out that we didn't much like him." Both felt that their integrity was being called into question by the other. Each was doggedly determined to stick by his principles and saw the other as ethically compromised. After Osnos canceled the contract they continued to spar, with Osnos suing to recover the $50,000 of the advance he had already paid out. Bouton believed he had never violated the termination agreement so refused to return any of the advance. Motions and cross-motions went flying, and after the judge somehow managed to rule against both of them, the case was settled.[12] To this day his tussle with Bouton rankles Osnos, and he prefers to remember it concluding with his emerging victorious and vindicated in the courts, although the record is far muddier and opaque than his recollection.[13] Really, nobody won.

Each described the other as operating in bad faith and went to court to prove it, but the truth was that the sort of bad faith Bouton was alleging was not the kind that could be determined in a court of law. Instead, it was the sort of existential bad faith Sartre contemplated when he wrote of the inkwell. An inkwell is simply an inkwell, he wrote in *Being and Nothingness*. It can be nothing else. But a person can don many hats and become many things, each of which is not himself. And whenever he throws himself into a role that is not true to himself, he is acting in bad faith.[14] Osnos accused Bouton of acting in bad faith by not investigating all sides of the GE issue, and under his definition of bad faith he had a point. But Bouton was not an investigative reporter. He was Jim Bouton, author of *Ball Four*. He approached his subjects his way. Compelling him to approach them as an investigative reporter would was, in Bouton's eyes, an act of bad faith in itself. When you signed Jim Bouton to a book deal, you were going to get Jim Bouton, nobody else. To expect anything different would be to expect him to compromise his personal integrity.

After l'affaire PublicAffairs he was on his own. Other publishers expressed interest but backed away as soon as they heard the GE angle. "We'd get a warm welcome walking in," Paula recalled of their efforts to sell the book at that time, "but then there'd be a sudden change of mood and then nothing." Jim was determined to find a publisher for the book, but Paula understood that the fear of retribution from a corporate behemoth like GE would make that impossible. "I knew from our experience of dealing with Wrigley that a corporation with deep pockets just keeps on coming. There's no way to win against that. You just have to find another way around." She finally persuaded him to let it go and self-publish instead. The game was rigged; they were now more convinced of this than ever. That's what his book, titled *Foul Ball*, was all about, and that's what was being driven home to them now, in their attempts to sell the book to other publishers. "There's a club, and you're not in that club and you'll never get in that club," she realized. The cross-pollination among the corporate club members meant that they'd take great steps to protect their own and do whatever they could to silence anyone who posed even a minimal threat. "*Foul Ball* had a sense of humor, but boy, it wasn't funny," Paula remembered. "I was appalled by what I got a close look at."

He decided to create his own imprint, Bulldog Publishing, and publish the book himself, throwing about $150,000 of his own money into the project to bankroll the printing, design, and publicity expenses.[15]

He released the book in June 2003, and, once again, just like in *Ball Four*, his targets overreacted and helped to publicize a book that, absent the sway of a traditional publisher behind it, would have had trouble being noticed otherwise. Two months before *Foul Ball* was released, the *Eagle*'s editorial page trashed it, writing that Bouton's "command of the facts is so tenuous, and his allegations so unfounded, that it is no wonder he is reduced to self-publishing the book." Postrelease, the weekly *Pittsfield Gazette* criticized it as "rife with errors, dubious quotes, naïveté and a lack of context." Those further from the scrum saw it differently, though. John Feinstein wrote that while the book wasn't in the same league as *Ball Four*, it was important and entertaining nevertheless. It told, he wrote, "a remarkable story, a sad one, in which the bad guys win." Writing in the *San Francisco Chronicle*, David Kipen remarked that the book was "delightfully funny, bittersweet, and altogether engaging." He also noted that, to those who still chirped that there was no way Bouton could have possibly written *Ball Four*, the same voice is infused throughout *Foul Ball* even though Len Shecter had been dead for three decades.[16] The *New York Times*, though, ignored it because it was self-published (subsequently the e-book edition was published by RosettaBooks, which still sells it nearly two decades later). As such its reach was muted, despite the encouraging reviews from here and there around the country. Sales were "extremely modest," says Paula.

Regardless, Bouton was happy with both the fight and the book, as was Elitzer. "We got our message out there," Elitzer said, despite the obstacles, which aligned themselves against them all along the way. They fought until it became obvious they were going to lose and cost their investors a lot of money and then pulled out before that happened. "We gave it everything we had, right up until we decided that we had to fold our tent. Most any other person probably would have tossed in the towel long before." As for whether he had another book in him, Bouton laughed off the suggestion. "I like to keep about 30 years between books," he said at the time. "So look for me in about 30 years with an exposé of the nursing home industry."[17]

39 A Mile in Bowie's Shoes

The battle over Wahconah Park married his romantic love of baseball's old ways with his penchant for stirring up trouble and led him right into another opportunity to engage in both. This time, his adventure began when he met John Thorn in April 2004. Both had been called as "expert witnesses" in an ESPN stunt putting the Yankees' spending habits on mock trial at the Bergen County Courthouse in Hackensack, New Jersey. It was during a break in filming when he and Thorn got to talking and Thorn informed him of the 1791 Pittsfield ordinance. This led both of them into a deep dive into baseball history, ultimately forming the Vintage Base Ball Federation (VBBF), where games would be played as they might have been back in the nineteenth century, when the game was two words instead of one, and where Jim Bouton, of all people, would be seated as its commissioner. This gave him an opportunity, on a smaller scale, to see what baseball might have looked like from Bowie Kuhn's perspective. While Bouton had spent the three decades since *Ball Four*'s publication opining how he'd be the antidote to the dolts who were actually running the game if they'd only put him in the commissioner's chair, when it actually happened at the VBBF, things turned out pretty much as they had in the bigs under Kuhn's leadership. Turned out, running a baseball league, whether one word or two, was a lot harder than it looked.

The excitement generated by the revelation of the Pittsfield ordinance confirmed to Bouton what he already suspected: It wasn't only the hard-core baseball historians who were fascinated by the game's history. There was a critical mass that was also drawn to it, and if he could reach them, he'd be able to make his point about Wahconah while making a few bucks in the process. Greg Martin realized that as well. Martin had recently gotten involved in putting together vintage "base ball" (as it was spelled in the nineteenth century) tournaments in Hartford and saw enough of an opportunity there to justify starting up his own business catering to it. His Vintage Base Ball Factory sold period uniforms and equipment to the amateur historians/ballplayers who spent their weekends trying to re-create the game as they believe it existed before the creation of the modern game. Martin had picked up *Foul Ball* and read a few chapters, realizing quickly that there might be a way to grow his company via Bouton and his passion for Wahconah Park. He Googled Jim, then emailed him, asking whether they might get together to consider the possibilities.

Martin's idea was to play a vintage base ball game at Wahconah Park, with his company supplying the uniforms and equipment. Bouton was intrigued. He was able to get ESPN excited about it, too. So much that it agreed to broadcast the game on its ESPN Classic channel on July 3, 2004, with Bouton's Pittsfield Hillies taking the field against former Red Sox hurler Bill Lee's Hartford Senators. Toward the end of the game Bouton took the mound to the cheers of the crowd, pitching a few innings with mixed results. The game was a smashing success. The parking lot was jammed hours before the game, the stands were packed, and everybody seemed to have a good time. Susan Sarandon and Tim Robbins showed up, many fans decided to become part of the show by dressing in period costumes, and even Paula got into the act, making her way through the stands at one point holding a sign arguing for women's suffrage. Lost among the revelry was the fact that this celebration of old-time base ball wasn't exactly historically accurate. Among other incongruences, the players were brought onto the field in antique cars that dated from the 1920s and '30s, even though the game itself was being played pursuant to rules from the 1880s, and the period costumes were actually from various eras throughout the late nineteenth and early twentieth centuries. "It was kind of an old-time base ball celebration that spanned a long period," Thorn recalled. "The inspiration may have been a 1791 document, the ballpark may have been constructed in 1892—or at least the first ballpark on that site was constructed in 1892—and the fans with their bowler hats and walking canes and fluffy dresses [represented] various vintages." Nobody seemed to care. Soon enough, they would.

Martin saw a business opportunity in games like these. Bouton was more hesitant, but eventually Martin convinced him that they should try to schedule another game, this one recalling the days of barnstorming baseball with a team of barnstormers playing a "Negro League" All-Star squad in Birmingham, Alabama. And if that went well, maybe, Martin thought, they could even try to re-create the world tour Albert Spalding organized in 1888, where he assembled two teams to travel the globe, ostensibly promoting the new American game but, really, promoting Spalding's burgeoning sporting-goods empire. In his own way Martin saw himself as not that dissimilar from Spalding, with his feet in both the baseball and the sporting-goods businesses. Maybe things could work out for him the way they had for Spalding more than a century earlier. Martin was thinking big. Let's try the Birmingham game, Bouton said, and then we'll see what we have.

Again, he was able to convince ESPN to broadcast it on its Classic channel. The game was scheduled to coincide with Black History Month and was played at Rickwood Field, the oldest standing ballpark in America, predating Wahconah by a decade. Bouton coached the Bristol Barnstormers, and former Red Sox star George Scott coached the Birmingham Black Barons. The game was designed to re-create the look and feel of baseball as it existed in the 1940s. Again the game was a success. At one point during a lull in the action Martin sat down next to Bouton in the dugout and said that this could become a regular thing. You know what we should be doing? Martin said, We should be doing a vintage base ball tournament—a World Series of vintage base ball. Bouton turned to him and said, "You know what? I like that idea."

Bouton saw fun; Martin saw a way to grow his business. Their concept, the Vintage Base Ball Federation, would mimic the Little League World Series, only for adults and with a history lesson attached that would go down as honey and not vinegar. Vintage clubs from around the nation would compete every year in their tournament, much like the Little Leaguers did every August. And they would not only have to pay an entry fee but would have to purchase their uniforms and equipment from somewhere, most likely Martin's Vintage Base Ball Factory. Now it was Bouton who was thinking big. It would be a national phenomenon, he believed, with clubs coming from all over the country. The possibilities were endless. One problem, though—vintage base ball was a niche sport that was played only in pockets here and there, with each club adhering to its own set of rules, playing by what it believed the rules were in, say, 1863 or 1886 or whenever. Much like two-word base ball really was back during that time period there was little uniformity in rules or customs from one town to the next or even one club to the next. Putting them all on one field and expecting them to agree even to the ground rules would be a challenge, to say nothing of playing the games themselves.

Bouton put together a board of directors for the VBBF full of cleanup hitters. He would be the chairman and chief executive officer and serve as the league's commissioner. Frank Deford, John Thorn, and former baseball commissioner Fay Vincent would also be board members. The kickoff celebration was scheduled to take place at Delmonico's Restaurant in New York, the place where Spalding held a celebratory dinner upon his return from the world tour in 1889. It was a lavish affair—like Spalding's was—designed to connect the VBBF to the history of the game through Delmonico's, but even here something was just a bit off. "Alas, Delmonico's has had many, many locations," Thorn said. "So the connection between Delmonico's and baseball's history is by name only, rather than by connection to this particular site. There was a spiritual connection but not a geographic one." To Bouton that was close enough. To others in the vintage base ball world, close enough would never be good enough.

Bouton's vision of the VBBF was that it would approximate the look and feel of nineteenth-century base ball. His league would cobble together "the most interesting rules," as he put it, from the period between 1860 and 1890 in order to present to the public a mixture of sport and theater.[1] Dressed in a brown derby and old-time vest, Bouton told the media assembled at Delmonico's that in his league, the umpires would be addressed as "sir," fans would be called "cranks," six balls would constitute a walk, and a foul ball caught on the bounce would be called an out. It would be "the game the way it was meant to be played," he said. "No batting gloves, helmets, wristbands, elbow pads, shin guards, sunglasses. No arguing with the umpire. No stepping out of the batter's box. No charging the pitcher or posing at home plate. No curtain-calling, chest-thumping or high-fiving. Just baseball."[2] Well, that depended on whom you talked to.

Because beyond the old-timey rules and phraseology, the VBBF would also have night games, which would have been as out of place in the nineteenth century as wristbands, along with some Vaudevillian skits in the stands that threatened to turn the history lesson on the field into something that more closely resembled slapstick. Watching this unfold, some began to wonder whether, sometimes, honey could be a bit *too* sweet. Before one game Bouton paid a bunch of actors to dress as Keystone Kops and take the field, threatening to shut the game down because it was being played on a Sunday. He had others dress as women from the Women's Christian Temperance Union roving the stands picketing against the evils of alcohol. He also had a routine involving gamblers waving large bills and trying to cajole the players to throw the game. "It's much more than a vintage baseball game," he told the *Times*. "It's a piece of living history."[3] Martin, who had spent the last few years dealing with the hard-core vintage base ball enthusiasts, who approached their pastime with the zeal of Civil War reenactors, braced himself for the trouble he knew was coming.

Reading about the burgeoning VBBF in the papers, more than a few players on the vintage clubs the league was hoping to attract to its tournaments considered Bouton's words to be heresy. He wasn't interested in the history, they believed; he was interested in running a business. They saw him as an opportunist, one who was swooping down into something they cherished and repackaging it as a sideshow for cheap laughs and as many bucks as he could get. His remark that the VBBF would be cherry-picking the "most interesting rules" from the nineteenth century was, to them, proof of his crass intentions. "If he would have chosen, say, 1864 rules, then the people watching would have said, 'Hey, this is how the rules were in 1864. Instead, his league was basically a hodgepodge," said Brad Shaw, a vintage base baller on the Flemington Neshanocks, who played by those 1864 rules and were part of the Vintage Base Ball Association (VBBA), an association that prided itself on historical accuracy above all else. "We thought he wasn't going to be true to history. His league was a show; it was entertainment. We had a problem with that. If someone goes into this for the history, they want it to be historically accurate. You don't expect a Civil War reenactor to do things that they did in the Spanish-American War."

It wasn't so clear who was being true to history and who was peddling fantasy, however. Bouton had taken in a few vintage games here and there along the way, including some put on by the VBBA. What he saw convinced him that the displays could not have been historically accurate, at least as far as the athleticism went. He saw players who were old and out of shape and who couldn't possibly have been even decent athletes in their younger days. As historians they may have been skilled; as ballplayers, their limitations were limitless. Perhaps they were true to the technicalities of the game they were playing, but those in the stands were clearly not getting a true picture of the athleticism of the game. During one such match he turned to Thorn and said, "You know, they play baseball like historians."

And when it came to the rules themselves, it wasn't at all clear that even they were an accurate representation of how the games were played back in the day. Thorn, the official historian of Major League Baseball, agreed that what they were watching was inaccurate. "It seemed to me that a slavish dedication to a particular rule book was false to history," he said. "It is unlikely that [teams] changed the way they played the game year by year in accordance with edicts from the National Association of Base Ball Players convention in New York.

Rather, the styles that seemed to work one year lingered for some years. As locally played, baseball was almost certainly an amalgamation of holdovers and local variance."

What emerged was a showdown over the soul of vintage base ball. At the annual convention of the Society for Baseball Research (SABR) in Seattle during the summer of 2006, Bouton addressed a room full of baseball historians and convinced them that his VBBF was not a sideshow, much to the amazement of Shaw, who assumed going in that the room would tear him apart. "It was me and a few other people on the panel debating against Jim," Shaw recalled. "The people in the audience are all about the history. They eat, live, and breathe baseball history. And we were about the history, and he was all about his VBBF. But because he's Jim Bouton and a terrific spin doctor, he turned the room against us." He followed that up with an open letter to the VBBA, hoping to smooth things over. He wrote that his VBBF "means no harm to the VBBA" and that the two organizations served different purposes—the VBBF was a business, whereas the VBBA was an organization. He then followed that up with a shot at the VBBA, noting that "whatever claims the VBBA may make with respect to rules in a given year, it certainly can't say that the polyurethane balls many of its teams use are in any way historically correct."[4]

The letter only inflamed things further. Martin, who knew the mind-set of the hard-core vintage base ballers better than Bouton, and whose sporting-goods business was at stake, begged Bouton to allow him to write the letter, but Bouton insisted on doing it himself, with the predictable results. "The players that were out there were taking this very personally," Martin recalled, "to the point where it started to impact my business. I was sent some email threads that were going around saying, 'Do not buy any products from Vintage Base Ball Factory.' This was how offended some of these players were." Customers he had worked with for years stopped returning his calls. He was being frozen out. By November 2006 his business had dried up. At that point he made a fateful, and fatal, decision, writing a check for $5,000 from the VBBF to his Vintage Base Ball Factory in order to keep it above water. "It was going to be a loan," he says. "It certainly was not intended to be anything shady. I didn't bring it up to Jim or the board of directors because I knew what the answer was going to be." When Bouton found out about it, he called Martin, asking him what was going on. Martin told him that he thought he was going about things all wrong, that he was trying to start out too big, that he was too controlling. And because of all that, Martin said, his business was practically out of business. The next thing he knew he was on a conference call with Bouton, Deford, Vincent, and the entire board of directors. They voted to expel him from the board. Shortly thereafter, Vincent decided that he didn't need the aggravation and resigned as well. The VBBF started to get a stink about it, and those with reputations to protect began to question why they were attaching their names to a small-time diversion that appeared to be on shaky footing.

The infighting between the two vintage base ball factions only intensified. The hard-core historians considered Bouton to be a philistine, one who was intent on putting on a Halloween costume party rather than a historically accurate representation of nineteenth-century base ball. Bouton and his VBBF compadres considered the hard-core folks to be out of touch and not all that accurate anyway. The VBBA "was a museum piece," Thorn said, one that was about as fun as a dusty diorama and not half as informative. The hard-core contingent was "somewhat delusional in thinking that they were actually re-creating 1863," says Gary Goldberg (Pops) O'Maxfield, a vintage player who lined up behind Bouton. There was no way to know what the game was really like back then; it was impossible to know just by looking at a set of rules. So why not relax and just have fun?

Despite the hard feelings all around, the VBBF was able to coax enough clubs to Westfield, Massachusetts, for a tournament in 2007 and another in 2008. The clubs were composed of talented players—these guys most definitely didn't play like historians. It was a tournament that was true to Bouton's approach to the endeavor in that "it combine[d] old-time values with modern business practices," as he told a reporter at Delmonico's.[5] The competition was real and impressive to watch, the stadium staff wore suspenders and newsboy caps, and the rules were an amalgam. "Harmless additions," he said at the event. And anyway he wasn't out to satisfy the historians; he was in this to have fun and put something on the field that people would pay to see. "From the fans' point of view, they really don't care," he added. "They like the fact that the players are brought onto the field on a horse-drawn hay wagon."[6]

It couldn't last. The disagreements ran too deep to provide the sort of foundation an enterprise like this needed to survive, and when the economy tanked in September 2008 that was it. The 2009 tournament was canceled, and the vbbf faded away.

Looking back on it, no matter what anybody may have said with regard to the historical accuracy of the games on the field, the battles off it did in fact mimic the very ones that were taking place during the nineteenth century over the preferred direction of the game. "Absolutely," O'Maxfield says when asked if at least the squabbling was properly representative of the era. "When you think about the fact that the National League started in 1876 and they actually were able to get eight teams together that would play by one set of rules, it's pretty amazing." As were the two vbbf tournaments. At least O'Maxfield and Shaw could agree on that much. "The funny thing was, this was not unlike what happened in the 1860s," Shaw says. "It was the fight between the amateurs and the professionals. The amateurs wanted to keep the game pure, but the professionals said that you can't keep the game pure if you're going to pay somebody because now there's another motive. Instead of a motive for playing as being enjoyment and camaraderie, now the motive is to make money—for the players as well as the owners. So this was history happening all over again." All of it makes O'Maxfield laugh. The fighting, the rivalries, the pettiness—all of it an accurate representation of "base ball" as it existed a century and a half ago. In this vein Bouton's vbbf was a smashing success that even the hard-core historians had to at least acknowledge.

Most ironic, though, was the fact that the battles between the vbbf and vbba put Bouton on management's side for once in his life. In advocating for a tournament based on fun, he was accused of seeking naked profits at the expense of the integrity of the game, just as he had accused Kuhn and NFL commissioner Pete Rozelle of doing. After spending a lifetime jabbing at the men who ran the games, condemning them for not appreciating their simple beauty, for discarding history for want of a buck, he now found himself not only in their chair but in their shoes as well. And, like them, he protested that he was wrongfully accused. The commissioner's seat, he realized, was in many ways a perpetually hot one. It was difficult if not impossible to balance competing interests such that all sides were happy. More often, nobody was. There was a futility to the role that would frustrate anyone with a mind-set of setting goals and then reaching them. For all he had said throughout his life about how he would and could fix all that was wrong with baseball if only they'd put him in the commissioner's office, his VBBF experience taught him that it would have most likely been a job that would exasperate him to no end. It was a thankless position that should have had "Must be willing to be the bad guy" in the job description. Not a job for someone who had spent his life striving to be the opposite.

40 Cashing Out

Jim "likes jumping off cliffs without a parachute," Paula said in the middle of the Wahconah Park scrum. "The trouble is, you don't know where your next dollar is coming from."[1] He always believed that he could make money. He would reassure a nervous Paula that she shouldn't worry about it; if they needed some, he could always think up a way to get what they needed. As he aged he held on to this belief, even while Paula was telling him that at some point other people simply wouldn't let him earn money in the ways he always had. They wouldn't hire him, wouldn't invest in him, for the simple reason that he was no longer the young man he once was. "He doesn't get that," she said recently. He was never interested in becoming rich; he simply wanted to have fun and work on the things he enjoyed. He didn't need the nest egg, he believed, because so long as he was doing what he loved, the money would follow. Or at least enough of it would. "I heard that around here a lot," she said. "'Don't worry about it. I can always do something. I can make a speech; I can write a book; I can write articles; I can make art and sell my art.' He has just always, since he was a little boy, believed that about himself." There was no individual retirement account, no investment portfolio for them to fall back on. There was just Jim. "We didn't quite believe in old age," Paula says. "Jim's notion of himself was that he was going to die suddenly, in the midst of running to accomplish something or do something. He would just keel over, and that would be it. There would be no slowing down; there would be no disease process or illness."

Which was why he barely hesitated to give up the one thing that would have given him the fat nest egg to see he and Paula through old age and beyond: Big League Chew. The mid-1990s were a tough time for the bubble gum—the 1994 baseball work stoppage that led to the cancellation of the World Series soured people on the game along with pretty much everything associated with it, including Big League Chew. Sales flattened, and the decade-long winning streak the gum had been on seemed to have finally ended. Laurie's death a few years later left him in a state of shock such that he had no patience for earnings reports and marketing ploys to right the ship. He just wanted to be done with it all. He just wanted to cash out.

He sat down with Rob Nelson and told him he wanted out. Nelson didn't have the money to buy him out in one fell swoop, so they agreed on a plan where Nelson would buy out his partner's share over a three-year period. Laurie's death "really put him in a funk," Nelson said, "and he did a lot of soul-searching and reevaluating of his own life. And he and Paula just decided that they thought Big League Chew had run its course." The agreement they eventually crafted resulted in Nelson keeping the rights to the Big League Chew brand when it came to gum and candy and Bouton keeping the Big League brand as it might apply to anything else. The deal matched their respective personalities: Nelson was comfortable being anonymous and well compensated; Bouton could never be comfortable with that. In fact, there was no Big League brand beyond the gum and candy at the time, and that's the way he liked things—there was a sense of the unknown, the unconquered, on his end of the deal. He would be free to make it up as he went along, to chart his own course, sail in a new direction.

Nelson was convinced that his partner was making a mistake. "We had a fundamental difference in terms of expanding the Big League brand," Nelson recalled. "Jim was always a big thinker and wanted to maximize the leverage that Big League Chew created, and I didn't want to do that. I looked at Big League Chew as a kind of WD-40. You come up with one product and just ride it into the sunset." Bouton thought that the strength of their creation resided within the words *Big League*, whereas Nelson believed that it resided within the word *Chew*. It was the bubble gum people responded to, Nelson thought, the way it was packaged and presented. Take the gum away, and there was nothing left. "I remember saying to Jim, 'It's like taking the *Jack* out of *Cracker Jacks*. When people look at a pouch of Big League Chew they say, 'This is really fun. This is a nice idea.' I can't see somebody looking at a bottle of Big League Root Beer and having the same kind of giddy feeling."

Over the years Bouton tried to expand the brand, with limited success. He tried Big League sunflower seeds, Big League fruit shreds. He thought there might be a market for Big League popcorn and Big League hot dogs. What would set Big League hot dogs apart from the dozens of others on the supermarket shelves? "It's Big League," Paula said. That wouldn't be enough. Nelson was pretty sure this was how things would ultimately wind up, so he tried to dissuade Jim from cashing out multiple times. "We don't have to do this," he told him more than once during the course of the three-year buyout period. "I think the brand is going to bounce back." But Bouton would not be dissuaded. "I didn't want the partnership to break up," Nelson says. "As it turns out, it worked to my advantage because I get to call the shots more, and I like that. But it wasn't my first choice." He never wanted to be put in the position where he'd have to turn to his former partner and say, "I told you so," but Jim wouldn't give him any other option.

Still, Jim and Paula refused to look back with regret. "I think, perhaps, if Laurie hadn't died, we might not have done that," Paula said. "But we were numbed out. We just couldn't function for a number of years. It was as if the light had gone out. So we handed it over, and it seemed like a good deal, and a fair deal, at the time." Although they've had reason to look back and reassess, to kick themselves over a deal that wasn't so great after all, they rejected that approach. "There's no point in dwelling on that," she added. "We don't look back. We're not bitter people. We just don't live in that space." They would acknowledge, however, that their decision wasn't the best. "Rob," Paula would say to him years later, "you did the right thing, and we made a big mistake."

Their mistake was in assuming, as they always had, that Jim would make something work, no matter what. The fact that Nelson went on to license his part of the company to Ford Gum, where it experienced a rebirth in the marketplace, making Nelson an even wealthier man, never became a sore point because they firmly believed at the time that while Nelson may have had the gum, they had Jim Bouton, which was even better. But then the market crashed in 2008, and then a few years after that everything would change. "We thought we would have the energy to work on the rest of the brand, but we didn't anticipate the downturn in the economy in 2008; we didn't anticipate how long it would take us to get back in the saddle, so to speak, after Laurie died," Paula said. And they didn't anticipate that in 2012 life would once again get in the way of Jim's dreams, rendering some of them unreachable for the first time.

41   The Butter-Yellow Box

On August 15, 2012, the fifteenth anniversary of Laurie's death, Jim suffered a stroke. It wasn't his first—he had suffered a smaller one previously that resolved spontaneously. But this one was treated the way most strokes are, with blood thinners. What the doctors didn't know at the time was that Jim had a condition known as cerebral amyloid angiopathy, which in many ways mimics the condition that causes Alzheimer's dementia. People with CAA are at increased risk for brain bleeds, and providing a CAA patient with a blood thinner is just about the worst thing a doctor can do.[1] At the time, though, nobody had reason to suspect CAA—Jim had regularly submitted to annual physicals, and his numbers were always excellent. He always looked younger than his age, and whenever the routine blood work came back it suggested nothing out of the ordinary. The combination of the blood thinners and the CAA ultimately resulted in a hemorrhage in the frontal lobe of his brain. Soon he was having trouble organizing information; he was repeating himself; he wasn't as quick mentally as he had been. When the CAA diagnosis came later on, it was a shot to the gut. He had already suffered some cognitive impairment, he was told, but most people with CAA progress into a state of full-on dementia within five years or so. When, or how, or even if, this would occur to him was an open question; CAA is not one of those diseases that causes steady, gradual decline. There can be no decline for years, and then all of a sudden it can be as if you've fallen off a cliff.

For a person who had seen obstacles as mere adventures to push through on his way toward achieving his goals, the news was devastating. When they received the diagnosis, Paula said, it was the first time Jim had faced what truly was an immovable object. "That was the hardest part for him," she recalled. "'You mean I can't get better? What do you mean I can't get better?' He didn't get that, *really* get that, for years." He'd had a rough week or so after the stroke in 2012 but was convinced that he would fully recover from it. It wasn't until almost two years later that the doctors realized that his cognitive issues were coming from something other than just the stroke. Even then, for a short time at least, "he thought, deep down, that he could conquer [it]," says Paula. "He would just keep going, do things, and it would all work out." But when the concrete reality of the diagnosis hit him—that he would not be able to overcome this, no matter what, it "plunged him into a despair I hadn't seen in him in forty years," she said. "That required some medication to handle."

He began taking antidepressants to help him cope with the finality of his condition and eventually was able to reach at least a measure of acceptance. For a time, Paula said, "we worked out how to live with this. We manage[d] to have fun and have a good time between the disappointing evidence that things [were] not getting better, but this is the thing he's had the most difficulty with since I've known him. Nothing has thrown him like the notion that he just can't get up and go to work at something." He thought his life would be the way he'd always lived it; he thought it would go on forever. "That was the biggest change since the diagnosis," Paula says. "It [became] very hard for him to hang on to that belief."

He began transferring control of his various businesses and interests over to Paula. He had done a little of that beforehand, but now he understood that she would have to become the one to make the important decisions. He could handle that, though, because he was never about business. It was the other losses that threw him. "I used to open my mouth," he said a couple years after the diagnosis, "and something witty and perfect would come out. And I wouldn't plan it or think about it; it just would happen. It was so lightning fast. And now I open my mouth, and nothing comes out." The loss of his gift, the one that made him Jim Bouton, depressed, frustrated, and, at times, enraged him. A low dose of Prozac helped to keep all of that in check. Otherwise, Paula wonders, "how can you live with that?"

The Prozac settled him; slowly, he began to adjust. One morning he awoke and reported to Paula that he felt "the absence of bad." To his neurologist this was progress; this was, in its way, success. Because a life with psychic pain of the sort Jim had is pure hell. Prozac removed the bad. But there was nothing that could restore the good. Making everything more poignant was the fact that he had, for a few years at least, a metaperspective on his decline. He was aware of everything he had lost or was in the process of losing. Unlike a person sinking into a different form of dementia, noticeable to others but invisible to the sufferer, he oftentimes recognized when something was diminishing before anybody else. "In the past," he said, "it was so much easier to do things. Now I can't access any of that. Even if I have a good idea, by the time I'm halfway through it I've forgotten what the first part was. It's a pain in the ass is what it is." He'd lost a lot, but his intelligence remained, sitting above the disability, fully recognizing the shape of what was happening. And that, in its way, was a profound sadness of its own.

Dementia is something the Boutons have had on their radar for a while. Jim's father, George, suffered from it for years until he died in 2012. He had been a boxer in the navy, and the brothers speculated that perhaps a blow, or too many blows, to the head caused it, but they never knew for sure. They used to take him to Yogi Berra Stadium in Montclair, New Jersey, every year for his birthday, where he would throw out the first ball before a game, something he looked forward to all year. But then his decline accelerated to the point where he couldn't even recognize the menu he was holding in the diner they went to on their way to the stadium, so they ended that tradition. They then watched the dementia eat away at him until there was nothing left. After he died the brothers donated his brain to Columbia University. A little while later they received a report concluding that their father had indeed suffered a longtime injury that perhaps could have been related to his boxing career, but then again it could have been caused by something else. Jim's brother Bob also developed a form of dementia, although, unlike Jim, he never suffered a stroke. Whether the three cases are related remains a mystery. In their own way each was different—Jim was never a boxer; Bob never suffered a stroke. The only commonality is that they were all Boutons.

Until another stroke hit him right after Christmas 2018, he would often appear to be okay, at least on the surface; Bobbie said he typically sounded fine when they would speak, Kitman pronounced him "still great," and even Pete said that his brother could stay in a conversation, keeping up for the most part, although searching for words on occasion. But even prior to his 2018 stroke, the longer a conversation lasted, the more obvious it became that there was a significant loss. He'd get halfway through a story and then stop, smacking the sides of his chair in frustration as the conversational thread disappeared before his eyes. "Let it go, babe," Paula would gently say. He'd look at her pleadingly, and then he'd do as she said. It would be up to her to finish the thought.

The loss of the ability to write was what stung most. Before the 2012 stroke it was second nature for him to write something pithy, something that could make you laugh and think all at once, "but I don't have the chops to do that anymore," he said shortly before his 2018 stroke. "That's what's missing in my life now." After *Foul Ball* he had planned to write a book on his childhood, telling the sort of tales that constitute the first few chapters of this book, but once the effects of his CAA hit hard he abandoned the idea. "It's too damn hard to do," he said, turning away from the notes he had taken, giving up on it altogether. "Just regular conversation" was difficult enough, he added. "Forget about trying to write something." For a few years Paula urged him to try to make it work, to figure out a way for him, perhaps with her help, to write the book, to no avail. "When he began to realize that he couldn't put a sentence together that he liked, he stopped using email, stopped looking at the computer, stopped writing," Paula says. "He just wouldn't hear of going back to that book. It was just 'I cannot do it; it'll be bad; there's no point.' I said, 'Why don't you just tell the stories?' Well, now even that is difficult." As was painting. For a time he tried, but what he produced was "not my idea of art," he said, so he stopped altogether. "Actually," Paula says, "I found some of the pieces that he sketched at the beginning [shortly after his diagnosis] interesting. But then he made the mistake of trying to do a human face, and he was so horrified by what came out on the page he just wouldn't look at it again."

Rather than continue to produce, he began the process of letting go. In late 2016 he put up for auction all of the notes, tapes, drafts, and correspondence that made up the primordial ooze of his masterpiece, *Ball Four.* Even the 978 pieces of paper that were the genesis for the soul of the book, the notes he jotted down on hotel stationery and air-sickness bags capturing the musings of Gene Brabender, Gary Bell, Doug Rader, and the rest of the Pilots and Astros, were put up for sale. For decades they were nestled in a butter-yellow box that made Paula nervous whenever Jim took them out to show an interested visitor. They were clearly his pride as he showed them off. This one is on Houston Astros stationery, he'd say, that one from the Jack Tar Hotel. He'd beam as he showed them, his eyes half on them and half on the memories they elicited. They were his children. He gave birth to them. He nurtured them, formed them, and then sent them out into the world where they were embraced by millions. Their success reflected back on him, and he'd be awash in it whenever he took out the butter-yellow box.

The "Ball Four Collection," as it was called, generated a lot of interest, just not enough. Bids came in high, but just short of the reserve. So they didn't sell. "We're not unhappy waiting," Paula said afterward. "I'm confident turning down something I thought was inadequate. A respectful and adequate offer from a party who can take care of it properly is what we're looking for, and we don't mind waiting. Maybe some people have to get past the notion that because it's about baseball it's somehow of less literary value." Finally, in late 2018, they found what they were looking for, selling the archive to the Library of Congress. "They understand the iconic nature of Jim's life," Paula said, so she felt comfortable handing off his life's work.

Once he was able to adjust to his new reality, he began to venture out in public, at least a little. He appeared at Drew University with Ira Berkow in 2015 with Paula at his side, helping him fill in the gaps. In July 2017 he headlined the annual SABR convention in New York, where he and Paula again charmed the crowd, telling old stories along with conveying the reality of what it's like to live with a degenerative brain disease. He was through running from it; now he not only had accepted it, but in true Jim Bouton fashion was determined to tell his audience what it was like from the inside. The morning of the SABR event an article appeared in the *New York Times* that painted a portrait of an addled Jim Bouton—he thought it was 1982, the article said; he didn't know his age; he was unable to answer a question regarding whether his Major League win total was closer to fifty or three hundred.[2] The article bothered his brother, Pete, who thought, "It was maybe technically accurate but really not descriptively fair . . . to portray him as, time for the Pablum, put a bib on him, is just not at all accurate." Most of those in the audience that afternoon had read the article and came braced for the worst. They were pleasantly surprised. For most of the hour he commanded the dais he was witty and relatively sharp, with Paula once again helping to steer him around the potholes he would encounter in the middle of a story. The event ended with the feeling in the room being that once again, and as had been the case many times before, the doubters had written Jim Bouton off prematurely. The Bulldog lived.

Yet even he knew that while the Bulldog was indeed alive, he was not well. As his CAA progressed it was claiming bits and pieces of him, mercilessly. Slowly at first but then rapidly. Until he became dependent on Paula for even the most basic tasks. By the end of the year his short-term memory had deteriorated to the point where any activity requiring even a modicum of focus left him confused and exhausted. By early 2019 he had trouble recalling basic facts or even signing his name—Paula finally had to start returning unfulfilled the autograph requests that still arrived in the mail. When it appeared as if he might slip away for good a couple of months later, Chip Elitzer's sons, Daniel and Sam, flew in from California to spend what would turn out to be their final moments with him. Sam had been an impressionable young teenager when he worked as a gopher for his father and Jim as they navigated the Wahconah Park ordeal, and the biggest impression left on him was the one made by Jim Bouton. He was determined to let him know that before it was too late. "One of the obviously painful things about dementia," Sam said afterward, "is that you're not sure what place you have in a person's memory. What was important to me was to tell Jim that it doesn't matter whether he remembers me. I remember him. I remembered who he was, who he is. I remember the greatness, the charisma, and the virtue. That struggle against injustice, that need to right wrongs, and represent people who were getting a raw deal. It was important for me to tell him that."

The prognosis had been nearly on the money—a small handful of years after the diagnosis he was in free fall. His long-term memory was still, for a time, not fully beyond his grasp, though, and when not receiving visitors he liked to spend his time indulging in a teenage passion—losing himself in the earthy cool defiance of *On the Waterfront*. On a seemingly endless loop it played, with Jim mouthing Brando's dialogue right along with him. That was me, he'd say whenever Brando's Terry Malloy came on the screen. After spending some months in home hospice care, Jim Bouton died on July 10, 2019. In what would be his final moments, after he'd lost the ability to speak, and then the ability to move his body freely, and when he appeared to be in the netherworld between life and death, Paula placed a baseball in his right hand for the final time. Immediately his fingers sprang to life, manipulating the ball here and there, searching for the seams. He then placed his first three fingers behind them and gripped the ball as tight as he could. And then he was gone.

Upon reflection it's clear that by the time he finally agreed to let me discuss this biography project with him in 2016, he knew that the end was, if not near, at least visible on the horizon. At a minimum he understood that his writing life was over; it was finally time to let someone else tell the story. The old Jim Bouton would have never ceded control like that. In discussing the parameters for this book, he and Paula were adamant that I explore all angles of his life; they imposed amazingly few restrictions. They didn't seek any form of editorial control or approval; I was free to tell the story as I saw it, just like Bouton did when he wrote *Ball Four*. Their only requirement, Paula stressed, was that they didn't want a puff piece; a hagiography wouldn't be true to who Jim Bouton was.

When, for a moment during our initial meeting in 2016, I slipped into fanboy mode and asked him to sign my beaten-up copy of *Ball Four* for my high school–age son, Alex, who (with perhaps a gentle nudge from Dad) had selected it as his "free choice" book to read over the summer, Jim—perhaps inadvertently, perhaps not—provided me with what I found to be something that might as well have been his battle cry as I began my work on his life's story. "Fuck 'em all, let it all hang out" was how he wanted to inscribe the book, a toothy smile exploding onto his face as he said this loud enough for Paula to hear, fully aware that this would gently pickle her. She overruled him. Don't you dare, she said. So he signed it as he usually did: "Smoke 'em inside," he wrote. Which is no doubt the battle cry of the army of *Ball Four* junkies, who even a half century later devour the book every spring as a preseason ritual, laughing and crying along with Jim Bouton before they drift off to sleep for the night, where they all hope to dream in baseball just like him.

Epilogue

The Cool of the Evening

There comes a point in every biography when the subject's legacy must be addressed, and here we are. What to make of Jim Bouton? It's true that most modern players have never heard of him, and while there remain legions of *Ball Four* fans, or "freaks" as they identify themselves on Facebook, there are legions more that couldn't pick Jim Bouton out of a lineup of degenerates rounded up from the roof of the Shoreham Hotel or identify the book as anything other than one of dozens of baseball books they might have seen in a bookstore at one time or another. On Father's Day 2018 I attended Old Timers' Day at Yankee Stadium with Jim and his family. It was the first time he had been invited back in years and marked the twentieth anniversary of his memorable return to the Yankee fold in 1998. It was a big day for Jim and Paula, but in the grand scheme of things, he was just another semianonymous old-timer to the scattered thousands who dotted the stands that hot June afternoon.

He was introduced near the end of the first group of old-timers announced, the ones who would occupy the third base side of the diamond and whom the brass had clearly decided weren't the ones people were coming out to see. The Frank Tepedinos, Al Downings, Graeme Lloyds, and Jeff Nelsons of the Yankee universe. The star attractions had reserved seats on the first base side, where they would be introduced last and to longer and louder ovations than their predecessors: Ron Guidry, Bobby Richardson, Don Larsen, David Cone,

Andy Pettitte, Paul O'Neill, and the biggest star of them all, Reggie Jackson. Once the Old Timers' game itself got under way Jim made his way toward us in the stands. "I didn't get to pitch," he said apologetically to the few dozen family members and friends who had come out to cheer him, as he headed toward an unoccupied seat. All of a sudden Paula found herself trying to contain a full-on sob. So much had changed from when they all did this back in '98. So much had taken place since then; so much had been lost so quickly. So little was left.

A few seats away an older man—he looked to be in his early sixties and wearing a weathered, sun-bleached Yankee cap—was taking all of this in with a confused look. He had a thick Bronx accent and was the right age to have been the target audience for the *All 'Bout Bouton* newsletter back in the day. He turned to me. "Who's that?" he asked. "Jim Bouton," I said. "Did he play for the Yankees?" he wanted to know.

Still, his impact on the game was outsized. It is relatively easy to tell the history of baseball without making mention of the greatest third baseman the game has ever seen—Mike Schmidt. It's nearly impossible to do so without at some point referencing the journeyman pitcher who won all of sixty-two games for the Yankees, Pilots, Astros, and Braves. When he became eligible for induction in Cooperstown in 1983 Ira Berkow wrote, somewhat in jest, that for singular contribution, Bouton deserved consideration; *Ball Four* was that much of a game changer.[1] Today MLB historian John Thorn sees it through a different lens. "Where is the lifetime achievement award in baseball?" he asks. "The Hall of Fame is not quite it. Larry Ritter is not in; Bill James is not in," he says. Nor is Jim Bouton. "When you have figures of monumental importance in the history of the game, for whom no honor exists," what do we do? he wants to know. "For me," he adds, "the cue for what ought to be the principal criterion is visible in the name of the institution—fame. Were you famous? Can the story of baseball be told without you? On that basis Bouton's in, Marvin Miller's in (he would in fact finally be elected in 2019), and certain people who are now in are out." Where do you put a Bill James or a Jim Bouton? "If they're not in the Hall of Fame, maybe there's a need for a People's

Baseball Hall of Fame," he suggests. Something that focuses more on impact than chumminess with the baseball establishment. Whatever it might be, he says, "It'd be nice for him to be no longer a prophet without honor."

Then he reconsiders. What does it matter, really, if he's enshrined on a plaque somewhere, entombed on a bust under which a few sentences are written that couldn't possibly hope to capture all he has meant to the game of baseball and how we watch it, understand it, and love it in a way we couldn't before he came along? Do we need a physical memorial to tell us what we already know, even if we don't know that we know it because of Jim Bouton? We have *Ball Four*; we have the legacy of his newscasts whenever we turn on *SportsCenter*; we have the subversive fun of Big League Chew; we have a wry, pointed, ironic approach to the game that we didn't have before the Chipmunks made him their muse. We have so much that recalls and channels him whenever we even think about baseball today. All of these are the monuments to Jim Bouton. These are what matter. These are what lasts long after the statistics are forgotten, after the physical facts of a player's career become as dusty as the plaque that purports to honor him. As much as some within the game might wish it to be otherwise, Jim Bouton courses through baseball's veins. When we talk about baseball during the last half century, we have no choice but to talk about Jim Bouton. And that, Thorn says, is the ultimate enshrinement. For it is of more enduring value than bronze, he believes, to have one's name writ on the wind.

Notes

1. Warm-up Bouton

1. Stephanie Fuller, "Jim Bouton's New Pitch," *Chicago Tribune*, July 11, 1971, 40.
2. Bouton, "Going Home," 48, 49, 50.
3. McDonald, "Big League Chew."
4. Bouton, "Going Home," 96.
5. "Knuckle-Ball Is Not a New Stunt," *Cleveland Plain Dealer*, March 15, 1908.
6. Picking, "Endangered Species," 17.
7. Shecter, "Jim Bouton," 48, 72.
8. Bouton, "Going Home," 96.
9. Klapisch, "The Next Chapter," 12.
10. Bouton, "Bronx Tales," 22; Angell, *The Summer Game*.
11. Jim Bouton, "Art/Architecture; Fantasy Baseball of Another Kind," *New York Times*, June 29, 2003, AR29.
12. Shecter, "Jim Bouton: Everything in Its Place," 72.
13. See "The Chip Hilton Series," http://seriesbooks.info/hilton.html, for an overall description of the tone of the Chip Hilton books as well as a summary of each of the twenty-five books in the series, originally published between 1948 and 1965.
14. Fuller, "Jim Bouton's New Pitch."
15. Shecter, "Jim Bouton: Everything in Its Place."
16. Gleason, "Legion Gave the Bulldog a Big Break," 24.
17. Gleason, "Legion Gave the Bulldog a Break."
18. Undated note contained in the butter-yellow box containing 978 sheets of notes, written by Bouton at some point during the 1969 season and that form the bones of what would become *Ball Four*. Currently available at Jim Bouton Papers (JBP), Manuscript Division, Library of Congress, Washington DC.
19. Gleason, "Legion Gave the Bulldog a Break."

2. Take a Hike, Son

1. Marion Clyde McCarroll, "Woman . . . Becomes Steel Window Expert," *Brooklyn Daily Eagle—Sunday Eagle Magazine*, August 28, 1927, 13.
2. Harry Cronin, "Jim's a Real Mound Artist," *New York Daily News*, October 6, 1963, 30.
3. Ferdenzi, "Pitching or Painting, Bouton Big Winner," 3; Til Ferdenzi, "Yanks Bouton . . . He's a Real Gem Dandy," *New York Journal-American*, August 31, 1963.
4. Ogle, "Bouton, Man of Talents," 44.
5. Ferdenzi, "Artist on Mound," 18.
6. Ogle, "Bouton, Man of Talents."
7. Dinerstein, *Origins of Cool*, 311.
8. Holmes, "Philosophy of the Beat Generation," 233.
9. Dinerstein, *Origins of Cool*, 344.
10. Bouton, *Ball Four*, 120.
11. John Leusch, "High School Sports Notes," *Newark Evening News*, March 2, 1965.

3. Joliet

1. Joseph Carragher, "Yankee Ace Stars at Home," *Newark Star Ledger*, September 22, 1963, Sports 1, 24.
2. Freehan, *Behind the Mask*.
3. Carragher, "Yankee Ace Stars at Home."
4. Shecter, "Jim Bouton: Every Thing in Its Place," 72.
5. Irene Janowicz, "Woman in the Family," *New York Mirror*, June 30, 1963.
6. Ferdenzi, "Pitching or Painting, Bouton Big Winner."
7. See Bobbie Bouton's scorecards, made available to and on file with the author.
8. Jerry Hagan, "Sportitorial: Western Student, Hurler for Yanks, Weds While on Leave from Fort Dix," *Kalamazoo Gazette*, December, 1962; Jerry Hagan, "Sportitorial: Houk Figured Ex-Bronc as Reliever but He Made Flag Clinching Easy," *Kalamazoo Gazette*, September 16, 1963.
9. Janowicz, "Woman in the Family."

4. You Should Write a Book

1. See letters from George Bouton, JBP.
2. Letter from George Bouton to Walter Laskowski (scout for the Philadelphia Phillies), November 3, 1958. On file with the author; JBP.

3. Letter from George Bouton to Jim, fall 1958 (specific date unknown). On file with the author; JBP.

4. Letter from Nicholas Kamzic (Milwaukee Braves scout) to George Bouton, undated. On file with the author; JBP.

5. Undated letter on New York Yankee stationery outlining the terms of Jim Bouton's contract. "I agree to sign a 1959 contract with the New York Yankees for the following terms: $5,000 a year for three years—total—$15,000; $500 a month salary for three years—Total—$9,000; $6,250 upon signing a New York Yankee Contract—$6,250. Grand Total: $30,250." The letter is signed by Art Stewart and on file with the author; JBP.

6. Letter from W. K. Fred to Jim Bouton, January 17, 1959. On file with the author; JBP.

7. See letters from W. K. Fred to George and Jim Bouton. Provided to the author by Jim Bouton and Paula Kurman and on file with the author; JBP.

8. Topps Chewing Gum contract addressed to George Bouton, along with the check for "Exactly Five Dollars," which remains uncashed, April 3, 1959, JBP.

9. Jim Bouton, "Did He Throw It on Purpose?," *New York Times*, July 11, 2000.

10. Jim Bouton, "Athletes Draw Fire, and People Stoke It," *New York Times*, May 10, 1987.

11. Ferdenzi, "Bulldog Bouton Earns Top-Dog Rating," 7; Carragher, "Yankee Ace Stars at Home."

12. Letter from Jack Sheehan to W. K. Fred, April 18, 1960. On file with the author.

13. Ferdenzi, "Bulldog Bouton Earns Top-Dog Rating."

14. Red Foley, "Jewelry Hobbyist Bouton Pretty Valuable Himself," *New York Daily News*, July 14, 1963, 104.

5. A Long Way from Amarillo

1. Bouton recalled his inaugural moment in the Yankee clubhouse in "Yankee Remembers 'The House That Ruth Built,'" September 19, 2008, www.cnn.com.

2. "Houk Calls Bouton Big League Timber," *Ridgewood Sunday News*, February 18, 1962.

3. See Shecter, "Jim Bouton: Every Thing in Its Place," 72.

4. Bouton, "Yankee Remembers."

5. Bouton, "Yankee Remembers."

6. John Drebinger, "Senators Win, 4–2, before 8–0 Loss," *New York Times*, May 7, 1962, 41.

7. "Blasé Yankees Whoop It Up in Ovation to Kid Hurler," 30.

8. Ferdenzi, "Bouton Takes Bomber Bow," 16.

9. "Mantle Doffs Lid to Bouton," 8; Ferdenzi, "Howard Booming Bouton," 7. In the article catcher Elston Howard likewise favorably compared Bouton's curve with Pascual's.

10. Steve Jacobson, "A New Chapter," *Newsday*, July 26, 1998, 62.

11. Undated note contained in the butter-yellow box, JBP.

12. Surface, "Johnny Sain Teaches the Power of Positive Thinking," 49. Unless otherwise noted, the sketch of Sain herein comes from this article along with the author's interview with Jim Kaat, who worked with Sain as a member of the Minnesota Twins.

13. Reidenbaugh, "Author Bouton Hits Jackpot," 7.

14. "Bombers' Celebration Is Routine," *New York Times*, September 26, 1962; Ferdenzi, "Ho Hum," 14.

6. Fucking Shecter

1. Bouton and Offen, *I Managed Good*, 114.

2. Poe, "The Writing of Sports," 173, 377.

3. Isaacs, "Out of Left Field," 95–96. Manuscript made available to the author out of the generosity of Isaac's daughter, Ellen, and on file with the author.

4. Poe, "The Writing of Sports," 174.

5. Isaacs, "Out of Left Field," 132.

6. Isaacs, "Out of Left Field," 95–96.

7. Isaacs, "Out of Left Field," 11.

8. Isaacs, "Out of Left Field," 15.

9. Isaacs, "Out of Left Field," 128–29.

10. See, for example, Isaacs, "Out of Left Field," 21–22. This was repeated to the author during his interviews with Vecsey, Jacobson, and Merchant.

11. See, for example, Ferdenzi, "Everybody Lends a Hand," 4.

12. Vecsey, "Can Jim Bouton Go Home Again?," 22, 64.

13. Leggett, "Out in Front with a New Look," 26.

14. See Dinerstein, *Origins of Cool*, 4–7, 226.

7. All 'Bout Bouton

1. "New York Yankees: Some Hope for the Rest of the League," 72.

2. Ferdenzi, "Bouton Nixes 'Cute Stuff,'" 5.

3. Gordon S. White Jr., "Bouton Hurt as Yanks Bow to Orioles; Cubs and Cards Tie Giants for Lead," *New York Times*, June 7, 1963.

4. Til Ferdenzi, "Yanks' Bouton . . . He's a Real Gem Dandy," *New York Journal-American*, August 31, 1963.

5. Herschel Nissenson, "How Barbara Felt after Jim Got K: OOOHHH!," *Bergen Record*, September 14, 1963.

6. Jim Bouton, "Righthander Jim Bouton of the Yankees Remembers a Storied Rivalry," *Boston Globe*, October 8, 2003.

7. John E. Meyer, "The Hot Corner," *Chicago Heights Star*, June 30, 1963. (After being pulled from a start against the White Sox in Chicago, Bouton emerged in the grandstand to conduct his interview with Meyer, commenting on his start as well as the game that was still in progress. Although in my interviews with him Jim asserted that leaving the clubhouse and entering the stands during the game was not an unusual practice at the time, follow-up with Major League Baseball's official historian, John Thorn, concluded otherwise. "This is news to me . . . and pretty great," Thorn said via email to me when I informed him of Jim's practice (December 4, 2017). "I can only surmise that it was unusual at the least, if not unique to Jim."

8. Leonard Shecter, "Bouton Has the Fans to Cool Off Athletics," *New York Post*, July 30, 1963, 63.

9. Leonard Shecter, "Fan Club," *New York Post*, October 1963 (specific date unknown).

10. Leonard Shecter, "Bouton Popped the Cork," *New York Post*, September 15, 1963.

11. Til Ferdenzi, "'Young Breed' Yanks Go Wild," *New York Journal-American*, September 15, 1963.

12. Arthur Daley, "In Delayed Tribute," *New York Times*, September 17, 1963.

13. Nissenson, "How Barbara Felt after Jim Got K."

14. Leonard Shecter, "Bouton Rooters Have Good Reason to Cheer," *New York Post*, October 1, 1963, 64.

15. Jim Bouton, "Series Sidelights," *Kalamazoo Gazette*, October 1963 (specific date unknown).

16. Rob Neyer, "When Jim Bouton Couldn't Quite Match Don Drysdale's Zeroes."

17. Leggett, "Koo-Foo the Killer"; Arthur Daley, "On the Edge of the Cliff," *New York Times*, October 6, 1963.

18. Shecter, "Bouton Popped the Cork."

8. A Threat, Not a Fine

1. Angell, "Four Taverns in the Town," 184, 197.

2. Sain and the Yankees' new manager, Yogi Berra, had not gotten along in many years. So when Houk was booted upstairs and Berra named the

new manager, Sain asked for a two-year contract in order to protect himself from Berra. Houk refused and cut Sain loose instead. According to Jim, Houk was likewise not enamored of Sain, who used to encourage his pitchers by saying, "Don't be afraid to climb those golden stairs" and demand from management a fair contract for their talents. Now that Houk was the man who would hear those demands, he preferred Sain to be elsewhere.

3. Shecter, *The Jocks*, 109.

4. Shecter, *The Jocks*, 120, 121.

5. John Drebinger, "Yogi Lays Down the Law in Inaugural Address," *New York Times*, February 18, 1964.

6. Bouton and Offen, *I Managed Good*, 104, 113.

7. Maury Allen, "Bouton Aims High," *New York Post*, January 6, 1964.

8. John Drebinger, "Yanks' Payroll to Hit $900,000," *New York Times*, January 14, 1964.

9. "Bouton, a 21-Game Winner, Spurns Yanks' First Offer," *New York Times*, February 13, 1964.

10. John Drebinger, "Tresh Sings $23,000 Contract, but Reniff and Linz Balk at Yankee Terms," *New York Times*, March 1, 1964.

11. John Drebinger, "Bouton Holdout Disturbs Berra," *New York Times*, March 8, 1964.

12. Nichols, "Harmon Killebrew and Jim Bouton," 28, 30.

13. John Drebinger, "Houk Says Bouton's Siege as a Holdout Will Cost Him $100 a Day," *New York Times*, March 10, 1964.

14. Til Ferdenzi, "Houk Hit 'Foul'—Bouton," *New York Journal-American*, March 10, 1964.

15. Tommy Holmes, "Houk Tells Bulldog: Sign or We'll Bite," *New York Herald Tribune*, March 10, 1964.

16. Phil Pepe, "Bouton about to Bow to Yankee Ultimatum," *New York World Telegram and Sun*, March 9, 1964.

17. Pepe, "Bouton about to Bow."

18. Ferdenzi, "Houk Hit 'Foul.'"

19. Jim Ogle, "Bulldog Bouton Lost His Bite, Not His Bark," *Newark Star Ledger*, March 10, 1964.

20. Jim McDonald, "Houk Swung Big Stick and Bouton Jumped," unknown newspaper, March 1964 (clipping courtesy of Bobbie Bouton-Goldberg and found within her scrapbook).

21. Phil Pepe, "Sain Knows Just What Bouton's Going Through," *New York World Telegram and Sun*, March 1964.

22. "Bouton OK's Yank Offer," *New York Daily News*, March 11, 1964, 1.

23. Joe Trimble, "Bulldog Stops Barking, Agrees to Yanks' 18G," *New York Daily News*, March 11, 1964.

24. "Bouton Takes the 18G's, Flies South Tomorrow," *New York World Telegram and Sun*, March 11, 1964.

25. Trimble, "Bulldog Stops Barking."

26. "'Bunt and Boost Your Value,'" 8.

27. "This Year's Crop of Unusual Stories Has a Serious Note," 6.

28. King, "Bouton Case May Bring Pitch for Arbitration Panel," 14; "Player Reps Say They'll Air Yank Threats in Bouton Case," 6.

29. See, for example, "Hobbies Give Yankee Pitcher Moments of Calm before World Series Storm," *Chicago Tribune*, September 27, 1963; Jack Powers, "Six Months of Army Life Made Jim Bouton a Winner," *Ridgewood Journal*, January 28, 1964.

30. Powers, "Six Months of Army Life."

31. "Baseball Bunglitis," 100.

32. In his interview with me Vecsey recalled Jim telling him that his elbow hurt but hedged a bit and said that it may have been his shoulder.

33. Ferdenzi, "Bouton Parboils Yank Rivals," 9.

34. "Basketball Frolic," 44. The spread ran in 1967 but noted that the games began three years earlier.

35. Ferdenzi, "Phil's Harmonica Rascal Skit Hits $200 Clinker," 7; J. Neyer, "Jim Bouton Remembers the 1964 World Series."

36. Neyer, "Jim Bouton Remembers the 1964 World Series," and interview with author.

37. Robert Lipsyte, "A Tired Bouton Asks Mantle for a Home Run and the Yank Slugger Delivers," *New York Times*, October 11, 1964.

38. "Bouton Says Arm Tightened in Sixth, but It Wasn't Cause for His Removal," *New York Times*, October 15, 1964; J. Neyer, "Jim Bouton Remembers the 1964 World Series."

39. "Bouton Says Arm Tightened in Sixth"; "Kink Can't Stop Bouton," 32.

40. "Bouton Says Arm Tightened in Sixth."

41. Steadman, "Only Two Yanks Able to Avoid Goat-Horn Tag," 22.

42. Enright, "Brock Still Bewildered by Series Scout Report," 7.

43. Jimmy Cannon, "A Pitcher's Morning," *New York Journal-American*, 1965 (specific date unknown).

9. The Bulldog and the Chipmunks

1. Barnea, "'Harmonica Phil,'" 6.
2. Addie, "Combination of Lane and Veeck," 14.
3. Milton Richman, "Bouton Feels Yanks Should Bend in Battle for Bucks," *Ridgewood Sunday News*, February 14, 1965.
4. Richman, "Bouton Feels Yanks Should Bend.
5. Isaacs, "Out of Left Field," 24.
6. Milton Gross, "Bouton Just Wants His Share," *New York Post*, February 10, 1965.
7. Dick Young, "Bouton, Howard Balk as Houk Heads South," *New York Daily News*, February 13, 1965.
8. See, for example, "Williams' Arm Heals before Ailment Reveled," wherein Young wrote that "Bouton fields his position as well as any pitcher in the majors." Young would toss small bouquets like this Bouton's way on occasion, but these became less frequent as the decade progressed.
9. Poe, "The Writing of Sports," 374.
10. Isaacs, "Out of Left Field," 309.
11. See, for example, Bruce Stark, "The Great Society" (political cartoon), *New York Daily News*, February 13, 1965, depicting two homeless men reading about Bouton's holdout and remarking that, in a way, he was just like they were—little guys going after big business.

10. Rebel without a Fastball

1. Leonard Shecter, "The Yankee," *New York Post*, July 16 (?), 1965 (exact date of article unknown).
2. "Bouton Appears Ready This Time," *Newark Star Ledger*, March 24, 1965.
3. Leonard Shecter, "Two Pitchers," *New York Post*, May 18, 1965.
4. Shecter, "The Yankee."
5. Shecter, "The Yankee."
6. Cannon, "A Pitcher's Morning."
7. Young, "Young Ideas," August 7, 1965, 20.
8. "Bad Season Prompts Bouton," 28.
9. Ferdenzi, "Bombers Hoping Winter Snooze," 12.
10. Ferdenzi, "It's Do-or-Die Year," 20.
11. Til Ferdenzi, "Will Yank Righty Be Right in '66?," *New York Journal American* (date unknown).
12. Joseph Durso, "Yankees Wrap Up Six in $128,000 Package," *New York Times*, February 9, 1966.

13. Ogle, "Yank Bulldog Bouton Winning Battle," 17.

14. Ogle, "Yankee Bulldog Growling, Ready to Chew Up the Enemy Swingers," 29.

15. Gabe Buonauro, "Return of Old-Time Form Makes Bouton Jubilant," *Bergen Record*, March 8, 1967.

16. See Shecter, *The Jocks*, 112–13. Shecter quotes from a 1967 article by *New York Post* writer Vic Ziegel on Bouton's campaign to become Yankee player representative.

17. Letter from Jim Turner to Bouton, January 21, 1966, JBP.

18. Ogle, "Bouton Sent Off to Syracuse," 6.

11. The Youth of America Is for Kids

1. Bouton and Offen, *I Managed Good*, 237–38.

2. Peterson, *Mickey Mantle Is Going to Heaven*, 145–46.

3. Shecter, *The Jocks*, 156.

4. Robert Lipsyte, "Flakes' Progress," *New York Times*, February 24, 1967.

5. Leonard Koppett, "The Brighter Yankees," *New York Times*, September 29, 1964.

6. Leonard Koppett, "Staid Yankees Get Zany Look with Help of Pepitone, Bouton," *New York Times*, April 26, 1964.

7. See Nathanson, *People's History of Baseball*, 108–45, for a deeper dive into the hows and whys of the changes in the business of baseball during the 1960s.

8. Bouton and Offen, *I Managed Good*, 238–39.

9. See Nathanson, *People's History of Baseball*.

10. Isaacs, "Hey Mike Burke," 53; Weintraub, "Yankee, Executive, Soldier, Spy."

11. Isaacs, "Hey Mike Burke," 55.

12. Weintraub, "Yankee, Executive, Soldier, Spy."

13. Isaacs, "Hey Mike Burke," 60.

14. Unknown title, *High Times*, June 1971. Although *High Times* proclaims that it dates back to 1974, Bobbie Bouton-Goldberg's scrapbook contains a photocopy of part of a *High Times* article on Jim with the month and year of the issue printed (printed in the publisher's script) beneath it.

12. The End of the Line

1. Dinerstein, *Origins of Cool*, 236 (emphasis in the original).

2. Shecter, "My Friend the Brother."

3. Vecsey, "Can Jim Bouton Go Home Again?," 64.

4. Robert Lipsyte, "The Line-Ups," *New York Times*, August 5, 1968.

5. Ogle, "Bouton, Man of Talents."

6. Bouton, "Returning to the Minors," 30.

7. "Statement by Jackie Robinson and K. C. Jones on Behalf of American Athletes Protesting South Africa's Readmission to the 1968 Olympic Games," issued by the American Committee on Africa and Jackie Robinson, February 8, 1968, www.africanactivist.msu.edu.

8. Frank Litsky, "65 Athletes Support Boycott of Olympics on S. Africa Issue," *New York Times*, April 12, 1968.

9. Bouton, "Mission in Mexico City," 64, 65.

10. Bouton, "Lobbying at the Mexico City Olympics," November 1968, www.africanactivist.msu.edu.

11. Bouton, "Mission in Mexico City."

12. Bouton, "Mission in Mexico City," 65. Bouton reported that the press chief, Bob Paul, called him a "reverse racist" and said, "You not only got yourself sent to Seattle, but you've got Larry James (a Negro gold medalist on the relay team) so confused he doesn't know what to think."

13. Beginnings

1. Ogle, "Yank Bulldog Bouton Winning Battle."

2. Young, "Young Ideas," April 27, 1968, 14; Goethel, "Twins Have a Fine Chance," 12.

3. Jim Ogle, "Houk's Prophecy Rings," 17.

4. Undated note written by Bouton calculating the breakdown of his 1968 salary, JBP.

5. Ogle, "Yanks Hail Return," 17.

6. Shecter, "My Friend the Brother."

7. Shecter, "My Friend the Brother."

8. Shecter, "My Friend the Brother."

9. Shecter, "My Friend the Brother."

10. Robert Lipsyte, "The Apprentice Junkman," *New York Times*, August 31, 1968.

11. Nichols, "A Ballplayer's Image," 29, 30.

12. Vecsey, "Can Jim Bouton Go Home Again?," 65.

13. See Richard Moss, "The Free Agency Issue: Why the Beef?," *New York Times*, September 27, 1987.

14. From Tell-Some to Tell-All

1. Shecter, *The Jocks*, 146, 147.

2. Wilson, "Bouton Book to Reveal Beer Slosher's Viewpoint," 47.

3. Vecsey, "Can Jim Bouton Go Home Again?," 66.

4. "The Top 100 Sports Books of All Time." *Ball Four* was ranked third, behind *The Sweet Science* and *The Boys of Summer*.

5. For a complete history of the World Publishing Company, see the archives kept at Case Western Reserve, https://case.edu/ech/articles/w/world -publishing-co/; and Kent State, www.library.kent.edu/world-publishing -company-records#series9.

6. Kramer, *Instant Replay*, 21–22, 149, 60, 150.

7. Shecter, *The Jocks*, 20–24, 4.

8. Isaacs, "Out of Left Field," 30.

9. See Hoffarth, "More on 'Ball Four' @ 40."

10. See D. Schaap, *Flashing before My Eyes*, 155–60.

11. Letter from Shecter to Bouton, February 24, 1969, JBP.

12. Durell, "Wonderful Writings of Donald Honig."

15. Take Your Pants Off, Bouton

1. Transcription of "tape #1," provided to the author by Jim Bouton and Paula Kurman and on file with the author; JBP.

2. Bouton, *I'm Glad You Didn't Take It Personally*, 187. World later promised an additional $10,000 to entice Bouton and Shecter to stay after Ed Kuhn left the company. World never paid the additional money, though, and then promised $5,000 instead. JBP.

3. Shecter to Bouton, March 12, 1969, JBP.

4. Bouton notes (undated), contained in butter-yellow box containing his 978 sheets of notes on the 1969 season, JBP.

5. Spector, "Jim Bouton: 'You Can't Just Go through Your Day.'"

6. Bouton and Offen, *I Managed Good*, 299.

7. Zimmerman, "Pilots Discover Blunt Weapon," 20; Zimmerman, "Mincher's Health Okay," 35.

8. Bouton note (undated), contained in butter-yellow box containing his 978 sheets of notes on the 1969 season, JBP.

9. See Jack Mann, "Jim Bouton, Reliever," *Washington Daily News*, 1969 (specific date unknown).

10. Bouton note (undated), contained in butter-yellow box containing his 978 sheets of notes on the 1969 season, JBP.

11. "Pitcher Jim Bouton Catching It Now," *San Antonio Light*, June 1970 (specific date unknown).

12. B. Bouton and Marshall, *Home Games*, 58.

13. "Jim Bouton: Speaking Freely," interview conducted by the First Amendment Center, May 20, 2003, www.firstamendmentcenter.org

14. Bouton note (undated), contained in butter-yellow box containing his 978 sheets of notes on the 1969 season, JBP.

15. See Shecter's copy of the original transcription of the manuscript, JBP.

16. Shecter to Bouton, September 1, 1969, JBP.

17. Shecter to Bouton, September 1, 1969, JBP.

18. Ed Kuhn to Theron Raines, September 16, 1969, JBP.

19. Undated "Dad's Comments" (two pages), JBP.

20. Arthur Abelman to Peter Ritner, February 19, 1970, JBP.

21. Abelman to Ritner, February 19, 1970, JBP.

22. Ritner to Shecter, February 20, 1970, JBP.

23. See documentation contained with the *Ball Four* collection, JBP.

24. JBP.

16. Fuck You, Shakespeare

1. George Vecsey, "Former Yankee, Now Owner of Salon, Hopes to Achieve Success with Astros," *New York Times*, March 3, 1970.

2. Spector, "Jim Bouton: 'You Can't Just Go through Your Day.'"

3. Fuller, "Jim Bouton's New Pitch."

4. Spector, "Jim Bouton: 'You Can't Just Go through Your Day.'"

5. Hoffarth, "More on 'Ball Four' @ 40."

6. Vecsey, "Can Jim Bouton Go Home Again?," 65.

7. Bouton notes (undated), contained in butter-yellow box containing his 978 sheets of notes on the 1969 season, JBP.

8. Bouton, interview with Red Barber, 1970, https://soundcloud.com /kenntomasch/red-barber-interviews-jim-bouton.

9. Kindred, "SportsWorld '98," 94.

10. Bouton, interview with Barber.

11. George Gopen, email exchange with author and detailed analysis of the writing of *Ball Four*, on file with the author.

12. Bouton, *Ball Four*, 154.

13. Bouton, *Ball Four*, 189.

14. Kipen, "Ball Four: The Final Pitch," 92.

15. Bouton, interview with Barber.

16. See transcriptions of the *Ball Four* tapes, JBP.

17. Shecter's copy of the transcription of the *Ball Four* tapes, JBP.

18. Shecter to Bouton, July 3, 1969, JBP.

19. Kahn, "Sports," December 1970, 14, 18.

20. Kahn, "Sports," May 1971, 16.

21. Vecsey, "Can Jim Bouton Go Home Again?," 65.

22. Hoffarth, "More on 'Ball Four' @ 40."

23. Undated note, JBP.

24. Hoffarth, "More on 'Ball Four' @40."

25. Shecter to Ritner, n.d., JBP.

26. Letter/contract from Cowles Communications, Inc., to Raines, March 26, 1970, JBP.

27. Shecter to Ritner, n.d., JBP.

28. Holtzman, "Jewish Fan Club for O'Brien?," 21.

29. See Reidenbaugh, "Author Bouton Hits Jackpot" (containing a breakdown of the print runs of the first edition of the book); and JBP.

30. See Bouton, "My Love/Hate Affair with Baseball," 82. The second excerpt, "Comeback," appeared in the June 16, 1970, edition, p. 60.

31. Shecter to Ritner, n.d., JBP.

32. See Freehan, "Never Touch a Superstar," 54.

33. "Author Bouton Gets Summons from Kuhn," *Washington Post*, May 30, 1970, C2.

34. See "The Talk of the Town," 39. The article quotes an unnamed player as saying, "Go get 'em, Shakespeare," but Bouton later wrote in *I'm Glad You Didn't Take It Personally* that the player was either Rose or Johnny Bench and the quote was "Shakespeare, you no-good rat-fink. Put that in your fucking book" (62). Later, the quote morphed into "Fuck you, Shakespeare!" and attributed by Bouton to Rose.

35. Dick Young, "Young Ideas," *New York Daily News*, May 28, 1970.

36. Robert Lipsyte, "Crack in the Clubhouse Wall," *New York Times*, June 1, 1970.

17. Protectors of the Holy Flame

1. Bouton, interview with Barber.

2. Bouton, interview with Barber.

3. See Reidenbaugh, "Author Bouton Hits Jackpot."

4. Charles Maher, "On False Pretenses," *Los Angeles Times*, June 6, 1970.

5. Burnes, "Flood Rap at Musial Draws Angry Rebuttal," 37.

6. "Voice of the Fan—Literary Equilibrium," 4.

7. Falls, "Athletes on Guard," 2, 34.

8. Twombly, "Beware of Snoopy Colleagues," 20.

9. Kahn, "Sports," December 1970, 25.

10. Kahn, "Sports," December 1970, 26.

11. Dick Young, "Young Ideas," *New York Daily News*, May 28, 1970.

12. Young, "Bouton Rates a Reprimand," 16.

13. Young, "Teammates Trusted Bouton," 16.

14. "Voice of the Fan—Bouton Isn't a Youth," 4.

15. See "Does an Athlete Have the Right to Tell It Like It Is?," 90.

16. Holtzman, "Appling Offers Tip for Youngsters," 14.

17. Anonymous letter to Bouton, June 15, 1970, JBP.

18. "Does an Athlete Have the Right to Tell It Like It Is?"

18. Against the Unwritten Rules of Baseball

1. Reidenbaugh, "Author Bouton Hits Jackpot."

2. Bill Mazer on an ESPN *SportsCenter* retrospective on the fallout from *Ball Four*, www.youtube.com/watch?v=yRUSLZ9J5c4.

3. Hirshberg, "Players Answer Bouton," 54, 55, 94.

4. "Bouton Rebuffed!," 30.

5. Joseph Durso, "Elston Howard Replies," *New York Times*, July 16, 1970.

6. "Mantle Upset over Sales of Bouton Book," *Washington Post*, July 26, 1970, D2.

7. See fan letters to Bouton, JBP.

8. Fan Letters to Bouton, JBP.

9. Letter from fan to Bouton, June 19, 1970, JBP.

10. Letter to Bouton, May 31, 1970 JBP.

11. Letter to Bouton, June 22, 1970. Bouton scribbled underneath the comment regarding his height: "Actually, 5'11½."

12. Flaherty, "Toots Shor among the Ruins," 226, 268.

19. Not Enough Sex

1. Christopher Lehmann-Haupt, "Not All Peanuts and Cracker Jack, Exactly," *New York Times*, June 19, 1970.

2. Rex Lardner, "The Oddball with the Knuckleball," *New York Times*, July 26, 1970.

3. David Markson, "As a Pitcher, He's a Very Good Writer," *Washington Post*, June 21, 1970.

4. Michael Gartner, "Right Down the Middle," *Wall Street Journal*, July 8, 1970, 18.

5. "Pitcher Says the Umps Isolate, Resent Ashford," *Baltimore Afro-American*, May 30, 1970.

6. Sam Lacy, "Another A to Z Hurrah for Jim Bouton," *Baltimore Afro-American*, June 5, 1971.

7. Young, "Young Ideas," September 12, 1970.

8. See "Ball Four No. 2 Book in Houston," *Norfolk Journal and Guide*, July 18, 1970.

9. Ira Berkow, "Bouton and the Write Stuff," *New York Times*, December 10, 1983.

10. "Jim Bouton Is Off Base, Says Bowie," *Chicago Tribune*, June 2, 1970.

11. Lipsyte, "Dying Game," 100, 102.

20. The Leni Riefenstahl of the National Football League

1. Whitlesey, "Nat Fans Filter Rumors," 50.

2. Bouton, *Ball Four*, 212.

3. Spink, "We Believe . . . ," 16.

4. Bergman, "Sure Dobson Takes Greenies," 47.

5. Jack Scott, "It's Not How You Play the Game, but What Pill You Take," *New York Times Sunday Magazine*, October 17, 1971.

6. Rudy Johnson, "Catcher for Mets in Antidrug Role," *New York Times*, June 13, 1971.

7. Murphy, "The Path to Power," 82.

8. Vogan, *Keepers of the Flame*, 9–10.

9. Vogan, *Keepers of the Flame*, 5, 17–18.

10. Vogan, *Keepers of the Flame*, 64.

21. Taking It Personally

1. "Bouton's 'Ball Four' Authors Astros' Loss," *Washington Post*, July 7, 1970, D2.

2. See "Jim Bouton: Speaking Freely."

3. Bouton, interview with Barber.

4. Rich Levinson, "Smoke Em Inside," unknown newspaper, 1970.

5. Wilson, "'Ball Four' Bouton Takes Walk to O.C.," 18.

6. Untitled article contained within Bobbie Bouton-Goldberg's scrapbook, publication not identified, August 3, 1970.

7. "'Ball Four!' Bouton Walks Out of Pros," *Paterson News*, August 11, 1970.

8. Robert Lipsyte, "Naked Came the Knuckleball," *New York Times*, August 13, 1970.

9. World Publishing spring 1970 catalog, JBP.

10. Settlement agreement between World Publishing, Inc., and Bouton and Shecter, January 13, 1971, JBP.

11. Hoffarth, "More on 'Ball Four' @ 40."

12. Genevieve Stuttaford, "More Chocolate Cake from Bouton," *San Francisco Sunday Examiner*, August 29, 1971.

13. Frizzell, "Mays, 40, Still Giants' No. 1 Success Factor," 7.

14. John Hall, "The Fink Returns," *Los Angeles Times*, June 2, 1971.

15. Young, "Young Ideas," June 19, 1971, 15.

16. Lacy, "Another A to Z Hurrah for Jim Bouton"; Deford, "With Any Luck"; Holtzman, "Pitchers Should Know How to Bunt," 12; William Gildea, "Bouton on Winning Streak of Two," *Washington Post*, June 1, 1971, D1.

17. "I'm Glad You Didn't Take It Personally," *New York Times*, July 11, 1971; Jonathan Segal, "The Games Some People Play," *New York Times*, December 5, 1971; Ed Rumill, "But, Jim, We Did Take It Personally," *Christian Science Monitor*, May 21, 1971; Robert Markus, "Along the Sports Trail," *Chicago Tribune*, June 23, 1971.

18. John Gregory Dunne, "Jim (Ball Four) Bouton Hurls Sequel," *Los Angeles Times*, July 20, 1971.

19. Bouton and Offen, *I Managed Good*, 166.

20. Bouton, "Reflections on Managing a Baseball Team," 153.

21. David Condon, "Bullpen Saves Bouton Again," *Chicago Tribune*, July 12, 1973.

22. Spander, "Never Wanted to Manage," 12.

22. Bad Stuff 'bout the Mets

1. Roger Beirne, "Jim Bouton: A New View on Sports," *Bergen Record*, December 10, 1970.

2. Dell Publishing advertising copy, JBP.

3. "Israel Lang Out to Become Football Bouton," *Washington Post*, August 16, 1970; "Johnny Sample's 'Confessions,'" *New Journal and Guide*, December 5, 1970.

4. Holtzman, "Finley Offers Advice to Daughter," 27.

5. Bob Ross, "Bo Recounts His Conquests," *Los Angeles Times*, June 10, 1973.

6. Bisher, "Another Peep Show."

7. Pepitone with Steinback, *Joe, You Coulda Made Us Proud*.

8. Tax, "Booktalk: With 'Balls,' Graig Nettles Takes a Few Cuts."

23. Not Selling Refrigerators

1. Howard Cosell, "Sports and Good-by to All That," *New York Times*, April 5, 1971.

2. Roger Beirne, "Jim Bouton: A New View on Sports," *Bergen Sunday Record*, December 10, 1970.

3. Grace Lichtenstein, "For 11 Years I Was Just a Ballplayer," *New York Times*, October 4, 1970.

4. Jim Bouton's WABC publicity biography packet, 1971, provided courtesy of Bobbie Bouton-Goldberg. The Cosell quip was his chosen quote.

5. Al Harvin, "Rucker Event to Open Saturday," *New York Times*, May 27, 1973.

6. Ed Runill, "Bouton Trades Mound for Movie Cameras," *Christian Science Monitor*, September 23, 1972.

7. "Knuckleballer," 40.

8. Ehrlich and Silva, "Jim Bouton."

9. Beirne, "Jim Bouton: A New View on Sports."

10. Olbermann and Patrick, *The Big Show*, 223. The remainder of Olbermann's comments within this chapter stem from his interview with the author.

11. Christmas card from Olbermann to Bouton, n.d., provided by Bouton to the author.

12. "Channel Chatter," *Philadelphia Evening Bulletin*, February 11, 1973.

13. Bouton, *I'm Glad You Didn't Take It Personally*, 18.

14. Fischler, "Yankees Greet Old Pal Bouton," 28.

15. Spoelstra, "Schultz Savors Edict to Ban Bouton," 42.

16. Frank Brown, "'Andy Lawson' Misses Out at Yankees' Tryout Camp," *Argus Press*, August 2, 1973, 16.

17. Brown, "Andy Lawson Misses Out."

24. The Most Famous Vasectomy in New York

1. Bouton, "One Man's Family Planning," 64, 65.

2. Wakefield, "Highlights of a NON-Event," 33, 35.

3. Holtzman, "Bouton's Bid Fails," 30.

4. See Deford, "A Magnificent Obsession."

5. "Stars on Film and on TV Delve into Politics," *New York Times*, June 4, 1972.

6. "Party Delegates Are New Breed," *New York Times*, June 25, 1972.

7. Thompson, "Fear & Loathing in Miami."

25. Are We Rolling?

1. Runill, "Bouton Trades Mound for Movie Cameras."

2. Allen Barra, "Baseball: Pitching Deep and Inside," *Wall Street Journal*, April 7, 2010, D7.

3. Jim Bouton, "Jim Bouton Bangs the Drum, Loudly," *New York Times*, September 30, 1973.

4. The draft is housed among the Jim Bouton Papers, JBP.

5. "People," August 24, 1970; Holtzman, "Movie of Bouton's Book," 47.

6. "People," April 30, 1973.

7. Dinerstein, *Origins of Cool*, 81.

8. Chandler, *Raymond Chandler Speaking*, 232.

9. Terrence Rafferty, "A Gumshoe Adrift, Lost in the '70s," *New York Times*, April 15, 2007.

10. David Thomson, "Robert Altman's Decade of Astonishments," *New York Times*, June 11, 2000.

11. Vincent Canby, "Altman and Gould Make a Brilliant 'Long Goodbye,'" *New York Times*, October 29, 1973.

12. Lindgren, "Pinup Goalie: Shep Messing."

13. Jordan, "After the Sundown."

26. One Smart-Ass and Four Lawyers

1. Koppett, "Bouton and Falls Called to Task," 4; "Libel and Slander," 256.

2. Koppett, "Bouton and Falls Called to Task."

3. *Webster v. American Broadcasting Companies,* New York County Superior Court, Trial Term, pt. 12, September 30, 1976, Stecher, J.

4. "Bouton Changes Teams, from Channel 7 to 2," *New York Times*, September 19, 1973.

5. Jordan, "After the Sundown."

6. Jordan, "After the Sundown."

27. You're a Long Time Dead

1. Bouton, *Ball Four*, 398.

2. Gordon Murphy, "Baron Regrets: No Jim Bouton," *Ridgewood Herald News*, August 13, 1970.

3. Kaplan, "Jim Bouton's Instant Replay."

4. See John Rowe, "Bouton Likes Met League Life," *Bergen Sunday Record*, August 12, 1973.

5. O'Gara, "Bouton Stalls in Comeback," 34.

6. Jack Mann, "It's Summer and Bouton Is on Mound," *Washington Post*, June 14, 1976, D1.

7. "Bouton Beats Walla Walla in Comeback," *New York Times*, August 10, 1975.

8. "Bouton Hopeful," *Kalamazoo Gazette*, date unknown.

9. See "Classifieds: 'Maverick Ballplayers," 52.

10. Twombly, "Portland Mavericks," 8.

11. Bertram, "Independent Mavericks Catch Portland's Fancy," 41.

12. Letter from Larry Dotson, Northwest League umpire, "Voice of the Fan," *The Sporting News*, January 25, 1975, 6.

13. "Portland Pilot Robinson Draws 1-Year Suspension," 28.

14. "Mavs Draw Crowd," 53.

15. McDonald, "Big League Chew."

28. The Battered Bastard of Baseball

1. Title unknown, *Fort Myers News-Press*, July 17, 1979.
2. Al Crombie, "Bouton Lives a Dream—Wins Again!," *Columbian*, August 10, 1975, 36.
3. "Mavericks Break Own Season's Gate Record," 40.
4. Spink, "We Believe . . . ," 12.
5. See *The Battered Bastards of Baseball*, directed by Maclain Way and Chapman Way (2014).
6. The other two witnesses were Joe Torre and Pete Rose.
7. Spector, "Jim Bouton: You Can't Just Go through Your Day."
8. "For Bouton, a Happy Return to Yankee Stadium," *Washington Post*, July 26, 1998, D2.

29. *Gilligan's Island* in Baseball Suits

1. Char Anderson, "Mrs. Bouton Tells Her Allegan Friends of Jim's New Venture," *Kalamazoo Gazette*, 1976 (specific date unknown).
2. Cyd Zeigler, "100 Most Important Moments in Gay History."
3. Albin Krebs, "Designated Actor?," *New York Times*, January 25, 1976; B. Bouton and Marshall, *Home Games*, 130.
4. "CBS Has New Pitch in Fall TV Comedy Called 'Ball Four,'" *Wall Street Journal*, April 7, 1976.
5. Gary Deeb, "'Ball Four' to Strike a Blow for Realism," *Chicago Tribune*, June 24, 1976, B8.
6. Epstein, "Ball Four, You're Out."
7. Ludtke, "Two Strikes on 'Ball Four.'"
8. Undated printout of Bouton's teleprompter notes regarding *Ball Four* television show, JBP.
9. Deford, "A Magnificent Obsession," 56.
10. Deford, "A Magnificent Obsession," 56.
11. Soni Bayles, "I'll Take the Credit—Any Credit!," *New York Times*, February 6, 1977.
12. Undated note from Vic Ziegel to Ginny Shecter, enclosing Shecter's unproduced *Ball Four* movie script, JBP; John J. O'Connor, "TV: Men-Boys, Inanity and Blood," *New York Times*, September 22, 1976; "Television Reviews," 54; John Schulian, "Early Mets Provided More Humor, Credibility than 'Ball Four,'" *Washington Post*, October 1, 1976, D6; Gary Deeb, "CBS'

Big Comedies Have Premiered but Network Brass Aren't Laughing," *Chicago Tribune*, October 1, 1976, A13; Scott Vernon, "TV 'Bombs Away,'" *Baltimore Afro-American*, November 13, 1976, 11; Epstein, "Ball Four, You're Out."

30. Too Old, Too Everything

1. Al Harvin, "Bouton's Latest Mound Debut a 3–1 Loss in Minor League," *New York Times*, April 16, 1977.
2. Jim Bouton, "The Ballad of Cone's Comeback," *New York Times*, January 13, 2001.
3. Deford, "A Magnificent Obsession."
4. Al Harvin, "People in Sports: Figueroa Gets 4-Year Pact for an Estimated $500,000," *New York Times*, February 3, 1977.
5. Bob Verdi, "Bouton Chases the Butterfly of Life," *Chicago Tribune*, April 17, 1977, B1.
6. Deford, "A Magnificent Obsession."
7. Deane McGowen, "People in Sports: Ali to Meet Shavers Sept. 29 in Garden," *New York Times*, July 21, 1977.
8. Deford, "A Magnificent Obsession."
9. Deford, "A Magnificent Obsession."
10. Holtzman, "Old-Timers May Demand Fees," 19.
11. "Bunts Beat Bouton," 40.
12. "For Bouton It's 'Strike Three' and You're Out of Baseball," *Los Angeles Times*, June 2, 1977, F4.
13. Morales, "Odom and Bouton Make Winning Mexico Debuts," 37.
14. "Suspension for Odom," 56.
15. B. Bouton and Marshall, *Home Games*, 152.
16. "A Maverick in a Maverick's Uniform," *Los Angeles Times*, July 21, 1977, E1.
17. "Bouton Is Back," 48.
18. "Sweepers Silenced," 48.
19. "A New Twist," 44.
20. "Bouton Shelled," 40.
21. Goldman, Dreier, and Goldman, "Jim Bouton Follows His Dream," 20.
22. "Yankee Staying Power," 42.
23. Goldman, Dreier, and Goldman, "Jim Bouton Follows His Dream."

31. Magic

1. Deford, "A Magnificent Obsession."
2. Deford, "A Magnificent Obsession."
3. Zimmerman, "Mariner Swap Bait," 16.

4. *Atlanta National League Baseball Club, Inc. v. Kuhn,* 432 F.Supp. 1213 (N.D.Ga. 1977).

5. Roy Blount Jr., "Jim Bouton, Comeback Kid," *New York Times,* May 22, 1978.

6. Lawrence Wright, "The Game That Brought Jim Bouton Back from Exile," *New York Times,* June 12, 1978.

7. Blount, "Jim Bouton, Comeback Kid."

8. B. Bouton and Marshall, *Home Games,* 162.

9. "Morning Briefing: Aaron Reviews Bouton; He Was a Snake in the Grass," *Los Angeles Times,* May 7, 1979, 2.

10. "Bouton Fans 7 in Pitch for Job," *New York Times,* May 11, 1978.

11. Wright, "Game That Brought Jim Bouton Back."

12. Deford, "A Magnificent Obsession."

13. Deford, "A Magnificent Obsession."

14. Spence Martin to Bouton, August 3, 1978, provided by Bouton to the author; Talese, "Frank Sinatra Has a Cold."

32. Dreaming in Baseball

1. Bouton, *Ball Four,* xv.

2. Wright, "Game That Brought Jim Bouton Back."

3. Deford, "A Magnificent Obsession," 56.

4. Pluto, *Greatest Summer.*

5. Wright, "Game That Brought Jim Bouton Back."

6. "Bouton Starts Another Chapter," *New York Times,* May 20, 1978.

7. "Bouton Beats Bunts," 41.

8. Bisher, "Discovery Came to Bill Lucas Only in Death," 39.

9. Deford, "Old 56 Comes Back at 39," 59.

10. "Kuhn Not Concerned," 33.

11. Deford, "Old 56 Comes Back at 39," 59.

12. Verrell, "Dodgers Open Some Daylight," 17.

13. Deford, "Old 56 Comes Back at 39," 59.

14. "The Week (Sept. 10–16)."

15. "Kuhn Not Concerned," 33.

16. Caruso, "Bouton Picks Up Speed," 34.

17. Deford, "Old 56 Comes Back at 39."

18. "The Week (Sept. 10–16)."

19. Caruso, "Braves Get Taste of Good Pitching," 34.

20. See Bisher, "Yes, Bouton Is Back," 2.

21. Young, "Young Ideas," November 18, 1978, 6.

22. "What They Are Saying," *New York Times*, December 17, 1978.
23. Caruso, "Ball 4 Author Bouton Takes Strike 3 Again," 35.

33. Mask of the Bulldog

1. Judy Klemesrud, "2 Baseball Wives Call It as They See It," *New York Times*, April 24, 1983.
2. George Vecsey, "Painful Memories," *New York Times*, March 7, 1983.
3. Deford, "A Magnificent Obsession," 56.
4. Wedge, "Reflections on Milton Erickson."
5. Bouton note (undated), contained in butter-yellow box containing his 978 sheets of notes on the 1969 season, JBP.

34. Hey, New York—Bouton's Back!

1. "Bouton Is Back," *New York Times*, January 15, 1979.

35. Lightning in a Pouch

1. The history of Big League Chew comes from the author's interview with Rob Nelson, supplemented by Dave Sheinin, "Rob Nelson Invented Big League Chew, and His Bubble Has Yet to Burst," *Washington Post*, July 14, 2015; and McDonald, "Big League Chew."
2. See *Jim Bouton Corporation v. Wm. Wrigley Jr. Company*, 902 F.2d 1074 (1990).
3. United States Patent Number 4,732,274 (March 22, 1988).

36. The Solo Artist

1. The recounting of the writing and publication of *Strike Zone* comes from the author's interviews with Jim Bouton, Paula Kurman, and Al Silverman, supplemented by Farina, *Asinof and the Truth of the Game*.
2. Gerald Eskanazi, "Off the Field, Pickets, Pictures," *New York Times*, October 5, 1987.
3. "A Call to the Commissioners," letter to the editor, *New York Times*, October 18, 1987.
4. Bouton, "Revisiting the 'Ball Four' Astros," 15.
5. "Call a Timeout," letter to the editor, *New York Times*, October 5, 1997.
6. Tyler Kepner, "The Trials of Jason Giambi," *New York Times*, January 31, 2005.
7. Undated "List of Players," with names, addresses, and Bouton's notes regarding their potential receptiveness to a request to discuss *Ball Four*, JBP.
8. Bouton to Stein and Day, November 21, 1980, JBP.

9. Robert Lipsyte, "Yankee Fans Agree: Season Is a Waste without a Title," *New York Times*, August 16, 1998.

10. Tom Dunkel, "In the Twilight, Bouton's Are Alive and Pitching," *Wall Street Journal*, August 11, 1995.

11. Bruce Watson, "Ball Park to Ballroom," *Daily Hampshire Gazette*, January 19, 1998.

37. Laurie

1. Blount, "Jim Bouton, Comeback Kid."

2. "Wrecker Nets $300,000 on Yankee Stadium Items," 21.

3. Brian Sullivan, "Once More, for Old Time's Sake," *Berkshire Eagle*, June 4, 1995.

4. George Vecsey, "Keep the Number, Cheo," *New York Times*, March 30, 1988; Malcolm Moran, "Still Excluded after All These Years," *New York Times*, July 14, 1990.

5. Sullivan, "Once More, for Old Time's Sake."

6. Ira Berkow, "Bouton Gives Eulogy for His Daughter," *New York Times*, August 19, 1997.

7. Dave Anderson, "Return of the Prodigal Yankee Old-Timer," *New York Times*, July 26, 1998.

8. Neal Travis, "Jim Bouton's Mantle Peace," *New York Post*, June 10, 1997.

9. Bouton, *Ball Four*, 90.

10. "Backtalk: 'For Bouton, Let Bygones Be Bygones,'" *New York Times*, June 21, 1998.

11. Allen St. John, "Baseball's Bolshevik Returns," *Village Voice*, August 4, 1998, 157.

38. Existential Bad Faith

1. Jim Luttrell, "Minor League Notebook: Charm Might Not Be Enough," *New York Times*, August 2, 2000.

2. Smolkin, "Wild Pitch."

3. Smolkin, "Wild Pitch."

4. See Bouton, *Foul Ball*.

5. Smolkin, "Wild Pitch."

6. "Stadium Plans Drop Back on the Table," *Berkshire Eagle*, August 24, 2001, 6.

7. "Jim Bouton: Interview, August 2003."

8. Frank Litsky, "Now Pittsfield Stakes Claim to Baseball's Origins," *New York Times*, May 12, 2004.

9. See *PublicAffairs v. Bouton*, No. 603769/03, Supreme Court of the State of New York—New York County (2003). The amount of the advance is noted within the parties' motions to dismiss.

10. "Jim Bouton: Interview, August 2003."

11. Zeitchik, "New Bouton Book Critical of PublicAffairs," 18. Bouton's perspective on this issue can be found additionally in *Foul Ball*, 334–36.

12. See *PublicAffairs v. Bouton*, order of Helen E. Freedman, Justice, October 22, 2004 (ruling on the motions); Zeitchik, "New Bouton Book Critical of PublicAffairs."

13. The court's ruling and accompanying opinion on the various motions are on file with the author.

14. Sartre, *Being and Nothingness*, 101–3.

15. "Jim Bouton: Interview, August 2003."

16. *Berkshire Eagle*, April 16, 2003; *Pittsfield Gazette*, December 11, 2003; Feinstein, "Foul Ball Tells True Tale"; David Kipen, "Stepping Up to the Plate," *San Francisco Chronicle*, July 27, 2003.

17. "Jim Bouton: Interview, August 2003."

39. A Mile in Bowie's Shoes

1. "Base Ball Like It Ought to Be, and Like It Was," *New York Times*, August 25, 2006.

2. "Base Ball Like It Ought to Be."

3. "When the Game Was Called Base Ball," *New York Times*, August 19, 2007.

4. "Bouton Responds to VBBA," which can be found on the VBBF's website, http://jimbouton.com/vintagebbf/news.html#a0.

5. Tim Arango, "Old-Time Pastime," *New York Post*, August 27, 2006.

6. Jimmy Golen, "Bouton Gives Fans a Real 'Old-Timer's Day,'" *Boston Globe*, August 19, 2007.

40. Cashing Out

1. Fred Bernstein, "Now Pitching for Wahconah, Jim Bouton," *New York Times*, April 10, 2003.

41. The Butter-Yellow Box

1. For more information regarding CAA, see Banerjee et al., "Increasing Impact of Cerebral Amyloid Angiopathy."

2. Tyler Kepner, "Jim Bouton, Author and Former Pitcher, Struggles with Brain Disease," *New York Times*, July 1, 2017.

Epilogue

1. Ira Berkow, "Bouton and the Write Stuff."

Bibliography

Addie, Bob. "Combination of Lane and Veeck Would Be Explosive." *The Sporting News*, February 27, 1965.

Angell, Roger. "Four Taverns in the Town." *New Yorker*, October 26, 1963.

———. *The Summer Game.* New York: Popular Library, 1972.

Appel, Marty. Interview with author, August 24, 2016.

"Bad Season Prompts Bouton to Alter Conditioning Ideas." *The Sporting News*, October 9, 1965.

Baer, Jill. Interview with author, July 22, 2019.

Banerjee, G., R. Carare, C. Cordonnier, S. M. Greenberg, J. A. Schneider, E. E. Smith, M. van Buchem, J. van der Grond, M. M. Verbeek, D. J. Werring. "The Increasing Impact of Cerebral Amyloid Angiopathy: Essential New Insights for Clinical Practice." *Journal of Neurology, Neurosurgery, and Psychiatry* 88 (2017): 982–94.

Barnea, Joe. "'Harmonica Phil' Struts Stuff at Manchester Fete." *The Sporting News*, January 30, 1965.

"Baseball Bunglitis." *Sport*, June 1964.

"Basketball Frolic." *Sport*, June, 1967.

Bell, Gary. Interview with the author, November 16, 2016.

Bergman, Ron. "Sure Dobson Takes Greenies, but Not as a Regular Practice." *The Sporting News*, March 13, 1971.

Berkow, Ira. Interview with the author, September 12, 2017.

Bertram, Nick. "Independent Mavericks Catch Portland's Fancy." *The Sporting News*, August 11, 1973.

Bisher, Furman. "Another Peep Show." *The Sporting News*, July 7, 1973.

———. "Discovery Came to Bill Lucas Only in Death." *The Sporting News*, June 2, 1979.

———. "Yes, Bouton Is Back." *The Sporting News*, October 14, 1978.

"Blasé Yankees Whoop It Up in Ovation to Kid Hurler." *The Sporting News*, May 16, 1962, 30.

Bouton, Bob. Interview with the author, September 14, 2016.

Bouton, Bobbie, and Nancy Marshall. *Home Games: Two Baseball Wives Speak Out.* New York: St. Martin's, 1983.

Bouton, Jim. *Ball Four.* Edited by Leonard Shecter. 1970. Reprint, New York: Macmillan, 1990.

———. "Bronx Tales." *New York Times Book Review,* June 1, 2012.

———. "Comeback." *Look,* June 16, 1970.

———. *Foul Ball: My Life and Hard Times Trying to Save an Old Ballpark.* Guilford CT: Lyons Press, 2005.

———. "Going Home to Rochelle Park." *New Jersey Monthly,* April 1981.

———. *I'm Glad You Didn't Take It Personally.* Edited by Leonard Shecter. New York: Dell, 1971.

———. Interviews with the author, 2016–2019.

———. "Mission in Mexico City." *Sport,* August 1969.

———. "My Love/Hate Affair with Baseball." *Look,* June 2, 1970.

———. "One Man's Family Planning." *New York Magazine,* April 10, 1972.

———. Papers. Manuscript Division, Library of Congress, Washington DC.

———. "Reflections on Managing a Baseball Team." *Esquire,* May 1973.

———. "Returning to the Minors." *Sport,* April, 1968.

———. "Revisiting the 'Ball Four' Astros." *The Sporting News,* August 21, 1989.

———. "Yankee Remembers 'the House That Ruth Built." www.cnn.com, September 19, 2008.

Bouton, Jim, and Neil Offen. *I Managed Good, but Boy Did They Play Bad.* Chicago: Playboy Press, 1973.

Bouton, Pete. Interviews with author, August 11, 2016; August 29 and October 4, 2017.

"Bouton Beats Bunts." *The Sporting News,* August 19, 1978.

Bouton-Goldberg, Bobbi. Interviews with the author, 2016–2018.

"Bouton Is Back." *The Sporting News,* July 30, 1977.

"Bouton Rebuffed!" *The Sporting News,* July 25, 1970.

"Bouton Shelled." *The Sporting News,* August 13, 1977.

Brosnan, Jim. *The Long Season.* Chicago: Ivan R. Dee, 2002.

"'Bunt and Boost Your Value,' Lopat's Lecture to Tartabull." *The Sporting News,* March 28, 1964.

"Bunts Beat Bouton." *The Sporting News,* May 28, 1977.

Burnes, Bob. "Flood Rap at Musial Draws Angry Rebuttal." *The Sporting News,* March 13, 1971.

Caple, Jim. "Wit, Wisdom and Social Commentary." June 15, 2000. http://static
    .espn.go.com/mlb/ballfour/caple.html.

Carragher, Joseph. "Yankee Ace Stars at Home." *Newark Star Ledger*, September
    22, 1963.

Caruso, Gary. "Ball 4 Author Bouton Takes Strike 3 Again." *The Sporting News*,
    January 6, 1979.

————. "Bouton Picks Up Speed with a Slo-Mo Style." *The Sporting News*, Octo-
    ber 7, 1978.

————. "Braves Get Taste of Good Pitching." *The Sporting News*, October 14, 1978.

Cerrone, Rick. Interview with author, July 16, 2017.

Champion, Marge. Interview with author, August 9, 2016.

Chandler, Raymond. *Raymond Chandler Speaking*. Edited by Dorothy Gar-
    diner, Katherine Sorley Walker, and Paul Skenazy. 1962. Reprint, Berkeley:
    University of California Press, 1997.

Charlip, Lou. Interview with author, September 22, 2016.

Charlton, Jim. Interview with author, September 21, 2016.

"Classifieds: 'Maverick Ballplayers, 1975 Tryouts.'" *The Sporting News*, March 8, 1975.

Colangelo, Jerry. Interview with author, November 22, 2016.

Colton, Larry. Interview with author, September 28, 2016.

Cronson, Howard. Interview with author, January 3, 2017.

Cunningham, Bruce. Interview with author, September 19, 2016.

Davis, Tommy. Interview with author, November 16, 2016.

Deford, Frank. "A Magnificent Obsession." *Sports Illustrated*, July 3, 1978.

————. "Old 56 Comes Back at 39." *Sports Illustrated*, September 18, 1978.

————. "With Any Luck, This Review Will Appear in Jim Bouton's 3rd Trea-
    tise, 'Son of . . . ,'" *Sports Illustrated*, September 20, 1971.

Dierker, Larry. Interview with author, February 20, 2017.

Dinerstein, Joel. *The Origins of Cool in Postwar America*. Chicago: University of
    Chicago Press, 2017.

"Does an Athlete Have the Right to Tell It Like It Is?" *Sport*, August 1970.

Dulane, Pierre. Interview with author, August 10, 2016.

Durell, Mike. "The Wonderful Writings of Donald Honig." December 15, 2015.
    http://seamheads.com/blog/2015/12/15/the-wonderful-writings-of-donald
    -honig/.

Ehrlich, Charles, and Rene Silva. "Jim Bouton: Willing to Talk about Any-
    thing." *High Times*, June 1971.

Elitzer, Chip. Interview with author, August 22, 2016.

Elitzer, Sam. Interview with author, April 23, 2019.

Enright, James. "Brock Still Bewildered by Series Scout Report." *The Sporting News*, November 14, 1964.

Epstein, Dan. "Ball Four, You're Out: How a Classic Baseball Book Became a Failed Baseball Sitcom." *Vice Sports*, September 22, 2016. www.sports.vice.com.

Falls, Joe. "Athletes on Guard." *The Sporting News*, June 20, 1970.

Farina, William. *Eliot Asinof and the Truth of the Game: A Critical Study of the Baseball Writings*. Jefferson NC: McFarland, 2011.

Fatsis, Stefan. Interview with author, February 8, 2017.

Feinstein, John. "Foul Ball Tells True Tale, Albeit an Unhappy One." July 29, 2003. www.aol.com.

———. Interview with author, June 1, 2017.

Ferdenzi, Til. "Artist on Mound—Bouton's Also an Ace at Easel." *The Sporting News*, July 2, 1966.

———. "Bombers Hoping Winter Snooze Will Put Bite Back in Bulldog." *The Sporting News*, November 6, 1965.

———. "Bouton Nixes 'Cute Stuff,' Pumps Hard to Win Fireman Job." *The Sporting News*, May 18, 1963.

———. "Bouton Parboils Yank Rivals by Booting Old Warmup Style." *The Sporting News*, June 27, 1964.

———. "Bouton Takes Bomber Bow as Jim-Dandy Hill Booster." *The Sporting News*, July 7, 1962.

———. "Bulldog Bouton Earns Top-Dog Rating." *The Sporting News*, July 20, 1963.

———. "Everybody Lends a Hand When Sore Arms Upset Yank Bull Pen." *The Sporting News*, September 12, 1964.

———. "Ho Hum—Bomber Clubhouse Quiet after Pennant Clincher." *The Sporting News*, October 6, 1962, 14.

———. "Howard Booming Bouton as Big Bomb-Thrower in Yank Future." *The Sporting News*, January 19, 1963.

———. "It's Do-or-Die Year for Bouton, Yanks' One-Time Hill Ace." *The Sporting News*, February 26, 1966.

———. "Phil's Harmonica Rascal Skit Hits $200 Clinker." *The Sporting News*, September 5, 1964.

———. "Pitching or Painting, Bouton Big Winner." *The Sporting News*, December 28, 1963.

Feuer, Richard. Interview with author, April 18, 2017.

Fischler, Stan. "Yankees Greet Old Pal Bouton with Icy Stares." *The Sporting News*, October 17, 1970.

Flaherty, Joe. "Toots Shor among the Ruins." *Esquire*, October, 1974.

Freehan, Bill. *Behind the Mask: An Inside Baseball Diary*. Edited by Steve Gelman and Dick Schaap. New York: World, 1970.

———. "Never Touch a Superstar." *Sports Illustrated*, March 2, 1970.

Frizzell, Pat. "Mays, 40, Still Giants' No. 1 Success Factor." *The Sporting News*, June 19, 1971.

Fulks, Sonny. Interview with author, October 12, 2016.

Gleason, Bill. "Legion Gave the Bulldog a Big Break." *The Sporting News*, June 22, 1968.

Goethel, Arno. "Twins Have a Fine Chance with Dean Setting an Example." *The Sporting News*, April 27, 1968.

Goldman, Paul, Peter Dreier, and Mimi Goldman. "Jim Bouton Follows His Dream." *In These Times* (September 28–October 4, 1977): 20.

Golenbock, Peter. Interview with author, January 25, 2017.

Gornie, Al. Interview with author, August 31, 2016.

Hirshberg, Al. "Players Answer Jim Bouton." *Sport*, October 1970.

Hoffarth, Tom. "More on 'Ball Four' @ 40 . . . From a Drunken Women's Title Suggestion to a Musical Number on the Roof Top of the Shoreham Hotel." Farther Off the Wall with Tom Hoffarth, September 20, 2010. www .insidesocial.com/tomhoffarth.

Holmes, John Clellon. "The Philosophy of the Beat Generation" (1958). In *Beat Down to Your Soul: What Was the Beat Generation?*, edited by Ann Charters New York: Penguin, 2001.

Holtzman, Jerome. "Appling Offers Tip for Youngsters." *The Sporting News*, July 25, 1970.

———. "Bouton's Bid Fails." *The Sporting News*, February 26, 1972.

———. "Finley Offers Advice to Daughter." *The Sporting News*, June 16, 1970.

———. "Jewish Fan Club for O'Brien?" *The Sporting News*, May 23, 1970.

———. "Movie of Bouton's Book." *The Sporting News*, November 27, 1971.

———. "Old-Timers May Demand Fees." *The Sporting News*, August 26, 1978.

———. "Pitchers Should Know How to Bunt." *The Sporting News*, June 12, 1971.

Honig, Donald. Interview with author, May 30, 2019.

Hoynes, Lou. Interview with author, October 5, 2017.

Isaacs, Stan. "Hey Mike Burke, Don't You Wish You Were the Boss of the Mets?" *Jock*, August 1969.

———. "Out of Left Field: A Sports Writer's Life." Unpublished memoir.

Jacobeit, Fred. Interview with author, September 2016.

Jacobson, Steve. Interview with author, July 12, 2016.

"Jim Bouton: Interview, August 2003." *Baseball Reliquary* (August 2003).

Jordan, Pat. "After the Sundown." *Sports Illustrated*, January 6, 1975.

Kaat, Jim. Interview with author, August 31, 2016; December 5, 2016.

Kahn, Roger. *The Boys of Summer.* New York: Harper & Row, 1972.

———. "Sports." *Esquire*, December 1970.

———. "Sports." *Esquire*, May 1971.

Kaplan, Jim. "Jim Bouton's Instant Replay." *Sports Illustrated*, August 31, 1970.

Kindred, Dave. "SportsWorld '98." *The Sporting News*, December 28, 1998.

King, Joe. "Bouton Case May Bring Pitch for Arbitration Panel." *The Sporting News*, March 28, 1964.

Kipen, David. "Ball Four: The Final Pitch." *Atlantic*, March 2001.

Kitman, Marvin. Interview with author, July 18, 2016.

Klapisch, Bob. "The Next Chapter." *The Sporting News*, August 29, 1994.

"Knuckleballer." *New Yorker*, October 24, 1970.

Koppett, Leonard. "Bouton and Falls Called to Task." *The Sporting News*, March 18, 1972.

Korman, Keith. Interview with author, October 3, 2017.

Kramer, Jerry. *Instant Replay*. New York: Signet, 1969.

"Kuhn Not Concerned." *The Sporting News*, September 30, 1978.

Kurman, Paula. Interviews with the author, 2016–2019.

Leggett, William. "Koo-Foo the Killer." *Sports Illustrated*, October 14, 1963.

———. "Out in Front with a New Look." *Sports Illustrated*, September 28, 1964.

"Libel and Slander . . . Public Figures." *ABA Journal* (February 1977).

Lindgren, Hugo. "Pinup Goalie: Shep Messing." *New York Magazine*, July 10, 2006.

Lipsyte, Robert. "The Dying Game: Why Baseball Has Gotten Too Big for Its Jockstrap." *Esquire*, April 1993.

———. E-mail interview with the author, July 18, 2016; December 22, 2017.

Ludtke, Melissa. "Two Strikes on 'Ball Four,'" *Sports Illustrated*, September 27, 1976.

"Mantle Doffs Lid to Bouton: 'Nearest Thing to Pascual.'" *The Sporting News*, May 25, 1963.

Marceau, Yvonne. Interview with author, August 10, 2016.

Marshall, Mike. Email interview with author, September 6–9, 2017.

Martin, Greg. Interview with author, August 31, 2016.

"Mavericks Break Own Season's Gate Record." *The Sporting News*, September 6, 1975.

"Mavs Draw Crowd." *The Sporting News*, June 19, 1976.

McDonald, Anna. "Big League Chew: An Oral History." May 5, 2015. www.foxsports.com.

McEvoy, Dermot. Interview with author, June 13, 2017.

Merchant, Larry. Interview with author, November 29, 2016.

Michalak, Brian. Email exchange with author, September 6, 2016.

Miller, Norm. Interview with author, February 18, 2017.

Morales, Tomas. "Odom and Bouton Make Winning Mexico Debuts." *The Sporting News*, June 25, 1977.

Murphy, Austin. "The Path to Power." *Sports Illustrated*, August 30, 1999.

Nathanson, Mitchell. *A People's History of Baseball*. Urbana: University of Illinois Press, 2012.

Nelson, Rob. Interview with author, May 8, 2017.

Neuman, Jeff. Interview with author, June 6, 2017.

"A New Twist." *The Sporting News*, August 20, 1977.

"New York Public Library's Books of the Century." (1995). www.nypl.org /voices/print-publications/books-of-the-century.

"New York Yankees: Some Hope for the Rest of the League." *Sports Illustrated*, April 8, 1963.

Neyer, Rob. "Jim Bouton Remembers the 1964 World Series." October 2014. www.foxsports.com.

———. "When Jim Bouton Couldn't Quite Match Don Drysdale's Zeroes." October 5, 2013. www.sbnation.com.

Nichols, Max. "Harmon Killebrew and Jim Bouton: A Ballplayer's Image." *Sport*, July 1965.

Offen, Neil. Interview with author, November 14, 2016.

O'Gara, Roger. "Bouton Stalls in Comeback." *The Sporting News*, May 13, 1972.

Ogle, Jim. "Bouton, Man of Talents, Still on Yank Hopeful List." *The Sporting News*, December 9, 1967.

———. "Bouton Sent Off to Syracuse to Revitalize Tender Wing." *The Sporting News*, June 17, 1967.

———. "Houk's Prophecy Rings True as Yankee Minutemen Deliver." *The Sporting News*, May 25, 1968

———. "Yank Bulldog Bouton Winning Battle against Odds." *The Sporting News*, March 30, 1968.

———. "Yankee Bulldog Growling, Ready to Chew Up the Enemy Swingers." *The Sporting News*, February 4, 1967.

———. "Yanks Hail Return of Downing as Key to Solid Starting Staff." *The Sporting News*, July 6, 1968.

Olbermann, Keith. Interview with author, May 5, 2018.

Olbermann, Keith, and Dan Patrick. *The Big Show*. New York: Atria Books, 1998.

O'Maxfield, Gary Goldberg "Pops." Interview with author, December 23, 2016.

Osnos, Peter. Interview with author, October 24 and 26, 2016; January 28 and 29, 2019.

"People." *Sports Illustrated*, August 24, 1970.

"People." *Sports Illustrated*, April 30, 1973.

Pepitone, Joe, with Barry Steinback. *Joe, You Coulda Made Us Proud.* New York: Sports, 1975.

Peters, Frank. Interview with author, September 16, 2016.

Peterson, Fritz. Interview with author, September 5, 2016.

———. *Mickey Mantle Is Going to Heaven.* Denver: Outskirts Press, 2009.

Picking, Ken. "Endangered Species." *The Sporting News*, May 13, 1991.

"Player Reps Say They'll Air Yank Threats in Bouton Case." *The Sporting News*, April 4, 1964.

Pluto, Terry. *The Greatest Summer: The Remarkable Story of Jim Bouton's Comeback to Major League Baseball.* Englewood Cliffs NJ: Prentice Hall, 1979.

Poe, Randall. "The Writing of Sports." *Esquire*, October 1974.

Pokotilow, Steve. Interview with author, January 18, 2017.

"Portland Pilot Robinson Draws 1-Year Suspension." *The Sporting News*, September 15, 1973.

Primo, Al. Interview with author, September 18, 2016.

Reidenbaugh, Lowell. "Author Bouton Hits Jackpot—with Bowie's Assist." *The Sporting News*, August 8, 1970.

Sartre, Jean Paul. *Being and Nothingness.* New York: Washington Square Press, 1993.

Schaap, Dick. *Flashing before My Eyes: 50 Years of Headlines, Deadlines & Punchlines.* New York: William Morrow, 2001.

Schaap, Jeremy. Interview with author, January 18, 2018.

Schalman, Lynne. Interview with author, April 17, 2017.

Shecter, Leonard. "Jim Bouton: Everything in its Place." *Sport,* March 1964.

Schillan, Joe. Interview with author, May 1, 2017.

Schonely, Bill. Interview with author, October 5, 2016.

Scribner, David. Interview with author, August 24, 2016.

Shaw, Brad. Interview with author, December 19, 2016.

Shecter, Leonard. "Jim Bouton: Everything in Its Place." *Sport,* March 1964.

———. *The Jocks.* New York: Bobbs-Merrill, 1969.

———. "My Friend the Brother." *Signature Magazine,* 1968 (specific date unknown).

Silverman, Al. Interview with author, August 30, 2016.

Smolkin, Rachel. "Wild Pitch." *American Journalism Review* (February–March 2004).

Spander, Art. "Never Wanted to Manage." *The Sporting News*, June 2, 1973.

Spector, Jesse. "Jim Bouton: 'You Can't Just Go through Your Day Tweeting Stuff That's Not Worth Anything." *The Sporting News*, September 23, 2013.

Spink, C. C. Johnson. "We Believe . . ." *The Sporting News*, September 20, 1975.

Spoelstra, Watson. "Schultz Savors Edict to Ban Bouton." *The Sporting News*, April 1, 1972.

St. John, Marco. Interview with author, July 10, 2017.

Steadman, John. "Only Two Yanks Able to Avoid Goat-Horn Tag." *The Sporting News*, October 31, 1964.

Stewart, Art. Interview with author, September 21, 2016; June 27, 2017.

Surface, Bill. "Johnny Sain Teaches the Power of Positive Thinking." *New York Times Magazine*, April 20, 1969, 49.

"Suspension for Odom." *The Sporting News*, July 23, 1977.

Swanson, Jim. Interview with author, September 16, 2016.

"Sweepers Silenced." *The Sporting News*, July 9, 1977.

Talese, Gay. "Frank Sinatra Has a Cold." *Esquire*, April 1966, 89.

"The Talk of the Town." *New Yorker*, October 24, 1970.

Tax, Jeremiah. "Booktalk: With 'Balls,' Graig Nettles Takes a Few Cuts at George Steinbrenner." *Sports Illustrated*, May 7, 1984.

"Television Reviews." *Variety*, September 29, 1976.

"This Year's Crop of Unusual Stories Has a Serious Note." *The Sporting News*, April 4, 1964.

Thompson, Hunter S. "Fear & Loathing in Miami: Old Bulls Meet the Butcher." *Rolling Stone*, August 17, 1971. www.rollingstone.com.

Thorn, John. Interview with author, December 22, 2016.

"The Top 100 Sports Books of All Time." *Sports Illustrated*, December 16, 2002.

Twombly, Wells. "Beware of Snoopy Colleagues." *The Sporting News*, June 20, 1970.

———. "Portland Mavericks—a Noble Experiment." *The Sporting News*, July 14, 1973.

Vecsey, George. "Can Jim Bouton Go Home Again?" *Sport*, July 1970.

———. Interview with author, July 7, 2016.

Verrell, Gordon. "Dodgers Open Some Daylight and Get That Sunny Feeling." *The Sporting News*, September 30, 1978.

Vogan, Travis. *Keepers of the Flame: NFL Films and the Rise of Sports Media*. Urbana: University of Illinois Press, 2014.

"Voice of the Fan." *The Sporting News*, January 25, 1975.

"Voice of the Fan—Bouton Isn't a Youth." *The Sporting News*, July 11, 1970.

"Voice of the Fan—Literary Equilibrium." *The Sporting News*, March 27, 1971.

Wakefield, Dan. "Highlights of a NON-Event." *New York Magazine*, September 9, 1974.

Wedge, Marilyn. "Reflections on Milton Erickson." *Psychology Today* (December 17, 2011). www.psychologytoday.com/us/blog/suffer-the-children/201112/reflections-milton-erickson.

"The Week (Sept. 10–16)." *Sports Illustrated*, September 25, 1978.

Weintraub, Robert. "Yankee, Executive, Soldier, Spy." May 6, 2015. www.grantland.com.

Whitlesey, Merrell. "Nat Fans Filter Rumors; Short Seeks Shortstop." *The Sporting News*, October 31, 1970.

"Williams' Arm Heals before Ailment Reveled." *The Sporting News*, August 31, 1963.

Wilson, John. "'Ball Four' Bouton Takes Walk to O.C." *The Sporting News*, August, 15, 1970.

———. "Bouton Book to Reveal Beer Slosher's Viewpoint." *The Sporting News*, April 11, 1970.

Wolff, Rick. Interview with author, April 28, 2017.

"Wrecker Nets $300,000 on Yankee Stadium Items." *The Sporting News*, June 29, 1974.

"Yankee Staying Power." *The Sporting News*, August 27, 1977.

"Yanks Knot Series on HRs by Maris, Mantle, Pepitone." *The Sporting News*, October 24, 1964.

Young, Dick. "Bouton Rates a Reprimand." *The Sporting News*, June 6, 1970.

———. "Teammates Trusted Bouton." *The Sporting News*, June 20, 1970.

———. "Young Ideas." *New York Daily News*, May 28, 1970.

———. "Young Ideas." *The Sporting News*, August 7, 1965.

———. "Young Ideas." *The Sporting News*, April 27, 1968.

———. "Young Ideas." *The Sporting News*, September 12, 1970.

———. "Young Ideas." *The Sporting News*, June 19, 1971.

———. "Young Ideas." *The Sporting News*, November 18, 1978.

Zeigler, Cyd. "100 Most Important Moments in Gay History: Moment #55: Jim Bouton's Ball Four TV Show Includes Gay Ballplayer." *SB Nation Outsports*, August 9, 2011, www.outsports.com

Zeitchik, Steven. "New Bouton Book Critical of PublicAffairs." *Publishers Weekly* (April 14, 2003).

Zimmerman, Hy. "Mariner Swap Bait: Stanton's HR Bat." *The Sporting News*, October 15, 1977.

———. "Mincher's Health Okay, and Pitchers Know It!" *The Sporting News*, July 25, 1969.

———. "Pilots Discover Blunt Weapon: The Bench." *The Sporting News*, July 25, 1969.

Index